DATE DUE FOR RETURN

The Corporate State and the Broker State

The Corporate State and the Broker State

The Du Ponts and American National Politics, 1925–1940

Robert F. Burk

Harvard University Press
Cambridge, Massachusetts, and London, England   1990

Library of Congress Cataloging in Publication Data

Burk, Robert Fredrick, 1955–
  The corporate state and the broker state : the Du Ponts and
American national politics, 1925–1940 / Robert F. Burk.
    p. cm.
  Bibliography: p.
  Includes index.
  ISBN 0-674-17272-8 (alk. paper)
  1. Business and politics—United States—History—20th century.
2. United States—Politics and government—20th century.
3. Du Pont family. I. Title.
JK467.B874 1990
322'.3'0973—dc20   89-15250
                                                        CIP

353211

Contents

Preface

This is the story of one generation of a powerful American family and its interventions in national politics. Traditionally the political intercessions of businessmen in the United States have not attracted great attention from scholars. The family under examination here—the du Ponts—has not escaped such neglect. The inattention is undeserved, for Pierre, Irénée, and Lammot du Pont, and their close colleague John J. Raskob, controlled a vast economic empire centered on the twin jewels of the Du Pont and General Motors corporations. Drawing upon the enormous financial power provided by that base, they plunged into many of the major political controversies of the 1920's and 1930's, including the prohibition repeal movement, the presidential campaigns of 1928, 1932, 1936, and 1940, the struggle for control of the Democratic party, and the effort to repeal the New Deal.

Besides being active in public affairs, the du Ponts were also energetic private correspondents who tried to place their political activities within a broader historical and ideological context. As such they stand as exemplars of an important segment of corporate America in the interwar years. Their notions of political economy can best be captured by three adjectives—"corporatist," "cosmopolitan," and "conservative" (a somewhat different "CCC"). They were corporatist in that they were products of, and champions of, the business corporation as an organizational construct. They held as articles of faith the superiority of the corporation's efficiencies of scale, its centralized administration of production, prices, and wages, and its abilities to reduce "damaging" competition and to exercise "industrial self-government." They believed that the corporation tested its executives' capacities to respond to changing technological realities and popular tastes better than any other institution of modern America, and that the property-holding "electorate" of the corporation—its stockholders—insured the necessary degree of accountability. Corporate leaders, they claimed, were far better prepared to meet the national and international challenges of twentieth-century public administration than untrained elected and appointed partisan officials, who had to cater to the irrational short-term passions and demands of a broader electorate and its varied "special interests."

The diverse business ventures of the family contributed to the creation of a national, standardized material culture and the secular values that accompanied the new mass-consumer society—values that were antithetical to traditional standards of taste, custom, morality, and independence. The du Ponts viewed as both inevitable and desirable the homogenizing changes of the age, and saw the rural populism and continuing political assertions of "island-community" localism as meddlesome and irrational. If (borrowing the terminology of historians Samuel Hays and Jackson Turner Main, among others) we may posit the existence in early twentieth-century America of a "community-society" or "localist-cosmopolitan" spectrum of social and political values, the du Ponts would have identified themselves at the "cosmopolitan," or "society," end of the scale. As part of a trans-Atlantic network of industrial capitalists, they scorned the parochialism, as they saw it, of their enemies' vision. Their most consistent and bitter adversaries in politics from the 1890's to the 1930's, the rural insurgent populists and progressives, stood for ideals they had already rejected— yeoman self-sufficiency, moral Puritanism, decentralized competitive capitalism, agrarian democracy, and foreign-policy isolationism.

The du Ponts put their corporate and cosmopolitan perspectives in the service of essentially conservative goals, in various senses of that term. Although they saw themselves as social moderns, they sought to restore the hierarchical ideals of the American polity of the Founding Fathers. They wished to recreate a single line of political and economic authority to replace the dual, though often interlocking, systems of public and private administration of their day. They were also conservative, in a manner more familiar to our own time, in opposing the use of government to redistribute wealth and power from the "haves" to the "have-nots." Besides seeing such reallocations as a threat to their interests, the du Ponts viewed the "statist demagoguery" of charismatic populists as a step leading inexorably to totalitarianism. To check these "irrational" tendencies, they looked backward to a pre-Jacksonian America ruled indisputably by the propertied, with only those owning a "stake in society" claiming the right of suffrage. They also believed that the size of an individual's holdings corresponded roughly to his ability and virtue. Their ideal America, then, did not have as broad a democratic base as actually existed, or as broad a base as was endorsed by their political adversaries. Nor did it entail an egalitarian economic order: the du Ponts favored a meritocracy.

Given the du Ponts' guiding political principles, it is clear that to call them "Jeffersonian," as has often been done, is a mistake. Part of the confusion has stemmed from the fact that the du Ponts' conservative Democratic allies in the 1930's employed the term to distinguish themselves from Franklin D. Roosevelt and the New Dealers. But the du Ponts' own views on the social origins, and the hierarchical distribution, of public power and virtue had a far greater affinity with those of the Federalists than with those of the Jeffersonians. Their urban, industrial, and financial sources of wealth were more compatible with a Hamiltonian philosophy. Nor did the du Ponts necessarily even believe, as has usually been supposed, in government decentralization and states' rights. When, for example, they assailed Roosevelt in 1935–36 for appropriating too much power in the federal government, it was not centralization that they condemned. If they and their allies could not *control* the machinery of economic stabilization, then it was better that the machinery be dismantled than be operated by their enemies. As their business careers demonstrated time after time, the du Ponts regularly sought to magnify, consolidate, and centralize their own power and prerogatives, while they struggled to keep their opponents— rival firms, outside unions, or political adversaries—decentralized, fragmented, and weak. For all these reasons the family championed the "corporate state," which provided government sanction for their economic hegemony, and bitterly resisted the broker state, which legitimized the rival claims of competing interests and maintained dual structures of public and private economic governance.

Sharper understanding of the du Ponts' ultimate objectives helps shed new light on many of the specific political controversies they became involved in. To take one example, "dry" defenders of prohibition in the 1920's consistently portrayed the family's commitment to repeal as a selfish ploy to reduce its own taxes and to shift the burden to consumers and a reestablished liquor industry. The du Ponts' supporters, in turn, portrayed them as defenders of individual civil liberties. Both characterizations contain some truth, but both define the family's aims too narrowly. The du Ponts led the repeal cause after 1926 for several additional reasons; they wanted to deal insurgency politics a decisive reversal, to test the family's national political clout, to attempt to direct a policy change outside the control of the major political parties, and to demonstrate the corporate managerial class's ability to craft public policy alternatives superior to those of partisan officeholders.

Similar distortions have clouded our understanding of the nature of the du Ponts' relationship with the New Deal of Franklin Roosevelt. The political warfare which accelerated in 1934 was not, as pro–New Deal contemporaries conveniently portrayed it, simply the continuation of a timeless "progressive" historical struggle between "Tory" reactionaries, wanting to dismantle the federal government and restore laissez-faire capitalism, and the Roosevelt administration, champion of the "people" versus the "interests." But resistance to the new policies was not, as later New Left historians characterized it, merely a smokescreen covering the willing cooptation of the New Deal by the corporate sector. If Roosevelt was a consistently vigorous adversary of corporate "reactionaries" such as the du Ponts, then why did Pierre du Pont and John Raskob serve in his administration in 1933–34? Conversely, if the New Deal was carrying out the du Ponts' agenda, then why did they turn against it and form the American Liberty League to voice their discontent?

In actuality, despite their disappointment that Al Smith or some other suitably sympathetic candidate had failed to attain the presidency in 1932, the du Ponts at first had seen some promise in the New Deal. Their early hope was rewarded with repeal of prohibition and, even more important, the creation of the National Recovery Administration. Under a like-minded proponent of "industrial self-government," Hugh Johnson, the NRA showed initial signs of becoming the instrument which would institutionalize the corporate state. Only when the New Deal gradually drifted to the left, away from the du Ponts' aims, did the family break its ties with the Roosevelt administration. Even though the New Deal had proved a boon to company balance sheets, by 1934 it had come to threaten something far more crucial to the family than profits—*power*. The emerging broker state was hardly antithetical to capitalism, but it raised the frightening spectre of business forced to share power with an independent government bureaucracy, outside industrial unions, and other interests that would be excluded from participation in a corporate state.

In the struggle over competing visions of the American political economy—between the du Pont corporate state and the New Deal broker state—the du Ponts lost, as was dramatically underscored in the 1936 election. In contrast, those corporate chieftains who were practical enough to admit that rival interests could no longer be ignored, and to display a more cooperative spirit toward a partisan federal government they could not completely dominate, retained and even enhanced their level of influence upon the personnel and policies of that government, with no small help from the emergency of World War II. These "corporate liberals," perhaps better described as "corporate pragmatists," became the principal long-term victors in the twentieth-century struggle between business and the federal government. By better understanding the du Ponts and other relative "losers" in that engagement, we gain a greater comprehension of the "winners" and the precise nature and extent of their triumph.

This study would not have been possible without the dedication and assistance of archivists and librarians at a host of research institutions. My special thanks go to the staffs of the Hagley Library, the Library of Congress, the Maryland Historical Society, Princeton University Library, Yale University Library, the Franklin D. Roosevelt Library, the New York State Library, the University of Kentucky Library, the State Historical Society of Wisconsin, the Kansas State Historical Society, and the Muskingum College Library. This project would also have been much more difficult and longer in germination without the generous financial support provided by a Mack Foundation grant from Muskingum College in the summer of 1986, an Albert Beveridge Grant from the American Historical Association and a National Endowment for the Humanities Travel to Collections award in 1987, and an NEH Summer Stipend in 1988. I am also indebted to colleagues John M. Cooper, Jr., of the University of Wisconsin and David Sturtevant and Lorle Porter at Muskingum College for their careful reading of the manuscript. Judy Woodard has labored many long hours both at the office and at home to prepare the typed version, and I am very grateful for her sacrifices. The editorial staff at Harvard University Press, notably Aida Donald, Elizabeth Suttell, Lila Weston, and Kate Schmit, have been constant sources of good advice and encouragement during the evaluation and revision process. To Tristan, Maxie, and Bruce, I extend my gratitude and occasional consternation at being distracted from the typewriter. Most of all, my thanks to Patricia Geschwent, for providing me with seven years of love and support; she will soon receive her acknowledged reward from her dilatory spouse.

The Corporate State and the Broker State

chapter 1

Barons of the Brandywine

"The business of America is business," proclaimed President Calvin Coolidge. And if ever an age seemed dominated in its patterns of popular thought and policy by the businessman, it was the Roaring Twenties. Propelled by an industrial expansion which rapidly outpaced war-ravaged Europe, America in the Twenties was a nation in the midst of an economic revolution. The many advances in mass production included assembly-line technology, mechanical coal-loaders, mine locomotives, power shovels, pneumatic drills, continuous strip sheet rolling, the Ross carrier for lumber, and automatic cigarmakers. During the decade the Czech term *robot* first entered the American vocabulary. The multitude of technological innovations spurred industrial productivity, lowered labor costs, and made available a wide variety of goods for the first time to the middle-class consumer. If the American worker avoided technological unemployment, he or she enjoyed, on average, a nearly 11 percent boost in real earnings from 1923 to 1928.[1]

Mass production created a modern national consumer society which now reached even the most remote countryside. Concrete mixers, dump trucks, and hydraulic finishing machines propelled the onward drive of road construction, rapidly trailed by the traveling salesman and the mail-order catalogue. The radio industry, but a feeble wireless telegraph service in 1920, grew by decade's end into a billion-dollar industry, with corporate advertising providing the lion's share of its revenue. The new consumerism permeated the postal service, too: by the Twenties 80 percent of all mail consisted of ads. With increased productivity also creating more leisure time, an exploding variety of service industries—from restaurants to recording companies to motion pictures—emerged to profit from it. Government expenditures at all levels likewise climbed for roads, libraries, parks, and—to meet the changing educational needs of the workforce—schools and colleges.

Like the towering skyscrapers making their mark upon the urban landscape, personal and corporate fortunes soared to meteoric heights. One source of the great fortunes was increased business consolidation into smaller numbers of giant firms. In the 1920s eight thousand mining and manufacturing companies disappeared within combinations. Five hundred utilities similarly were swallowed up, most by holding companies. By decade's end, the nation's two hundred largest nonfinancial corporations owned almost half of all corporate wealth and 22 percent of overall national wealth. Despite the popular lip service to isolationism, overseas investment also expanded, from $94 million to $602 million. Between 1922 and 1929 the undistributed earnings of American corporations averaged better than $2.5 billion per year. Stock dividends climbed a phenomenal 110 percent, from $3 billion in 1922 to $6.3 billion in 1929, as recorded on the new stock tickers.[2] The business community set the national standard of living, shaped Americans' material perspectives, and increasingly was viewed as the social class most capable of identifying and solving national problems. In other words, the businessman and business corporation were becoming the popular individual and institutional representatives of national progress and social modernism.

To be sure, the business culture of the Twenties contained its share of tinsel and abuses. With the spread of labor-saving technology, the continued availability of cheap labor (in spite of severe restrictions on immigration) and management pressures upon a predominantly nonunionized workforce kept wages lower than was wise from an economic or ethical standpoint. Worship of the new god of consumption by the middle class led millions to pursue a materialistic standard of life that plunged them into debt. The Brookings Institution estimated that of the nearly 27.5 million families in America, over 20 percent claimed incomes of less than $1000 per year, 40 percent earned less than $1500, and over 70 percent made less than $2500. The combined income of the lowest 40 percent was equalled by that of the wealthiest one-hundredth of one percent. Nearly 80 percent of American families held no aggregate savings, while the top 24,000 families (0.9 percent) controlled over one-third of national savings. Unemployment rose in industries displaced by new technologies, and the farm economy suffered from slackness in foreign demand and overproduction at home. These underlying weaknesses, and others, became all too apparent in the months and years that followed a particular Black Thursday on Wall Street in October 1929.[3]

But until that day of reckoning, the popular image of America of the Twenties was that of a materialistic Eden, and no one symbolized it better than the du Ponts. Aided by the springboard of World War I, the du Ponts of Delaware controlled the greatest industrial empire then known to history, an empire that included a wide range of products from chemicals to automobiles, synthetic fibers to leaded gasoline, and paints to food packaging. In the Twenties the du Ponts enjoyed their greatest economic triumphs. Drawing upon their impressive and expanding economic base, they played an increasingly prominent role in the political affairs of the nation for the next two decades.

The contributions to the material changes of American life made by the Du Pont corporation and its partners in the 1920's were truly staggering. The du Ponts secured foreign dye patents and processes that revolutionized the domestic clothing and paint industries. Their attractive "Duco" lacquers expanded consumer choice in the automobile industry, as did their development of tetraethyl lead for high-compression gasoline. Their scientists helped develop "shatterproof" glass for auto windshields. During their stewardship of General Motors, Chevrolet leaped forward to overtake Ford as the auto industry's sales leader. Their cellophane increased the market volume of the food industry. Du Pont produced one of the first inexpensive types of cellulose film for Hollywood. The company's Pyralin plastic led to higher sales of cheaper, lighter radios and other appliances. Neoprene, introduced in 1931, became valuable as a more resistant sealant than natural rubber. And the company's development of rayon and synthetic leather triggered a revolution throughout the fiber and apparel industries.

Nor were the du Pont's innovations merely technological. Whether for good or ill, the family and company were linked with nearly every major social trend of the period. The du Ponts pioneered the promotion of installment buying through the General Motors Acceptance Corporation. In advertising, they developed the most imaginative and efficient publicity bureau in American business, and the *Du Pont Magazine* became a leader in corporate public relations. Du Pont was one of the first large corporations to move production facilities to the South, signalling the beginnings of a long-term business trend. Family members were active in promoting road construction, public education, private pension plans, and aviation. Although not completed until the Depression, du Pont funds even played a major role in underwriting the construction of that symbol of urban ascendancy, the Empire State Building. Similarly, du Ponts were involved heavily in the Florida land boom of mid-decade and the Great Bull Market of the late 1920's.[4]

To put it simply, if the corporation was the representative institution of American material growth and progress in the Twenties, the du Ponts were its personal symbols. Whether in the halls of Congress or on the floor of the New York Stock Exchange, the name du Pont was acknowledged, respected, and feared. For the family itself the decade marked a dramatic transformation from the unglamorous grime of raw industrial production in munitions to the refinement of consumer research and production of synthetic materials, high finance, and modern, "high-rise" corporate management. From their lofty vantage point the du Ponts directed their financial legions into new avenues of investment. Among the most skilled "corporate raiders" of their time, they moved from acquisition to new market need to new acquisition—from munitions to chemicals and dyes; from those investments to others in General Motors and U.S. Rubber; and from there to leaded gasoline and partial ownership in Phillips Petroleum. Each prize served as a building block for an expanding family empire which advanced as a consequence not only of economic but also of political interventions. Already the du Ponts' home state of Delaware was labelled the "corporate state"—because of the laxness of du Pont–sponsored incorporation laws at the turn of the century and the family's longstanding enormous power in state government. Besides the economic clout provided by the family company and by the large General Motors investment, the du Ponts exercised additional leverage through their personal holding company, Christiana Securities; their own bank, the Wilmington Trust Company; their ownership of both of Wilmington's daily newspapers; and an expanded network of relatives, friends, and allies holding local, state, and national offices.[5]

Despite the many changes and expansions of the du Pont empire, however, it remained true to its early nineteenth-century origins in one very important respect—it was still a family operation with family ways. With rare exceptions the guiding officers of the empire were either direct descendants of company founding father Eleuthère Irénée du Pont or indirect heirs through marriage into the family. By the 1920's, four individuals dominated administration of the fortune, having seized the reins of power and held them vigorously since the winter of 1914–15. They were Eleuthère Irénée's great grandson Pierre S. du Pont, Pierre's younger brothers Irénée and Lammot, and longtime aide and partner John J. Raskob.

Of these four titans, Pierre du Pont clearly was the "anchor" of the family and company. Born in 1870, Pierre acted from the age of thirteen as a kind of surrogate father to Irénée, Lammot, and their eight other siblings following their father's death in a plant explosion at the family's Repauno, New Jersey, chemical works. Pierre and his brothers and sisters grew up in as self-contained a world as anyone could imagine. The family's traditional home on the banks of the Brandywine, Eleutherian Mills, was from its inception in 1802 a du Pont–owned village, complete with large manorial estates, smaller homes, churches, stores, a blacksmith's forge, and a doctor's office. There was no sharp dividing line between du Pont personal property, Du Pont company property, and the possessions of those who worked for the family firm. Even the family's transportation vehicles and bank accounts were kept in the company's name. But despite his ready access to the comforts of a privileged life, including an inspiring trip to the Philadelphia Central Exhibition at the age of six, Pierre did not enjoy an easy childhood. A physically weak child with a shortened tendon in his left foot, he hated horseback riding and never learned to swim. Rather than permit surgery on his son's foot, Pierre's father insisted that he undergo painful, and ultimately fruitless, stretching treatments at the hands of a Philadelphia physician. As a consequence of his physical shortcomings, Pierre developed a shy, taciturn personality that concealed an aggressive, compensatory inner ambition for power and success. Family members loved to tell of the young Pierre's recruitment of two of his younger siblings in a scheme to sell old paper to a local paper mill; Pierre purportedly received a ten-dollar payment but relinquished only one cent apiece to his partners.[6]

Pierre's sheltered existence continued through his schooling. He attended Phillips Andover Academy and the Massachusetts Institute of Technology in the exclusive company of cousins, brothers, and family friends. But upon his graduation from MIT in 1890, he found his advancement in the company blocked by family elders. After serving as a research assistant at the company's laboratory at Carney's Point, New Jersey, where a new variant of smokeless powder was being developed, Pierre left to pursue street railway ventures in Lorain, Ohio (where the later Cleveland reform mayor Tom Johnson was a partner), and Dallas, Texas. In 1899, frustrated at having been shut out of a prominent executive position when the family's old business partnership dissolved and a new corporation, E. I. du Pont de Nemours and Company, was created, he joined forces with his equally discontented cousin T. Coleman "Coly" du Pont in Kentucky. Three years later, amidst the great merger mania of the early Progressive Era, Pierre, Coly, and cousin Alfred I. du Pont capitalized on the death of chief executive Eugene du Pont to seize control of the family corporation. With Pierre serving as the financial mind of the triumvirate, the company absorbed former rivals and cartel partners in the gunpowder business, triggering the collapse of the cartel—the Gunpowder Trade Association—itself.[7]

Pierre did not complete his full ascent to family and company power, however, until 1915. In the winter of 1914–15, being aware of Coly du Pont's need for investment capital for the proposed Equitable Life Insurance Building in New York, Pierre joined his brothers Irénée and Lammot, brother-in-law R. R. M. "Ruly" Carpenter, and John Raskob in negotiating the purchase of Coly's stock over Alfred's objections. After a series of brutal court and stockholder contests, Pierre then ousted Alfred from any further management role in the company and consolidated his power, marking the completion of his recovery from the early days of "exile." He served as company president until 1919, when Irénée's assumption of command freed him to pursue the General Motors Corporation. Again, through adroit stock maneuvering and aided by his brothers and John Raskob, Pierre seized decisive power in GM from William Crapo Durant. He then ran GM as its president until 1923, when his appointed successor, Alfred Sloan, replaced him.[8]

Business—especially the business of empire building—dominated most of Pierre's adult life. He even delayed marriage, for example, until his career was well under way. When he did take a wife, as with so many of the du Ponts, he married a cousin, Alice Belin. Even then, given that the couple did not have children, Pierre's attentions remained focused upon his ambitions for himself, his "extended" family, and his economic empire. Given his own habitual shyness and distaste for the public spotlight, a public career in politics was out of the question. Only by World War I did he overcome his shyness enough even to give local speeches in Wilmington for the Red Cross. His reclusiveness, unfortunately, also contributed later to the lurid speculations about the purportedly sinister backroom machinations of Pierre and his siblings as "merchants of death" and "anti–New Deal facists." But although, in contrast to brother Irénée, Pierre loathed public attention, he did have an abiding passion for economic and civic affairs and a love of the exercise of power in both arenas. While he orchestrated the outlines of family and company policy for many years from backstage, others spoke and acted publicly in his behalf.[9]

If Pierre was the family's modern patriarch and ambitious guiding hand, younger brother Irénée cast a more aggressive public profile as a conspicuous consumer and an industrialist. It was he, more than Pierre, who fit the Twenties' popular mold of the boosterish business tycoon. His physical appearance underscored the image, for Irénée was more robust than his older brother and rarely was seen in public attired in less than the best-tailored three-piece business suits and furbished with his trademark pipe. More aggressive in espousing the family's anti-government rhetoric, and more viscerally Republican in his politics, Irénée frequently lacked the patience and public circumspection of Pierre. On occasion his intemperate nature resulted in personal or political embarrassments for the family. But without question business success drove Irénée every bit as much as Pierre, if for apparently less refined reasons. As a junior executive the young Irénée had made a practice of playing his own version of Monopoly on Thursday nights with colleague John Raskob and others, the group pretending themselves to be the Du Pont Company's executive committee. Because of his older brother's shrewd maneuverings, of course, the dream had become a reality by 1915. Irénée then joined Pierre, Lammot, and Raskob on both the board of directors and the company executive committee, and from 1920 to 1926 he commanded Du Pont's daily operations as its president. It was Irénée, also trained at MIT as a chemist, who was responsible for the strategy which captured a host of German dye patents after World War I and who administered the company's maturing expansion into the chemicals field.[10]

Despite their academic training, both Pierre and Irénée expanded the family business empire less through immediate enhancement of its own basic research capability than through "corporate raiding" of various kinds. Their strategies included not only the financial takeover of market-related firms, but also the acquisition of others' technical innovations by means of licensing and patent exchanges. In contrast, Lammot, the youngest of the du Pont inner circle, was in both appearance and behavior more suited to the ascetic aspects of product research and cost accounting. More frail-looking than either of his brother partners, but similarly MIT-trained, Lammot lacked the expansive vision of Pierre and the colorful personality of Irénée but was a greater master of the laboratory and the bottom line. Following Pierre's takeover, he moved to the head of the company's organic chemicals division. In 1926 he assumed the company presidency, a position he held until 1940. Under the stern, somber Lammot, Du Pont played a greater leadership role within the National Association of Manufacturers (NAM). Lammot also became a personal symbol of business rectitude during the worst days of the Depression through such actions as bicycling to work through the streets of Wilmington, his briefcase attached to the handlebars.[11]

The one company insider in the 1920's who was not a family member was nonetheless probably the closest in personality and outlook to Pierre. John Jakob Raskob was born the son of an Alsatian immigrant cigarmaker and an Irish mother in Lockport, New York. Like Pierre, he had witnessed the death of his father at an early age and had assumed responsibility for supporting a large family. Some nine years younger than the Du Pont chieftain, Raskob initially became acquainted with him through a common business associate, Arthur Moxham. The two young men found in each other a remarkable compatibility of personality and ambitions, and when Pierre commenced his Dallas street railway venture, Raskob accompanied him as his personal secretary. From that moment until the 1920's, he rarely left Pierre's side through a series of ambitious business gambits. When Pierre's group of investors took over the Du Pont corporation, Raskob was a prominent participant and became company treasurer. When Pierre seized GM, he did so at the advice of Raskob, who subsequently became its new treasurer and chairman of its finance committee.[12]

Although Raskob, an ardent Catholic, differed from his mentor in having many children, in most respects he reflected and even magnified Pierre's own ambitions and weaknesses. A small, quiet, fastidious man, Raskob also had to overcome his natural shyness in public forums, and he did so more successfully. Like Pierre, but to an even greater extent, he was more excited by corporate financial dealing and the "lure of the hunt" than by the nuts and bolts of daily company administration. A corporate visionary in his own right, Raskob predicted an age of greater leisure, expanded installment buying, and enlarged stock ownership by workers in the companies they served. Because of his own stock manipulations and his bullish promotion of common stock ownership, he became known by the late 1920's as the "Wizard of Wall Street" as well as "the financial genius of the Du Pont Company." Also like Pierre, his visions and ambition did not stop at the water's edge of politics and government. Raskob's own partisan and policy interests eventually peaked in the period from 1928 to 1932, when through his budding friendship with Al Smith he held the chairmanship of the Democratic National Committee.[13]

With their positions of immense economic power secure by the early 1920's, each of the du Pont inner circle lived the lavish life of a modern-day feudal lord, complete with huge estates and elaborate personal amusements. Among the family's twenty-four different estates in Delaware and southeastern Pennsylvania, Pierre resided at Longwood in Chester County, Pennsylvania, some seventeen miles north of the company's Wilmington headquarters. Reflecting his love of landscaping and horticulture, the estate contained a thousand acres of Japanese waterfalls, trees, exotic plants, sunken gardens, and six greenhouses for rare tropical species. Pierre's private refuge also included a 1200-

seat open-air theater for private entertainments, immense multi-level fountains highlighted by beams of colored lights, a transplanted Norman bell tower, and a 10,000-pipe organ which required fourteen railroad cars to ship to Longwood. To play the instrument, Pierre hired Firmin Swinnen, the organist of Antwerp Cathedral. Within a splendid estate that rivalled Versailles in grandeur, he resided in a comparatively modest thirty-room mansion at its center, staffed by over one hundred servants and protected by a $7 million life insurance policy that barred him from flying his private airplane.[14]

Although other du Ponts may not have required all of the private comforts enjoyed by the reclusive Pierre, their public consumption often was more conspicuous. Irénée, master of the 514-acre Granoque (a Francophile spelling of Great Nock) estate, claimed a seventy-room mansion, a sixty-foot yacht, and a lavish winter home on the north coast of Cuba, dubbed "Xanadu." Lammot, who had been given their mother's estate, St. Amours, by Pierre, possessed a seventy-six-foot yacht and a summer estate in fashionable Fisher's Island off Long Island. For renovations for the New York house, he stripped the woodwork from the finest old homestead mansions of Maryland's Eastern Shore. Raskob, with a reported net worth by 1928 of $100 million, owned his own Delaware estate, Archmore, as well as a farm in Maryland and a residence in his financial nerve center, New York City. Devoted to Catholic philanthropy, he received membership in the Knights of the Order of St. Gregory the Great for his generous gifts to the Hospital of Infant Jesus in Rome and for a million-dollar grant to the archdiocese of Wilmington.[15]

The du Ponts' lavish pastoral estates, although suggesting a link to family traditions, were in important respects misleading. The lion's share of their wealth came not from the land but from an industrial empire geared primarily to growing urban consumer tastes. Similarly, though they might live the private lives of landed gentry, their business perspectives were those of academically trained corporate technocrats and managers. Under their leadership, Du Pont gradually was emerging as a leader in fundamental laboratory research and as a sponsor of industrial academic fellowships. Their way of blending the old and new was the advocacy of a hybrid of paternal, Social Darwinist, and managerial elements in their empire's personnel organization. Du Pont the company in the 1920's was a mixture of the most up-to-date concepts of streamlined corporate organization and earlier, even preindustrial, notions of family, gentry, and hierarchy. As did other corporate managers, the du Ponts sought new methods to retain the close-knit, "family" spirit of employees at all levels within the company, to balance power and prerogatives efficiently between lieu-tenants and the central leadership, and to maximize production by substituting the cooperation of complex units for the individual skills of the smaller enterprise, but without violating honored company traditions.[16]

As vice-president and acting general manager, Hamilton Barksdale had been the central figure in the early twentieth century in estab-lishing evaluation guidelines for executives, creating a system of family administrative "understudies" to ease subsequent succession prob-lems, and forming a development department for product research and market analysis. Most important, management philosophy had been put into place which valued decentralized management but held each division's performance and coordination with overall company objec-tives accountable to a dominant central executive committee. In the du Pont empire, with the inner circle of Pierre, Irénée, Lammot, and Raskob occupying key positions on the executive and finance com-mittees, the watchwords of their own version of an industrial federalism were "decentralized management, centralized control." Under Alfred Sloan, General Motors likewise adopted an organizational plan that emphasized decentralized daily management while financial and policy control were centralized in a committee prominently featuring Pierre's circle of du Ponts.[17]

Such management concepts were readily reconciled with the long-standing du Pont distaste for drawing outside the family for managerial expertise. Departmentalization gave young du Ponts—the new ver-sions of Pierre and his brothers—opportunities to test their mettle and emerge from within an inbred company version of "survival of the fittest." The performance standards for executives established by Barksdale in the early 1900's provided Pierre's generation with more "scientific" criteria for selecting future leaders. Within this organi-zational scheme, individual departments operated within the company much as individual firms within a cartelized industry would, subject to the overall regulation of base pricing, product line, and profits set by the central executive committee. With these organizational concepts in mind, it took no great leap of insight for Pierre and his colleagues, by extending the same principles, to advocate the private central reg-ulation of entire industries through self-policing trade associations, or, even more ambitiously, the subordination of the entire national in-dustrial economy to the dictates of a single, overarching corporate "supercouncil."

Throughout the 1920's, company organization at Du Pont was considered an "essay in federalism." It followed a hierarchical pattern which included a small leadership group at the top (usually about five members), a somewhat larger body of advisors and policy consultants beneath it, and further below a series of specialized functional departments. As with any such "federal" system, however, the dangers of rigidity, inadequate coordination, and policy paralysis through an overly effective system of checks and balances were genuine. For that reason, the du Ponts' version of "industrial federalism," like its political counterpart, contained its own informal, flexible code of rules and prerogatives. On the one hand, pleading the independence of subordinate departments could allow the executive committee to compartmentalize and contain labor and regulatory problems at a local level (a kind of corporate assertion of "states' rights"). On the other hand, local autonomy still could be circumvented when the central committee deemed it convenient, given its overall financial clout. In actuality, then, the du Ponts' heralded decentralized management often was most useful in cloaking and legitimizing the centralization of executive power.[18]

Examples of the flexible use of a supposedly decentralized, "Jeffersonian" structure for neo-Hamiltonian ends were numerous, but perhaps the best example of Du Pont managerial "flexibility" could be seen in the company's ongoing relationship to its work force. The du Ponts saw industry-wide or craft-wide trade unions as invading "antibodies" hostile not only to company harmony but even to worker self-interest. For over a hundred years, the family nurtured a paternal relationship between managers and workers, each engaged in a mutually advantageous partnership of interest in the company's welfare. At the heart of this tradition was a hierarchical structure resembling the master-apprentice traditions of the European guilds. Young male du Ponts learned their business and "earned their spurs" on the job; they knew their employees as individuals, even influenced their religious preferences and dress. The company provided rental housing and modest death and disability aid for loyal workers and their families, trained employees' children in the values of duty and obedience at the Brandywine Manufacturers' Sunday School, and sponsored the construction of Episcopal and Catholic churches on Du Pont property. The forces of time, increased scale of operations, and technology had reduced the closeness of that prior association, but old assumptions of a continuing partnership of interest instead of an adversarial management-labor relationship died hard. As late as 1920, Coly du Pont still insisted that at the company an employee who needed a raise could simply rely upon his boss's good judgment: "If he has the right stuff in him, and he isn't afraid to expend plenty of body or brain sweat to make himself a bigger and broader man, the matter of salary will work itself out quite satisfactorily in the end." After all, Coly had added, "I never asked for a salary raise in my life."[19]

One of Du Pont's methods of preserving the allegedly harmonious, nonunion system of employee relations was to retain an obtrusive hierarchical structure while integrating journeymen into the ranks of management as foremen. Periodic slowdowns and job insecurity within the industry, increasing mechanization, and competition from foreign immigrants and rural migrants for lesser-skilled jobs also helped the company keep workers in line. During World War I, the company augmented its supervision of its workforce and also guarded against foreign sabotage by establishing a 1400-member police squad and an employee spy network. On the strength of its journeyman practices, in 1921 the company formed its own employee representation system, the Works Council, composed of decentralized joint committees of plant management and workers. The same year, prompted by memories of the labor unrest and Red Scare of the immediate postwar period, administrative representatives of both Du Pont and General Motors were among the founding members of the ten-member (later twelve) Special Conference Committee. The organization, intially including members from Du Pont, GM, Bethlehem Steel, General Electric, Goodyear, International Harvester, Irving Trust, Standard Oil of New Jersey, U.S. Rubber, and Westinghouse, was used to share information and strategies on how to forestall unionization as well as to map strategy on economic policy concerns. Beginning in 1923, Du Pont also contributed $2000 a year to the League for Industrial Rights (formerly the Anti-Boycott League) in its efforts to maintain the open shop. An internal public relations campaign was mobilized to encourage worker identification with the firm, utilizing the slogan, "You are a Du Pont man." An employee education course, entitled "How Our Business System Operates," or HOBSO, taught workers the dangers of "un-American" labor radicalism.[20]

Not all the du Ponts' efforts to maintain a traditional level of control over their workers were coercive or propagandistic. Pierre, John Raskob, and other company leaders sincerely believed that worker loyalty and cooperation did, and should, produce tangible rewards. Accordingly, they were leaders in the expansion of employee benefits in the 1920's known as "welfare capitalism." Du Pont had established its first pension plan for salaried employees back in 1904. In 1919, the company established a group life insurance plan for workers, and by the end of the Twenties extended it to cover sickness and accidents. For senior executives, however, benefits proved more generous, including stock bonuses and, beginning in 1927, a trust fund to provide executives with low-interest loans to finance stock options. In both Du Pont and General Motors, the driving force of "welfare capitalism" was Raskob, and from his position as GM's finance committee chairman and treasurer he made the automobile giant his testing ground. Even before the du Ponts' takeover of GM, the manufacturer's previous ownership had created a bonus plan for employees. Following an enlargement of the benefits programs the next year, the company had begun renting or selling housing to employees on a deferred payment basis. By the end of 1929, some 35,000 GM employees lived in company-owned housing. Employees also were permitted to contribute up to 10 percent of their earnings, if less than $300, to a savings fund into which the company agreed initially to match the worker's contributions and fixed the interest rate at 6 percent.[21]

Raskob, however, subsequently added his own innovations. In December 1926, he created a group insurance plan in which employees with at least three months' seniority could be protected up to $1000, with costs shared between the worker and the company. Payments could be received either in lump sum or in installments of twenty months in case of death or permanent disability. In 1928, he enlarged the plan to include larger death benefits, as well as health and nonoccupational accident insurance. GM also made contributions to a recreational and educational organization called the Industrial Mutual Association in Flint, Michigan, to fund the activities of its workers there. But Raskob's main emphasis was upon designing schemes to promote employee stock investment in the parent company. To him, stock ownership conferred a kind of "industrial citizenship," which led to more loyal, "responsible" (as in nonstriking), and productive workers with a direct "stake" in the company's fortunes. The strong parallels between Raskob's vision of industrial citizenship through stock ownership and the commonly held belief of many wealthy Americans, including the du Ponts, in the virtues of property qualifications for political citizenship, voting, and officeholding illustrated a persistent underlying unity between the du Ponts' economic and political philosophies.[22]

Under Raskob's guidance, GM's matching contributions to its employee savings plan were made in the form of purchases of stock in the company's investment fund. Employees were not permitted to pull out of the savings fund without forfeiting their investment fund holdings as well. As GM stock soared in value in the decade, however, the company scaled back the level of its contributions to the investment fund from fifty cents on the dollar in 1922 to twenty-five cents by 1933. Because of the mandatory tie-in to the savings plan, 89 percent of company workers participated. But when, as in 1924, Raskob offered employees a preferred stock subscription plan allowing employees to buy up to ten shares on the installment plan, with payments of two dollars a share above the regular dividends for five years, only 3342 employees took part.[23]

What Raskob's stock ownership schemes showed was that Du Pont management's interpretation of "welfare capitalism" placed a much greater emphasis upon executive capitalism than worker welfare. By generating additional demand for company stock among workers, such plans boosted the value of the du Ponts' own holdings. They were also cheaper than wage increases or company-wide bonus plans. For example, GM limited its own 1922 bonus plan to employees making at least $5000 a year. In the American chemical industry, where Du Pont was the industry leader, wage costs were over 17 percent of the value of products in 1919, but by 1933 the figure tumbled to less than 12.5 percent. In times of economic downturn and hardship such as the post–World War I recession, the du Ponts had not hesitated to invoke wage cuts or layoffs, insisting upon their unlimited prerogatives to do so. Nor did they hesitate to do so later, when business conditions again soured. Even in times of prosperity such as the Twenties, the du Ponts' management structure "worked" through exerting great pressure from the top upon departments to generate a high rate of return on capital, with performances rewarded by bonuses and punished by firings. High rates of return often were generated by squeezing labor costs, by speeding up the production lines, or by shifting operations into the poorer, less regulated and less unionized South, where wages averaged 44 percent lower than in the North.[24]

In 1924, after establishing the "rayon" name in synthetic fabrics, the Du Pont company built three new plants near Richmond and Waynesboro, Virginia, and at their World War I–era "Old Hickory" plant site in Tennessee. It was revealing of the du Ponts' view of their economic imperatives, in particular the need to accelerate worker productivity for the sake of greater profits, that when Irénée was asked to foresee the most revolutionary future benefit chemistry could bestow upon humanity, he replied, "I think it is likely that material will be found which, taken into the human system, will accomplish the results of eight hours of sleep. This will change the active existence of a man from 16 hours a day to 24 hours a day."[25] Nonetheless, with such beliefs and policies shielded beneath the glitter and promise of the post-recession Twenties, the du Ponts enjoyed widespread respect and admiration as technological and managerial innovators and as guardians of the public welfare. The growing popular admiration and personal success only encouraged Pierre, his brothers, and Raskob to seek new horizons—to extend their economic and social principles and defend their prerogatives in the strange arena of national politics.

chapter 2

Anti-Insurgent Politics

The Twenties may have witnessed the ascendancy of the American entrepreneur to popular acclaim, but the decade was not devoid of political conflicts or concerns for businessmen. Many of the era's political battles arose from the interplay of two divergent trends—the rise of the centralizing, managerial impulses of a corporate economy and the stubborn persistence of decentralized democratic ideals rooted in what the historian Ellis Hawley has called "village values." Traditional social mores were being challenged by a corporate-sponsored consumer mass culture, which carried with it relaxed and secularized moral standards, national managerial bureaucracies, and looser family and marriage ties. But the traditional village society could and often did fight back in the name of the "people versus the interests." Conflicts over prohibition, the Klan, anti-trust policy, public ownership of utilities, federal taxation, farm relief, and crime often fed upon the economic, ethnic, and cultural divisions of a nation marked by urban-rural tensions and a "cosmopolitan-localist" spectrum of popular values.[1]

In the arena of business-government relations, at least four competing models of political economy vied for popular and official favor. Two of them, the decentralized, enforced-competition model of Louis Brandeis and the federal-regulated corporate economy of the New Nationalism, appeared to observers in the 1920's to be losing ground. A third, the concept of a national interest-group pluralism which acknowledged labor unions, farm organizations, and consumer interests as separate and coequal government-brokered powers alongside business, had not yet experienced its day in the sun. Instead, the vision of business-government relations which appeared most likely to carry the field in the 1920's was a form of national self-regulation of business through trade associations. According to the advocates of the "new capitalism," enlightened corporate stewards should be allowed greater freedom to monitor industrial practices through collective private association and consultation, with government serving but a modest role as an anti-trust watchdog, as an information source, and as a friendly jawboner.[2]

This concept of industrial self-government also had variations, which often stemmed from differences in the scale and market power of individual business firms. For much of the "secondary tier" of American industry, cooperation by companies within distinct industries did not convey to a few industrial giants dictatorship over price, wage, production, or trade secrets decisions. Nor did it call for an additional layer of centralized corporate control above the level of the individual trade associations. This limited version of the new capitalism coincided with Secretary of Commerce Herbert Hoover's views on trade associationism. Among the leaders of the most highly integrated, expanding, and powerful national corporations, however, complete economic centralization seemed but the logical culmination of steady growth in business scale and organization. One such leader was Pierre du Pont. His own company's experiences in a highly voluntaristic, but also more thoroughly centralized, economic planning process during World War I had only reinforced this conviction. He maintained that a corporate "supercouncil," similar to the War Industries Board or the Special Conference Committee, could become the basis for an even broader corporate stewardship of national policy. He insisted, however, that national planning and decisionmaking *must* be kept in private corporate hands in the process, for, he claimed, "Government system, or lack of system, is drastically opposed to business methods."[3]

Immediately after World War I, Pierre turned down an invitation from fellow Delaware native Josiah Marvel to enlist in a superpatriotic society, United Americans, designed to head off the threat of socialism and to defend private property rights. In its broad outlines the organization resembled in some respects the American Liberty League, sponsored by the du Ponts in the 1930's. But in 1920 Pierre concluded, after conversations with Irénée and Raskob, that "a more practical plan would be that of organizing a council through individual effort, with the hope that the studies and recommendations of this well-chosen body of men might eventually command respect and, perhaps, lead to their becoming a potent factor in legislative matters." Such thinking shaped the formation of the Special Conference Committee, consisting as it did of representatives from Du Pont, General Motors, and eight other prominent corporations.[4]

It was, nonetheless, the supreme irony of the du Ponts' postwar

the insurgents, the special intensity of their hatred for demagoguery and class politics drew upon another, more direct, local example—the family's political sparring in Delaware with ousted cousin Alfred I. du Pont.[8]

Alfred du Pont was in nearly every personal respect the opposite of his cousin Pierre. While Pierre was responsible, stoic, and private, Alfred was embarrassingly theatrical, unstable, and flamboyant. Whereas Pierre's sense of family honor was strong, Alfred caused a scandal when he divorced one cousin and married another under questionable circumstances. Once Alfred found himself ousted from power in the Du Pont Company, he launched a protracted campaign of political revenge upon both Pierre and Coly. As Coly became increasingly active in Republican state politics as a defender of company interests, Alfred cast his lot as a progressive in opposition to the family. He formed the Delaware Trust Company in competition with Pierre's Wilmington Trust. After purchasing the Wilmington *News,* he used the press to castigate his cousins and espouse insurgent reforms. He spoiled Coly's small presidential boomlet in 1916 within the Delaware Republican delegation by endorsing Theodore Roosevelt, and then supported the Democratic opponent of Pierre's great-uncle Henry A. ("The Colonel") du Pont in the U.S. Senate campaign that fall—the first in the state's history conducted by popular vote rather than by the state legislature. By then encouraging the entry of a third-party Progressive candidate, and having the *News* assail the Colonel's record as "labor's enemy," he succeeded in blocking Henry's bid for re-election.[9]

Alfred's heyday as a progressive champion in Delaware, meddlesome though it had been, proved short-lived. He managed to mastermind the election of an officer in the Delaware Trust Company as reform mayor of Wilmington, blocked Coleman's appointment to the U.S. Senate in 1918, and launched a tax reform campaign in the state. But having already lost his court fight to regain leadership in the Du Pont Company and facing personal financial difficulties, he was forced to sell his most effective propaganda vehicle, the *News.* To his dismay, the newspaper soon found its way into the control of Pierre's faction. In Delaware's "Dirty Deal" of 1921, he failed to block Coly's appointment to the Senate following the resignation of the man he had helped elect in 1916, Democrat Josiah Wolcott. By 1923, Alfred was effectively finished as a political threat to the family in his native state. Moving south, he began carving out a new sphere of wealth and political influence in Florida that would last until his death in 1935.[10]

With both Alfred and the Senate's progressive insurgents as recent examples, Pierre and his partners, despite the positive political trends of the Twenties, felt threatened by the potential mischief of government, especially at the federal level. In the years since Pierre's initial rise to company leadership in 1902, they had accumulated a long litany of complaints: (1) the periodic efforts of government to "violate economic law" by launching anti-trust suits against big business, (2) regulatory harassment of the du Ponts' policy prerogatives in labor relations and other fields, (3) the threat of government competition with industry through creation of state-operated firms, (4) government "confiscation of property" through the tax system, (5) demagogic rabble-rousing by Congress through the mechanism of committee investigations, and (6) the dangerous expansion during the Progressive Era of constitutional experimentation through the amendment process. If continued, these trends would result, they were convinced, in the complete conversion of the American republic into a direct democracy and ultimately, through demagogic political manipulation, into a statist, communist dictatorship.

Ever since 1907, the threat of federal anti-trust suits directed at the du Ponts' empire had been taken very seriously. Sparked by a Congressional investigation of the company's monopoly of government-acquired dye patents, Theodore Roosevelt's Justice Department filed an action that in 1911 resulted in a decree forcing the divorce of Du Pont from its Atlas and Hercules explosives subsidiaries. Nonetheless, Du Pont executives continued to fill the leadership ranks of both companies. Passage of the Clayton Act in 1914 and the establishment of the Federal Trade Commission also made the family nervous. But even short of anti-trust threats to the empire, the dangers posed by federal regulatory statutes and agencies led the du Ponts to take special steps. Fearing exposure of trade secrets by federal inspectors, in 1908 the company began insisting that no government representatives be given access to a plant without first signing a security pledge. A year later, Pierre decreed that no information would be released by any employee without prior headquarters approval. Following the outbreak of World War I in Europe in 1914, Du Pont refused to provide the Secretary of War with information on the company's foreign munitions contractors. Requests for trade secrets were not answered until 1918, after the U.S. government had placed its first major wartime TNT order with Du Pont.[11]

American entry into the war in 1917 created new opportunities for cooperation between big business and government through the War Industries Board and other agencies. But for the du Ponts, the new prospects were at best a two-edged sword. Government contracts boosted company profits, but they also increased the risks of government meddling and control. In 1916, the company urged Congress to permit it to develop a water-power site and nitrogen-extraction plant, only to receive a bill authorizing the government to build its own facility. According to the New York *World,* angry company officers ordered employees not to wear Wilson reelection buttons, although Pierre denied the story. By the end of 1917, the government urged Du Pont to submit proposals for the building of a series of five federal munitions plant, including a Tennessee facility dubbed Old Hickory. Despite the company's proposal to build the plants on a cost-plus basis with only a one-dollar fee, the War Industries Board and Secretary of War Newton Baker objected to the government's assumption of the financial risks of construction while guaranteeing Du Pont large operating profits and management control. As a result, the original contract was cancelled. Only one plant—Old Hickory—was built, and even that caused ill will. Three years later a House investigating committee headed by Illinois Representative William Graham accused Du Pont of building it unnecessarily and bilking the taxpayers out of $116 million.[12]

Another prime example of the federal government's threat to the du Ponts emerged as a consequence of the Trading-with-the-Enemy Act of 1918. Under the law the Alien Property Custodian, A. Mitchell Palmer, seized all German-owned property in the country, including dye patents. His successor, Francis P. Garvan, was named president of an organization created by the du Ponts and other chemical firms, called the Chemical Foundation, to purchase the patents for distribution to private companies. Following a protracted suit by the Justice Department to regain the patents obtained by the du Ponts through the efforts of Garvan and the Chemical Foundation, the federal challenge was withdrawn in January 1924. Nonetheless, the suit generated considerably more adverse publicity for the du Ponts, occurring as it did in the midst of revelations in 1923–24 of other Harding administration scandals in the Alien Property Custodian's office.[13]

By the mid-1920's, the fear of executive branch regulation and interference with company prerogatives had eased. But another kind of threat—that of property confiscation through the federal tax system—had not. In 1913 the first indication of what many wealthy Americans labelled a new federal assault on private property was signalled by the ratification of the Sixteenth Amendment to the Constitution. Within three years, annual income taxes on individuals had risen to $173 million, taxes on corporations to $172 million. In 1916, congressional insurgents pushed for $26 million in excess-profits taxes, with munitions manufacturers a major target. Although reductions were inserted in the Senate's final bill, the "Munitions Tax" still imposed a 12.5 percent surcharge on the net profits of explosive sales, retroactive to January. Irénée du Pont later estimated that the company paid 90 percent of all the moneys collected under the measure by the federal government. In contrast, tax protection legislation for the du Ponts in the form of a tariff bill targetting foreign dye imports took four years to pass, clearing the Congress only in 1922.[14]

Such limited tax relief, in the du Ponts' view, hardly substituted for an otherwise escalating burden of federal income, estate, inheritance, and corporation levies in the 1920's. After World War I, individual and corporate income taxes rose to $1.42 billion in 1921, $1.9 billion in 1925, and almost $2.4 billion by 1928 (with the total almost equally split between individual and corporate obligations). It was not, of course, that such increases actually prevented real growth in the incomes of wealthy Americans and corporations. But nonetheless, the impact of higher tax bills was to impress upon the du Ponts and others in similar circumstances that they were being "singled out" as a class for unprecedented confiscation. And, in fairness, the charge did have some validity. As historian Mark Leff has noted, by the late 1920's taxable incomes of over $50,000 a year still amounted to only 24 percent of the reported national total of personal income but provided the source for approximately 80 percent of the income taxes collected. Taxation of the wealthy was for both congressional insurgents and their pro-business enemies a symbolic power struggle that each fought with equal fervor. Corporate interests including the du Ponts opposed such evolving features of the tax code as the estate tax, dual taxation of income at both the state and federal levels, separate classification of property into private and corporate categories, and rate progressivity. Increasingly they advocated both reductions in income and estate taxes and their replacement by more regressive alternate forms of taxation, such as a federal sales levy.[15]

The du Ponts placed great hopes in the efforts of Treasury Secretary Andrew Mellon in the 1920's to eliminate the "soak the rich" features of the federal tax system. Until his tenure, federal officials had seldom even considered the idea of wholesale tax rebates. But under Mellon, controller of a vast aluminum fortune and a primary stockholder in both Mellon National Bank and Gulf Oil, tax savings through revisions and rebates amounted to over $6 billion. The Revenue Act of 1921 reduced by 60 percent the levies taken in on annual incomes of over $300,000, lowered the maximum surtax on incomes over $2 million from 65 percent to 50 percent, and abolished the excess-profits tax, saving corporate stockholders another $1.5 billion. But despite the rate relief, the steep rise in personal and corporate fortunes in the 1920's itself meant that the du Ponts' actual tax obligations still rose. According to Pierre's calculations, the "average tax collections" of the family and the company at all levels of government per year for the period 1923–1926 came to $1.8 billion.[16]

Pierre and his brothers welcomed Mellon's additional efforts to reduce taxes on the wealthy through a proposed cut of the maximum income surtax to 25 percent in 1924. But with congressional insurgents in opposition to the plan, not only was it defeated but an anti-Mellon Senate investigation, headed by James Couzens of Michigan, was launched. The revenue bill enacted actually hiked inheritance taxes upward to 40 percent on estates worth over $10 million, forcing Pierre to accelerate the timing of his decision to "sell" personal stock holdings to younger family beneficiaries before the new law took effect. Pierre, citing a population of some 160 du Ponts, endorsed Secretary Mellon's assertion that the concentration of great fortunes was no danger in America because of the tendency over time toward disperson of wealth within families. President Coolidge drafted a letter of rebuke to the Senate, and Irénée du Pont seconded him in the *New York Times*. "Their [the Senate's] recent actions are as bad as anything in red Russia," he blustered. "It is time to call a halt. The idea that the Senate should take exception to President Coolidge's note and even suggest that it be expunged from the record is the most preposterous thing that has happened in Washington." Mellon in turn expressed similar alarmist sentiments, claiming of the congressional actions that, "Carried to excess, they differ in no way from the methods of the revolutionists in Russia."[17]

The last institutional bastions of government against such "radical" forces in Congress, the du Ponts believed, were the courts and the Constitution. The federal judiciary appeared in safe hands, with the Supreme Court upholding "yellow dog" labor contracts, striking down federal child labor statutes, placing unions more tightly under anti-trust restrictions, and in general applying substantive due process and contract-right requirements in a manner to circumscribe government regulatory activity. But how useful would such protections of the courts remain if their legal and political underpinnings were removed by way of constitutional amendment? The Progressive Era had witnessed the unleashing of federal amendment campaigns designed to hurdle various political barriers to moral and economic regulation by the state, to extend forms of "direct democracy," and to generate new forms of taxation. In most cases those same campaigns had been spearheaded by the same rural, populistic insurgents the du Ponts detested. The result had been the ratification of five amendments to the federal constitution within eight years, including the income tax, the direct election of senators, prohibition, and woman suffrage amendments. In all cases the du Ponts had either privately maintained serious doubts or had openly opposed the changes. With a national child labor amendment and an equal rights amendment for women under consideration by Congress and the states in the 1920's, and other possible changes being discussed, the threat of additional constitutional experimentation remained a serious one.[18]

It has become almost commonplace to dismiss the political continuities between the Progressive Era and the 1920's, and to see little real threat to business power in the maneuverings of the insurgents. At the time, however, the du Ponts did not view matters so sanguinely. After all, the fruits of economic power and political respect that recently had been gained could also be lost, especially given a political process that provided so much leeway for the rabble-rousing demagogue. One source of Pierre's 1924 diatribe against popular politics, for example, was the threat of a La Follette-led third-party movement—a movement which did become a reality and which put forth a platform advocating such constitutional experiments as the direct popular election of the president and the requirement of a national referendum before any congressional adoption of a war resolution. Besides blocking the Mellon tax initiatives, Midwestern rural insurgents in Congress also threatened in the McNary-Haugen bill to use the federal tax power to underwrite American farmers, and they orchestrated efforts to increase utility regulation and public ownership of power facilities. When both the Harding and Coolidge administrations attempted to sell the Muscle Shoals hydroelectric and nitrate facilities in Alabama to private industry, they successfully delayed action. As the clearest sign of the insurgents' stubborn determination and enduring clout, in 1928 Congress even passed a bill authorizing limited federal development of the Tennessee Valley, although Coolidge would kill the measure through a pocket veto.[19]

From the early years of the century until the mid-1920's, the family's political responsibility for countering the "radical" influences of congressional insurgents had belonged to an older cadre of du Ponts, in particular Henry and Coleman. "Colonel" Henry, a graduate of West Point and son of Gilded Age family patriarch "Boss" Henry du Pont, was known as the "Junker of Delaware" for his well-waxed Vandyke beard and for his vigorous defense of the railroads in particular and of big business generally. After a decade of effort, he won a seat in the Senate in 1906, from which he served as a stalwart member of the Republican Old Guard. He opposed the Clayton Act, the Adamson Act (giving the eight-hour day to interstate railway workers), various pieces of labor legislation, and woman suffrage, while backing tariff and military preparedness bills. Defeated for reelection in 1916 amidst charges by the opposition of the Senate's worst rate of absenteeism, Henry's role as congressional defender of family interests was then assumed by Coly.[20]

T. Coleman ("Coly") du Pont, a Republican national committeeman and chairman of the party's Speakers Bureau since 1908, was a founder of the pro-preparedness National Security League in 1915. He subsequently fought suspected radicalism and promoted pro-business Americanism through the American Association of Foreign Language Newspapers, boosted the presidential candidacy of Warren Harding in 1920, and chaired the Inter-Racial Council, which opposed the restriction of immigration. Appointed to the Senate in 1921, after several previous bids for the office, Coly pushed through the dye tarriff protection legislation the family sought. An opponent of the soldiers' bonus, he enthusiastically endorsed the Mellon tax program. But by 1924, his Senate record also was marred by illness and absenteeism. Already in his sixties, he began to consider retirement soon after the Coolidge landslide of the fall swept him into a full Senate term. He finally retired in 1928 upon discovering that he had cancer.[21]

With the passing of the "old guard," it was time for one or more of Pierre's generation to assume political responsibilities, but prior to Pierre's retirement as General Motors president in 1923 and Irénée's resignation as active Du Pont head in 1926, neither of them had been willing or able to pull themselves away from the daily problems of business administration. Pierre's reclusive nature and his disdain for partisan politics also ruled out his seeking direct elective office. He, his brothers, and John Raskob had been attentive to political issues and campaigns in the past, but their role had been limited largely to providing financial contributions to like-minded—usually Republican—candidates. In 1912, in the aftermath of the Roosevelt-Taft Justice Department's anti-trust campaign, Pierre had seen the Democrat Woodrow Wilson as the least dangerous White House possibility and had voted for him. By 1916, however, he had changed his mind and, hoping to promote America's preparedness for entering the war in Europe on the Allied side, had given $92,000 to the campaign of Charles Evans Hughes. More money, $12,378, had followed from Pierre to the Republican campaign of Warren G. Harding in 1920.[22]

For his part, Irénée, who had always been a more stalwart Republican partisan along the lines of Colonel Henry and Coly, had given $22,832 to the GOP in 1919–20 and provided $10,000 of the family's $34,000 to Coolidge in 1924. John Raskob, in contrast, was more inclined to follow Pierre's avowedly nonpartisan lead, having told a reporter in 1919 that he was a "thoroughly independent voter." But he, too, usually had found himself giving to the GOP on policy and ideological grounds, including donations of $1000 to New York Republicans in 1922 and $5000 to the Delaware party organization in 1924. After Pierre's resignation of the GM presidency in 1923, however, both his and Raskob's political activities broadened. Raskob urged Pierre's brother Lammot to enlist the Du Pont Company's support of a greater policy lobbying role by the U.S. Chamber of Commerce. Raskob himself joined the Chamber's finance department, as well as the Ex-Serviceman's Anti-Bonus League. Pierre, following his "sale" of stock holdings to family inheritors in 1924, began to assume a much greater role in Delaware state government. In April, the same month in which he verbally blasted the electoral process, he attended the grand opening of the Kennett Pike highway, which Coly had pushed and he had extensively underwritten.[23]

Pierre's most important new state public venture, however, was the upgrading of Delaware's public schools. Determined to prove his case for the superiority of enlightened private stewardship, he, along with Raskob and the Reverend James H. Odell, revived a moribund 1919–20 school modernization plan. Before the 1920's, the state's black schoolchildren were taught in sheds because of laws prohibiting the taxation of whites to pay for black facilities. With many white schools also horribly substandard, an estimated 20 percent of Delaware's youths could not even write their names. In 1924 Pierre arranged his own appointment to the state board of education, donated over $4 million of his own money to finance the replacement of one hundred dilapidated buildings, gave another $2 million to the state university, and revised the school code to reduce local control of funds and text-book selection. He used the power of his position to force local districts to provide matching funds for the construction program. Named School Tax Commissioner the next year, he (ironically, given his views on governmental tax "confiscation") found himself the state's main collector of income, franchise, inheritance, estate, and occupational taxes in Delaware. Under his administration, all state income taxes were directed to the school program.[24]

By the end of his third term as the state's tax administrator, Delaware would rise to tenth in the nation in literacy rate. According to one observer, "In Delaware schools the children chirp George Washington, Abraham Lincoln, and Pierre du Pont in the same breath." The *Outlook*, hailing Pierre as "hero of the schools" and Coly as "hero of good roads," cited their examples as "a case of expert knowledge both in school matters and road building, and business genius applied to collecting taxes, which up until now have never been satisfactorily gathered." In Pierre's own perspective, his willingness to assume the responsibilities of school financing and tax collection in an honest, efficient manner underscored the validity of his assertions about the virtues of "disinterested" private stewardship of public policy. He felt assured that the tax system, if administered by managers like himself, rather than by the "wrong people," would not be employed as a demagogic weapon against wealth, but would be instead used to pursue genuinely worthy social aims. Following an extended vacation to Europe with his wife in late 1925 (including a sojourn to Italy for new ideas for his gardens and fountains), Pierre returned refreshed and heartened by the acclaim that his civic efforts in Delaware were receiving.[25]

Emboldened by the popular reception to his venture into policy administration and aware of Coleman's fading value as the family's political protector, Pierre, along with his brothers and Raskob, began in late 1925 investigating other avenues for demonstrating their rejuvenated faith in corporate public policy administration. Motivated by a contradictory mixture of economic optimism and a continuing concern over populistic threats to their prerogatives, they sought a major public debate into which they could channel their belief in private policy stewardship, their disdain for rural insurgency, their fears of government regulation, competition, and confiscation, and their hope of a gentrified, managerial political process. Already one particular national issue was becoming a dramatic example of their concerns, and an example of the broad capacity for harm inherent in constitutional manipulation and in declining popular respect for class, order, and hierarchy. That issue—to which the du Ponts would bring their personal and financial resources directly to bear—was prohibition.

chapter 3

The Opening Wedge of Tyranny

Prohibition of the manufacture, transportation, and sale of alcoholic beverages, the issue to which the du Ponts turned in 1926, was the most controversial of the constitutional experiments of the Progressive Era. In November 1913 (the same year as the ratification of the Income Tax Amendment), the Anti-Saloon League launched a public appeal for a national prohibition amendment. Spurred by concern over liquor's role in promoting crime, poor health, family abuses, and working-class economic maladjustment, the prohibition crusaders garnered additional allies during World War I because of anti-German patriotism and pro-conservation sentiments (it was argued that grain and farmland should be devoted to other agricultural products, not spirits). Hoping to improve the health of workers and productivity of the war economy, Congress passed an emergency measure which defined intoxicating beverages as those with an alcohol content of over 2.75 percent and barred their traffic after July 1, 1919. Legislators also approved for submission to the states a postwar constitutional amendment prohibiting the manufacture and distribution of intoxicating liquor. By January 1919, forty-four states had ratified the measure, and under its provisions prohibition took effect a year hence. Needing an enforcement statute to accompany the new amendment, Congress in October of that year enacted the Volstead Act, which created a prohibition bureau within the Treasury Department, redefined the meaning of "intoxicating liquors," and set federal penalties. As defined by the Volstead law, an intoxicating liquor was one with an alcohol content of but 0.5 percent, effectively prohibiting the use not only of hard liquors but even light wines and beer.[1]

Prohibition had its expected critics—the brewers and distillers, their workers, saloonkeepers, and hotel and restaurant industry spokesmen—but in addition, many well-to-do Americans viewed the law as a new example of the federal government's growing threat to private property, individual liberty, and personal choice. After all, through the prohibition measure the government, agitated by rural insurgents, had embarked on nothing less than the destruction of an entire industry by fiat. One such affluent critic of prohibition was Captain William H. Stayton. Afready fifty-seven years old at the time of the amendment's enactment, Stayton was best described as an old-fashioned Washington lobbyist, and one with a particular bent toward anti-government, conservative, and pro-defense causes. As a young man, he had, while wooing the commandant's daughter, graduated thirteenth in a class of seventy-five at the U.S. Naval Academy. After ten years' service, he resigned his commission and earned two law degrees from the Columbian (later George Washington) University. Following careers as an admiralty lawyer, a steamship company manager, and a speculator, as well as serving as a Spanish-American War volunteer, Stayton became president of the naval academy's Alumni Association and, more important, executive secretary and chief lobbyist of the "big-navy" lobby, the Navy League, in Washington from April 1916 to January 1918. As a Delaware native and a visible advocate of military preparedness, including federal funding for the Merchant Marine and production speedups opposed by shipyard unions, Stayton was known by John Raskob and representatives of the du Ponts as well as by other war industry executives.[2]

Although Stayton was not shy about lobbying for greater federal financial aid for the shipping industry, he professed great alarm at the other tendencies toward centralized government control of industry in the Wilson Administration. As he later related to H. L. Mencken, "I found myself particularly alarmed by two movements that were running parallel; one, to provide the passage of a child labor amendment, so that the management of the family would be taken out of the control of parents, and, second, an effort to pass a Federal prohibition amendment." Although his role as a spokesman for naval armament led him to set aside his bias against federal activism when it was beneficial to his clients, Stayton at least in theory still clung to a states' rights view of the Constitution and opposed the gradual accumulation of power at the national level.[3]

Stayton wanted to put together an effort to block prohibition months before the end of World War I, but friends and patrons persuaded him in the spring of 1918 to postpone consideration for the war's duration. On the day after the armistice, however, he launched his new crusade by creating the Association Against the Prohibition Amendment. From the organization's inception, Stayton maintained that one of its primary purposes was to educate the public on the broader subject of a "proper" interpretation of the Constitution and on the need to keep state powers out of federal hands. The AAPA's prospectus described the Eighteenth Amendment as an improper delegation of state regulatory and police powers to the federal government. The organization's immediate objectives were to keep the country from going "bone-dry" in 1920 and to make the Eighteenth Amendment inoperative by promoting state nullifications of enforcement. Stayton's first recruits were former Navy colleagues and business clients, but his first big contribution, from John A. Roebling, son of the builder of the Brooklyn Bridge, for $10,000 in 1920, came in too late to offer any hope of heading off prohibition's implementation.[4]

Stayton showed a grudging admiration for the organizational skill of the enemy, the Anti-Saloon League, and patterned his movement's structure after it. Following the AAPA's incorporation in Washington in December 1920, the Anti-Saloon League proved an effective grassroots mobilizer of swing votes in primary and general elections, pushing state legislative candidates and congressmen toward a dry stance. Stayton, however, found his counter-efforts very slow going. By the midterm elections of November 1922, the AAPA claimed 457,000 members nationwide, but such figures were likely inflated. In any event, by February 1924 the total claimed fell to less than 400,000. Despite renewed membership growth from 1925 on (to over 725,000 in 1926), membership in wet organizations at the grass roots remained behind that of the drys. Worse yet, given the need of broad-based support spanning many states to effect repeal, AAPA membership remained concentrated in urban centers of Northeastern, industrial Midwestern, and West Coast states such as New York, Ohio, Illinois, and California. In vast stretches of the rural South, Midwest, and West, the wets attracted a sparse following. Membership figures themselves, in any case, gave but minimal measurement of the intensity of members' commitment, since belonging to the AAPA required only a one-dollar annual contribution.[5]

Membership deficiencies were accompanied by financial weakness. Beyond the Roebling contribution, few large donations had been forthcoming in the AAPA's early years. By 1923, in a clear indication of the organization's floundering finances, the AAPA had altered its initial policies to allow contributions from representatives of the liquor industry up to a level of 50 percent of its total annual income. Although needed, contributions from the industry undercut AAPA claims to be the vanguard of a principled opposition to prohibition and fed AAPA opponents' charges that it was nothing more than a paid mouthpiece

of the liquor trade. Stayton himself was forced to subsidize his struggling organization to the tune of $1000 a month for the first five years.
In the same five years, the AAPA collected but $800,000 in total
contributions and dues, not only illustrating fundraising difficulties
but also casting renewed doubts on the movement's membership
claims.[6]

Stayton tried his best to bolster the organizational effort. In 1921,
state divisions were created, both to oversee state election activities
and to relieve Stayton of some responsibility for direct recruitment of
members and contributions. Although the state chapters were asked
to turn over a quarter of their receipts to the national headquarters,
few did so. Pennsylvania and Maryland state divisions were created
in 1921, and the following year New York formed not only a state
chapter but also a separate women's committee. The California AAPA,
also constituted in 1922, claimed 25,000 members by 1924. In other
states it was deemed wiser not to create new chapters but to absorb
existing "modification leagues," such as those in Minnesota and Ohio
and the Constitutional Liberty League in Massachusetts. By 1926, the
AAPA claimed twenty-five state branches but, reflecting the same
recruitment difficulties as the national office, not one was located in
the South and only a few were in the Plains states or the West.[7]

Supplementing the state organizations were small groups of prominent citizens, or "voluntary committees," formed independently or
within unaffiliated cooperating bodies, such as the New York Yacht
Club's Voluntary Committee. But despite the AAPA's efforts to ab-
solve its cause from ethical taint by recruiting the "moral guardian-
ship" of women, it remained virtually all male as well as restricted by
region. In New York and Pennsylvania, anti-prohibition women's
groups known as Molly Pitcher Clubs had been formed, but they would
disappear by 1928. A small women's organization headed by Miss M.
Louise Gross did continue under a series of names, but without notable
impact. Nothing demonstrated the political weakness of the wet cause
in the early 1920's more clearly than the juxtaposition of the AAPA's
public urgings to candidates to endorse repeal and its humbling hesitancy in revealing the sparseness of its membership rolls. Making
matters even worse, the numerically superior Anti-Saloon League
hunted down lists of AAPA-endorsed candidates and targetted them
for electoral reprisal with disturbing success.[8]

Owing in part to Stayton's insistence that the AAPA's message be
rooted within a deeper conservative opposition to the rural populistic
and government-centralizing influences of the Progressive Era, he
found it difficult to build bridges of cooperation with agrarian, working-

class, and labor groups. Combined with the organization's weakness in the South and West, and the requirement that repeal be ratified by three-fourths of the states, Stayton's failures led to internal disagreements over both the immediate tactics and ultimate objectives of the AAPA. Should the organization bow to the reality of its limited resources and seek the lesser goal of modification of prohibition laws, or should it push resolutely for absolute appeal? The AAPA's own slogan, calling for "Beers and Light Wines NOW, but no Saloons EVER," mirrored its members' ambivalence. In recognition of its limited political clout, and needing a victory to bolster members' enthusiasm, Stayton listed his gradualist priorities in April 1922 as (1) the legalization of beer and wine for home consumption; (2) the amendment or repeal of the Volstead Act providing a reduced, national standard of enforcement; and, only then, (3) the repeal of the Eighteenth Amendment itself.[9]

Working within Stayton's enunciated strategy, the AAPA won isolated victories, most notably in New York. In January 1919, the same month as the ratification of the Eighteenth Amendment, a Republican-controlled state legislature approved prohibition over objections by Democratic Governor Alfred E. Smith that it be put to a statewide popular referendum. In April 1920, the legislators opted for a less stringent definition of intoxicating liquors, a 2.75 percent standard signed into law by Smith. Following the Harding landslide, however, which swept into power Republican Governor Nathan Miller, a new 1921 state enforcement statute known as the Mullen-Gage law brought the state back into conformity with the Volstead Act. With the AAPA's help, the 1922 elections then returned Smith to the governor's chair on a platform pledging return to the 2.75 percent level. The state legislature, going even further, opted on May 3, 1923, to repeal Mullen-Gage in full. After a series of public hearings and well-publicized agonizing over his decision, Smith signed the enforcement repeal measure on June 1.[10]

As part of its gradualist approach, the AAPA also joined forces with the American Federation of Labor, the Modification League of New York, and the Constitutional Liberty League of Massachusetts in a 1922 joint legislative lobbying group urging modification of the Volstead Act to set the alcohol content standard at 2.75 percent. Hearings were held by the House Judiciary Committee in April and May 1924 as a preconvention partisan warmup for platform debates, without result. At the 1924 national party conventions, the wets, if anything, lost ground. The Republicans moved away from their 1920 silence on the issue to hint at a pro-enforcement position. Attempts to pass a minority plank against prohibition at the Democratic convention generated considerable noise but actually garnered fewer votes than another minority proposal calling for a condemnation of the Ku Klux Klan. More damaging, the wets' presidential hopeful, Governor Al Smith, was denied the party's nomination.[11]

The AAPA's failure to steer either party toward repeal, when combined with a Coolidge landslide that favored the "drier" major party, led some wets to urge promotion of popular noncompliance and nonenforcement of existing laws rather than continued legislative modification and repeal efforts. Given Stayton's traditionalist views, advocacy of civil disobedience was rejected as undermining the broader respect for law and order. Instead, Stayton decided to accentuate the AAPA's long-term effort to convince politicians that support for prohibition was risky by orchestrating state referenda urging modification and repeal. In 1922, a *Literary Digest* subscribers' poll indicated that 38.6 percent favored existing laws, 40.8 percent supported modification, and 20.6 percent wanted total repeal. A closer analysis showed that of factory worker respondents, 62 percent backed repeal and only 9 percent enforcement. In four state referenda that fall, Ohio overwhelmingly rejected modification, but Californians only narrowly endorsed their state's enforcement act, Illinois voters opted for modification by a two-to-one margin, and Massachusetts citizens declared by a four-to-three ratio their opposition to the Bay State's enforcement act. Three years later, a *Collier's* poll of 263,583 respondents indicated that over two-thirds were dissatisfied with prohibition, over 60 percent believed it was not being enforced, and a similar number did not believe it could be.[12]

Changing politicians' minds on prohibition through the weight of popular opinion, however, required an extensive public education and propaganda apparatus that would feature newspaper columns and editorials, magazine articles, lectures, and testimonials by well-known and respected spokesmen—and, above all, the money to fund such efforts. The financial demands of a serious propaganda effort, combined with the AAPA's failure to out-organize its dry opponents at the grass-roots membership level, led Stayton by late 1925 and early 1926 to emphasize even more than before the recruitment of a moneyed and prestigious core of loyalists to his cause rather than the solicitation of a direct-mail mass membership. This approach was encouraged by a mutual friend of both Captain Stayton and the du Ponts, Federal Judge George May of Wilmington. It also appealed to the Captain's own well-developed social elitism. Then as later, when considering the virtues of an elitist versus a grass-roots clientele, Stayton's preference was for those who "wore coats" over those who walked around "in shirtsleeves on a Saturday or Sunday."[13]

The AAPA's shift in tactics and recruitment in the mid-1920's proved well suited to the growing unease among wealthy Americans over the rise of crime and bootlegging, the loss of social decorum and order, and the additional federal intrusions of various kinds upon their professional and personal prerogatives. Stayton noted the mood in a letter he cited before an April 1926 Detroit AAPA meeting: "The people are not very much interested in the question of wet and dry . . . Prohibition is not a real disease, but merely a sympton of a very great and deep-seated disease—the disease of plutocracy, of centralization of government from Washington in public affairs that extends now into the home and to the dinner table." Already included among the AAPA's elite membership were the humorist Irvin S. Cobb, Illinois Central Railroad president Stuyvesant Fish, former mayor of New York City Seth Low, and Guaranty Trust Company head Charles H. Sabin. Now, however, others were adding their names to the AAPA roster— none with more prominent reputations and more copious coffers than the du Ponts.[14]

At first, the du Ponts played a very minor role in the AAPA's efforts. John Raskob was the first to be contacted by Stayton's organization, through solicitation letters and questionnaires in late 1919 and again in 1920. He did not join the AAPA until June 1922, when he sent in the minimum one-dollar fee, and he refused invitations to appear at the House Judiciary Committee's prohibition hearings in April 1924. Irénée and Lammot du Pont also sent in their initial membership fees the same summer of 1922. By November Irénée's interest in the cause had grown sufficiently that he upgraded his membership to a "Class B" status, with a ten-dollar contribution. He was content to remain at that level in 1925.[15]

Pierre du Pont proved the most hesitant to take the plunge into prohibition politics. Besides his inherent shyness, he was a virtual abstainer from alcohol who had enforced a dry rule in company plants during World War I. Plant managers had been empowered to "properly decline to employ a man who uses intoxicants at any time on or off the job." When Raskob, Irénée, and Lammot joined the AAPA in 1922, an otherwise sympathetic Pierre refused on the grounds that the organization appeared to be merely a front for the liquor trade. Pierre's influence within the family and the company was such, however, that without his personal enlistment to the cause, involvement by other du Ponts would probably have remained at their initially low levels.[16]

Pierre's mobilization began to occur in 1925 and was motivated by

the fear of increased federal power generated by tax debates, his growing interest in Delaware state policy issues, and the specific emergence
in the state legislature in March of the Weer bill. The Weer bill was
a proposal to strengthen Delaware's prohibition enforcement statute
by allowing police to enter private property, arrest citizens for mere
possession of alcoholic beverages, and sentence convicted first offenders
to jail terms. Alarmed at another example of the extension of government's right to confiscate property, Pierre the businessman was also
becoming concerned at reports of prohibition's effects on worker moral
and respect for law—reports confirmed by plant managers who complained of worsening productivity and bootlegging. When the U.S.
Prohibition Commissioner hinted that all privately owned liquor
should be seized, Pierre's response was to become a Class B subscriber
to the AAPA in November. As yet he still disavowed interest in taking
on more responsibility, declining a position on the AAPA Advisory
Board on the suggestive grounds that "I do not care to become a
figurehead only."[17]

At the beginning of 1926, Pierre decided, with some prompting by
Irénée, to assume a greater leadership role in the AAPA. Irénée organized and even financed a chapter of the AAPA in Delaware by
offering to pay the one-dollar dues of 5000 state residents unable or
unwilling to do so themselves. Pierre chaired and hosted an exploratory
meeting of the Delaware chapter at the Wilmington Playhouse on
January 21, and the next month he donated an additional $100 and
became a director of the state organization. Pierre also joined a national
AAPA "committee of fifty," whose task it was to study the systems of
liquor control in other countries and to propose recommendations for
the organization to advocate in legislative testimony and in propaganda
literature. Contributions of each of the du Ponts rose gradually in
1926, with Pierre extending $5250 to the national AAPA and $1100
to the state chapter. Raskob, in turn, gave $750 to the national office.
Pierre and Irénée also agreed to "loan" $5000 each to the national
AAPA in the early fall and contributed smaller amounts to underwrite
the costs of local events and meetings.[18]

The du Ponts gave a variety of reasons for the new vigor of their
commitment to the cause. Among the motivations certainly was the
simple wish to be able to continue enjoying a private social activity
without fear of property confiscation or arrest. Another was the desire
to rid the country of one source, of many, of political debauchery and
demagoguery. As Pierre had put it, prohibition helped create both
"the bootlegger and the bribe taker." Pierre also cited the tax money
squandered because of an outlawed liquor industry, claiming that both

lost liquor taxes and the revenues wasted on prohibition enforcement could be redirected to worthier causes, such as a federal effort to eradicate tuberculosis or a reduction of individual and corporate income taxes. For his part, Raskob, father of twelve children ages five to twenty-one, fretted that prohibition's effect in eroding respect for law among the young could unleash a revolutionary spirit that might spawn "Bolshevism." As the lone Catholic in the du Pont inner circle, he also noted the frequent connection between advocacy of prohibition and nativist religious bigotry.[19]

The most thorough accounting of the du Ponts' motivations was supplied by Irénée in an angry, but undelivered, reply to an article by William Allen White in *Collier's* magazine. He maintained that (1) prohibition laws actually had promoted the abuse of liquor, not abstinence; (2) a rich source of tax revenue was being wasted and the moneys diverted to bootleggers and corrupt agents; (3) prohibition was a violation of states' rights; and (4) prohibition represented "the opening wedge to a breaking down of our whole theory of Government by legislating through the Constitution." Irénée also condemned prohibition's role in encouraging the use of denatured industrial alcohol as an illegal ingredient in beverages, given the accompanying public health hazards. To Coleman du Pont he blamed the Eighteenth Amendment for "untold corruption of Governmental employees," the "demoralization of the young," and the sacrifice of "hundreds of millions of governmental income." Pierre, for his part, did admit that alcoholism created its own health miseries, but nevertheless he insisted that "the right of the majority to interfere with the liberties of a minority" was the central issue. "The welfare of a very small percentage of 'would-be' alcoholics," he charged, "is not as important as the security of the American ideal, by which I mean the right to choose one's course."[20]

Such reasons helped explain why the du Ponts enlisted in the fight against prohibition. What they did not explain, however, was why so much of their participation in that fight should take place outside, rather than within, the structure of the major political parties. Why choose the AAPA as the family's primary repeal vehicle, given its less than impressive performance to date? Although he modestly claimed that Irénée "is more actively interested in the Association than I have been," it was Pierre's view of the value of nonpartisan political stewardship which guided the family on this particular course. In October he wrote that the very words "Republican" or "Democrat" were "to me as the red flag is to the bull." Disillusioned with electoral partisan "politics as usual," he preferred to build a nonpartisan Delaware

AAPA and, through it, build a wise liquor program from the ground up, rather than merely channel funds to an established political party in the uncertain hope of influencing its policies. He claimed, "The only way that we can straighten out our political affairs is to start at the bottom and see that each separate entity be placed on a business basis in charge of qualified people." In this regard Irénée initially was less visionary than his older brother. Contributing $37,500 to the Republican party in 1926 with the stipulation that it be spent only on repeal candidates, Irénée placed early emphasis upon trying to "accomplish certain specific results now and again," rather than intending a long-term participation "in the game."[21]

Pierre's comments on the need to start "at the bottom" and to restructure the processes of politics applied both to government officialdom and to the AAPA's own leadership. In 1926 the AAPA was still an antiquated "one-man show" with Stayton at the helm, aided only by national secretary Gorton C. Hinckley, field secretary Louis Livingstone, and a tiny staff. When Stayton appeared in the spring before a Senate Judiciary subcommittee studying modification, and then a special Senate panel investigating campaign irregularities, he scored a few public relations points, but he also exposed the clumsiness of the campaign's efforts to date. AAPA publicity had been limited to small pamphlets and fliers, irregular issues of clip sheets featuring newspaper reprints, and two short-lived newsletters, *The Minute Man* in 1922 and the AAPA *Bulletin* in 1923. As the 1926 midterm elections approached, the AAPA's tactics remained timid and its effectiveness limited by squabbles between local chapters and the national office. As one example of the organizational chaos, the Wisconsin AAPA chose to back conservative Republican Irvine Lenroot for the U.S. Senate in defiance of a national AAPA endorsement of his primary opponent, John J. Blaine.[22]

Despite the national AAPA's ineptness, the du Ponts had reason to hope that public sentiment, as measured by state referenda, was turning away from prohibition. Most encouraging were improvements in the West, despite losses in California, Colorado, and Missouri. In Montana, 54 percent of the voters endorsed repeal of the state's enforcement act. In Nevada, a proposition urging creation of a national constitutional convention to consider modification or repeal garnered a three-to-one margin. Pierre became increasingly convinced that an all-out, massively funded assault on prohibition could prevail as early as 1928. On the basis of his researches into liquor policy in Quebec and Great Britain, he supported in place of prohibition a reconstituted, regulated, and taxed liquor industry which would dispense alcoholic beverages in moderation and indirectly would reduce tax burdens on individuals and businesses. To attain the immediate goals of repeal and reconstitution of the liquor industry, he insisted upon a change in tactics away from the limited referenda strategy and toward an aggressive campaign geared at generating national legislation and state repeal conventions.[23]

As a necessary foundation for their ambitious timetable, both Pierre and Irénée pressed Stayton to step up the recruitment of corporate benefactors in the fall and winter of 1926, using the tax savings argument as the prominent theme. Just before the November elections, Stayton issued a memorandum indicating that he had targeted some 2000 individuals who paid taxes on incomes of $100,000 or more for a special appeal. The du Ponts lent their powerful voices to the effort. Irénée claimed that one of his companies would have saved $10 million in corporate taxes if the United States had imposed the British level of taxation on legalized beer. Using a 1914 estimate placing beer production in the United States at 66 million barrels, he calculated that if American brewers were taxed at the British rate the Treasury would receive over $1.3 billion in revenues—more than the total of federal individual and corporate income taxes. If workers were willing to pay but a three-cent levy per glass on "mild, wholesome beer," Irénée concluded, it would "enable the federal government to get rid of burdensome corporation taxes and income taxes," take the "snoopers and spies out of offices and homes," and even promote European economic recovery and war debt repayment by increasing foreign spirits sales to America. Pierre, citing "our average tax collections" at $1.817 billion from 1923 to 1926, claimed that legal liquor trade could both eliminate federal income taxation *and* pay off the federal debt in less than fifteen years.[24]

The appeal to corporate titans received an impressive response. Motivated by fears similar to those of the du Ponts, such men as Pennsylvania Railroad president W. W. Atterbury, Philadelphia investment banker Robert K. Cassatt, Edward S. Harkness, railroad financier Arthur Curtiss James, Robert T. Crane of Chicago's Crane Company, merchandiser Marshall Field, publisher Charles Scribner, retired Packard Motors president Henry Bourne Joy, New York investment banker Grayson M.-P. Murphy, Maryland's William Cabell Bruce, Carnegie Institute president Samuel Harden Church of Pittsburgh, and former Republican Senator James W. Wadsworth of New York (himself a 1926 victim of dry opposition in his reelection effort) answered the call. The results could be measured in dramatically higher contributions by year's end and continuing financial sustenance in 1927. Owing in large measure to the special targeting of wealthy businessmen, the AAPA's receipts for the last six months of 1926 alone totalled about $128,000, and in 1927 the yearly income reached about $250,000. Another sign of the change lay in the fact that 1926 was the last year in which the AAPA received a majority of its funds in amounts of $100 or less. By 1928, the percentage of funds made up by smaller donations would fall to only 22 percent of the organization's total.[25]

Although Pierre du Pont's own financial contribution temporarily dropped to $500 in 1927, his emotional investment and his organizational activities continued to deepen. In December 1926, he assumed leadership of a Delaware committee of manufacturers and employees seeking repeal of the Klair Law (the state's 1919 prohibition enforcement statute) and laws against shipping liquor dating back to 1917. In the same month, *Current History* carried his article, "Commendable Features of the Quebec Plan," which labelled prohibition a failure and urged consideration of Quebec's system. In that Canadian province, a government commission with a monopoly on sales and distribution administered a system of outlets which sold hard liquor one bottle at a time and wine in unlimited quantities. Licensed taverns sold beer by the glass, licensed stores dispensed beer in bottles, and licensed restaurants could sell drinks with meals. Pierre lauded the approach for making less intoxicating liquors more accessible than stronger ones and noted that Quebec's government received one-fifth of its revenues through liquor sales. Within the Du Pont Company, he also lobbied other executives to endorse the wet cause. Responding to the assertion of company officer H. Fletcher Brown that prohibition had contributed to American prosperity in the 1920s, Pierre countered that the true sources of national affluence were the automobile boom, credit buying, and "a period of high wages and freedom from strikes." The usually reticent Pierre even appeared on Delaware radio programs and public forums to declare his convictions.[26]

Reminded by rumors of a Justice Department–FTC anti-trust investigation against Du Pont and General Motors that prohibition was but one example of government's reach, Pierre increasingly viewed the AAPA's revitalization as not just vital to the repeal cause but useful as an experiment in corporate leadership, in reversing the consequences of demagogic democratic processes, and in formulating policy on "sound" business principles. He wrote, "It is futile for people to dictate government by committing representatives to certain policies, or to know the qualifications of candidates." The average voter, he insisted, "must learn to leave these matters to those who do know, trusting them to carry out their work." He despaired of the wisdom of the "masses" in a democracy, "no matter what their education or qualifications may be." Instead he favored encouraging mass apathy as a means of insuring that "those who are qualified by force of character, learning, or any other attribute, would naturally gravitate into the governing class." Pierre insisted that "the above is exactly what happens in corporations," and, although he promoted better schools by donating his time and money, he maintained that "our endeavor should be to discourage the unintelligent voter . . . If we let the mass of voters alone, they would not vote, and there would be some chance for intellectually capable people to operate governmental affairs the same way that they are permitted to operate corporate affairs."[27]

Within the family's inner circle, Pierre was not alone in his long-range estimation of the stakes involved in his heightened national political activity. John Raskob agreed to serve on the AAPA's advisory committee, and he had already begun to use his position on the U.S. Chamber of Commerce's board of directors to push repeal, tax reduction, opposition to restrictions on foreign rubber imports, and other family causes. But most important, Raskob was cultivating a promising friendship with the man considered the likely Democratic nominee for President in 1928, Governor Alfred E. Smith of New York. Although usually a voting Republican (one who as late as the end of 1927 gave $5000 to the New York GOP), Raskob was drawn to the "Happy Warrior" by their shared devotion to the Catholic faith, their detestation of prohibition, and their mutual love of New York City's cultural and social life. Both were sensitive to any slights to their religion, saw themselves as "rags to riches" testimonies to private initiative, and enjoyed the fast company of Broadway producers, racehorse owners, and (ironically, given Pierre's views of current politics) Tammany politicians.[28]

Exactly when the Raskob-Smith friendship began is difficult to trace precisely. Broadway producer Eddie Dowling later claimed that the two men first met in 1922 at a benefit dinner hosted by Cardinal Patrick Hayes in behalf of the German Oberammergau Passion Players. According to Dowling, they renewed acquaintances in 1926 because of Raskob's desire to satisfy himself that there was no foundation to rumors of corrupt dealings between Smith and unlicensed milk dealers. Apparently satisfied, Raskob reportedly offered Smith a campaign contribution of $50,000 (historian Kenneth Davis placed the offer at $25,000), but on legal advice reduced it to the allowed limit of $5000. If this account is accurate, Raskob's actions indicated that as early as 1926, the same year that the du Ponts' anti-prohibition activities expanded, he considered Smith a promising national standard bearer of the family's policy views. Again according to Dowling, further financial arrangements cemented the political partnership. Raskob purportedly arranged through an intermediary, investment banker James J. Riordan of County Trust Company, to have the banking firm receive additional GM and Du Pont assets in return for Raskob's appointment to the bank's board of directors and Smith being named chairman of the board. Although other sources could not trace the blossoming of the Raskob-Smith friendship earlier than a 1927 meeting arranged by Smith supporter and contractor William F. Kenny, it is nonetheless clear that by 1927, at the latest, Raskob was assuming a role as a prominent benefactor of the Democratic presidential hopeful.[29]

By the fall, after Pierre's return from a late summer vacation to Europe, the du Ponts and other AAPA leaders were professing newfound optimism toward the coming year's political possibilities. On November 1, Stayton wrote Pierre that the time was ripe for a "new stage" in the repeal fight. The next day secretary Hinckley of the AAPA forwarded to Pierre a draft of a new legislative proposal for the House Ways and Means Committee, calling for "Federal Income Tax Relief" by legalization and taxation of light wines and beer at the same rate as cigarettes. The proposal projected a revenue of $1.2 billion per year, or more than the amount paid by corporations in federal taxes in 1926. Following up on his own campaign to create state repeal conventions for consideration of any forthcoming federal amendment, Pierre had already begun ordering copies of each state constitution and had analyzed the state ratification procedures employed for the Eighteenth Amendment in anticipation of legal challenges.[30]

Despite the improving political climate for modification or repeal, however, grumbling persisted over Stayton's capacity to lead a successful fight. As early as the congressional hearings on modification in April 1926, Grayson Murphy had complained to Senator Wadsworth that Stayton was a poor leader because of ill health and opined that the AAPA needed a "keen, well-informed political organizer." Murphy's views, which had grown more vehement in subsequent months, were also endorsed by Boston lawyer and Constitutional Liberty League head Julian Codman, whom Stayton suspected of selfishly trying to take over his organization. In the aftermath of his own 1926 reelection defeat at the hands of the dry legions, Wadsworth, a Yale graduate, student of William Graham Sumner, and a long-time champion of conservative causes as well as a "gentleman farmer" with 35,000 acres in New York's Genesee Valley, concurred upon the need for new blood.[31]

By late 1927, Wadsworth, Murphy, Codman, and other prominent repeal activists were prepared to advocate a complete overhaul of both the AAPA's organizational structure and its executive leadership. Wadsworth arranged for a "summit" meeting to be held at his Washington home in mid-December. While ostensibly consulting Stayton on the guest list, he also sounded out the Captain's own plans for the coming year. Although Stayton revealed his own grand objective of raising $3 million in support of a campaign for a national prohibition referendum, Wadsworth pressed him to consider a different strategy as well as a reorganization of the AAPA, so as to provide him with "active assistance in an executive way."[32] As events would show, the single most crucial sponsor of the reorganization effort, and its greatest long-term beneficiary, was none other than Pierre du Pont.

chapter 4

A State of Revolution

On December 12, 1927, a group of eighteen prominent opponents of prohibition, including Pierre du Pont, met for a two-day summit conference at the home of ex-Senator James Wadsworth. Dissatisfied with the repeal movement's progress to date, the conferees, led by Pierre and Wadsworth, agreed to assemble two committees to formulate recommendations on the future structure and strategy of the campaign. The two reports then would be discussed at a second summit gathering scheduled for January 6, 1928. The committee on policy objectives was top-heavy with the wet movement's experienced Northeastern political hands, consisting as it did of state repeal leaders William Bell Wait and Austin G. Fox of New York, U.S. Senator Walter Edge of New Jersey, Stayton, Wadsworth, and Codman, its chairman. The organization committee, in contrast, featured the group's corporate titans, with Charles Sabin and Edward Harkness joining Stayton on the panel and Pierre serving as its head.[1]

In the intervening three weeks, Pierre worked behind the scenes to increase his leverage in the AAPA. He recruited additional financial backing from among his East Coast acquaintances, which elevated further his already considerable economic clout within the movement. He also engaged in backstage consultations with Julian Codman concerning their respective reports. Codman even drafted a rough organizational plan for Pierre's use in late December. Although Pierre rejected his suggestion of a new title for the AAPA, he otherwise found much to recommend in Codman's proposal, for the authority lines charted in it mirrored the organizational principles within the du Ponts' own economic empire. A national board of directors, anticipated to number about fifty, would be selected both for its prestige and, because it would have a broad geographic and professional range, for its scope. Stayton would be "kicked upstairs" to the prestigious, but less active, position of chairman of the board. Real power, however, would be centered in an executive committee of five to seven members, which would formulate policy and oversee the AAPA's day-to-day finances. The national headquarters would be directed by a president chosen for his administrative and public political skills, who, like the board chairman, would be responsible both personally and financially to the executive committee.[2]

When the crusaders reconvened at Wadsworth's house in January, the results of their deliberations demonstrated that Pierre's orchestrations had paid off. Codman's committee did recommend, to Pierre's dislike, abandonment of an immediate repeal drive in favor of the lesser goal of modification and urged the AAPA's termination in favor of decentralized state activity. Those proposals, however, quickly were shelved by Pierre's supporters. Instead of Codman's policy proposals, the majority adopted Pierre's terse four-page organizational report, along with its more ambitious immediate policy objectives. Soothing Stayton's feelings by commending publicly his efforts, insuring him a continuing role, and keeping the AAPA name that the Captain had originated, Pierre in his report nonetheless called for sweeping structural changes and set the lofty goal of immediate prohibition repeal. For all practical purposes, Pierre had purchased Stayton's "stock" and had accomplished a "leveraged buyout" of the AAPA, just as he had lined up cousin Coly during the Du Pont Company's power struggle of 1914–15. To ease the concerns over leadership of Wadsworth and others among the AAPA's professional politicans, Pierre proposed that Henry Curran, former Republican candidate for mayor of New York City and a friend and Yale classmate of Wadsworth, be named as the association's new president. AAPA headquarters accordingly were to be moved to Curran's New York home base. Also reflective of a closing of ranks with Wadsworth (who was less "immediatist" and more partisan than Pierre), but one that still retained Pierre's operating control, was the proposed composition of the executive committee. The central body was enlarged to include brother Irénée, Stayton, Harkness, Murphy, Sabin, Benedict Crowell, and Curran, with Pierre serving as its chairman. Solidifying Pierre's hold was the group's endorsement of his key recommendation that both Curran and Stayton be paid not out of general funds, but out of a special fund guaranteed by board and executive committee members, with the du Ponts the largest bloc of contributors.[3]

For the next two months, ironing out organizational details and raising funds preoccupied the du Ponts. All nominees except Harkness accepted their appointments to the executive committee, which met at first on a weekly basis. The appointment of Henry Curran—an outspoken, aggressive politico with a wooden visage resembling Buster Keaton—as president became official on January 15. Following direct consultations with executive committee members, Pierre and Stayton recruited additional candidates for the board of directors, including such luminaries as W. W. Atterbury of the Pennsylvania Railroad, Charles M. Schwab of U.S. Steel, Henry H. Westinghouse, Paul W. Litchfield of Goodyear, Fred Fisher and Charles F. Kettering of General Motors, Eldridge R. Johnson of the Victor Talking Machine Company, and R. L. Agassiz of Calumet. All but Schwab, Westinghouse, and Litchfield accepted, as did AAPA stalwarts James, Joy and, as expected, John Raskob. Author-editor Fabian Franklin and educator Samuel Harden Church also enlisted, although Elihu Root, President Nicholas Murray Butler of Columbia University, and former Senator Oscar W. Underwood of Alabama declined. Automatically enrolled in the board of directors were the attendees of the December and January summit conferences. As a sign of recognition of the need for political allies in the election year, a director's invitation was even extended to, and accepted by, American Federation of Labor vice-president Matthew Woll. In contrast to the executive committee, however, the board of directors (organized by state representation rather than by "industrial group," as Pierre would have preferred) rarely met and served mostly as "window dressing."[4]

With the executive committee in charge of solicitation, financial contributions of corporate leaders in behalf of the AAPA mushroomed well beyond the levels of 1926–27. The emerging pattern of financial support would have surprised no one familiar with the du Pont philosophy of "decentralized management, centralized financial control." Beginning in March the du Ponts dramatically increased their own levels of underwriting to far outdistance any others as the AAPA's chief benefactors. Pierre and Irénée donated $15,000 apiece toward the national office's immediate expenses, and each pledged $25,000 more at the end of June for the next year's operating costs. John Raskob pledged $25,000 per year for the next two years, plus an additional three-years' underwriting contingent upon satisfactory progress toward repeal. To pay the $25,000 and $10,000 annual salaries of Curran and Stayton, Pierre and Irénée, Lammot, and Raskob agreed with Sabin, Harkness, and Thomas Phillips to give $5000 each per year for the next five years. In 1928 the three du Ponts and Raskob gave over $130,000 more to the AAPA ($42,000 from Pierre alone), greater than the entire amount collected by the association in the last half of 1927 and more than it had garnered in any year prior to 1926.[5]

The burgeoning of the du Ponts' investment in the AAPA raised basic questions among contemporaries, as well as later historians, concerning the breadth of the organization's real popular base and the possibility of a du Pont "hidden agenda." From 1928 until the ultimate triumph of repeal in December 1933, spending by the AAPA averaged $450,000 per year, with a 1930 peak of $820,000 that included a deficit of over $100,000. In attempting to counter the claim that the AAPA had become a "rich man's front," spokesmen pointed out that the new levels of income and expenses still only approximated those of the Anti-Saloon League during its campaign to enact prohibition. This defense missed the point, however, that notwithstanding the large gifts from John D. Rockefeller, Henry Ford, and S. S. Kresge, the Anti-Saloon League had relied upon a broader base of modest contributors. In 1928 the AAPA received only 22 percent of its donations from gifts under $100, compared to 53 percent in 1926. A shift toward financial centralization clearly had occurred.[6]

Even the summary percentages, however, actually understated the steady evolution of economic control into a small number of hands, most notably those of the du Ponts. From 1928 through 1932, the three du Pont brothers alone provided $400,000 to the association, and business associates and close allies Raskob, Jasper Crane, James, and Harkness each gave between $64,000 and $70,000. These seven individuals, guided by Pierre, were responsible for almost 30 percent of the AAPA's entire income over the five-year span. In 1929, the association's eighty directors donated about $300,000, or an average of less than $4000 per director. But the AAPA's top fifty-three givers that year generated three-quarters of its funds, and the directors, though constituting less than one percent of the contributors, still provided 65 percent of the income. In contrast, nearly 8000 gifts of up to $25 produced under 10 percent of the organization's moneys. From 1930 until repeal, owing to a growing list of Depression-era small donors, gifts in amount under $100 constituted over 90 percent of the total number of contributions, but in only one year—1930—did such gifts exceed 15 percent of the AAPA's total income. The surest sign that mass-based funding was no longer essential to the du Pont–led AAPA was the decision that after 1928 dues requirements for membership would be dropped. The change made the oft-presumed equation between association membership and an intense individual commitment to its activities even more tenuous than before.[7]

What can explain the du Ponts' shift from modest participation in the repeal movement to direct control of its leading organizational vehicle, the AAPA? It could not be any fixation of Pierre's with the desire to drink liberally. As Irénée noted of his elder brother, "No one cares less for drink—he seldom takes it and does not even patronize bootleggers." According to a resolution made by the new executive committee, the chief issue at stake was the "distortion of our Federal Constitution by compelling it to carry the burden of a task which is an affair for the police power of each of our forty-eight separate and sovereign states."[8] But not even that statement of principles told the full story. Once involved in a cause, Pierre had never been able to bear not being in charge of the effort, and he insisted on running the repeal effort on the principles that he had tested in his business career. Always an empire builder, he thrived on the challenge of wielding power in and building up—not merely contributing to—an organization that promised to reshape a major national social policy.

As Pierre privately admitted, it was not the prohibition issue for its own sake that he was primarily interested in. He wrote in February, "The collateral issues outweigh the liquor question." Clearly included among the "collateral issues" were the threats of crime and federal taxation. Both privately and in an April article in *Current History* he reiterated his claim that legalized and taxed liquor would "warrant the abolition of the income tax and corporation tax." But even those reasons, important as they were to critics of social disorder and government confiscation of wealth, were only surface manifestations of a far grander, and more revolutionary, corporate managerial vision. As Pierre put it, "Personally I believe that the Association will bring together on public questions a body of men who may be lead [*sic*] to a greater interest in other questions of government entirely apart from politics." In short, Pierre's ambition was that the AAPA could become the foundation for the far more extensive public use of corporate administrative panels, with the power to direct research on and design and implement policies to address a broad range of American economic and social issues. A clue to the kind of public administration he hoped to foster could be found in his response to a private correspondent that "we believe in the Constitution of the United States as it was prior to 1919"—although upon reflection he might well have set the date back further, to 1913. Irénée echoed Pierre's hopes for the AAPA less than a year later, in February 1929, when he confessed to his brother, "It really seems to me that some day there may be great need of an organization which can bring together a large proportion of the big industrial men of the country so that they may act in unison."[9]

On the specific matter of liquor control, Pierre was never content merely with the repeal of prohibition but intended to replace it with a salutary alternative. By the early summer of 1928, his preferred corrective no longer was the Quebec plan for a governmental monopoly, but instead the Swedish system of a licensed private monopoly. As late as May he still waffled between the two, insisting, "We do believe that it is better that the Government or responsible people should handle the liquor trade rather than the bootleggers or the low-class politicians who formerly ruled." But influenced by his detailed researches into the "Bratt system" of Sweden, a month later he declared, "Personally, I advocate turning the whole liquor business over to a corporation organized by substantial people, to be operated at a reasonably small profit, the Government to obtain all profits above the agreed amount." All the du Ponts desired resumption of a legalized liquor trade as part of a general shift away from taxation of the wealthy and toward more regressive avenues. It was also likely, however, that when Pierre referred to management by "substantial people," he envisioned his own AAPA colleagues as worthy candidates to administer a legalized monopoly. As he had done for the contract for the Old Hickory nitrate plant in World War I, Pierre suggested that under corporate administration the government would be allowed to assume control of the liquor trade if it agreed to reimburse the capital invested by the private operators.[10]

As an outgrowth of Pierre's personal interest in analyzing policy alternatives to prohibition, the AAPA created a formal research department in the spring of 1928. On the basis of recommendations by an internal committee in April, both a research division and an information department were formed. John G. Gebhart, a former social worker with the Social Science Research Council, was tabbed as the research department's head, and he hired a staff of three full-time and several part-time assistants with a first-year budget of $100,000. Besides expanding Pierre's efforts at statistical analyses of prohibition and research into the liquor control systems of other nations, Gebhart's office increasingly provided the raw data employed in the AAPA's propaganda efforts. Hard facts and figures now buttressed the arguments presented in newspaper articles, editorials, cartoons, and pamphlets.[11]

Before launching the AAPA's full-scale assault on prohibition at the upcoming nominating conventions, Pierre wanted to gather additional information on grass-roots sentiment, both to satisfy himself that the timing was right and to have ready opinion data with which to exert more pressure on party leaders. In order to get a firsthand indication of the feelings of a cross-section of voters in his own immediate surroundings, and also to screen out any "nonbelievers" from his personal entourage, in February he issued a private questionnaire to family members, servants, and staffers entitled, "To Those Living at Long-wood and Interested in Its Welfare." As both a propaganda device and gauge of sentiment in his native state, in late April Pierre also commissioned a prohibition questionnaire to about 100,000 registered and taxpaying voters in Delaware. With Pierre's confidence bolstered by the limited polling, the AAPA zeroed in on the platform committees of the major parties. In 1920 and 1924, both parties and their national tickets had skirted the prohibition issue with vague statements on the need for popular compliance with, and honest enforcement of, existing law.[12]

With the Republican gathering scheduled first, prominent AAPA Republicans Irénée du Pont, Wadsworth, Curran, and Joy hoped against hope to steer their party away from its drift toward support for prohibition. Back in February, Irénée had made inquiries with a friend in Dubuque, Iowa, about likely presidential nominee Herbert Hoover's position, and he had not been reassured by the response. A week before the opening of the Kansas City convention, on June 6 John Raskob attempted to influence both parties by issuing over 100,000 copes of a public letter in which he termed prohibition an "unsound" economic policy. But at the Republican convention, despite platform committee testimony for a wet plank by Nicholas Murray Butler, Wadsworth, and Curran, the delegates adopted a pro-enforce-ment plan authored by insurgent Senator William E. Borah. In his acceptance speech weeks later, Hoover also chose to trumpet the dry position by opposing repeal, urging "efficent enforcement," and de-scribing prohibition as "a great social and economic experiment, noble in motive and far-reaching in purpose."[13]

The du Ponts in particular were disillusioned by the Republicans' performance and by Hoover's remarks. In a letter to Ogden Mills, Undersecretary of the Treasury and an operative of the Hoover plat-form committee, Raskob blasted the prohibition law as unworkable and a clear failure. Aged Coleman du Pont, ever the GOP loyalist, tried to mollify his cousins, but conceded, "I think the Republicans could have put up a much stronger candidate than Hoover, and I agree with you it may be wise to go through sweat to straighten things out." He cautioned Raskob against hanging all his hopes on the Dem-ocratic party, however, claiming that "by making either Party wet or dry, it would be much harder to change the law." In an angry letter to Republican fundraiser Herbert N. Straus, Pierre vigorously excor-iated the Republicans' prohibition stance and warned Straus that if the Democrats offered a better alternative on the issue, he would prob-ably contribute to them.[14]

Even before the disappointments at the hands of the Republicans, it had become increasingly clear that chances for a wet platform were much better in the Democratic party, despite the obstructive presence of its rural Southern and Western wing. Most of that hope was rooted in the anti-prohibition record of the Democrats' likely presidential nominee, Raskob's friend Al Smith. Besides the encouragement offered by the budding friendship, AAPA leaders Stayton, Sabin, and Murphy were nominal Democratic party members and hoped to have better luck with their platform committee than their Republican colleagues had enjoyed. In the larger sense, Smith's apparently growing conservatism on economic issues also was heartening, and he was accumulating an impressive list of Wall Street benefactors that included William F. Kenny, Harry Payne Whitney of Standard Oil, M. J. Meehan, copper magnates W. A. Clark and John Ryan, candy manufacturer George W. Loft, and financiers Bernard Baruch, Thomas Fortune Ryan, and Francis P. Garvan. As for the financial ties between Raskob and Smith, they had been extended in March when Raskob had arranged a deposit with his broker of an account in Smith's name of 1000 RCA shares, worth well over $100,000. On the eve of the June 26 Houston convention, hoping to boost the wet cause and accelerate corporate recruitment for the Smith campaign, Raskob dramatically endorsed the Happy Warrior in a public statement.[15]

The Democratic convention proved somewhat less than an unmitigated triumph. Smith's forces, trying not to alienate rural delegates completely, pledged an "honest effort" to enforce the Eighteenth Amendment. Wets, however, were reassured by resolutions committee chairman Key Pittman of Nevada that the platform did not prevent party candidates from advocating repeal. Smith himself favored a national referendum as a first step toward the return of liquor control to states and municipalities. Winning the nomination easily, he rejected Raskob's advice that he form a solidly wet ticket by choosing a pro-repeal running mate and named Arkansas Senator Joseph Robinson. But in turn, overruling the advice of political advisers Belle Moskowitz, Joseph Proskauer, and Franklin Roosevelt, Smith did select Raskob as his campaign manager and as his choice as chairman of the Democratic National Committee (DNC).[16]

If the du Ponts and Raskob had their obvious reasons for cultivating Smith's favor, the governor had his own motivations for reciprocating. He hoped above all that Raskob's prominent role in the campaign would help him in recruiting additional business support and funds from Eastern industrial states. When combined with his personal compatibility with Raskob, Smith's need for business backing in the campaign against Hoover overrode any fears he may have had of alienating Democratic prohibitionists, agrarians, and progressives when he recruited Raskob. As the *New Republic* noted, "It is not enough [for the Smith campaign] to be wet and popular. The business support is absolutely essential in those [industrial] states, and Smith knows it. That is why Raskob was picked."[17]

Raskob immediately plunged into his dual role as repeal spokesman and Smith's campaign chief. In accepting, he claimed disingenuously that he was not a politican and had never been "affiliated with any party either nationally or locally." Asserting that his candidate was a "strong advocate of less Government in business and more business in Government," he privately sought to reassure a skeptical Irénée of Smith's fundamental "soundness." Given Irénée's Republican loyalties and his attentiveness to Coly's advice, Raskob had a tougher sell to him than to older brother Pierre. He maintained, "Governor Smith's ideas of protecting big business are quite in accord with yours and mine." He added, "Personally, I can see no big difference between the two parties except the wet and dry question, and, of course, some say the religious question, which I think both of us agree should form no part of politics."[18]

To bolster Smith's chances of carrying his home state by strengthening the state ticket, Raskob courted Franklin Roosevelt as the Democrats' New York gubernatorial candidate. Roosevelt wisely returned a $250,000 "loan" extended by Raskob but accepted a direct $25,000 gift (the first installment of what would eventually total $100,000) to the Warm Springs Foundation, which helped release him from ongoing fundraising obligations to the charity. Raskob also sought to link the Democratic party directly with the fight against prohibition by issuing in July an AAPA questionnaire on modification to the approximately 2300 delegates who had attended the Houston convention. Although most drys simply refused to send back their responses, the new party chairman claimed that the overwhelming approval of modification by those who had replied placed the party on record on the side of the wets. He followed up the initiative to Democratic delegates by requesting from AAPA president Curran a list of prominent wet Republicans, with the intention of soliciting from them an "open statement" of endorsement of Smith.[19]

Raskob already was becoming, however, a mixed blessing at best for the Smith campaign. Not really understanding the details of the agricultural plank of the party platform, which supported the McNary-Haugen bill and which had been drafted by advisers George Peek and Hugh Johnson, both he and Smith gave it the briefest of endorsements.

As a result, they damaged further the candidate's already slim chances in farm states. Raskob's decision at the end of July to move Smith's campaign headquarters from their traditional lodgings in New York's Biltmore Hotel to the General Motors building also fed accusations that the campaign had been captured by big business. In his first major press conference of the general election, on August 1, he floundered even more by appearing to attribute all opposition to Smith solely to intolerance and bigotry. The irrational, nativist claims of papal domination of the Smith cause were in turn fed by press revelations that Raskob had attempted to arrange a political truce between the Catholic church and the government of Mexico through the good offices of the Vatican's Monsignor Guiseppe Pizzardo and U.S. Ambassador Dwight Morrow.[20]

Raskob's central failure, however, was his inability to pry away a majority of business support from the Republicans, especially from outside New York City. The *New Republic* noted, "There is a certain amount of resentful comment in business circles, largely based on the fact that Raskob is, and has been, connected with the stock end of General Motors rather than the constructive end." Although Raskob himself gave approximately $540,000 to the campaign effort in the form of direct contributions and loans, and endorsed promisory notes for another $150,000 afterward to cover lingering debts, neither he nor Pierre could even guarantee du Pont family solidarity behind the Smith ticket, much less win over the hearts and minds of other corporate leaders.[21]

Within the AAPA inner circle, Pierre endorsed Smith on the basis of his position on prohibition and gave the campaign $50,000. Henry Curran also publicly announced for the New York governor. James Wadsworth declined, however, and Irénée du Pont, remaining true to his Republican loyalties, cast his vote for Hoover while restricting his $22,000 contribution to the Delaware Republican party to "suitable" (that is, wet) candidates. Brother Lammot, despite his opposition to the Eighteenth Amendment and his admission that "there is no radical difference in principle between the two parties," also voted the Republican ticket and gave $42,300 to the GOP. By August partisan bickering within the family had reached serious enough proportions that Coly du Pont's son Frank and du Pont in-law Ruly Carpenter, both state Republican fundraisers, negotiated a truce under which no family members would oppose the GOP in Delaware and Pierre would support Smith only at the national level. Guided by the agreement, Carpenter contributed $15,000 to the Republicans, his brother Walter gave $3000, Coly du Pont $10,000, company executive Charles Copeland $500, and Pierre's cousins William and A. Felix du Pont $2500 each.[22]

Raskob's prominence in the Smith campaign also drew recriminations from within General Motors. When asked to head the Democratic party, Raskob informed Pierre but not other GM officers, who were nervous at the appearance of the company endorsing a presidential candidate, especially a Democrat and an underdog. Before he was able to notify company president Alfred Sloan of his new post in early July, Raskob was detained by his son William's sudden death in an automobile accident. As a consequence, at the moment he publicly accepted the position of party chairman on July 11, he had still not sought approval from other GM executives for the decision. The mood of officers within the automobile giant hardly was improved by a drop in company stock prices following Raskob's announcement. Sloan, insistent that GM avoid any direct political affiliation, demanded Raskob's resignation from the finance committee. Raskob instead pleaded for a leave of absence. Leaping to his friend's defense, Pierre, citing his AAPA activity, attempted to employ his company leverage by threatening to resign his own position on the finance committee.[23]

To Pierre's surprise, Sloan enlisted other du Ponts and pulled an end run around his threat. Polling the board of directors, the GM president found that a majority favored Raskob's resignation but would not accept Pierre's. Championing that position was Pierre's own brother Irénée, who lobbied that "the other resignation be not accepted" because it was based upon "loyalty to a friend rather than the necessity of the case." At the directors' meeting, Raskob's resignation was approved and Pierre's denied, the board granting him a leave of absence instead. Even more unsettling for the new Democratic chieftan was Sloan's decision not merely to release Raskob's simple resignation statement and the GM president's reply to the press, but to declare in a major public address at Flint, Michigan, that "GM is not in politics." To underscore that message to his workers, officers, dealers, and stockholders, Sloan had his speech reprinted and distributed at company expense.[24]

Having been outflanked by Sloan—and with his own brother's assistance—Pierre could do little to prevent Raskob's public ostracism from GM. "The only way that we can improve political service is to get better men," a frustrated Pierre lamented to Coly. "We cannot get the best from corporations if we impose the penalty of resignation from corporate work at the same time." Raskob also resigned his memberships on the executive committee of the Missouri-Pacific Railroad and the boards of directors of Texas and Pacific Railroad, Gulf Coast Lines, and Denver and Rio Grande–Western Railroad, all part of the Missouri-Pacific system. Actually, the "sentences" could have been much worse. Both Raskob and Pierre were allowed to remain on GM's board of directors, and Raskob was permitted to rejoin the finance committee after the election. Du Pont family influence on the company remained high even during the general election period, for Lammot assumed Pierre's post as chairman of the board and Pierre remained on the finance committee. Also remaining on the GM board were Irénée and Henry F. du Pont and in-law Donaldson Brown.[25]

Pierre was more committed to repeal and Smith's election than ever before because of the GM showdown, defiantly declaring, "We are now in a state of revolution quite as much as the country was in 1776." As for Raskob, his enthusiasm was bolstered by rumors that if elected, Smith might name him Secretary of the Treasury and Pierre Secretary of State. When asked for his response, he cryptically replied, "I believe that there is a destiny which shapes our ends. I'm positive it was so in my case." But in actuality Raskob's effectiveness as a rallying point for business support of Smith had collapsed, and the collapse threatened to drag down the wet cause with it. The AAPA launched its own campaigns for wet state, local, and congressional candidates, citing prohibition enforcement "atrocities," and eyed reapportionment bills with a wary gaze for their likely effect on the wet-dry balance in Congress. Pierre and noted prohibitionist Irving Fisher, an economist at Yale University, carried on a debate in the press over the costs and benefits of prohibition.[26]

Despite the best efforts of Raskob and Pierre, their causes were both about to receive disheartening defeats. Although Smith's own presidential campaign outspent that of his rival Hoover (only the second time in history that a Democratic presidential effort cost more than that of a Republican), 74 percent of the funds raised came from within New York State alone. It also left a $1.5 million shortfall, given the $5.3 million spent. A substantial portion of the corporate community, especially that outside Raskob's own Wall Street circle, remained loyal to Hoover and the GOP. Within even GM, five Fisher brothers and Alfred Sloan each gave $25,000 to the Republican ticket, and $100,000 was sent to Hoover from GM's Fisher Body subsidiary, despite Sloan's earlier claim of company nonpartisanship. Combining all levels of election expenditures, the GOP actually outspent the Democrats by about $2 million. Shaping that pattern of giving was the central fact that for the business community prohibition simply was less important an issue than economic prosperity and the faith in Hoover's ability to sustain it.[27]

Herbert Hoover defeated Al Smith in the presidential contest with 21.4 million votes, or 58.2 percent, to the Democrat's 15 million votes and 41.2 percent. The strategy to link the wet cause with the Smith campaign backfired, for out of fifty-six House and Senate races in which the AAPA had intervened, Hoover's coattails prevented victory in all but nineteen. Of those nineteen contests, eleven wet winners were incumbents, and in five others the AAPA had endorsed both major candidates and by doing so had made it impossible to lose. Quite simply, as Henry Curran put it, "We were licked." Rural and dry Democrats such as Texas Governor Dan Moody openly attributed the outcome to the blundering of Raskob, whom he described as a "cynical commercialist with an alcohol complex." Even Raskob aide Jouett Shouse admitted privately that his boss had "perhaps emphasized to an undue extent the Prohibition feature of the campaign." As part of the post-election fallout, Commerce Secretary-designee Robert P. Lamont publicly resigned from the AAPA, and Coleman du Pont, citing illness and facing public charges of questionable 1920 financial dealings with Teapot Dome figure Harry Sinclair, quit the U.S. Senate in December. Gloating over Pierre's gloom was outcast cousin Alfred, who wired the president-elect from Florida, "By virtue of your success, our country has been preserved from a threatened catastrophe, the result of which one does not care to contemplate."[28]

Aside from the partisan races, there actually were some reasons for hope amidst the gloom. State referenda results continued to indicate shifts in popular favor away from prohibition and toward repeal. In June, a repeal referendum in North Dakota had been defeated by a narrow margin. In November, Montana voters refused to reinstate a prohibition law which had been removed two years earlier. In Massachusetts, a 60 percent majority voted to direct their House and Senate representatives to back repeal legislation, and a state repeal referendum carried easily. In general, repeal was more popular than the presidential vote suggested, and the ballots in Montana and Massachusetts demonstrated the point. By the next April, a 63 percent majority in Wisconsin would overturn the state's dry enforcement law.[29]

Nevertheless, even under the most positive assessments the foundation had not yet been laid for a successful national repeal program. The 1928 results meant that fundraising would have to be sustained over several more years, and additional recruitment and organizational alliances would be necessary to increase the AAPA's political clout. With such aims in mind, the 1929 financial target was placed at $750,000, which would also help lay the groundwork for a 1930 congressional election push. The goal proved too ambitious to reach, for only about $457,000 was raised in 1929, but it still represented nearly double the AAPA's 1927 income. Of the 1929 funds, the association's eighty directors contributed almost $260,000, not even counting another $40,000 from the 1928 post-election period earmarked for 1929. Nine individuals alone gave $25,000 each for the headquarters' salary and operating expenses, including Pierre, Irénée, Lammot, Raskob, and Fred Fisher. Pierre gave an additional $18,500 in direct contributions for AAPA programs. To further coordinate the financial solicitations, the executive committee approved creation of a formal, six-member finance committee, with Raskob serving as a member and Lammot du Pont its chairman.[30]

Building up the AAPA's grass-roots strength, especially among women, and its support among professional groups was a more arduous task. Among the actions taken in 1929 were the enlargement of the association's Authors and Artists Committee, the creation of a lawyer's organization called the Voluntary Committee of Lawyers, the establishment of a women's branch entitled the Women's Organization for National Prohibition Reform (WONPR), and a young men's auxiliary, the Crusaders. The Authors and Artists Committee, under the leadership of Kentucky humorist Irvin Cobb, swelled to almost 600 members by 1930. The Voluntary Committee of Lawyers (VCL), founded in January 1929, was headed by Joseph H. Choate, Jr., an AAPA board member, son of a former ambassador to Great Britain, and a partner in the New York law firm of Evarts, Choate, Sherman, and Leon. Other key figures in the VCL included Chicago law partners James H. Winston and Ralph Shaw, later active participants in the du Pont–sponsored Liberty League. The VCL recruited prominent members of the bar, sought public denunciations of prohibition from bar associations, and attempted to influence fellow lawyers serving in the state legislatures and Congress. New York City served as the VCL's center, although both Chicago and Philadelphia claimed strong chapters. Partly because of the committee's efforts, from 1928 to 1930 bar associations in New York and Philadelphia, as well as in Boston, Detroit, Washington, D.C., St. Louis, San Francisco, and Portland, endorsed repeal. State bar associations in New York, Nevada, and Virginia followed suit, and the American Bar Association did likewise in 1930.[31]

The VCL operated as an independent legal arm of the AAPA, but the organizational linkages between the AAPA, the WONPR, and the Crusaders were much closer. In a very real sense both branches were "blood relatives." The WONPR, created in the spring of 1929 as a counter to the Women's Christian Temperance Union (WCTU), was

headed by Pauline Morton Sabin, the wife of AAPA executive committee member Charles Sabin. Mrs. Sabin was in her own right a
prominent New York Republican, having served as a national com-
mitteewoman from 1924 to 1929. In addition, she was the grand-
daughter of a former Nebraska governor and U.S. Secretary of
Agriculture, daughter of a Secretary of the Navy, and niece of the
founder of the Morton Salt fortune. By 1928 she had become an outspoken critic of prohibition. Following Hoover's inauguration she resigned from the Republican National Committee, denounced the
President's prohibitionist stance, and began recruiting for the
WONPR. Lending support to the notion that the WONPR was but
a wives' auxiliary to the AAPA was the presence of Pierre du Pont's
wife, Alice Belin du Pont, and Mrs. Henry B. Joy on the new organization's 125-member national advisory council. In the span of two
months, three organizational meetings were held in New York, and
Mrs. Sabin inaugurated membership tours in the East and Midwest.
On May 28 twenty-four women from eleven states launched publicly
the WONPR, having rejected an alternate name—the Women's Legion for True Temperance.[32]

Under Mrs. Sabin's direction, the WONPR filled its advisory committee with women from twenty-six states, established a small office
in New York, and paid its first month's expenses. Within a year, it
claimed over 100,000 members and thirteen state branches. Despite
the constant charges that the organization was but an artificial extension of the AAPA (charges supported by the fact that after the 1928
debacle Pierre's executive committee had openly discussed the need
for an effective women's auxiliary), Mrs. Sabin proved a skilled political operative. Not the least of her success consisted in keeping rival
M. Louise Gross and her Molly Pitcher Clubs at arms' length from
the WONPR's efforts. Using the opposition WCTU's clout as its
benchmark, by December 1931 the WONPR would claim to have
surpassed it in membership. Like the assertions of the AAPA, however,
such claims were hard to verify, given that membership in each could
not be matched against any dues requirement.[33]

Also formally launched in May 1929 was the Crusaders, a young
men's organization headed up by thirty-nine-year-old Cleveland oil
company president Fred G. Clark, a World War I associate of the
AAPA's Benedict Crowell. Once again strong family ties existed with
the AAPA, for among the new group's members were the sons of
Charles Sabin and Lammot du Pont. If the WONPR's organizational
blueprint was the WCTU, the Crusaders' model was the American
Legion, for it was structured like a veteran's organization, complete

with a national "commander" and state and local "battalion commanders." The first chapter sprouted in Cleveland, with 4000 attributed members, and the national leadership established a goal of ten million recruits paying one dollar in dues each. The Crusaders never approached the goal, however, and remained a disappointment to the AAPA leadership.[34]

Besides encouraging the launching of the VCL, WONPR, and Crusaders, the AAPA in 1929 undertook new state campaigns in May and June. In the process, it absorbed the Constitutional Liberty League of Massachusetts as a state subsidiary. Not all opportunities for acquisition and growth through merger were accepted, however. The limits of the AAPA's new "empire building" within the wet movement reflected Pierre du Pont's elitist and hierarchical notions of the necessary qualifications for takeover candidates. Unless such organizations explicitly accepted, and were accountable to, the central direction of the AAPA and its executive committee, Pierre resisted even loose cooperation with them in the repeal effort. As an example, the Federal Dispensary Tax Reduction League, founded in 1923 by Denver physician Frederick W. Buck, sought AAPA affiliation, but because it paid its fundraisers a 50 percent commission, Captain Stayton urged its rejection on the basis that it was merely a "moneymaking scheme." To Pierre he asserted, "I have never known these people to do any actual work, and I have known them to do things which were harmful." Pierre followed the Captain's advice, but even in the case of potentially more fruitful ties with the wet lobbies of labor unions, he consistently pressed for control rather than just cooperation. Pierre also approved abandonment of support for the disappointing Molly Pitcher Clubs even before the establishment of the WONPR.[35]

Increases in the propaganda effort of the AAPA accompanied the organizational shakeups and expansions. The research and publicity bureaus inaugurated a series of pamphlet on aspects of the prohibition problem in March 1929 with *Scandals of Prohibition Enforcement*. The publication stressed the rampant official crime and corruption generated by prohibition by looking at five specific cities—Chicago, Pittsburgh, Detroit, Buffalo, and Philadelphia. Although the du Ponts wanted the pamphlet released six months earlier as an anti–Hoover administration vehicle, the research department was not ready to push the project forward until the spring. It was followed in May by an analysis of prohibition's effect on taxation, entitled *The Cost of Prohibition and Your Income Tax*, which claimed that the Volstead Act cost the federal treasury approximately $36 million in 1928. Repeating a familiar litany, a liquor industry taxed at 1918 rates for consumption levels equal to those of 1910–1914, the brochure stated, would have produced $850 million in federal revenue and $50 million more in state and local moneys. Adding up the costs of enforcement and lost taxes, the AAPA claimed a net loss of $936 million in 1928 and asserted, on the basis of a federal individual income tax figure of $833 million in 1928, that such income levies could be nearly eliminated if liquor were legalized. Reissued and updated in a second edition the following year, with estimates of $951 million in lost federal moneys and individual income taxes of $1.096 billion in 1929, the tax pamphlet became the AAPA's most popular single piece of literature: 209,000 copies were printed, and its finding were circulated to newspapers with a combined readership of 80 million.[36]

Other literature in the AAPA's series hammered at the social costs and the unenforceability of prohibition. In July, *Canadian Liquor Crossing the Border* claimed that only 5–10 percent of the better than a million gallons of liquor being "spirited" across the northern border was being captured. Another pamphlet, *Measuring the Liquor Tide,* attempted to establish the finding that alcoholism and alcohol-related deaths had actually increased since the advent of prohibition. *Reforming America with a Shotgun: A Study of Prohibition Killings* claimed that attempts to enforce the Eighteenth Amendment had cost 1000 deaths of civilians or police, although the federal government itself counted but 286. *Prohibition Enforcement: Its Effects on Courts and Prisons* in turn asserted dramatic increases in the federal caseload, which had forced plea bargaining and lighter sentences in order to ease overcrowding in dockets, jails, and prisons.[37]

As Pierre had always insisted, AAPA criticisms of prohibition were followed by the presentation of alternatives to the status quo, although they tended not to attract as much attention as the more sensational "attack" pieces. In a series of eight pamphlets, the AAPA presented other methods of liquor control compiled from other countries, including those of Quebec, Great Britain, Denmark, and, in particular, Sweden, where a privately financed and publicly supervised monopoly with a guaranteed profit limit of 7 percent sold beer and wine in unlimited quantities and rationed spirits sales. The program generated tax revenues that constituted fully one-sixth of Sweden's government moneys. Pierre's own proposal, *A Plan for Distribution and Control of Intoxicating Liquors in the United States,* incorporated the idea of a state-regulated private monopoly (described as an "incorporated monopoly") administered "by a private corporation" in the manner of a public utility. He added suggestions to oppose the sale of liquor by the drink in public places (that is, the return of the "saloon") and backed user licensing requirements and examinations—such as those for automobile operators—for liquor purchasers and prohibitions on sale to documented alcoholics and children under eighteen.[38]

Despite his organization's frequent use of states'-rights and civil-libertarian arguments against the prohibition law, Pierre's views demonstrated that he was not troubled at the prospect of regulatory controls on private individuals' access to liquor. This should not have been surprising, given his assumption of such prerogatives over his own workers in the past. What the AAPA proposals showed was that the du Ponts were not against a centralization of the liquor industry or the regulation of individuals' social conduct from above. What they did oppose was the assertion that government, employing "demagogic" democratic processes, could legally confiscate or outlaw a "legitimate" private enterprise. What was in dispute to Pierre and his family followers was not the wisdom of regulating individual behavior, but in whose hands the power to formulate and carry out such national policies should be held. Could a "responsible" liquor program be entrusted to partisan politics, which featured the irrational swings of "direct democracy" and the self-serving concerns of an appointed bureaucracy of career politicians; or should it instead be controlled by "enlightened" corporate managers chosen for their "superior" managerial skills, resources, and social vision? For the du Ponts, clearly the latter course was far more preferable.[39]

While in the aftermath of the 1928 disappointments Pierre rallied the AAPA behind his broad objectives, John Raskob did the same within the Democratic party. In the wake of Smith's overwhelming defeat, he was determined to restructure the Democratic National Committee into an effective vehicle not only for repeal but for the broader corporate managerial vision he shared with the du Ponts. Despite the fall's misfortunes, the Raskob-Smith financial relationship continued to grow. In January, Raskob transferred the balance of the stock account he had created ten months earlier for Smith, with a profit for the former governor of over $25,000. But if Smith personally had weathered the financial rigors of the campaign quite well, the Democratic party had not. Chairman Raskob had accumulated a $1.5 million debt and the party apparatus lay moribund in the aftermath of the elections. Raskob diligently collected over $1 million in contributions from himself, Pierre, Herbert Lehman, Bernard Baruch, William F. Kenny, and others to stave off immediate financial collapse, but approximately $400,000 of campaign debts remained. To cover the rest, in late November he placed a promisory note for the same amount with the County Trust Company of New York, whose directors included himself, Smith, Kenny, and James J. Riordan, and he sought new pledges from other Smith allies in order to redeem the note later. In addition, in early January he arranged for the DNC to purchase radio time for an appeal for funds. A follow-up letter and sales of a volume of campaign speeches generated another $125,000.[40]

Despite the financial struggles, Raskob was determined to build "an organization which parallels, as nearly as conditions will permit, a first-rate business enterprise operating all the time, spending money effectively and meeting the real issues at hand." Blocking his path were rural and dry Democrats, who blamed him for the 1928 disaster and claimed that he was trying to buy the party for his own pet causes. To a significant extent they were right, for Raskob by his own estimate already had endorsed a loan note of $150,000 and had become liable for $400,000 more. By the end of 1930 he had contributed about $875,000 more to the Democratic party, and he asserted to Al Smith that his commitment entailed the personal sacrifice of a GM contract worth "about $1,500,000." Raskob undertook such burdens because he agreed with Pierre that the stakes of success or failure were high. As he opined to the superintendent of the Anti-Saloon League of Michigan after the election, prohibition was breeding "a lack of respect for law in our institutions; it is but a short step to such lack of respect for property rights as to result in bolshevism."[41]

As Raskob was painfully aware, ever since 1915 the Democratic party had toyed unsuccessfully with the idea of a full-time, permanent staff. Under his predecessor Cordell Hull, reorganization had been attempted but had collapsed under a similar weight of defeats and red ink. Historically the national chairman's role was that of an election-year fundraiser and publicity promoter. Raskob, however, drew the lesson that the 1928 defeat was not a personal failure but the result of an inadequate organization, and he scheduled an April 19 dinner with prominent Democratic senators and former Smith operatives at his New York apartment to urge a wholesale overhaul of the DNC. Also invited and in written consultation with the chairman, although not in attendance at the meeting, was Governor-elect Franklin Roosevelt of New York. Through a May 5 article by Charles Michelson of the New York *World*, Raskob made public his intentions to create a permanent party headquarters in Washington, D.C., under the daily direction of aide Jouett Shouse, whose official title would be chairman of the executive committee of the DNC. The permanent headquarters would conduct ongoing publicity and research efforts, as well as administer the process of further reducing the party's debt and raising an additional $200,000 for its own operations.[42]

In tabbing Shouse, Raskob (labelled by colleagues as "soft-spoken little Johnny") recognized that he lacked the presence, patience, and political acumen to oversee directly the Democratic party's nuts-and-bolts administration. Shouse, a longtime party operative, had proven his value during the 1928 campaign and had travelled a winding ideological odyssey to his new post. Elected to the Congress in 1914 from Kansas as a Wilsonian Democrat, he served as Assistant Secretary of the Treasury after his reelection defeat in 1918. In 1924, as a delegate to the national convention, he cast his initial ballot for the arch-enemy of Smith and the wets, William G. McAdoo, only to switch to eventual nominee John W. Davis. By 1928, he had maneuvered his way into the Smith camp and, despite having voted for prohibition as a congressman, professed to be ardently opposed to it. A Kentucky native, Shouse exuded the charm of a bourbon Democrat, and he was seldom seen without his dapper walking stick, pince-nez glasses, and spats. To underwrite the veteran Washington insider's services to the party, Raskob personally contributed from $15,000 to $30,000 a month to Shouse's headquarters operation and paid his salary, beginning with an original installment of $20,000 in late May. By the time of Shouse's resignation as executive committee chairman in mid-1932, Raskob's payments to Shouse totalled $232,500.[43]

At the annual Jefferson Association dinner on June 10, Shouse publicly acted as the mouthpiece for Raskob's agenda. "A political party," he declared, "is in many regards like a business organization, and unless it is run on business principles its chance of success is greatly lessened." What Raskob wanted, with Shouse serving as his principal implementer, was to make the Democratic party's decisionmaking structure as much like that of Du Pont, General Motors, and the AAPA as possible. He specifically urged a "nationalization" of party control by suggesting that each state party organization be required to coordinate its publicity and fundraising with the national headquarters—his own variation of "decentralized management, centralized control."[44]

Given the greater procedural and political roadblocks to revamping a party of such varied constituencies, however, Raskob was forced to adopt less comprehensive and more informal methods of control of the national committee. The DNC's official structure remained much the same as before, consisting of a male and a female representative from each state, the District of Columbia, and the various territories, and five party vice-chairmen, adding up to 110 members in all. An advisory committee, a secretary, a treasurer, a sergeant-at-arms, and an eight-member executive committee rounded out the formal organization working under Raskob. Raskob hoped, following the du Pont blueprint, to make the executive committee, then consisting of himself, Shouse, former Smith aides Peter Gerry, Herbert Lehman, Belle Moskowitz, and James Hoey, Governor Roosevelt, and George Van Namee (Roosevelt's 1928 campaign manager), the party's decisionmaking hub. Soon, however, conflicts within the panel between the Smith and Roosevelt factions would lead him, along with Shouse, to attempt greater behind-the-scenes orchestration and merely employ the executive committee, in Charles Michelson's words, as a "device of legitimation."[45]

In an effort coordinated with the AAPA's own push to step up its propaganda campaign, Raskob in the late spring advocated the hiring of a full-time publicity chief for the DNC. In mid-June, Shouse announced the hiring of Michelson, the New York *World*'s former Washington correspondent, for the post. By July 1 Michelson had already assembled a small staff, which began issuing reprints of party statements to reporters, news agencies, and DNC members and other propaganda material, including a newsletter, to weekly magazines and newspapers lacking a Washington bureau. Michelson's office also arranged occasional radio time for leading Democratic figures, especially anti-Hoover congressmen.[46]

Raskob in 1929 also asserted for himself an enlarged role as national party spokesman on a variety of policy issues, an unusual procedure for a party chairman in a nonelection year. In May he advocated the creation of a national securities investment fund, or "workingman's trust," to sell stock to Americans of modest means. To provide such individuals with loans for the purchases, he even suggested the establishment of an accompanying national finance company. In July, he and Shouse solicited prominent Democratic politicians to issue statements of opposition to the proposed Hawley Tariff bill not on purely traditional anti-tariff grounds but on the basis that the legislation vested excessive rate-setting powers in the executive branch rather than Congress. Later in the summer, Raskob authored one of the most famous popular articles of the 1920's for the *Ladies' Home Journal*, entitled "Everbody Ought to Be Rich." Returning to his theme of expanded popular ownership of common stocks, he argued that if every American invested but $15 a month in such issues, twenty years later the investments would be worth $80,000 each.[47]

Raskob's pronouncements on public issues as DNC chairman were carefully coordinated with Pierre du Pont's efforts on behalf of the AAPA. As might have been expected, their coordination was greatest on the question of prohibition repeal. Back in April 1929, Raskob had requested and received permission from Pierre to transmit the AAPA research department's published comparison of federal penalties for prohibition violations with those of other, more violent, crimes to prominent Democratic senators, in the hope that the effort might encourage Congress to reduce the seemingly disproportionate statutory punishments for Volstead violations. While pursuing his DNC tasks, Raskob also continued to serve on the AAPA's finance committee. By November he was sending out financial solicitations on AAPA letterhead to all 1928 contributors to the Democratic party's campaign fund.[48]

By the fall of 1929, anticipating a major push to secure wet control of the Congress the next year, Pierre not only was using Raskob's position to solicit wealthy Democrats but was seeking the membership lists of the American Medical Association, the American Bar Association, the U.S. Chamber of Commerce, and other business and professional groups. He also was hard at work on a draft amendment to the Constitution that would both overturn the Eighteenth Amendment and establish a system of state-licensed private corporations to operate a reopened liquor trade. Having totally abandoned any interest in mere modification of the law, Pierre now sought the AAPA board's decisive endorsement of the objective of immediate and total repeal.[49] But neither he nor John Raskob could anticipate just how dramatic the political effects of "Black Thursday" and the stock market crash of October 1929 would be. The triggering of the greatest economic crisis in the history of the United States would generate far more lasting effects upon the repeal cause, and upon the du Ponts' broader policy hopes, than had their own efforts to date—and certainly far greater consequences than any seer that autumn could have foretold.

chapter 5

Depression and New Opportunities

The severity of the Wall Street crash of October 1929 caught the du Ponts as much by surprise as the rest of the country. In September company stock had reached an all-time high of 231 on the *New York Times* index of leading industrial issues. By Black Thursday, it had plummeted to 80. General Motors stock, having offered a 150 percent dividend in 1928 and risen to an index mark of 78, broke to 33. With a touch of bravado, John Raskob predicted, "Prudent investors are now buying stocks in huge quantities and will profit handsomely when this hysteria is over." In November, however, in an article for the *North American Review,* he came out for the forty-hour week and the Monday celebration of all holidays save Christmas as an economic stimulus to "head off socialism." Pierre du Pont, after attending a series of management conferences at the White House, also publicly expressed optimism. But business associate James J. Riordan, president of County Trust and an underwriter of the Smith campaign to the tune of $50,000, issued his tragic verdict on the unfolding economic disaster by committing suicide. Raskob and Smith appeared as pall-bearers at his funeral. By January, a continuing plunge in stock prices was reproduced in mirror image by a climb in unemployment, from 450,000 at the time of the crash to over four million. By the first anniversary of Black Thursday, the figure topped five million.[1]

The crash was the beginning of an extended period of economic trials both for the nation and the du Ponts. The family resorted to special measures to ease the personal burden. Even after the crash, Raskob, who had purchased huge blocks of GM and RCA stock at margin cost and sold them at full market value, owed taxes on some $6 million in 1929 profits. Pierre was in a similar tax predicament. Since income tax laws permitted investors to deduct their capital losses from stock income, the two arranged to sell each other approximately

$4.5 million worth of securities at a loss before year's end and to claim the net losses on their tax returns. In November Pierre bought $4,606,000 of Raskob's stock portfolio and sold $4,582,750 of his own to his friend. In January, after the start of a new tax year, the two bought back their stocks. Pierre sent Raskob a check on January 6 for $5,254,154, which Raskob deposited two days later and transmitted a return payment for $5,289,500. The transaction, although of dubious legality, immediately saved Pierre over $600,000 in taxes. Even so, $4.5 million in taxes remained on Pierre's estimated 1929 income of $31.5 million, the highest individual obligation in the nation.[2]

Although the growing economic crisis was a major worry for the du Ponts, it nonetheless represented a new opportunity for the cause of prohibition repeal. As businessmen, economists, and politicians scrambled for an antidote to the Depression, advocates of orthodox measures such as tax and spending cuts and balanced budgets grew more receptive to AAPA claims that a legalized liquor industry and its tax revenues could assist such remedies. For labor unions, whose focus was on reversing the decline in employment and stabilizing hours and wages, the return of legal liquor promised additional employment opportunities and increased purchasing power. Ironically, because they were slow to recognize the long-term nature of the crisis, the du Ponts did not fully exploit the economic arguments for repeal immediately after the crash. By 1932, they more than corrected their initial oversight. They had used the tax saving arguments for repeal for several years, and to that extent they were prepared to take advantage of the crisis to attain their 1930 electoral goal of a wet Congress.[3]

Before the effort could be launched, however, a series of internal AAPA squabbles had to be settled. Many of these disputes could be traced back to the differing tactical viewpoints of the Wadsworth and Pierre du Pont factions of the organization. In the fall of 1929 a minor flap already had arisen over president Curran's attempt to transfer finance department employees in the national office to his control within the accounting department. Raskob, as a member of Lammot du Pont's finance committee, demanded instead that the finance department be solely responsible for all daily administration of fundraising and that it operate directly under the charge of the finance committee and, through it, the executive committee. A more important issue was Pierre's stated goal of immediate repeal, which the experienced political professionals, mainly Republicans, around Wadsworth and Curran viewed as an unwise abandonment of the more "realistic" objective of modification of the Volstead Act. As Republican loyalists, Wadsworth and Curran did not want the AAPA deliberately shutting itself, and them, off from the GOP. They also, being less concerned than Pierre about post-repeal liquor policy management, saw little election-year value in continuing the organization's policy research studies. Instead they preferred even greater efforts to construct a grass-roots electoral following and to build alliances with unaffiliated organizations and labor unions sympathetic to repeal. On December 1, Wadsworth argued with Pierre that "instead of having a few thousand members we must run the number into six figures, perhaps more." He insisted, "We have finished our research work and need not spend any more money in that direction."[4]

Pierre accordingly was forced to scramble to quell the discontent over his insistence on immediate repeal. Faced with skepticism even within the executive committee on the political wisdom of "immediatism," he effected an end run by securing the endorsement of the AAPA board of directors on February 4. He did not get all that he wanted, however, as the board reached no decision on his request to have his specific draft amendment, on which he had labored for months, adopted. Pierre also staved off attempts to gut the research division's activities, although in a partial concession to critics its publications turned more toward election-year propaganda themes than to detailed analysis of the prohibition law and its alternatives. The AAPA also accommodated Wadsworth's wishes for a mass membership drive in 1930, but Pierre successfully staved off for the time being formal alliances and information-sharing with the AFL and other pro-repeal groups.[5]

In spite of the quarrels, by the spring of 1930 the AAPA was in as formidable a position as it had ever been. Spurred by an election-year rush of contributions, and not yet suffering from the drying up of corporate coffers as a result of the Depression, the war chest mushroomed. The three du Pont brothers, Raskob, and five business associates alone gave over $200,000. Total cash receipts for the year reached the record total of nearly $760,000. Even the number of contributions from modest donors, and their dollar value, climbed. In 1930 the AAPA received 28 percent of its income from over 21,500 givers of less than $100 each. A clear indication of the association's financial health was the fact that in 1930 no contributions were accepted from brewers. The AAPA had allowed brewer donations up to 5 percent of total income prior to 1927, 7 percent in 1928, and 2 percent in 1929. Membership also soared, from 150,000 in early 1930 to 360,000 by year's end. The VCL's roster grew to over 2500 and its budget rose to $15,000, the only year it reached that level. The WONPR's progress enabled it to hold its first national convention in Cleveland in April, and the Crusaders expanded from a local to a national association. The Authors and Artists Committee, for its part, grew to over 600 members and supplied an increasing volume of cartoons, articles, and editorials to the nation's press.[6]

Utilizing its expanded resource base and professional expertise, the AAPA under Pierre's guidance cast an ambitious two-pronged challenge to the Eighteenth Amendment. The first objective was the election of a Congress that would be willing to pass a repeal amendment and submit it to the states. The second scheme, equally dear to Pierre's heart, was an effort to repeal prohibition by initiating a direct court challenge of the ratification procedures used by the states. Although the Supreme Court had already upheld the amendment's ratification methods in the *Hawke v. Smith* and *National Prohibition Cases* of 1920, the New York County Lawyers Association had reopened the question in late 1927. In early 1930, AAPA member and Lawyers Association representative Selden Bacon argued that because of Tenth Amendment limits on amendment powers as stated in Article V of the Constitution, appropriate ratification methods had to be based upon whichever's rights and powers—the individual's or the states'—would be most affected. Since the Eighteenth Amendment clearly restricted individual freedoms, Bacon maintained, it legally could have been ratified only by popularly elected state conventions and not by state legislatures. Following a conference on March 31 between Bacon and Curran, Stayton, and Pierre, the next day the AAPA executive committee approved printing 25,000 copies of his findings in pamphlet form and backed his test case in a Newark, New Jersey, federal court.[7]

Congressional hearings in the spring further heightened the AAPA's visibility and damaged the credibility of its critics. From February to April the House Judiciary Committee held modification hearings, as it had done four years earlier. Since that prior occasion, however, prohibition agents had been made civil service employees, federal enforcement appropriations had been boosted, and, under the "Jones Five and Ten Law" sponsored by Washington Senator Wesley L. Jones, maximum penalties had been increased to five years in jail and/ or a $10,000 fine. AAPA spokesmen Grayson Murphy and John Gebhard testified in behalf of easing the law, but the most sensational of the hearings' headlines centered on Pierre du Pont and his motives in directing the repeal cause. Prospective witness Frank G. Atwood charged that in an exchange of private letters in 1928 and early 1929 Pierre had indicated his intention to take control of a national liquor monopoly following repeal. In fact, as Pierre's public release of his August 27, 1928, letter showed, all he had expressed to Atwood had been his hypothetical opinion that, if he magically possessed the sole authority to design the post-repeal structure of a legal liquor industry, he would prefer establishing a licensed private monopoly with a fixed profit percentage.[8]

Nonetheless, in August, Pierre did express confidentially his preference that the organizers of any post-repeal liquor monopoly be "directors of the AAPA, as far as possible all of them," and that liquor corporations might either be "more than one in each state, or one corporation might control in more than one state or in all of the states." The comments suggested that Atwood may have gauged accurately Pierre's ambitions, but his firsthand testimony as to Pierre's actual words had failed to support his charges. In mid-April an emboldened Pierre in House committee testimony blasted the Eighteenth Amendment, ironically, as an illegal document because it had never been properly ratified by popular will. He declared disingenuously, "No one should refuse to submit questions to a vote by the people. To refuse is to invite reference to that court of last resort referred to in the Declaration of Independence, in those words of unmistakable meaning: 'Whenever any form of government becomes destructive of these ends, it is the right of the people to alter or abolish it.' "[9]

Stung by Pierre's testimony, prohibition supporters tried to retaliate with their own populistic appeals. Already the Anti-Saloon League, citing the presence of fifteen out of twenty-eight General Motors directors as AAPA members, had insisted that the repeal effort was being orchestrated by the wealthy for selfish purposes. On the day of Pierre's Congressional appearance, the WCTU's Dr. Mary Harris Armor charged "big business" with seeking repeal so that "the poor man will drink the liquor to pay their taxes." In addition, the Republican majority on the Senate Lobby Investigation committee, stung by conflict-of-interest charges leveled at GOP chairman Claudius H. Huston, counterattacked by raising Democratic party chairman John Raskob's ties to the wet cause. Raskob misleadingly denied any personal role in the AAPA's activities or any attempt to commit the party officially to repeal. However, committee subpoenas of AAPA financial records and testimony by Henry Curran and William Stayton yielded proof of Raskob's financial contributions to the organization of nearly $65,000 since early 1928. Despite renewed calls from Southern Democrats for his dismissal on the ground that his AAPA contributions had helped defeat the party's own dry candidates, the chairman defiantly announced, "I have no intention of resigning." The political storm surrounding Raskob, like the furor following the presidential election, gradually blew over.[10]

In spite of Raskob's covert efforts to steer the Democrats toward repeal, Pierre and other AAPA leaders still hesitated to throw all their eggs in one basket. The reluctance stemmed partly from May poll results of the *Literary Digest,* which indicated that only 30 percent of its 4.8 million respondents now favored prohibition, while an almost equal number favored modification and a 40 percent plurality endorsed repeal. A New York *Herald-Tribune* survey of 110 daily newspapers in 36 states, despite omitting such overtly "wet" publications as the *New York Times, Washington Post,* and the *Herald-Tribune* itself, showed that the wets had rallied from a two-to-one deficit in 1919 to an even press split in 1930. More important, the wet papers carried a far greater circulation, and gains were recorded even among smaller nonmetropolitan dailies. Given the general shift against prohibition, abandonment of a nonpartisan stance could possibly cost the AAPA political support by alienating wet Republicans, rather than add to it.[11]

To capitalize on the momentum, the AAPA's research department issued a new edition of its *Cost of Prohibition and Your Income Tax* pamphlet, with updated 1929 federal income-tax and potential compensatory liquor-tax figures of $951 million and $1.096 billion, respectively. But the organization's partisan posture remained unsettled, a state reflecting Pierre's own uncertainties. Hoping to aid the general repeal cause, he had even contributed $100 in November 1929 to the National Women's party, although he professed doubts "as to the advisability of having such a party." In actuality the Republican party no longer was a welcome haven for wets, having drifted steadily in the opposite direction since at least 1924. Besides Mrs. Sabin's well-publicized defection from the GOP, Henry Bourne Joy had resigned from the Detroit Republican Club in December, and James Wadsworth, although consenting to attend the New York State GOP convention, had declined delegate status so as not to be bound by any dry platform resolutions. Even Republican loyalist congressman James M. Beck of Pennsylvania, a champion of states' rights and an AAPA director, publicly attacked his party over prohibition on the House floor, drawing parallels between the GOP's reluctance to take the lead on a present-day issue of personal liberty and the failure of the Whigs to confront the slavery question in the 1850s.[12]

Nor did all the Republican organizations across the country lean toward the drys. GOP platforms in Connecticut, New Jersey, Washington State, and Wisconsin openly backed repeal. Illinois and Rhode Island Republicans pledged to abide by the verdict of popular referenda. Nonetheless, the general closed-mindedness of Republican leaders to wet arguments led disgruntled party activists, most prominently in Pennsylvania, to propose forming a third, "Liberal" party and to seek AAPA backing. The ringleader of the plan, Carnegie Institute president and AAPA director Samuel Harden Church of Pittsburgh, even urged at the association's February 4 board meeting that a national Liberal party devoted to states' rights, individual liberty, war debt claims reduction, and prohibition repeal be launched. Because of his lingering uncertainties over Raskob's ability to "deliver" the Democrats, Pierre du Pont encouraged Church's schemes while remaining personally noncommittal. Following the February session he expressed doubts that "we have the necessary elements for party formation present in today's situation," but only a week later he sounded more positive: "My objectives are all withdrawn. A new party will be successful if the backing is obtainable."[13]

While continuing to humor Church's efforts, Pierre took the time to instruct his colleague on the proper content of his party platform. Especially sensitive to any attacks on economic monopolies in a pro–free enterprise plank, he asserted, "I think it wise to dissociate the public mind from the idea that some evil monster called a 'monopoly' will injure our country if industrial combinations are permitted." Wet Pennsylvania Republicans, led by Church, formed a Liberal party in May and backed AAPA director Thomas W. Phillips for the GOP gubernatorial nomination against dry Gifford Pinchot and moderate William Vare. Despite the help of other wealthy AAPA members such as Robert Cassatt, W. W. Atterbury, and Baldwin Locomotive president Samuel Vauclain, Phillips garnered only 281,000 votes in the primary, not only insufficient to win but having the effect of throwing the election to Pinchot.[14]

Waiting in the wings were Raskob's Democrats. Compared to the GOP they certainly offered more promise, with fourteen state platforms (including those of New York, New Jersey, Massachusetts, Pennsylvania, and Illinois) already on record for repeal. The fledgling Liberals of the Keystone State, having failed to nominate a wet Republican, even endorsed Democratic gubernatorial hopeful John Hemphill. But could the Democrats, so long in the political wilderness, deliver the goods? To position the party not just on prohibition but on economic issues, Raskob, in a published letter of June 12 to Senator Joseph Robinson of Arkansas, declared his opposition to the proposed Hawley-Smoot tariff duties. Although most congressional Democrats predictably opposed the bill's higher rates as a continuation of their party's longtime commitment to low tariffs, Raskob's own objections centered on the proposal for a presidentially appointed commission with the power to make adjustments in specific duties. In keeping with the du

Pont philosophy, the DNC chairman preferred the creation of an expert private commission with the power to make rate recommendations with such rulings then subject to congressional approval. At the same time, he also endorsed modest proposals for a limited federal public works program for the growing numbers of the unemployed.[15]

Money problems, however, continued to haunt Raskob's partisan efforts. As of April 1930, the pledges previously made by pro-Smith New York Democrats to pay off the $400,000 loan note held by County Trust still had not been paid. But rather than launch a new fundraising campaign to cover the debt, against advice Raskob demanded payment of pledges made in the 1928 campaign. Traditionally such pledges seldom were redeemed, but instead simply were forgiven by the party once subsequent general contributions had been collected to cover the amounts. Not surprisingly, then, many of the notesigners refused to comply with the chairman's demand. After receiving sharp criticism of his methods from Bernard Baruch and other signatories, Raskob reluctantly contented himself with getting ten of them to extend their pledges for additional time, backed by his own personal endorsement. With his own financial ties now even more extended, and given his continuing subsidization of the Democratic headquarters, Raskob estimated that only $50,000 was available in party coffers for the fall's House and Senate campaigns.[16]

If the Democrats lacked funds for electoral activities, however, their publicity apparatus in Washington, D.C., was scoring heavily against Herbert Hoover. The propaganda campaign was so devastating that Baltimore *Sun* columnist Frank Kent charged Raskob and party publicity chief Charles Michelson with orchestrating a "smear Hoover" effort. By September 1, the party headquarters had issued 406 public statements (three-quarters of them authored by congressional Democrats). Ever since the October 1929 crash, Michelson had exhorted newspaper columnists and cartoonists to pick up the Democrats' message. Day-to-day operational head Jouett Shouse scheduled a series of radio addresses for October and early November featuring himself, Raskob, and former presidential candidates James Cox and John W. Davis as spokesmen for the party. Meanwhile, although he publicly denied it, Raskob allocated the national committee's sparse campaign funds so as to weed out drys. By the November elections, only one congressional race (a Senate contest in Montana) featured a wet Republican against a dry Democrat.[17]

For its part, Pierre's AAPA was more than ready to make up for the Democrats' financial paucity and supplement its propaganda campaign. By the fall of 1930, the organization, citing feature articles in

600 million newspaper copies and 154 million magazine issues across the nation, claimed three times the readership of 1928. AAPA-sponsored news stories reached an estimated nine million more Americans. Four million pamphlets had already been distributed. In October the organization issued a new publication, *Does Prohibition Pay?*, which argued that the Eighteenth Amendment had neither increased consumer savings nor generated the prosperity of the 1920's. AAPA efforts had already paid off a month earlier with the adoption of a repeal resolution by the national Veterans of Foreign Wars convention. Before the election, the AAPA also released the results of an American Bar Association members poll that indicated a two-to-one majority for repeal. The organization's campaign efforts managed to outspend even its impressive revenues, with outlays of over $800,000. Sensitive to charges that the AAPA was attempting to "buy" the election for its wealthy sponsors, Pierre claimed that the du Pont family investment of over $150,000 averaged but about $1000 per person. In doing so he carefully sidestepped the fact that the lion's share of family contributions had come from just himself, Irénée, and Lammot.[18]

Even before the general elections, Pierre had personally "loaned" $4400 for poll watchers and voter recruiters upon request of Delaware's Democratic candidate for the Senate, Thomas F. Bayard. After his return from a European vacation that lasted from late September through October, the usually reticent Pierre gave an election-eve radio address on station WDEL in Wilmington in behalf of his repeal plan and implicitly endorsed Bayard over Republican opponent Daniel Hastings. Over nationwide radio the same day, John Raskob blasted away at Hoover's tariff policy, advocated creation of a coast-to-coast highway construction program, and endorsed the idea of a five-day work week at five-and-a-half-day pay levels in order to boost consumption. Pierre's special and unusual efforts in behalf of Bayard did not pay off, as the Democrat lost to Hastings. But around the country there was little other cause for disappointment with the election returns. Riding a wave of popular discontent with Hoover's economic policies, the Democrats gained fifty-three seats in the House, giving them a majority, and eight Senate seats, leaving them but one shy of the GOP. Eighteen out of thirty-one contested governorships also went to the Democrats. Although most races probably were not decided on the basis of the prohibition issue, the stronger correlation between Democratic candidates and the pro-repeal stance that Raskob had striven for meant similar advances in Congress for the wet cause.[19]

The 1930 election returns confirmed for Pierre du Pont that the Democratic party was the vanguard of the repeal fight. Estimates provided by AAPA president Curran indicated that the number of openly wet House members had jumped from 76 to 146. Not surprisingly, Pierre now relayed his better judgment against any further third-party agitation to Samuel Harden Church. "I am much interested," Pierre conveyed to Church, "in the plans of Mr. John J. Raskob, who, if permitted, will make something of the Democratic party." Church remained a stubborn advocate of his dream, even proposing the formal creation of a national Liberal party for 1931. Raskob, however, immediately arranged his own meeting with Church in early January to head off the idea.[20]

Besides the promise contained in the Democrats' campaign successes, Pierre's renewed drive for passage of a repeal resolution by Congress was dictated by the failure of legal challenges to prohibition. Although on December 16, 1930, Judge William Clark sided with the AAPA in its test of Eighteenth Amendment ratification procedures, two months later the Supreme Court in *U.S. vs. Sprague* reversed the ruling. But if Pierre hoped for congressional action to end prohibition, he knew that the Republican party would be of less help even than before, with the November returns having made it even "drier." A prohibition supporter, U.S. Senator Simeon D. Fess of Ohio, now became the GOP's new chairman. Even former diplomat Dwight Morrow, having run for the Senate in New Jersey as a wet, opted to follow the Hoover line once elected.[21]

As the new year dawned, however, Pierre's greatest new source of irritation with the Republicans became the issuance of the Wickersham Commission report. The eleven-member panel, officially titled the National Commission on Law Observance and Law Enforcement and headed by former Attorney General George W. Wickersham, had been created by President Hoover in May 1929 following campaign pledges for a prohibition study. When it was formed, however, Hoover expanded the body's mandate to examine the broader question of criminal justice and federal law enforcement. Critics charged Hoover with a subterfuge intended to water down the commission's impact and findings. Except for the release of a letter from Wickersham to a national governors' conference urging greater state enforcement efforts, and a brief interim report calling for minor changes such as the transfer of the prohibition bureau to the Justice Department, the commission maintained an uncomfortable silence regarding its inquiry.[22]

When the report was finally released in January, wet leaders, including Pierre du Pont, were struck at the disparity between, on the one hand, the gloomy content of the bulk of the study and, on the other, the report's optimistic final recommendations and Hoover's bullish characterization of it. The facts of the report actually appeared to buttress AAPA claims of prohibition's failure. As Pierre decried to Curran, "How the recommendations could have been drawn from the facts is beyond me." Making matters more confusing were the separate conclusions of individual commissioners, which when added up did not correspond to the report's summary vote of endorsement of the prohibition law. Of the eleven members, nine noted a lack of respect for the prohibition law and six appeared to endorse immediate change. Two favored absolute repeal, five endorsed phasing in the Bratt liquor system of Sweden as an alternative, and two others indicated a willingness to support repeal if a renewed test of enforcement failed. Only one commissioner unequivocally favored retention of the Eighteenth Amendment. Nonetheless, the published conclusion of the report and Hoover's own response both took that stance, lending credence to the supposition that the White House had pressured the panel into its collective judgment.[23] New York *World* columnist Franklin P. Adams caricatured the commission's findings:

> Prohibition is an awful flop.
> We like it.
> It can't stop what it's meant to stop.
> We like it.
> It's left a trail of graft and slime,
> It don't prohibit worth a dime.
> It's filled our land with vice and crime,
> Nevertheless, we're for it.[24]

Although personally dismayed at the report, Pierre du Pont and other wet leaders soon realized that the public furor it generated actually bolstered their cause. Certainly the body of the investigation provided the AAPA with even more factual ammunition with which to assault the Eighteenth Amendment. The Great Depression, however, was proving an even greater boost in the war against Herbert Hoover. By the previous November's elections, national unemployment already had topped five million, and by year's end it had neared six. After the elections, Hoover invited Pierre, Alfred Sloan, Henry Ford, and other leading industrialists to a White House conference intended to promote private wage and price stabilization measures. Hoover hoped that the industrialists would coordinate a national effort "on their individual behalf" to forestall further "movement for wage reduction." In return Hoover sought and received similar pledges from labor leaders to forestall demands for higher wages in contract negotiations. On November 23, Hoover, while continuing to rule out a federal public works program, wired the nation's governors seeking their local encouragement of the "energetic yet prudent pursuit of public works."[25]

Despite Hoover's entreaties, unemployment continued to soar through the winter, reaching eight million in January, and his voluntary stabilization program soon crumbled. Although Hoover had taken first steps toward greater federal intervention in relief assistance, public works, farm aid, and stock market regulation, he already was reaching the limits of his activism. Having created the Federal Farm Board in 1929, he remained unwilling to use it effectively to reduce the volume of food production. Although he encouraged local public works creation, he rejected calls for a $1–3 billion federal program issued by the National Unemployment League and by even his own Emergency Committee on Unemployment. Although he backed creation of the Federal Employment Service to help states coordinate their job promotion efforts, he vetoed legislation to replace the FES's twenty-four independent offices with a grant program to states linked to minimum job standards. And although he lauded expanded local and private relief efforts, he refused to move in the direction of direct federal aid and regulations.

For their part, the du Ponts were only now beginning to comprehend the full dimensions of the national economic plunge. Personal setbacks and growing direct contact with the destitute brought partial, belated recognition of the depth of the crisis. In October 1930, John Raskob joined the Emergency Unemployment Committee of New York and began service on its board of directors. The committee, which stayed in operation through April, coordinated the collection of moneys obtained through various private sources, such as Catholic Charities, the Charitable Organization Society of New York, Jewish Social Service, and the New York Association for Improving the Condition of the Poor. Funds raised (amounting to $8 million by the end of 1930) then were channeled to New York's Emergency Work Bureau, mostly in the form of $5-a-day wages for park and sanitation jobs. Reflecting the voluntaristic, anti-welfare assumptions of the committee, only a small proportion of the money went as direct relief rather than as work relief. None was used to pay the overhead of any permanent welfare organization. Besides his administrative contribution, Raskob also personally gave $5000—a sizable sum, but far smaller than John D. Rockefeller's $1 million offering.[26]

In Delaware, the du Pont brothers similarly were becoming involved in local and state voluntary relief efforts. In November 1930, Pierre recommended to the late Coleman du Pont's son-in-law, Governor C. Douglas Buck, that the state launch construction of a new highway running parallel to Du Pont Boulevard as a special public works project. A receptive hearing by the Delaware Highway Commission was assured, since Coly's son Francis was its chairman. The following month Pierre joined the Mayor's Emergency Unemployment Relief Committee in Wilmington, which from January through May 1931 raised funds for food, coal, and rent for needy families and allocated moneys through the Associated Charities of Wilmington (later renamed the Family Society). For his part, Lammot du Pont served as a director of Associated Charities. The organization also created a special fund for temporary roadwork projects, including road widening and painting of bridges and poles, which employed 300 workers per week. As with New York City's aid program, Wilmington's approach emphasized work wages rather than direct relief for the able-bodied unemployed, who were paid only for time on the job with no allowances granted for bad weather. As of early February, the committee had received private pledges of $90,000. By its termination in May, it had raised contributions of about $275,000. Of that total, Pierre had donated $10,000 and Irénée $30,000, with two-thirds of Irénée's amount specifically directed to the special road maintenance fund.[27]

Although their own difficulties paled by comparison with those of the unemployed, the Depression's effects also were felt in direct ways by the du Pont inner circle itself. As one example, in 1929 John Raskob had become intrigued by the thought of acquiring or redeveloping the Enyan Corporation's real estate property in Manhattan, which included the old Waldorf-Astoria Hotel. In August of that year, he had convinced the corporation's directors to demolish the hotel and to build a massive new office building, the Empire State Building, on the site. Within two years, he had arranged the renaming of the corporation as Empire State, Incorporated. Pierre and Al Smith had been persuaded to invest in the new venture, and Smith was named company president. But as a result of the economic crisis, the building could not entice enough tenants, and 1931 losses were so bad that, despite Pierre's stake in the project, Raskob had grave difficulty even convincing Du Pont president Lammot to move his company's New York offices into the property.[28]

Such difficulties, nonetheless, did not induce the du Ponts to abandon their economic orthodoxies. Even John Raskob, despite his party loyalties, chose not to blast Hoover for his caution. In October 1930 he joined the American Association for Labor Legislation—not to agitate for greater federal activism but to exert a "moderating" influence. After the November elections, he wrote the President to promise that the newly acquired strength of congressional Democrats would not be used for "radical" economic remedies. Privately he chastised Hoover for his criticism of, and implied threats to regulate, the New York Stock Exchange. The Du Pont Company, although it extended loans to current employees in financial straits, refused to expand the program to those already laid off, and the state of Delaware provided no unemployment insurance. Despite that fact, Pierre attacked schemes to increase the government's role either in unemployment relief or in "workfare" programs that would violate business prerogatives. He specifically blasted an idea suggested to Governor Buck that workhouse labor be employed in auto repair shops on the grounds that the shops would compete with private firms.[29]

Growing agitation for government-financed old-age pension relief further alarmed the du Ponts, particularly given the nature of its advocates. Family nemesis Alfred I. du Pont, having returned to Delaware and having wangled an appointment as chairman of the state's Old Age Welfare Commission, quickly proposed a pension program funded by state payroll taxes. In a move to dramatize himself as well as the issue, Alfred as far back as November 1928 had begun personally mailing monthly checks to some 1600 elderly recipients—beneficence that eventually totalled about $350,000. Both Pierre and John Raskob immediately assaulted the idea of a state program, the latter claiming that such assistance was "better supplied by interested relatives and friends than by paid workers." Following Pierre's personal intercession with the governor, Buck agreed that state aid would have to be limited to the truly needy, and the state could simply not afford to pension all elderly residents. In the spring of 1931, the state legislature nonetheless did pass a modest penion bill, and Alfred sent out his last check on July 1. At the national level, too, Pierre attempted to head off other expansions in the government's welfare programs, writing congressman Robert Houston to urge defeat of a "maternity bill" designed to appropriate $1 million to the states for hospital services. As the clamor for state interventionism spread, the du Pont's fears of "native Reds" led to greater receptivity among them to solicitations by self-appointed anti-communist organizers. Irénée personally donated $3000 to retired Major General Amos A. Fries, past president of the Washington, D.C., chapter of the Sons of the American Revolution and founder of the anti-radical American Security League, for his brand of "anti-Red activities."[30]

As the Depression continued to worsen in 1931, the du Ponts' fears of domestic radicalism were counterbalanced somewhat by the boost the crisis gave to their economic arguments for prohibition repeal. In January, the American Federation of Labor formed a National Committee for Modification of the Volstead Act, headed by Matthew Woll, to spearhead its own repeal drive. By September, both the Veterans of Foreign Wars and the American Legion formally enlisted in the cause. AAPA propaganda, and Pierre du Pont's private correspondence, increasingly reflected the growing preoccupation with the economic advantages of repeal. Both cited the beneficial effects of a legalized liquor industry on employment, the farm economy, the federal budget, and the possibilities of reductions in other government levies. In keeping with Pierre's orthodox belief in a balanced governmental budget and low income taxes, the AAPA churned out *The Need of a New Source of Government Revenue*. It claimed that the eleven years of prohibition had cost the federal treasury $11 billion in potential revenues which could have been used to avoid deficits and enable other means of stimulating the economy.[31]

The AAPA's return to the tax argument, even within the larger context of an economic recovery plan, drew fire from drys accusing the du Ponts and their supporters of selfish motives. The Anti-Saloon League claimed that while wet backers, such as Alfred Sloan of General Motors, contributed to the repeal cause, they privately placed bans on alcohol consumption by their employees. Sloan vigorously denied the charges. The dry lobby also accused Irénée du Pont, as it had for over a year, of promoting repeal in order to reduce his profit and income taxes by half. Spokesmen claimed that the du Ponts had no intention of using tax savings to promote immediate reemployment within their empire but instead, citing Irénée's projection of GM's post-repeal tax bonanza of over $10 million, planned to earmark the savings for either higher dividends or lower car prices. By 1931, however, the public found more sensational the charges circulating against the dry leadership. Anti-Saloon League superintendents in Missouri, New York, and Kansas faced personal scandals. Even Bishop James Cannon, Jr., head of the Methodist Board of Temperance, Prohibition, and Public Morals and one of the most prominent national advocates of the Eighteenth Amendment, found himself accused of stock manipulation, World War I–era profiteering and flour hoarding, and other personal peccadilloes.[32]

Although the AAPA was winning the propaganda war, the Depression by 1931 also was cutting into the organization's finances. During the severe downturn of the winter of 1930–31, contributions by donors at all levels shrunk as economic needs and other charities made more pressing claims for help. The AAPA set a post-election financial goal for 1931 of 140 percent of 1930 revenues or, more bluntly, a million dollars. But while the du Ponts themselves generally maintained their

high levels of funding, and John Raskob renewed solicitation of previously untapped GM, Du Pont, and Missouri-Pacific directors, contributions from small donors in particular plummeted. The number
of gifts under $100 fell by nearly 14,000, to under 8000, and overall
receipts fell to slightly more than $475,000, about the 1929 level. The
decline occurred despite claims of membership gains, with the AAPA
citing figures of 400,000 and the WONPR 300,000, most of them non-
paying members.[33]

Similar financial woes afflicted the Democratic party, necessitating
John Raskob's continued underwriting of party headquarters. But, as
with Pierre's role in the AAPA, Raskob's financial preeminence gave
him reassurances of steering the Democrats' policy directions. During
the spring and summer of 1931, he pushed harder than ever to make
his agenda that of his party, and he took pains to coordinate the efforts
with those of Pierre in the AAPA. In January 1931, Pierre informed
Stayton of Raskob's request "that I write down for him some thoughts
in regard to individual rights under the Constitution." At the top of
Raskob's own agenda was a "home rule" plank, similar to proposals
of Al Smith in 1928 and Pierre in 1929, which would allow each state
by popular referendum to opt out of the prohibition law. Because the
Wickersham report's furor had already painted Herbert Hoover into
a "dry" political corner on the issue, even Raskob loyalists such as
Jouett Shouse and Joseph P. Tumulty had urged delay on any specific
action by the National Committee. The Republicans' agonies, they
had argued, made an open declaration by the Democrats unnecessary.
Nonetheless, Raskob pressed ahead with the plan for the DNC's scheduled March 5 meeting.[34]

Grumbling already had surfaced over previous attempts by the
chairman to assume a policy spokesman's role, as he had done in his
post-election message to Hoover on economic policy. Accusations that
Raskob, having "bought" the party, now was trying to dictate its
policies were leveled by columnist Frank Kent in February. Supporters
of New York's popular governor, Franklin D. Roosevelt, for the 1932
presidential nomination similarly suspected in Raskob's maneuvers an
intent to set the stage for a Smith revival. In contrast to Raskob and
Smith, Roosevelt's own career was marked by the caution with which
he approached the prohibition issue. Seeking to avoid alienating either
wets or drys, as governor he ordered New York law enforcement personnel to cooperate with federal officials, but at the 1929 national
governors' conference he spoke for state prohibition control. At the
state's party convention in 1930 he endorsed repeal, only to back away
from the pledge at the start of the general election. On September 9,

1930, after popular sentiment indicated clear support of repeal, Roosevelt publicly agreed. Eyeing the upcoming presidential season, the governor and his backers still feared the loss of Southern and rural progressive support if the repeal cause was pressed too forcefully. Raskob's home rule tactic accordingly was viewed as a ploy to force Roosevelt into a divisive policy position over a year before the nomination.[35]

Attempting to counter Raskob, Roosevelt forces at the New York Democratic Committee meeting of March 3 adopted a resolution disavowing the right of the National Committee to advise or impose upon party nominees positions on controversial issues, and sent copies of the resolution to all DNC members except Raskob and Shouse. Facing a rebellion by Roosevelt supporters and Southern and Western Democrats, Raskob grudgingly agreed to defer consideration of the issue. Nonetheless, in his speech to the National Committee on March 5, he included a general plea in behalf of "Jeffersonian" principles, urged eventual adoption of a wet plank, and criticized partisan attacks upon the business community. An angry Raskob refused to relent following the meeting, instead firing off a telegram to Roosevelt indicating his determination to "insist and demand" that the Democrats take an "honest" prohibition stance rather than adopt a "mere pussy-footing law enforcement plank." Publicly attacking the enforcement tactics of federal officers, which he asserted included wiretaps and illegal searches, Raskob also maintained that if he *had* pressed the home rule resolution before the DNC it would have carried by a 70-30 margin. "In line with good democratic doctrine," however, he claimed to have deferred immediate action in order to allow time for "selling the South."[36]

In an April 4 letter to the DNC membership, Raskob pressed them to assume a policymaking role by formulating and sending proposals to national headquarters by September 1. His own list included a plea to "take the government out of business and relieve trade from unnecessary and unreasonable government restriction," a call for tariff revision by Congress, opposition to "government pricefixing schemes," limited farm relief, a voluntary and cooperative system of old-age and unemployment insurance, a five-day week without pay reductions, easing of the Sherman Anti-Trust Act, opposition to utility holding company regulation by the federal government, and, most urgently, either prohibition repeal or legislation establishing a national referendum on a home rule plan. Working in close consort with the chairman was Jouett Shouse, who publicly attacked prohibition and endorsed the home rule proposal in a speech to the Women's National Democratic Club.[37]

As Raskob's extensive "laundry list" of planks suggested, prohibition repeal was but one part of a general effort to steer the Democrats in a conservative, pro-corporate direction. His farm policy consisted of opposition to either production quotas or government subsidies; instead it endorsed a plan by California fruit packer E. Clemens Horst that combined prohibition repeal, the idling of federal lands, tariffs on agricultural imports, and anti-dumping measures. His desire to remove anti-trust restrictions on business collusion was both a continuation of longstanding du Pont doctrine and a response to increasing calls for "industrial self-government" and centralized economic planning. Most prominent among the advocates of such coordination was General Electric president Gerard Swope, who in September called for the compulsory cartelization of major industries into federally sanctioned national trade associations. Such national councils, containing business, labor, and government representatives, would be empowered to regulate production and price levels within their industries and establish "codes of fair practices." Although Raskob in his statements indicated no objection to centralized industrial councils and the suspension of anti-trust enforcement, and the du Ponts actively favored such ideas, he and his du Pont colleagues did not share Swope's enthusiasm for government and labor representatives on such panels.[38]

By the middle of July, Raskob still was predicting that the three primary issues of 1932 would be "the international situation, the tariff question, and the prohibition question." Of the three, prohibition continued to receive his greatest attention. All his actions were carefully screened beforehand with the du Ponts. Privately, Pierre du Pont pressed Raskob for a firm Democratic commitment to the wet cause. Using Samuel Harden Church's threat of a third party again as leverage, Pierre warned that if the Democrats' Southern wing prevented a "definite commitment against prohibition," a third party would be a "good thing." By mid-October, he was pointing out for Raskob's edification, while professing to minimize them, the differences between the AAPA's repeal amendment and the Democratic chairman's home rule scheme. Describing the variances as "only a difference in procedure," Pierre nonetheless noted that Raskob's plan contained the flaw of allowing prohibition to remain in place in a state even after repeal until an alternative liquor control program had been formally passed by its legislature and ratified by a state referendum.[39]

In response to Pierre's prodding, Raskob prepared a letter targeted at, and carefully limited to, the more than 90,000 contributors to the 1928 Smith campaign and polling them on whether they preferred home rule or immediate repeal. The wording of the repeal amendment specified in the letter was provided by Pierre. It called for ratification by popularly elected state conventions which would feature equal apportionment by district so as to avoid rural overrepresentation. Irénée, also given the opportunity to screen Raskob's letter, enthusiastically concurred, "I think you have 'hit' on an entirely proper plan to get the consensus of opinion of those who are really interested in a political party. I have little doubt of what that opinion is going to be." Bolstered by the du Ponts' approval, Raskob issued his "poll" at the end of November, and made plans to present its findings to the DNC in January as a way to pressure the party into an open endorsement of a wet plank in 1932. When Raskob's letter leaked to the press, and the *Washington Post* decried his attempt to split the party on prohibition, Pierre predictably rallied to his defense.[40]

Repeal was not the only matter upon which Raskob and Pierre du Pont consulted closely. In mid-October, Pierre relayed through Jouett Shouse his general views on the content of a desirable Democratic platform. Included in his list were opposition to any proposals on federal unemployment insurance beyond the mere study of the issue, avoidance of direct condemnations of the Hawley-Smoot Tariff but support for modest downward tariff revision, insistence upon corresponding cuts in government pay if federal employees' work hours were reduced, defense of utility holding companies, and opposition to any anti-trust plank which engaged in demagogic appeals against the "extortion of monopolies." Not just the platform but Democratic fundraising also was coordinated with the du Ponts. With the party deficit having risen to $700,000 by the end of August, in late September Raskob issued appeals for more pledges to 1928 contributors, setting a goal of $1.5 million for the prenomination period. Former nominee John W. Davis, a reliable ally, was tabbed as general chairman of the "Victory Fund." In addition, under the sponsorship of Raskob, Shouse, Charles Michelson, and Joseph Tumulty, special groups of donors of over $2000 each, called Minute Man Clubs, were formed, and claimed about 600 members by the end of October. Despite his lack of a formal party identification, especially as a Democrat, Pierre was invited to serve on the national committee of the Victory Fund. Raskob's gesture also insured Pierre's rebuffing of last-gasp overtures from Samuel Harden Church to accept chairmanship of his quixotic Liberal Party National Committee.[41]

The du Ponts and John Raskob recognized that the political stakes had never been higher than they would be in 1932. Underscoring the urgency was the fact that as gloomy as the winter of 1930–31 had been, the national economic situation entering the 1931–32 holiday season boded even worse. Delaware had passed an old-age pension bill, but the government budget continued to drop deeper into the red. Declining motor vehicle and income tax revenues were being stretched to the breaking point just to fund the state's highways and schools. In expectation of harder times, in Wilmington the Mayor's Emergency Unemployment Relief Committee had been reconstituted in September, and Pierre once more signed on as a member. Following entreaties from the Hoover administration, Pierre also accepted a position on a business advisory committee to the President's Organization for Unemployment Relief. But with the national jobless total having climbed past nine million in October, even the Du Pont Company was forced to cut the workweek of salaried employees to five days, and du Pont–dominated U.S. Rubber adopted wage cuts. Irénée du Pont, who contributed $4500 to Wilmington's work relief effort that winter, publicly urged the President not to seek a balanced budget through income tax increases, warning that to do so would cut into his and others' private charitable efforts.[42]

With schemes proliferating among popular circles for centralized economic planning, corporate cartelization, and state-run capitalism, even Al Smith boldly advocated that "a mild form of dictatorship, honestly operated, honestly intentioned, must be set up, or else we will simply have the promise of relief on paper."[43] It was in that darkening climate of apprehension and nervous expectation that the du Ponts prepared to launch their most ambitious fight yet for conservative corporate stewardship of national affairs. By the beginning of 1932, it was now a struggle to be fought out primarily within the confines of the Democratic party.

chapter 6

Uncertain Victory

At the close of 1931, Pierre du Pont and John Raskob had already established the immediate objective of electing a Congress that would adopt a prohibition repeal amendment. Their longer-range goals included the establishment of a centralized, private liquor industry and, more broadly, the transformation of the Democratic party into an organization committed to the principles of limited federal government power and private corporate stewardship. In order to achieve both the short- and long-term objectives they sought, they placed the maximum importance on a third target—the blocking of Franklin D. Roosevelt as the Democratic party's presidential nominee and his replacement by a candidate, preferably Al Smith, more attuned to their political perspectives.

As early as the fall of 1931, with Roosevelt still resisting adoption of an unequivocal wet plank by the DNC, Raskob and his party allies had been meeting irregularly to map anti-Roosevelt campaign strategy. Besides FDR's waffling on repeal, his courtship of the party's rural and progressive elements made the du Ponts uneasy. Roosevelt's own privileged economic background provided a reassuring counterweight, but the du Pont inner circle remained concerned about his apparent lack of "sound" fixed principles on a range of "vital" issues, his attempt in 1928 to block Raskob's appointment as party chairman, and the "radical" notions of some of his advisors. Meetings with Raskob at the Empire State Building to plot out anti-Roosevelt strategies included such Democratic notables as Jouett Shouse, Al Smith, Bernard Baruch, Governor Albert Ritchie of Maryland, former Secretary of War Newton Baker, and, representing presidential hopeful John Nance Garner of Texas, Sam Rayburn.[1]

The names of candidates floated by Raskob at strategy conferences reflected the du Ponts' continuing preference for a man of "sound business principles" over a professional political "demagogue." Among the trial balloons floated were those of GE executive Owen Young, Newton Baker, and even the obscure Melvin Taylor, president of the First National Bank of Chicago. Baker, citing his fragile health (he had suffered a heart attack in 1928 while campaigning for Smith), declined, and neither of the others generated any enthusiasm from the political experts at the meetings or from those in the "test" states of Kentucky, Texas, and Illinois. Al Smith, the one figure most looked to for leadership, agreed on the necessity of blocking Roosevelt but continued to show little personal enthusiasm for campaigning, despite entreaties by Raskob. By a process of elimination, the vigorous lobbying of Baruch, and the growing awareness that it would take an experienced electoral politican and orator to defeat another, Governor Ritchie inherited the early role of point man for the anti-FDR effort. Even this preliminary "choice" required the direct approval of Pierre du Pont. Following a letter in November from Raskob to Ritchie informing him of Pierre's personal interest in and support for his possible candidacy, a week later the party chairman, the Maryland governor, and Al Smith met in New York to plan out a campaign itinerary. Ritchie immediately launched a cross-country series of speaking engagements to increase his visibility as a candidate. Many political outsiders, however, still viewed him as nothing but a stalking horse for the still-reticent Smith.[2]

To the du Ponts and Raskob, the specific identity of the presidential nominee, so long as it was not Roosevelt, was of less importance than the assurance of his commitment to repeal and a broad pro-business philosophy. As a major part of the effort to link the Democratic party and its candidates with such viewpoints, Jouett Shouse in December mapped out a publicity program for Raskob intended to spotlight him as the Democrats' policy spokesman. The thoroughness of the campaign, in fact, even suggested to some insiders that in the absence of other candidates with business executive experience, Raskob perhaps was contemplating tossing his own hat in the ring. Shouse included in the chairman's projected publicity onslaught interviews and signed articles for the Sunday *New York Times,* a motion picture interview at his home with Graham McNamee, a magazine article, and prearranged luncheons with prominent editorialists Walter Lippmann, Samuel Blythe, Clinton Gilbert, and Frank Kent designed to "enable these writers to discuss Mr. Raskob's opinions and policies from actual personal contact." Even a Southern editor would be solicited to write a public letter to the chairman inviting him to explain his "remarkable interest in the party"— springboard both to disavow selfish motives in his huge financial stake in the party and to portray himself as one who "sincerely believes in the party system of government."[3]

Among other parts of the high-profile campaign lined up for Raskob by Shouse were a national trip "around the circle" to sound out leaders, contributions of a series of position papers to the press, and posings for still photographs with Democrats from all regions and political persuasions (especially supporters of Roosevelt-rival Garner). Shouse even contemplated having Raskob appear before a Congressional hearing as a witness on a range of "important principles in which the Democratic party is vitally interested." Without expressly stating the chairman's personal motive in this strenuous effort, Shouse declared, "It is believed that the definition of such an authentic picture in the public mind will greatly increase the popular acceptance of Mr. Raskob's ideas, will strengthen his leadership, and will greatly facilitate the execution of his plans."[4]

Raskob's most pressing objective was to force a DNC commitment to a home rule or repeal plank at its scheduled January 9, 1932, meeting in Washington, D.C. On January 5 he released the results of his November poll of contributors: 91 percent of the 25,000 respondents favored one or the other wet positions. Attempting to outflank Roosevelt in advance of the meeting, Raskob did not include him among the list of featured speakers at the January 8 Jackson Day dinner. Instead, former presidential nominees Cox, Davis, and Smith were chosen for the major addresses. Stung by the continued criticism that he was imposing an extreme policy plank on the party, Raskob insisted that the home rule option was intended as a middle ground. "What I have been trying to do," he declared, "is find some ground on which the wet and dry element in our party could be brought together and in that way get rid of the question and then fight the campaign on sound economic lines."[5]

Drys and Roosevelt Democrats had other ideas, choosing once more to block an open endorsement of home rule. The New York governor preferred to sidestep the prohibition question entirely in order to lead a united party into the fall campaign. In addition, a victory over Raskob and his segment of the party would boost even further his personal prestige among rural Democrats and progressives. Finding that he lacked the committee votes to prevail, Raskob was forced into a face-saving compromise in which he employed Virginia's Harry F. Byrd, a dry but otherwise a supporter of the chairman's conservative economic policies, as a negotiating intermediary. Under the compromise Raskob agreed to drop the home rule questionnaire from the meeting agenda, but the proposal would be referred to the party's platform committee for consideration at the summer's Chicago convention. In an additional display of Raskob's weakness, Roosevelt forces also elected their candidate for secretary to the national committee by a wide margin. Emboldened by his success within the DNC, Roosevelt followed it up with an open declaration of his presidential candidacy. Raskob could only take solace in the fact that his efforts had forced the platform committee to confront the prohibition issue.[6]

Despite his second rejection before the DNC, Raskob, following suggestions of Pierre du Pont, publicly endorsed in early February a revision to Article V of the U.S. Constitution requiring any future amendments to be ratified by elected state conventions rather than state legislatures. The prohibition issue, however, remained but the most visible manifestation of the growing confrontation between Raskob and Franklin Roosevelt. A less publicized focal point of conflict was Raskob's election-year vehicle for redeeming party debts and raising 1932 campaign dollars, the Victory Fund. Both the structure of the operation and its reliance upon former Smith campaign benefactors led the Roosevelt organization to conclude that it was little more than a Raskob-Smith slush fund. Nor were the New York governor's supporters reassured by the presence of conservative John W. Davis as the Victory Fund's general committee chairman.[7]

The fund's Victory Campaign was issued a public send-off by party chairman Raskob at a dinner party of January 14 in New York City, coordinated with state celebrations the same evening. Roosevelt campaign workers could at least count on a minimum degree of equal representation by regions, given that the general committee of the Victory Fund required a male and female representative from every state. But Raskob's other creation, the "Minute Men of the Democratic National Committee," was an even more exclusive club of donors and had the overt aim of increasing business influence on the party and keeping it informed of "national political trends." Already Raskob in his address to the DNC on January 9 had agitated rural and progressive Democrats by his comparison of the U.S. government with an industrial corporation—equating the president with a corporate chief executive, the Congress with the board of directors, and the voters with stockholders. Accordingly those same party representatives were not reassured by the prominence of Raskob, Smith, and Shouse on the Minute Men's executive committee. Further confirming the linkages between the DNC hierarchy and Wall Street wets was Charles Sabin's presence on the special Bankers and Brokers Committee to the Victory Fund. As of mid-January, the fund had raised $500,000 in contributions and pledges toward its $1.5 million goal, but the lion's share came from Smith backers such as William F. Kenny, Bernard Baruch, Herbert Lehman, and Raskob himself. The chairman also continued to subsidize his headquarters to the tune of $15,000 a month, and he gave $25,000 more to the Victory Fund in February. In May, he absolved the DNC of payment due him on two notes, matching an indirect "contribution" of yet another $100,000.[8]

Publicly Raskob and Shouse both claimed that their frenetic solicitation of funds from former Smith backers was not part of a deliberate stop-Roosevelt strategy. In a letter to New Mexico's Governor Arthur Seligman, Shouse insisted, "There is no desire on our part to dictate the nominee of the Convention." Raskob in turn blamed the Roosevelt camp for the slowness of Victory Fund collections, along with the conflicting claims upon potential donors posed by relief and charity efforts. But Raskob's actions, and those of his subordinates, spoke louder than his words. On January 23, Jouett Shouse issued a press statement urging state party conventions to send uninstructed delegates to Chicago—a clear anti-Roosevelt move. The chairman's continuing personal underwriting of the party drew a stinging rebuke from the *New Republic,* which called for an end to "one-man control." It concluded that Raskob, "on his part, tempted by the prospect of dictating a platform, naming a candidate, and perhaps running an administration, has connived rather than protested at the rising obligation . . . The debts that Chairman Raskob was influential in incurring, Banker Raskob has taken up."[9]

The steady decline of the national economy during the winter only escalated the stakes of political victory or defeat for the combatants on both sides. As for the du Ponts themselves, even though shielded from the most grievous signs of want, they could not avoid noticing the growing legions of unemployed on Wilmington's streets. By the end of 1931 the city's Citizens Committee had raised about $800,000 for relief assistance, with Pierre a major contributor. In January 1932, responding to an appeal from cousin William du Pont in behalf of the Family Society, Pierre extended an additional $36,000. Upon returning from his winter vacation in Cuba, in late January Irénée gave $5000 and another $10,000 by early March. The Mayor's Emergency Unemployment Relief Committee, which had been reconstituted the previous September and remained in existence until June, managed to collect another $670,000, of which $265,000 was allocated as direct wages and the remainder paid for the financing of relief services and construction jobs administered by the state highway department. The du Ponts, faced with such relief requirements, could no longer cling to the notion that the country was merely going through a modest, corrective recession.[10]

Faced with a depression now well into its third year, the du Pont brothers searched for economic panaceas. Irénée endorsed a proposal of company economist E. E. Lincoln for a federal sales tax to balance the federal budget and opposed any additional increases in the income tax. By April, having read avidly Samuel Crowther's pamphlet, "Your Money," he began championing the cause of credit expansion and economic stimulus through "trade acceptances"—a means of extending installment credit directly from manufacturers to retail purchasers. The ever-orthodox Lammot complained that federal defense and public works spending had risen to dangerously high levels by 1932 and advocated government budget cuts. Pierre, concerned at the potential legislative impact of embarrassing disclosures of Wall Street shenanigans by the Senate's Pecora committee, lobbied Senator John Townsend of Delaware in opposition to any attempts to cap the volume of securities assets held by commercial banks. He also decried proposals to separate investment banking functions from commercial banking, fearing the relocation of central financial power in the hands of political appointees on the Federal Reserve Board in Washington, D.C.[11]

Pierre himself continued to vest his faith for recovery in prohibition repeal and in the pro-corporate guidance of a revitalized Democratic party. Having made his second payment of a $25,000 pledge to the Victory Fund in early January, he was disappointed at the DNC's subsequent rebuke of Raskob. Nonetheless, he remained committed to Raskob's party as his, and the country's, best hope. Despite Samuel Harden Church's earlier prediction that Pierre's longtime friend would not be able to "swing the Democratic National Convention over to his liberal and sensible ideas," in February Pierre again ruled out the creation of a third party as unwise and belated. Instead, he pressed Jouett Shouse to steer the Democrats unequivocally toward repeal. "The greatest industry in this country," he maintained, "is now untaxed and is carried on by gangland at the expense of those good citizens who are trying to do an honest business." Pleading with his brother Lammot to commit the family company to the cause, he claimed that repeal would "almost eliminate" the need for income taxes and would stimulate recovery. Lammot, however, adamantly countered, "I don't believe that taxes and economics are fundamental factors in the Prohibition question. The fundamental factors are social and involve personal rights and liberty"[12]

The strategic disagreements between Pierre and Lammot on the prohibition question were a direct result of a longstanding divergence in their views. Pierre, never a convinced GOP loyalist, had confidence in the promise the Democrats offered as a vehicle for the family's policy perspectives. Lammot, in contrast, was never able to bring himself to take any actions that could be construed as open criticism of President Hoover and the GOP. But in spite of Lammot's reluctance to choose between his loyalties to repeal and to the Republican party, the prohibition question had already been transformed into a partisan barometer. Democratic frontrunner Franklin Roosevelt in February repeated in a Buffalo speech his 1930 call for states' freedom to determine their own liquor regulations. In March 1932, for the first time House Democrats forced a roll call on repeal in the form of a discharge petition for a home rule resolution—a vote which failed by a margin of 227 to 187 but put individual congressmen on record in advance of the upcoming elections. A spring *Literary Digest* poll indicated that out of almost 5 million respondents, nearly three-quarters favored outright repeal. Even John D. Rockefeller, Jr., son of the prohibition movement's original financial benefactor, endorsed jettisoning the Eighteenth Amendment.[13]

The AAPA jumped on the election-year bandwagon. President Henry Curran called upon both major parties to back a public referendum on repeal. The WONPR and the Voluntary Committee of Lawyers issued similar demands to Democratic convention delegates. The VCL's Joseph Choate authored a resolution, signed by fifty-three other attorneys and directed at both Hoover and prominent Democratic hopefuls, which declared, "The question of whether the Republican or the Democratic party shall run the government is subordinate to the question whether our traditional form of government is to continue at all." John Raskob spoke in equally monumental terms, warning of prohibition's contribution to the creation of a "supergovernment that most of us as yet cannot see."[14]

The du Ponts' campaign for firm platform commitments to repeal, in fact, was proceeding far better than their plans for a cooperative Democratic nominee. At the beginning of the year, Pierre and Raskob put Senator Harry Byrd of Virginia and Governor Ritchie of Maryland under active consideration as presidential material. Attention turned in February, however, back to Al Smith, following his "indirect declaration" of candidacy—consisting of a refusal to prevent supporters from launching a delegate effort in his behalf in Massachusetts. Privately Jouett Shouse expressed his doubts about Smith's electability, citing the anti-Catholic bigotry of 1928. But Smith was now more eager for the fight with Roosevelt, having catalogued a list of real or imagined snubs from his former protégé and still viewing him as an "ineffectual young man." Following a Raskob endorsement, with Smith's backing, of a Republican proposal for a federal sales tax and a Roosevelt address appealing for government action in behalf of the "forgotten man," Smith launched into an open assault on the New York governor. "I will take off my coat and fight to the end," the no-longer-Happy Warrior insisted, "against any candidate who persists in any demagogic appeal to the masses of the working people to destroy themselves by setting class against class and rich against poor." Raskob covertly endorsed the Smith effort, and Shouse urged Democrats to cooperate by sending uninstructed delegations to the Chicago convention.[15]

Already well aware of the animosity of the party chairman toward his campaign, Roosevelt wisely backed out of participation in April 13 Jefferson Day ceremonies in Washington, D.C. Roosevelt's fears that other speakers would "gang up" on him were well justified. The featured party oracle, Al Smith, again used the occasion to blast his rival as superficial and a reckless demagogue. Two weeks later, on April 29, Roosevelt demanded ironclad assurances that the party's Victory Fund collections, having climbed to the $360,000 mark, would not be utilized in any way prior to the convention as part of an effort to block his nomination. Without such assurances, FDR threatened, his own campaign backers in the Midwest, West, and South would cease all further contributions to the fall campaign. Roosevelt also continued to lobby in the resolutions committee for a platform plank written by A. Mitchell Palmer and former party chairman Cordell Hull, which endorsed state referenda on the prohibition question but refused to bind individual party candidates to endorsement of repeal.[16]

Despite Raskob's actions, however, the nomination battle against Roosevelt already was slipping away in early 1932. Both Smith and FDR did score victories in the spring's primary and state convention contests—Roosevelt in New Hampshire and Pennsylvania, Smith in Massachusetts, Rhode Island, and Connecticut. In California, a pro-Garner slate headed by former presidential candidate William Mc-Adoo carried the day. But although Roosevelt was denied a clear first-ballot margin going into the convention, he claimed 690 delegates, swamping Smith's 209, and his support was far more broadly based than his rival's. Raskob futilely attempted to revive the idea of an Owen Young presidential boomlet in May before a dinner gathering of businessmen that included Gerard Swope, Jesse Straus, and Vincent Astor.[17]

Given Raskob's failure to head off Roosevelt, the du Ponts' policy objectives, now ranging far beyond repeal to include new official structures for corporate guidance of the staggering economy, took on greater immediacy. To ensure "sound" economic policies, Raskob and Pierre floated the idea of a nonpartisan national executive committee to administer national policies. To Professor Edwin R. A. Seligman, Raskob lamented the inability of the United States to establish British-style coalition government during crises. He endorsed formation of a "nonpolitical body with almost autocratic powers," to be titled the "Emergency Economic Committee" or the "Peace Crisis Board." The panel, drawing heavily upon corporate expertise and personnel, would be authorized by Congress to dispense aid in the form of loans either to state and local governments or to private firms from a $5 billion "property loan" fund. The body would be additionally empowered to act as a provisional legislature when Congress was not in session, to override anti-trust rulings of the Interstate Commerce Commission and the Justice Department, and to prepare reports to Congress on such wide-ranging economic questions as war debt reparations and the gold standard.[18]

Raskob's proposal closely mirrored those of other leading industrialists in the late spring of 1932. For months businessmen had been meeting privately in small groups to map common economic strategy, including Irénée du Pont's "Friday night committee" in Wilmington and the "Owen Young committee" in New York. Henry I. Harriman, on the eve of his election as national president of the U.S. Chamber of Commerce, publicly urged the reorganization of the Federal Trade Commission to allow greater self-regulation in industry and, echoing the Swope Plan, he proposed that "business itself establish its economic council to consider the fundamental problems that affect all business." By the end of May, Raskob had refined his own proposal, contained in a letter to Senate Democratic leader Joseph Robinson of Arkansas, into a call for a ten-member bipartisan board consisting of five Democrats (preferably Al Smith, Owen Young, Bernard Baruch, John Nance Garner, and Robinson) and five Republicans (including former president Coolidge and former vice-president Charles Dawes). As for Irénée, growing alarm now led him, despite the caveat that "all we need is confidence and its offspring, credit," to confess, "If things continue to get worse, we may have a general breakdown of the economic structure. If it gets so bad that we have to call out the militia to suppress rioting, it may be time to consider the country in a state of war and have a dictator, either one man or a group."[19]

While Raskob lobbied in Washington for corporate economic centralization, Pierre did likewise within his circle of business associates.

In a letter to Alfred Sloan, he castigated the Sherman Act and claimed, "If you or any other leader could call together others of ability and make agreements for the benefit of industry in general or your particular branch, some good might result." To business economist Gilbert Montague, Pierre added, "I am sure that businessmen in general do not wish to be governed by a trade commission or any other federal body. It would be preferable to modify the trust laws so that those engaged in industry might collectively govern their industries." At the top of Pierre's list of specific policy recommendations were a national sales tax and slashes in federal spending directed toward the goal of a balanced budget. To his frustration, the Congress refused to include a sales tax in its 1932 revenue measure. To Modern-Bond Corporation president S. C. Bond, he insisted, "The Government is in no different position from the larger corporations, which, under contracting business, are obliged to reduce employment and activities in order to operate within their income. The Government should do the same thing." Pierre did endorse Delaware's existing levels and types of taxes, dismissing the state's franchise and incorporation levies on the grounds they constituted but a "very indirect burden" and insisting that gasoline taxes and automobile license fees did "not cause complaint." Given his special role in building Delaware's public schools, he even supported maintenance of the state's income tax for education funding, although he lamented its application to but "a very small percentage of the population." Over the longer term he endorsed the abolition of both federal and state inheritance levies, but for the moment he acknowledged that because 80 percent of such federal revenues were returned to the states, immediate repeal would have devastating fiscal consequences for Delaware.[20]

Besides budget cuts and a federal sales tax, however, Pierre still looked to prohibition repeal and restoration of a taxable liquor industry as a primary means to balance the budget and provide the revenues for an orthodox formula for economic recovery. Using the family's traditionally heavy contributions to the GOP as a lever, in late May Pierre warned Republican fundraiser Lee Warren that no donations would be extended by brothers Irénée and Lammot or in-law Ruly Carpenter until the party adopted an acceptable position on prohibition. Pierre delivered a similar message on his own behalf to both parties, warning the Democrats, for example, of his decision not to give any additional moneys at either the national or state level "until this decision [repeal] is reached." With similar motives in mind, the AAPA's board of directors, despite Pierre's lingering skepticism, voted to join forces with other pressure groups in a lobbying alliance called the United Repeal Council. The WONPR, the Crusaders, the VCL, the American Hotel Association, and the Republican Citizens' Committee Against National Prohibition enlisted in the alliance, and the American Federation of Labor, through AAPA member Matthew Woll, participated in the planning talks although it declined formal membership. At the beginning of the year Pierre still had held out against "a general consolidation of the various associations," fearing a loss of administrative control. Jealousies between AAPA president Curran and Crusaders' head Fred Clark also had delayed the formal unveiling of the repeal council. By the end of the spring, however, it was in place and prepared to lobby the platform committees of both major parties.[21]

In advance of the Republican convention, Curran wrote to each delegate in May urging repeal through the method of popularly elected state conventions. On the eve of the GOP gathering in Chicago, the United Repeal Council held its first national meeting on June 7 in the same city and, in a move which eased Pierre's fears, chose him as its overall chairman. Echoing Curran's prior appeal, the council formally urged the Republican convention to adopt a repeal plan drafted by Pierre, Mrs. Sabin, and the other organizations' leaders. Pierre, James Wadsworth, and Nicholas Murray Butler personally testified before the GOP platform committee in its behalf. In addition the Republican Citizens' Committee, having been created the previous December by disaffected wet party activists, lobbied individual delegates and delegations. Among their number exerting pressure either in person or by mail were Lammot du Pont, Joseph Choate, and Thomas W. Phillips. Aided by Chicago *Tribune* publisher Robert McCormick, wet leaders Raymond Pitcairn, Pauline Sabin, Matthew Woll, and Butler restated their warnings to the GOP at a pre-convention rally in the Chicago Coliseum. Wets, prompted by the rumor that a politically desperate Herbert Hoover might be willing to compromise on the prohibition plank, flooded the White House with telegrams.[22]

Once the convention formally opened, however, wet hopes rapidly were dashed. Hoover's appointments secretary turned away a delegation from the Voluntary Committee of Lawyers, as well as a request for an audience from the U.S. ambassor to Sweden intended to provide a briefing on the Bratt system to the President. The platform deliberations were dominated by Secretary of the Treasury and Hoover lieutenant Ogden Mills, and the majority plank on prohibition merely muddied the waters. The resolution seemed to approve putting prohibition reform to a popular choice by means of a constitutional amendment and elected state conventions, but in the same breath it endorsed continued federal liquor control as a noble aim and refused to obligate Republican candidates or office holders (especially Hoover) to support any specific change in the prohibition law. On the convention floor the administration's plank carried by a 690 to 460 vote. Pierre blasted the decision, insisting that the Eighteenth Amendment's failures could never be remedied at the federal level. Wadsworth labeled the plank a "fraud," and Curran termed it completely unsatisfactory.[23]

In marked contrast to the Republicans, the upcoming Democratic convention, also scheduled for Chicago in late June, showed every promise of an anti-prohibition platform. But in the view of Raskob and Pierre, the primary Democratic obstacle to broader success on a range of platform issues, and on long-term political and policy objectives, remained the Roosevelt candidacy. Pierre alluded to the upcoming struggle on June 20 when, preparing to leave once more for Chicago, he observed, "I do not believe the prohibition issue will occupy so prominent a place, and will be more quickly disposed of. The question of a candidate seems the important one before us." The struggle between pro- and anti-Roosevelt forces for control of the convention machinery had broken out into the open as early as April. When the arrangements committee met in the spring to consider the choice of convention officers, it became apparent that Raskob's ally Jouett Shouse had marshalled substantial DNC support to be convention keynoter—a possibility that the Roosevelt forces could not accept.[24]

Faced with an open split in party ranks, Harry Byrd of Virginia negotiated a compromise between the two camps in which Roosevelt's preferred choice, Senator Alben Barkley of Kentucky, would be keynoter and temporary convention chairman and Shouse would be given the permanent convention chairmanship. Amid hints from both Raskob and Shouse that in orchestrating the deal Byrd had done their bidding and had secured what they had actually sought all along, the two then demanded Roosevelt's firm acceptance of the bargain. By telephone Roosevelt indicated that he did not object to the arrangements committee "commending" Shouse for the post, but by June, insisting that "commending" did not mean the same as "recommending," Roosevelt instructed campaign manager James Farley to inform the press that his delegates would seek the election of the famous Teapot Dome investigator and U.S. Senator, Thomas Walsh of Montana, as permanent chairman of the convention.[25]

Besides the insurgent, anti-business symbolism of the Walsh proposal, Raskob, Shouse, and their du Pont backers all decried Roosevelt's "bad faith" in backing out of the April deal. In truth, both sides were guilty of double-dealing—Shouse for long having violated any pretense of official neutrality in the party's presidential selection process, Roosevelt for violating the spirit of the April compromise by playing semantic games and end-running the arrangements committee. With the atmosphere further soured by the beginning of the convention on June 27, and with Roosevelt short of the delegate strength needed for a first ballot nomination, the floor vote on the choice of permanent convention chairman became an early test of strength for both sides. Following an opening address by Raskob to delegates that extolled Shouse's virtues, John W. Davis spearheaded the anti-Walsh fight on the floor. Walsh prevailed, but the narrowness of the 626-to-528 margin, far short of the two-thirds needed for a presidential nomination, bolstered Raskob's and the du Ponts' hopes. The result also forced the Roosevelt camp to suspend efforts to seek immediate repeal of the two-thirds rule, settling instead for a pledge by the rules committee to recommend it at the 1936 convention.[26]

In his opening call to the delegates, Raskob, besides pleading Shouse's case, took the opportunity to plead for a platform plank unequivocally committing party candidates to repeal through the state conventions method. Roosevelt lobbied for a version written by A. Mitchell Palmer and Cordell Hull favoring state referenda but not imposing binding commitments upon candidates. After sharp divisions emerged within the platform resolutions committee on June 28 between advocates of Hull's plank and Raskob's favorite, drafted by Senator David Walsh of Massachusetts, the full committee the following day voted by better than a two-to-one margin for the "wetter" plank. Faced with another sign of possible erosion of his support, Roosevelt released his delegates from previous pledges to vote for Hull's proposal. In the early morning hours of June 30, after five hours of floor debate, including a ten-minute gallery ovation for Al Smith and the unfurling of a huge "End Prohibition" banner by the Crusaders, the repeal plank prevailed by an overwhelming margin of 934.75 to 213.75. Only eight state delegations stuck by the Hull proposal once released from their pledges by Roosevelt.[27]

Roosevelt's surrender on the prohibition issue was but one of many strategic retreats his forces made in order to preserve his nomination. Besides the statement on prohibition, the Democratic platform adopted by the delegates issued watered-down calls for banking and monetary reform, lower tariffs, controls on crop surpluses, and increased federal loans for state relief efforts, while it committed only to old-age and unemployment insurance "under state laws," urged federal withdrawal from private enterprise "except when necessary to develop public works and natural resources," and set the goal of a balanced budget through spending cuts of 25 percent. When combined with some rapid between-ballot maneuvering, however, Roosevelt's sacrifices in the platform succeeded in supplanting the momentum of the "stop-Roosevelt" coalition.[28]

When the presidential balloting began at 5 A.M. on July 1, Roosevelt still lacked the necessary two-thirds, and holding a strategic bloc of delegates was Texas' Garner, backed by William Randolph Hearst and William McAdoo. The Raskob–Shouse–du Pont faction, still trying to put together a coalition of former Wilsonites and urban Democrats that would block Roosevelt's nomination, employed Bernard Baruch to lobby Al Smith into throwing his strength to Newton Baker, who was more acceptable to a wider range of delegates than Smith. But after stemming a slippage of delegate strength before the fourth ballot with the aid of Southern and Western Democrats, including Louisiana's Huey Long, the Roosevelt forces struck the decisive deal with Garner. Relishing the moment, William McAdoo, remembering how Smith had blocked his nomination in 1924, mounted the speaker's platform amidst gallery jeers to cast California's forty-four votes for Roosevelt. Within minutes the nomination was FDR's, in exchange for Garner being offered the second spot on the Democratic ticket.[29]

Although they won major victories on the platform, which suggested the possibility that they could still steer (forcibly if need be) Roosevelt into "sound" policies, the du Pont–Raskob group found it hard at first to swallow their disappointment. Following the nominee's surprise announcement that he would fly from Albany to accept the nomination and address the convention in person, Raskob, Shouse, and Smith huddled at breakfast. A glowering Smith, lamenting, "I was four years ahead of my party, and look what happened to me," left for New York rather than greet his rival. Raskob, still party chairman in name until after the general election, could not do likewise, for he was required to host a DNC dinner for Roosevelt at the convention's close. For his part Roosevelt only confirmed Raskob's estimation of him as an unprinicpled opportunist by blithely ignoring the long platform fights, congratulating the delegates for their "courage" in adopting a repeal resolution and endorsing the platform "100 percent." Eight weeks later at Sea Girt, New Jersey, Roosevelt completed his expedient conversion to outright repeal by explicitly endorsing it.[30]

Even though Roosevelt's remarks could have been taken as a genuine attempt to heal party wounds, Raskob remained bitter toward the nominee. On July 5, he fumed to Harry Byrd that the party faced disaster when it "is turned over to a radical group such as Roosevelt,

Hearst, McAdoo, Senator Long, Wheeler, and Dill, and is taken out of the hands of such men as you, Governor Ritchie, Carter Glass, Mr. Reed, Colonel Breckinridge, Governor Smith, John W. Davis, Pierre S. du Pont, Governor Cox, Governor Ely, Peter Gerry, etc." The chairman saved his most vituperative comments for Shouse's confidence, asserting that while "the Party at heart is still good," the "scum, in the way of the radical element, has just come to the top and will be skimmed off in pretty vigorous fashion at the proper time." Despite Byrd's sympathetic words that "you and Jouett have been treated very badly," Raskob continued to boil. By late July, referring to an invitation from Roosevelt to discuss party campaign finances, he averred, "I hope he confines the discussion to finances, as I would rather not discuss other questions with him." Sharing his superior's sentiments, Shouse telegraphed perfunctory congratulations to the nominee after the convention, but a month later he declined to assume more than the most limited campaign efforts on Roosevelt's behalf.[31]

Pierre du Pont was as disappointed at the Roosevelt nomination as Raskob, but in view of the platform successes (and perhaps also the less direct personal consequences of defeat for him than for the lame-duck party boss), he maintained a more philosophical stance. In both the pledges of budget economies and the prohibition plank, he found much to praise in the Democratic platform. The manner in which Roosevelt had been forced to accept these and other modifications also gave him hope for the future of a Democratic administration. To Samuel Harden Church, Pierre expressed a willingness to consider backing the creation of a Roosevelt-Garner Liberal party slate in Pennsylvania as a half-way house for GOP wets unwilling to vote for Hoover. He also took special pains to ease the financial worries of Jouett Shouse, given his imminent departure from the official ranks of a Roosevelt-controlled Democratic party apparatus. As a signal of the AAPA's abandonment of the Republicans, and in response to Henry Curran's divisive record as AAPA president, Pierre arranged for Shouse's ascension as the organization's day-to-day chief administrator at a salary of $25,000 plus a $15,000 expense account. To help Raskob balance the Democrats' books before he left his post, Pierre also persuaded the DNC chairman to give an additional $25,000 to the party and added $15,000 more of his own to go toward the payment of debt notes still held by his friend.[32]

It was a cruel irony to John Raskob that despite clear indications that Roosevelt's campaign organization would not use party funds to pay off debts owed him until campaign needs were first met, the national party apparatus he had helped build now waged a supremely successful fight against Herbert Hoover. Even with help from his friends, the lame-duck chairman still held personal obligations for $300,000 of remaining debts. Employing the DNC publicity apparatus constructed by Charles Michelson, Roosevelt ran a noncontroversial campaign, avoiding specifics on such issues as collective bargaining rights for labor, federal aid for housing and mortgage relief, or taxes. Attacking Hoover in general terms for supposed fiscal profligacy, the Democratic candidate then issued equally vague calls for additional federal unemployment relief and public works for the states. Decrying a claimed tendency toward federal centralization, Roosevelt proceeded to call for increased national regulation of utility companies and the stock market.[33]

To put it simply, Franklin Roosevelt was content to let growing public frustration and animosity toward Herbert Hoover win him the election, rather than espouse specific economic remedies that might prove controversial. Given the political calamity for Hoover of the worsening depression, his campaign strategy was wise. According to the Federal Reserve Board, industrial production had dropped 50 percent from pre-Depression levels, and factory payrolls had been slashed 65 percent and employment 44 percent. The jobless total stood at over 13 million by the summer, and over 4000 banks had failed. Further condemning the incumbent's chances of reelection was the ugly sight in July of the forced removal of the ragged "bonus army" of squatter veterans and their families from the capital and the burning of their shanties. Democratic campaign literature could hardly have been more effective in casting an image of an administration, and a president, cruelly hardened toward human misery. In the du Pont's own state of Delaware, the continually mounting need for relief funds and shrinking local resources led to the launching of a new "Block-Aid" solicitation program in Wilmington, spanning from June to October. The private relief effort, which served over 3800 indigent families in the city and over 450 more throughout New Castle County, received $10,000 in help from Pierre du Pont in August.[34]

The ever-worsening business outlook amidst the election-year fervor fed renewed calls from the business community for unprecedented peacetime centralization of economic planning. In a poll of its members, the U.S. Chamber of Commerce reported that 90 percent of its respondents favored national planning of some sort, preferably in the hands of private industry. Growing corporate desperation, combined with the spreading awareness of Hoover's doomed political chances, led to a gradual, partial shift of corporate support and money toward Roosevelt. Desertions from GOP ranks accelerated when the Democratic candidate privately expressed interest in the Swope model of industrial planning. For one rare moment, the economic and political circumstances of 1932 produced a temporary "marriage of convenience" between corporate conservative titans such as Pierre du Pont, Edward Harkness, and Jesse Straus and insurgent progressives Robert La Follette, Jr., Hiram Johnson, and George Norris.[35]

Within the du Ponts' AAPA circle, splits resurfaced over the issue of whether support for prohibition repeal required endorsement of the Democratic ticket, given the two parties' divergent platform stands. In the executive committee, Pierre presided over a collection of three avowed Republicans—brother Irénée, Wadsworth, and Robert Cassatt. Five days after the Democratic convention, the WONPR's national executive committee opted on its own to endorse Roosevelt, with Pauline Sabin's picture appearing on the cover of *Time* to commemorate the occasion. Within days the Crusaders, however, chose not to endorse either ticket, and Fred Clark complained to Pierre about the lack of prior consultation from the WONPR. Pierre himself, of course, had already endorsed the Democratic platform and had given money to the party. Nonetheless, even he hesitated to oppose wet Republican candidates for state and congressional office. On July 22 he issued a press release indicating that the AAPA would continue its policy of supporting individual candidates on a nonpartisan basis. The policy remained the same despite Roosevelt's Sea Girt remarks in late August, which sounded like an AAPA press release in their denunciations of prohibition for its effect on social order and its violation of states' rights. Pierre also resisted calls from Raymond Pitcairn for the United Repeal Council to endorse Roosevelt on the grounds that bipartisan congressional help would be needed to pass any repeal amendment. In protest, Pitcairn resigned his seat on the council.[36]

Within the du Pont family, other than Pierre (whose support for the Democratic ticket was strictly pragmatic), most of the rest continued to publicly support Hoover without enthusiasm while they aided wets in other races. By late September, aggravated by rumors that a President Roosevelt might name McAdoo Treasury Secretary and dramatically increase federal public works spending and securities regulations, Irénée reaffirmed his loyalty to the national GOP. While chairman of the Delaware state AAPA, Irénée gave out over $10,000 to the state Republican party as well, making sure that it was earmarked for wet candidates. When new national president Shouse requested permission from Pierre to issue a pre-election radio speech for the Democrats, arguing that it would strengthen his post-election lobbying leverage with Southern Democrats, Irénée expressed the loudest opposition to the scheme.[37]

With Shouse now at the helm, the AAPA focused most of its resources on congressional races on a nonpartisan basis, although the clear platform differences between the parties tended to be reflected as well in their candidates. If the membership figures of 550,000 for the AAPA and 1.1 million for the WONPR could be believed, the groups now also constituted a substantial voting bloc. At Shouse's direction AAPA headquarters had been permanently shifted to Washington, D.C., the research office closed, and newsman Robert Burr hired to supervise publicity for an all-out, state-by-state electoral push. From June 1 to November 1 the national organization spent $300,000, or one-quarter as much as the Democratic party. Usually, though not always, the money went to Democratic candidates. While the Crusaders distributed a campaign book, *The New Crusade,* and the VCL lobbied the legal profession, the AAPA released its last pre-election pamphlet, a summary of previous arguments entitled *Thirty-two Reasons for Repeal,* in late September. Jouett Shouse barnstormed the country, giving pro-repeal speeches in Baltimore, Detroit, and St. Paul. Even Al Smith campaigned in the Northeast, albeit indifferently, against Hoover and for repeal, although not explicitly for Roosevelt. A partial financial ledger of du Pont family contributions to the AAPA campaign read: Pierre, $50,500; Irénée, $30,500; and Lammot, $30,100. All of them, privately or publicly, stressed to colleagues the economic reasons why prohibition had proven a disaster and held out the promise of reduced federal taxes and compensatory liquor revenues with repeal.[38]

As the campaign reached its climax, a confident Pierre already envisioned the shape of the post-repeal liquor industry. Given the likely fate of both Hoover and dry Republicans generally, there seemed little reason for pessimism. As early as July, he proposed to brewer August Busch a plan for supervision and control of liquor production and distribution by a single large corporation, placed under contract to state regulatory commissions. The contracts would spell out hours of sale, prices, and tax levels on the industry. According to Pierre, the plan would avoid "political manipulation and depredations." In order to maintain public confidence in the integrity of the new system, he advocated that the monopoly company draw a broader number of nonbrewers from the corporate ranks into its board of directors. Only a week before the election, Pierre reiterated his urgings to the major brewers and distillers to abandon decentralized competition and "make a combination of some kind and agree to accept the responsibility of the trade," acknowledging that such a change would result in the "elimination of the small dealer and small saloonkeeper."[39]

Buoyed by early predictions of an anti-Hoover landslide and determined to win the wet cause maximum credit and benefit for a Roosevelt landslide, Pierre personally endorsed the Democratic ticket publicly on election eve and had the statement carried by the Associated Press. Even Raskob set aside his resentment of Roosevelt in behalf of the larger cause long enough to give a nationally broadcast radio appeal for the election of a Democratic Congress, which he pledged would work for prohibition repeal, a balanced budget, an income tax cut, and a national sales tax. With the state already set for a Roosevelt landslide, Election Day was almost an anti-climax. Roosevelt garnered 22.8 million votes to Hoover's 15.75 million, and carried 32 of the nation's 36 largest cities; 282 counties voted for a Democrat for president for the first time in their history. And according to the *New York Times*, the newly chosen Seventy-third Congress would contain 343 wet House members and 61 pro-repeal Senators, paving the way for passage of a repeal amendment and its submission to the states. In separate state referenda, the voters of Arizona, California, Colorado, Louisiana, Michigan, New Jersey, North Dakota, Oregon, and Washington overturned enforcement laws, and Wyoming and Connecticut voted to petition the Congress to remove the Eighteenth Amendment.[40]

Surveying the happy tidings several days later, Pierre du Pont, while still repeating campaign rhetoric blaming prohibition as "directly responsible for our income taxes," was looking forward to the new administration and the new Congress with optimism. Defending his role in shaping the outcome to Eldridge Johnson, he claimed that "the greatest part of our reckless spending has been accomplished under complete Republican control of Congress." Replying to his friend's fears of the "radicals" around the President-elect, Pierre reassured, "As to Mr. Roosevelt's surroundings, I have every hope that the men mentioned by you will not be his advisors. At least, I am so advised on what I believe to be reliable authority."[41] With an otherwise potentially unreliable Roosevelt held on course by a Congress elected with substantial AAPA backing and by a conservative, pro-business platform, Pierre could now dream that a new day of enlightened corporate stewardship of national public administration was about to dawn.

chapter 7

A Brief Honeymoon

Pierre du Pont's anticipation of the consequences of the Democrats' electoral triumph in November 1932 could not mask the misery of the bleakest winter of the Great Depression. With Hoover powerless and the Congress unwilling either to take strong independent action or to cooperate with the lame duck, the nation suffered through a four-month "interregnum of despair." Whatever their elation at the prospects for repeal, the du Ponts were now feeling the weight of three years of business decline in their financial empire. Lammot du Pont had been forced to order the layoff of over 7000 company workers, including hundreds of chemists and engineers, in order to preserve the traditional 10 percent profit yield on invested capital. Other segments of the family empire had been hit even harder. General Motors' sales to its dealers had plummeted nearly 75 percent since 1928, and its profits had fallen to less than $8.5 million. (By contrast, Du Pont Company profits still stood at $26 million in 1932.) GM's motor vehicle division alone had lost almost $7 million in profits by 1932, resulting in a payroll cut of 60 percent and a workforce reduction of nearly 50 percent to 116,000 employees. GM had survived an inroad into its market share by Ford in 1929–30 (due to introduction of the Model A), recovering its predominance with a 43 percent share in 1931, but overall industry sales continued to shrink.[1]

The du Pont family empire's problems were but one example of the broader collapse of the American industrial economy and its durable goods sector. Manufacturing production in general had dropped 48 percent between 1929 and 1932. According to the Bureau of Labor Statistics, wholesale nonagricultural prices had plunged over 23 percent. With government funds rapidly drying up at all levels and deficits rising, public works construction had fallen from $12.3 billion in 1929 to $2.8 billion by the end of 1932. Most ominously, by early 1933

unemployment stood at, give or take a half-million Americans de-
pending on the estimate chosen, almost 30 percent of the workforce.²

In Wilmington the du Ponts witnessed directly the swelling ranks
of a nation in want. In anticipation of the bleak months ahead, the
summer's Block Aid program collected some $268,000 in twenty weeks,
but it expired on October 31, 1932. Even at its peak the effort assisted
only about 900 of the destitute, while many more suffered from the
drying up of governmental relief. In-law and state governor C. Douglas
Buck appointed Pierre du Pont to a state unemployment relief study
commission, which at the end of September estimated the state's unemployed at 18,000 (about 90 percent of the total in New Castle county
alone) and the necessary relief moneys for the year beginning November 1 at $2.5 million. The commission urged that two-thirds of the
money be spent on direct aid by the state and the rest channeled into
work projects such as road grading, sewing, and mosquito control.
Left unaddressed, however, were such deepening problems as long-
term aid for the unemployed and medical assistance for the needy.³

In mid-November, Pierre personally contributed another $45,500 to
the Mayor's Emergency Unemployment Relief Committee of Wilmington. But private charity was no longer adequate to meet the
mushrooming need, which seemed to mandate a greater governmental
role. Nonetheless, displaying the consistency of his creed, Pierre still
insisted that any new relief efforts, even if they involved governmental
moneys, be administered by a private corporation. Given the vast
influence of the du Ponts in state government, it came as no great
surprise that his view prevailed. Upon Pierre's recommendation, a
Temporary Emergency Relief Commission began duties on December
1, with a seven-member executive committee consisting of four private,
at-large members and Delaware's three county relief directors. Du Pont
business associate Jasper Crane served as its chairman.⁴

In other ways, too, Pierre continued to prescribe orthodox medicine
for the Depression's economic ills, including the oldest remedy of all—
simply letting the crisis run its full downward course. Reflecting a
greater insulation from, and a distrubing callousness toward, the plight
of the needy, he told brother Irénée, "To my mind the likely end to
the depression is when the existing commodities have reached such a
low point that it will necessitate resumption of manufacturing, mining,
etc., in order to provide the needs of the country." He asserted, "It
must be remembered that our population is no less than it was and
everybody is being fed, clothed, housed, etc." Pierre admitted, however, that the people were receiving such necessities "perhaps at a less
rate than heretofore." He concluded, "We must realize that much

contentment can be had through operations at a less rate of speed than prevailed when everything was booming."[5]

The du Pont inner circle did have its own tribulations that winter. In a move that both Pierre and John Raskob interpreted as political retaliation by the Hoover administration, in December the Revenue Bureau launched a tax investigation into their 1929 stock-swapping transaction. Also troubling was the uncertain degree of influence the Roosevelt administration would allot them in making personnel decisions. Through intermediaries Raskob and Al Smith the du Ponts relayed their preferences as choices for Secretary of State and U.S. Ambassador to Poland—Homer Davis and Pierre's brother-in-law Lammot Belin, respectively. But by mid-December Raskob already was warning his friends that his influence on cabinet selections was nil, and he continued to fret over the party's inaction in reimbursing his huge obligations in its behalf. Seeking to increase the outside political leverage of the du Ponts and their allies, Jouett Shouse urged Pierre to buy the New York *Evening Post* and install Al Smith as its editor. After Smith disavowed interest in the project to Pierre in late January, however, the idea was dropped.[6]

The immediate policy focus of the family remained prohibition repeal, especially given the continuing belief that an overall economic recovery program would be best left to private hands. Toward that end they had "invested" heavily in a desirable outcome. By the end of 1932, the three du Pont brothers had given a total of $400,000 to the AAPA since 1928, and John Raskob, in addition to his offerings to the Democratic party, had donated about $70,000 more. Their organizational vehicle for repeal claimed to be at its peak in membership, and its board of directors had swelled to 435. Although the AAPA spent less money in 1932 than it had in 1928, in part because of the Depression's effect upon financial contributions, the cause had been swept toward fulfillment by the Democratic landslide. With the task of electing a pro-repeal Congress now accomplished, efforts shifted to pressuring national and state legislators to quick action on a repeal amendment. The AAPA's new president, Jouett Shouse, as a Washington insider and former DNC executive was well positioned to be of maximum benefit to that aim. Adding to the repeal lobby's clout was the AFL's decision, relayed by Matthew Woll to Pierre in November, to link a Labor's National Committee for Modification of the Volstead Act as a partner to the United Repeal Council.[7]

The speed of congressional consideration of a repeal amendment nonetheless surprised even the du Ponts and their AAPA associates. On December 5, immediately following the convening of the lame-duck session, Democrats introduced a proposal for a new repeal amendment. The resolution, sponsored by Vice President-elect Garner, fell short of the necessary two-thirds by only six votes even in the "old" House of Representatives, boding well for the fate of a similar measure in March. Among the 144 voting against the measure were 81 lame ducks. According to advocate James Beck, even the December effort might have succeeded if it had been proposed in a less openly partisan manner and not been pushed on the first day of the session.[8]

Speed was of the essence to the AAPA, for if Congress could act on a resolution and send it to the states by February (before many of their legislatures would adjourn), the repeal movement might shorten the timetable by as much as two years. On January 9, 1933, without AAPA backing, the Senate Judiciary Committee reported out a resolution authored by lame-duck Republican John J. Blaine of Wisconsin which promised continued federal enforcement cooperation to states opting to remain dry and required ratification of repeal by state legislatures rather than elected state conventions. AAPA lobbyists, headed by Shouse, held firm for outright, total repeal and the ratification by convention, despite Blaine's assertion that state legislatures would act more quickly. In speeches before the Kentucky WONPR and a national radio audience, Shouse sought to appease dry congressmen by insisting that the AAPA's main aim was the repeal of the use of federal power to prohibit an economic activity or social institution, not to prevent states or communities from exercising local control if they so chose. Necessitating a conciliatory approach was the fact that two-thirds of the Republican-controlled Judiciary Committee had supported the Blaine resolution, and further floor action was being stalled because of a filibuster by Huey Long. With Senator Joseph Robinson, despite his dry leanings, prodding his fellow Democrats to implement the party's promise of repeal, on February 16 the Senate amended the Blaine resolution on a 45 to 15 vote to provide for convention ratifications. On a much narrower tally of 33 to 32, the provision continuing federal enforcement machinery to prevent the "reemergence of the saloon" in dry states was deleted. With these changes, the full Senate passed the repeal measure 63 to 23, as did the House four days later on a 289 to 121 vote. Both parties provided majorities in favor of the resolution, although Democrats gave it far larger margins.[9]

In anticipation of congressional passage of a repeal resolution, the AAPA and the VCL already had discussed in Chicago the previous June a "model" proposal for states to use in drawing up their ratification conventions. In the aftermath of the fall elections, Joseph Choate explored the legal complexities with A. Mitchell Palmer. Palmer asserted that state ratification procedures had to be established by the Congress, although former Solicitor General James Beck claimed that the states could set up their own methods on their own initiative. Although Choate agreed with Palmer, his VCL colleagues were divided on the issue. In order to save the states time, the VCL executive committee in late January voted to prepare a model bill for their consideration, assuming that if Congress later ruled out the proposed format changes would then be made. While Shouse lined up state lobbies to push the model bill, Choate and Columbia University law professor Noel Dowling drafted its specific language. Completed one day before congressional passage of a repeal resolution, the draft called for a procedure in which at-large rather than district delegates would be selected from competing slates of pro- and anti-repeal candidates. Delegates would be bound by their stances on one or the other slates rather than act at the convention as independent decisionmakers. Candidates for the slates would be chosen on the basis of the number of petition signatures compiled, giving the AAPA a great organizational advantage. With the AAPA generating petition signatures for its hand-picked candidates, the conventions would then, in an ironic contrast to the du Ponts' usual distaste for "direct democracy," exist merely to ratify the verdict of a popular referendum.[10]

Besides prompting hasty planning for state repeal procedures, the rapid march of the repeal resolution through the Congress revived Pierre's pursuit of organizational plans for the post-prohibition liquor industry. On January 3, Pierre asked brewer August Busch about the legitimacy of a solicitation he had received from an Ernest L. Klein to join "an association of the brewing industry." Busch confessed not to know any such person. But three weeks later, the St. Louis brewer personally wrote the secretary of the U.S. Brewers' Association, R. A. "Rudy" Huber, to urge the appointment of AAPA president Jouett Shouse as head of a reorganized liquor trade association similar in structure to Pierre's earlier suggestions. Busch gave Pierre credit for the idea on February 1, claiming that he was following his advice that a "capable man" be placed at the industry's head and that the industry be reshaped through outside leadership in order to provide "responsible" liquor control. He added that that very day Huber was offering the suggestion to the brewers' association meeting in Chicago. Apparently, however, other brewers did not welcome outside guidance as much as Busch. A month later, Busch reported back that Huber's message "did not meet with much encouragement or success because of the lack of funds in the Association to carry out such a plan as proposed."[11]

By the time Busch's discouraging report reached Pierre on March 1, the inauguration of President-elect Franklin D. Roosevelt was but three days away. Tension continued to mount in the capital and across the nation. The rate of bank failures had accelerated, causing dozens of states by March 1 to close or restrict operations of their financial institutions. The city of Newark, New Jersey, had defaulted on its public payroll. Over one week the Federal Reserve Board reported that a quarter-billion dollars in gold had poured out of the country's monetary system. In New York it was announced that several thousand relief workers would be dropped from the rolls because of insufficient funds. Farm prices, factory production, retail trade—all continued to plummet. Farmers in Iowa and other parts of the Midwest could be seen displaying shotguns to fend off the foreclosure sale. The nation waited—as did the du Ponts—frightened and anticipating.[12]

What unfolded, beginning on the fourth of March, 1933, would forever be remembered as the most remarkable, chaotic, energetic, and creative burst of domestic presidential leadership and legislative enactment in the history of the United States. Before a subdued gathering on that cold, cloudy day, the new president asserted, "The only thing we have to fear is fear itself," and promised "action, and action now." The lights burned late that night and for most of the next three months in the marble buildings along Pennsylvania Avenue, as the new administration plunged headlong into the frenetic period of activity dubbed simply "the Hundred Days." Following extension of an emergency national "bank holiday" and the convening of a special session of Congress on Thursday, March 9, presidential proposals and legislative enactments burst forth in a rapid-fire staccato of activity. By 9:00 P.M. on the ninth, Roosevelt had already signed an emergency banking measure into law. The next day the president asked for an "economy bill" that included the controversial proposal that veterans not be paid the bonuses they had agitated for the previous summer. Despite outcries from the American Legion and other veterans' groups, Congress complied within five days. The next day, March 16, Congress complied with another request, this time to modify immediately the Volstead Act so as to legalize the manufacture and sale of beer and light wine.[13]

On the same day that Congress approved the Volstead modification, Roosevelt asked for a sweeping new agriculture bill, the Agricultural Adjustment Act, designed to raise farmers' purchasing power through crop restriction, relieve pressure on farm mortgages, and increase the value of bank loans to agriculture. On the twenty-first, authority for the Civilian Conservation Corps, a public employment program for young men in reforestation and soil conservation projects, was requested of the Congress. Roosevelt asked the same day for legislative approval to provide additional grants of federal moneys to the states for direct unemployment relief via the Federal Emergency Relief Act. Before month's end, the administration had asked Congress for federal supervision of investment securities transactions and new financial disclosure requirements for companies trading securities in interstate commerce.[14]

In April, the president called for the creation of a public corporation, the Tennessee Valley Authority, to generate electric power, promote soil conservation, and support economic development in the Tennessee River basin, as well as new legislation intended to head off home mortgage foreclosures. On May 4 came bills for consolidation of railroad management under a national coordinator of transportation and for the regulation of railroad holding companies. And as the culmination of the Hundred Days, an omnibus measure entitled the National Industrial Recovery Act proposed creation of the National Recovery Administration as "a great cooperative movement throughout all industry" to centralize industrial planning, maintain employment and wage levels, and head off destructive price competition and overproduction. An added part of the measure was a large program of direct federal employment relief in construction projects, the Public Works Administration. By mid-June, all of the initiatives, albeit with modifications, had become law.[15]

The incredible pace of presidential initiatives left the du Ponts, along with the rest of the country, breathless. Not all actions met with their immediate approval. When Roosevelt decried the actions of "hoarders" in his fireside chat on the banking crisis, Pierre defended the practice as a natural human reaction and criticized the president's inclusion of the remark. Nonetheless, brother Irénée dutifully surrendered his gold pieces, accumulated for twenty years from Wilmington Trust as a director's fee. When the president took steps to depreciate the dollar, Lammot expressed reservations, claiming, "Nothing can be more important to business than absolute certainty as to the basis of money." Roosevelt's governmental economy bill, however, made the du Ponts smile with pleasure. And despite lingering worries about the new leader's assumption of unprecedented emergency authority in peacetime, John Raskob conceded to Senator James Couzens of Michigan in mid-March. "There are times when it is necessary to recognize a dictatorship." Two weeks later Raskob praised the administration's farm mortgage relief plan and the president's fealty to the 1932 party platform. By the end of May he was even willing to offer the estimation, "Never in my whole life have I been so mistaken about a man and his ability as I was about Franklin Roosevelt."[16]

Above all else, the specific policies that led du Ponts to see the Roosevelt of the First Hundred Days as a benign "dictator" were immediate modification of the Volstead Act and the creation of the National Recovery Administration. On April 7 modification went into effect, and after only one week the federal government collected $4 million in barrel taxes and license fees. The new revenues from legalized wine and beer, and their promise of possible tax reductions in other areas, eased the sting of Congress's refusal to adopt a federal sales tax in March and the passage of higher taxes on large incomes and inheritances. The best grounds for optimism, however, was the creation of the NRA. Drafted by presidential advisors Hugh Johnson and Rexford Tugwell, and modelled in part after the industrial self-government schemes of Gerard Swope and the U.S. Chamber of Commerce's Henry Harriman, the National Industrial Recovery Act was hastily thrown together as an alternative to a "thirty-hour" employment bill pushed by Senator Hugo Black of Alabama. Black's measure, endorsed by the American Federation of Labor, would have forbidden interstate commerce in commodities produced by workers employed for more than five days a week or six hours a day and had been designed to spread out available work among a larger proportion of the workforce.[17]

Within the administration, sharp divisions existed between advocates of large public works spending to absorb the unemployed and advocates of government-industry partnerships to create and enforce production, wage and hour codes. The eventual legislation contained both. The National Recovery Administration was assigned to form industry-wide councils, staffed by both public and private representatives, for the purpose of drawing up "codes of fair competition" for presidential approval. Firms participating in the codes, being exempted from the anti-trust laws, would establish a system of voluntary self-regulation combined with a governmental licensing power to prod businessmen into line. In section 7a of the bill, labor received a vague guarantee of the right of organization and collective bargaining with their employers, along with equally general provisions for fair wage and hours standards in the industry codes. Public works advocates, in turn, received an appropriation of over $3 billion for that purpose.[18]

Although suspicious of even the modest role given to government appointees in the new NRA apparatus, Pierre du Pont was reassured by the prominence of Hugh Johnson, a former Smith advisor, in the bill's crafting, and by the "careful attention" of the American Manufacturers Association and brother Lammot in watering down the collective bargaining and wage and hour guarantees. Pierre fretted over "the large powers lodged with the President of the United States," which made him "shudder," but he hoped that "business recovery may prevent the need for these." As for the public works segment of the NIRA, he grudgingly admitted that "under existing conditions we are obliged to swallow something of the kind," although he wished that the job projects were more substantial than "useless, ornamental post offices and the like." Given his suspicions on how the new recovery machinery might be abused, Pierre accepted the invitation of Secretary of Commerce Daniel Roper to that department's Business Advisory and Planning Council three days before Roosevelt signed NIRA into law on June 16. Shortly after the NRA's creation, he also signed on as a member of its new Industrial Advisory Board at the urging of Gerard Swope.[19]

Creation of the NRA marked the beginning of a protracted struggle between conflicting economic interests, both inside and outside the administration, with different conceptions of the new agency and its role in recovery. Was the NRA's administrative machinery intended to be an institutional embodiment of economic pluralism, or of unimpeded corporate management? Was it intended to facilitate central government planning of the economy or industrial self-government? Reflecting the bureaucratic power struggles for control of recovery policy within the administration, NRA chief administrator Johnson quickly circumvented attempts at oversight by a cabinet-level Special Industrial Recovery Board chaired by Roper. A second foray into cabinet supervision through an Executive Council created in July, with Frank Walker as executive secretary, similarly collapsed. Johnson's steady accumulation of administrative control over NRA, as it happened, suited du Pont objectives nicely. As a "veteran" of the War Industries Board, Johnson took the mission of building industrial "cooperation" with the government to the extreme of discounting the validity of other, conflicting claims made by consumers, labor unions, and small businesses. Johnson permitted the formality of a consumer advisory board to NRA while he consistently ignored its counsel. The Labor Advisory Board, chaired by Secretary of Labor Frances Perkins, was similarly treated.[20]

In contrast to his treatment of other interests, in the name of industrial cooperation Johnson willingly served the objectives of the larger corporate representatives within NRA. Included among their concerns were their fears of outside unionization and of the sharing of market decisionmaking and pricing with consumers, labor, and smaller firms. Johnson's willingness to cater to the needs of industrial titans was illustrated by his soliciting them for names of executives to staff the NRA's national and state codemaking and administering committees. Pierre, for his part, was asked to provide candidates from Pennsylvania, Maryland, and Delaware. After corresponding with brother Lammot, W. W. Atterbury, Raskob, Stayton, Andrew Mellon, and several other prominent Mid-Atlantic businessmen, he provided Johnson with suggestions from Delaware but opted not to intrude upon the prerogatives of industrialists from the other states. With the aid of corporate code-drafters, by September Johnson had drawn up guidelines for ten major industries, and hundreds of others had agreed to adopt a "blanket code." The blanket code had been approved by Roosevelt in late July in order to relieve the pressure upon the fledgling NRA's drafters from a flood of businesses for separate authorized codes. The chemical industry's code, drafted with major Du Pont Company influence, set minimum wages at 35–40 cents per hour when the industry was still paying 56.5 cents. Maximum hours, which had already dropped to 41 hours a week and would reach 38.5 hours by early the next year, were set at a 40-hour week.[21]

The biggest potential threat posed by the NRA to the du Ponts, given their dominance over the initial code-making process for their industry, was the possibility that collective bargaining rights might be granted to noncompany unions. Independent unions could erode the family's longstanding personal control over its labor policies and its workers. Despite Johnson's reassurances, the beginning of NRA code-drafting created great unease among labor managers not only at Du Pont but also at General Motors and other parts of the empire. Company spokesmen succeeded in installing in the chemical industry code a labor provision preserving for management the right "to engage, promote, or release employees." But GM's Alfred Sloan, worried about the implication of section 7a for his industry, warned that he would not "subscribe to the Industrial Recovery Act" as long as "the possibility deepens for the American Federation of Labor to organize." Working through its trade lobby, the National Automotive Chamber of Commerce, GM signed on with the NRA only after obtaining a clause which gave employers the power to "exercise their right to select, retain, or advance employees on the basis of individual merit, without regard to their membership or non-membership in any organization."[22]

GM also sought and received assurances from Hugh Johnson that the vague promise of collective bargaining did not require proof of *good faith* negotiation in the form of a compromise agreement. As Johnson soothingly stated, "The fact that you bargain with the men doesn't mean you have to agree." Buttressed by the NRA chief's reassurances, the National Association of Manufacturers drew up model informational notices on section 7a for posting on employee bulletin boards, and its legal department issued its own highly restrictive interpretation of the NRA's labor guarantees. GM, for its part, held divisional meetings in July to begin establishing Du Pont–style employee associations on a corporation-wide basis, both to forestall outside union organization drives and to establish the groundwork for opposing the principle of majority, or single-union, representation in plant negotiations in favor of nonunion and multiple bargaining agents. Withing such employee associations, only individual rather than collective grievances were traditionally held to be the legitimate subjects of consideration.[23]

The public promises to labor in the NIRA, nonetheless, led to expectations among national union leaders that the federal government had strengthened their hand in their recruitment drives. The predictable consequence of the clash between these raised expectations and persistent resistance to them by employers was a dramatic increase in strikes and work stoppages in the late summer and fall of 1933. Although the family's firm grip on company employees through its carrot-and-stick paternalism warded off immediate unrest at Du Pont plants, turmoil prevailed elsewhere, especially in the coal, apparel, tool and die, hosiery, and movie industries. In the first half of 1933, no single month had seen more than 603,000 man-days of labor lost to strikes, but in July and August the numbers climbed to 1,375,000 and 2,378,000, respectively. By the end of the year, more man-days had been lost than in any year since 1921. Faced with the onslaught, concerned with the possible effects of prolonged strikes on overall recovery, and pressured by union and public representatives on the NRA's labor and industrial advisory panels, the administration created a new arm of the NRA, the National Labor Board, in August. Chaired by New York's Senator Robert Wagner and consisting of three representatives each from labor and business, the National Labor Board was assigned the task of mediating strike disputes, but the executive order creating it took months just to be formally prepared and implemented.[24]

In the hosiery workers strike, a solution which would become known as the "Reading formula" emerged as the Roosevelt administration's preferred method of getting workers back on the job. In it, a back-to-work order was joined with company assurances not to fire returning strikers, to permit secret balloting to choose workers' official bargaining agent, and to leave further resolution of differences to the new National

Labor Board. Unfortunately, unrest in the steel industry's "captive" bituminous coal mines was not so easily resolved. Despite the "Appalachian agreement," in which the United Mine Workers won the right to a dues checkoff in workers' contracts, but not guarantees of the eight-hour day or the union shop, showdowns persisted in the Frick mines in Pennsylvania. Presidential intervention produced a back-to-work order and a code board, consisting of Gerard Swope, George L. Berry, and Filene's department store executive Louis Kirstein, which never met. Under industry pressure, the NRA's number-two man, Donald Richberg, also assured steel executives that the NRA did not consider a union dues checkoff a working condition formally protected by federal law, and Johnson concurred. Despite Roosevelt's overruling of Johnson and Richberg on October 4, the companies continued to refuse recognition to the UMW. Following a procedural resolution in late October, miners returned to work. Supervised representation elections were held at U.S. Steel and other "captive" mine sites, in which the UMW won in twenty, lost in nine, and tied in one. But even after the balloting, none of the steel companies issued contract offers to the newly chosen UMW bargaining representatives within the required ten-day period.[25]

The du Ponts were convinced that continued union agitation would kill the promising degree of recovery achieved in the administration's first six months, as well as threaten their own long-term interests. According to the Commerce Department, national income had risen from $3.5 billion in March to $4.2 billion by October. The Federal Reserve Board's index of industrial production, with a 1923–25 standard of 100, climbed from 59 in March to 91 in August. By October four million more Americans had found jobs, and according to the economist Robert Nathan, unemployment had dipped from approximately 30 percent in March to less than 22.5 percent in October. John Raskob fretted, however, that if the NRA shifted from its early philosophy of voluntary cooperation and industrial self-policing to a more coercive approach, especially in its labor policy, it would "wreak [*sic*]" industry. Pierre echoed the concern, claiming, "I am a believer in the NRA and am hopeful of some good results from it," but adding, "I believe that those who are heavily burdened would help themselves if their attitude were made a little more tolerant and if they would assume that adherence to the rules would be observed without force." He continued to fret over "the powers that are being placed in the hands of the President and his advisors," but admitted, "the 'big job' is being done and it is not right nor fair to find fault." Nonetheless, citing Henry Ford's continuing refusal to cooperate with the NRA, he lamented that it was "a pity that his determination to remain outside the NRA is not looked upon in better spirit by those in Washington."[26]

Besides the summer's economic boomlet, the best news received by the du Ponts in the fall of 1933 was the accelerating pace of prohibition repeal. The success of the repeal effort, as it turned out, helped delay the public surfacing of the family's discontent with the overall direction of New Deal economic stabilization and labor policies. Eleven states already had established repeal conventions within a month after congressional approval of the resolution, and thirty-nine did so within four months. In all, forty-three states, with Georgia, Kansas, Louisiana, Mississippi, and North Dakota the lone abstainers, called conventions. AAPA members, not surprisingly, dominated wet delegate slates across the contry. On April 3, Michigan had become the first state to select convention delegates, and by the end of June, sixteen more had endorsed repeal in delegate elections. By mid-July, three dry bastions—Alabama, Arkansas, and Tennessee—had fallen. By the beginning of November, thirty-three states had ratified a repeal resolution, leaving only three others required to end the Eighteenth Amendment. Nearly three-quarters of the more than 21 million participants in the state balloting had backed repeal, and only two states, the Carolinas, had opted to retain prohibition. To no one's surprise, the du Ponts' home state of Delaware had been one of the earliest endorsers of repeal. Following the scrapping of the Klair Law in February and the passage of a state liquor act, the state's repeal convention, with Pierre serving as its chairman, had completed the formalities on June 24.[27]

With prohibition repeal nearly complete, Pierre continued to find NRA chief Hugh Johnson's steady support of corporate prerogatives reassuring in spite of his growing fears of labor unrest. The elder du Pont still insisted, despite his lingering qualms over the degree of presidential power in making and interpreting industrial codes, that if kept in "safe" hands the NRA still held out the promise of providing bureaucratic means to legitimize the "corporate state." He particularly was delighted at Johnson's October address to the American Federation of Labor, in which the NRA chief intimated that within his agency's cooperative rubric, unions would become unnecessary and strikes superfluous. Further reassuring was the replacement the same month of Alexander Sachs as head of the NRA's Research and Planning Division with former GM sales manager Stephen De Brul. De Brul, in the later assessment of a critic, "first sabotaged and then suspended" the centralization of collecting and reporting of state data and recommendations necessary for truly effective government supervision of industry's compliance with the new codes. Given his general satisfaction with the direction the NRA was taking and his wish to avoid antagonizing the White House, Pierre was embarrassed to learn in mid-November that his earlier, admittedly mild criticisms of administration policies and powers nonetheless had been published. Immediately he fired off an apologetic letter to the president and, referring to his service on Secretary Roper's business advisory panel, concluded in it, "You may know that my fears in regard to your surroundings are answered in the fact that I am now serving under one of your advisors." Roosevelt's reply was equally warm. "That is an awfully nice letter of yours," he returned, "and I appreciate it."[28]

The next week, on November 24, Pierre received further indications that the White House intended to continue its rapprochement with the business community. Roosevelt transmitted to him a formal appointment to the recently created National Labor Board as a replacement for the late E. N. Hurley. The president specifically may have sought in appointing such an anti-union representative as Pierre to encourage still-recalcitrant companies to accept NLB oversight. By October several manufacturing companies already had refused to follow the "Reading formula's" call for NLB mediation, and in November the National Association of Manufacturers openly assailed it. Even before accepting the appointment, however, Pierre already was receiving confidential NRA policy memoranda from Johnson. When he released prematurely the contents of one such internal document, detailing future rights and responsibilities of corporations under NRA codes, to other industrialists, he drew a private rebuke from Johnson. Only after pressing Johnson to accept his view that government appointees to NRA should not view themselves as ultimately accountable to labor or consumers, but only to the overall code authority itself as a body which refused to acknowledge adversarial economic interests, Pierre accepted the NLB appointment on November 29.[29]

Pierre did not know it, but his own rapprochement with the Roosevelt administration, and the more limited ones of his brothers and John Raskob, were about to crumble. In no small measure the erosion was the product of disappointing new economic circumstances. By November, the summer boomlet was showing clear signs of halting. The index of industrial production, 91 in August, now slipped back to 76. Additional declines seemed likely, given the predicted resurgence of unemployment and production slowdown in seasonal industries over the winter. On November 8, Roosevelt responded with an executive order divesting some funds from the Public Works Administration to a Civil Works Administration charged to create smaller-scale, immediate work opportunities. The du Ponts and other business conservatives lamented both the economic slowdown and the response to it, but pressure from the political left to do still more was building. Milo Reno's Farm Holiday Association even led strikes and disruptions of trains carrying agricultural produce in an attempt to raise farm prices and incomes.[30]

The NRA now received growing criticism not only from labor, consumer, and small business groups, but also from larger corporate interests for its failure to spark additional recovery. Gerard Swope publicly advocated the replacement of NRA with a superorganization of industry representatives under U.S. Chamber of Commerce auspices, and the December NAM convention gave the agency but a tepid endorsement. John Raskob privately fretted that the new CWA's government job handouts might erode individual initiative in the country. Pierre, accepting election in December as chairman of the NRA's Industrial Advisory Board, seconded that "the Federal Government should not go into projects with a view to competing with existing private investment." At General Motors, Alfred Sloan continued to worry about the potentially deleterious effects of NLB rulings on his company's labor policies, despite Pierre's reassuring presence on that panel.[31]

With their economic anxieties about the future again rising, the du Ponts looked forward with special appreciation to the long-anticipated "Christmas bonus" of prohibition repeal—the cause which had been a focal point of six years of personal political struggle. Confident of victory, the VCL had already disbanded in early November, with its treasurer, Harrison Tweed, balancing final accounts by writing out a personal check for $6.66. In New York, James Wadsworth already had testified before the state's Liquor Control Board in behalf of establishing a Quebec or Bratt system of alcohol management. In Delaware, Pierre had been appointed to chair a five-member panel to draft a new state liquor control law. The committee's product was a proposal calling for the creation of a state commission either to operate a liquor monopoly or (as subsequently turned out) to license private retailers, with beer available for consumption only at the place of purchase. Fears of high initial capital investment costs in the midst of the Depression killed hopes for any far-reaching adoption by the state of a Quebec or Bratt plan. Instead the legislature within two months created the office of State Liquor Commissioner to oversee the licensing process for a relegalized liquor industry. Pierre was named to the post.[32]

While post-repeal state arrangements were already being prepared, at the national level the Roosevelt administration, caught by surprise at the speed of the process, created in October an interdepartmental wine and spirits committee to make federal recommendations. On November 9, suggestions were presented to the president and the cabinet. Roosevelt himself, bolstered by advisors Tugwell, Roper, Harold Ickes, and Henry Wallace, apparently preferred a federal monopoly of wholesale liquor traffic, combined with retail sales regulation and federal import controls as part of any reciprocal trade agreement. With Roosevelt's endorsement, the liquor industry was brought under the NRA code umbrella on December 4 in the form of the Federal Alcohol Control Administration. Under codes drafted with the supervision of the new agency's chief officer, former VCL head Joseph Choate, private firms were issued licenses and regulations covering labeling, advertising, production levels, pricing, and arrangements between wholesalers and retailers.[33]

Despite their earlier expressions of preference for centralized control and management of the liquor industry, the du Ponts were uneasy when such authority was entrusted to hands other than their own. They also sensed that in his actions, and in public statements by James Farley, the president was trying to claim excessive personal credit for what they believed was their own achievement in killing prohibition. Nonetheless, they prepared to celebrate the completion of the repeal goal—the ratification of the repeal amendment by the decisive thirty-sixth state. By the first week in December, the only real suspense left was deciding which among three candidates—Pennsylvania, Ohio, or Utah—would put repeal over the top. Utah, by deliberately drawing out its convention proceedings, "won" the honor at 5:32 P.M. Eastern time on December 5. The AAPA's Victory Dinner was held that evening at the Waldorf-Astoria Hotel, where Pierre presented each director with an inscribed cocktail glass and William Stayton an engraved bowl. Those assembled agreed to carry out arrangements to wind up the organization by year's end. At a contrastingly somber WONPR celebration at Washington's Mayflower Hotel (owing to the recent widowhood of Pauline Sabin), the women's vanguard in the repeal fight disbanded two days later.[34]

Once the air of celebrations lifted, however, second thoughts immediately arose about the wisdom of dismantling a political apparatus that had proven to be a successful experiment in corporate policy recommendation and political action. With the New Deal not yet conclusively set on a safe long-term course, would it not be wiser to keep the organizational network intact for future needs? The Crusaders believed so, opting not to even go through a formal disbanding. From Washington, the AAPA's daily administrator, Jouett Shouse, agreed, warning his colleagues of the pending dangers of federal centralization at the Victory Dinner and again three days later in Philadelphia. Despite his weariness of the political struggle, Pierre concurred, having already admitted to Grayson Murphy that "We may have to resort further to this method of change at a time when our representatives fail to carry out the will of the people." The day after the Victory Dinner, the AAPA board of directors founded Repeal Associates, with Pierre the chairman of an executive committee including Cassatt, Crowell, Murphy, Shaw, Stayton, and Wadsworth, which was to act as a watchdog on state liquor regulation. More important, the executive committee members of the defunct AAPA agreed among themselves to continue holding informal meetings with the idea of "the formation of a group, based on our old membership in the association, which would, in the event of danger to the Federal Constitution, stand ready to defend the faith of the fathers."[35]

chapter 8

Deserting the Ship of State

As 1934 dawned, the du Ponts observed the maturing New Deal with a mixture of budding skepticism and stubborn hope. Pierre, the family "insider" within General Johnson's NRA bureaucracy, still refused to abandon his dream that the recovery program would institutionalize corporate economic stewardship. Johnson remained sympathetic toward the need to steer NRA away from broker-state pluralism and toward corporate-directed economic nationalism. The NRA head's steady opposition to adversarial labor-management structures, the closed shop, and majority plant representation also bolstered Pierre's hopes. But others within the family circle, less disposed to patience with the Roosevelt administration to begin with for either personal or partisan reasons, already had begun firing public broadsides at the New Deal.

The fundamental danger that the du Ponts increasingly perceived in the New Deal was its threat to the economic prerogatives that the family had built up over decades. The emerging dispute between the Roosevelt administration and the du Ponts was not, and never had been, a quarrel between centralizers and decentralizers. The du Ponts actually had been more fervent advocates of centralized economic decisionmaking than many of the New Dealers. What was in dispute was in whose hands such massive decisionmaking power would be lodged, and which economic clienteles it would serve. Should national economic and social policy be controlled by an elected administration and its appointed bureaucracy, or by a cartel of the du Ponts and like-minded business leaders? Should national decisionmakers consider themselves accountable to a range of adversarial "special" interests (in a manner contrary to the du Ponts' traditional paternalism), or should they accept dictation from a corporate sector claiming to possess a less parochial economic vision and greater managerial competence?

It was not just on the political right that rumblings could be heard against the New Deal. In November 1933, Dr. Francis Townsend devoted full attention to building his old-age pension movement, Old-Age Revolving Pensions, Ltd., which was formally incorporated on January 24. Senate insurgents, including Nye, Borah, and Edward Costigan of Colorado, blasted the NRA in early January for having fostered control of the electric light bulb industry by General Electric. What particularly alarmed business conservatives about these developments was that the President appeared increasingly more responsive to the pressures from the left than to those from the right. In reaction to growing agitation for greater relief assistance, the Roosevelt administration created the Civil Works Administration in November. Increased deficit spending and experimental measures, such as gold purchases to drive down the dollar, were criticized for being unorthodox and led to the dismissal of the protesting Dean Acheson as Undersecretary of the Treasury and the resignations of conservative economic advisors Thomas Hewes, James Warburg, and Dr. Oliver Sprague of Harvard. The administration's diplomatic recognition of the Soviet Union on November 6, after sixteen years of isolation, further alarmed the right. Rumors of the President's apparent intention, soon to be confirmed in his message to Congress, for even more stringent restrictions on stock exchange practices than those contained in his 1933 legislation sent more shudders through Wall Street.[1]

By early 1934, the lengthening laundry list of the du Ponts' criticisms of the New Deal included FDR's tinkering with the currency, spending increases and unbalanced budgets, rising labor militancy, public power projects "in competition" with private industry, government absorption through the U.S. Army of private air mail service, banking regulation, "demagogic" congressional investigations and provocations by New Deal backers, and a supposedly rising number (according to accusations by such professional "red-hunters" as Dr. William Wirt) of communists in government. One of the earliest public salvos by a member of the du Pont circle had been issued by Al Smith in an open letter to the New York Chamber of Commerce weeks before, on November 24. According to the disgruntled Smith, the New Deal's failing lay with "inexperienced young college professors . . . who are ready to turn 130 million Americans into guinea pigs for experimentation." Suggesting his eagerness to lambast the administration further, Smith had assumed editorship of the *New Outlook* magazine as a forum for further public broadsides.[2]

Others in the inner circle gradually joined in the chorus of criticism, their words having been sharpened by personal disappointments. By

late December, Jouett Shouse confirmed to his mentor John Raskob
that his hopes of becoming the head of the brewers' trade association
had disintegrated in the face of brewer disagreements over the industry's NRA code and resentment of August Busch's attempt to stage-
manage Shouse's ascendancy. As a substitute, Shouse now offered his
services to the du Pont family as its paid Washington lobbyist. "With
the tremendous extension of federal activities such as has occurred
during the last nine months, their [the du Ponts] need to keep in close
touch with Washington and with the departments here must be ob-
viously greater." The need for such help appealed to company president Lammot, for having admitted that "the year 1933 has witnessed
an adventurous attack by the administration upon the political, social,
and economic ills of the country," he then announced that Du Pont
would have to abandon its employee stock investment plan because
of the "onerous" requirements of the 1933 Securities Act. As for Raskob, his private solicitations of the President to take on industrial
economist Fred I. Kent as a confidential policy advisor had been
rebuffed. In addition, his advocacy of the "Deane plan" (a 1933 "revolving fund" scheme to boost consumer purchasing in which workers
employed at less than regional and national averages of work hours
would receive compensation paid out of taxes on wages of workers
working more hours than those same averages) had been similarly,
albeit politely, rejected at a December 27 White House meeting with
Roosevelt, Harry Hopkins, Frances Perkins, and Hugh Johnson. Even
Pierre complained by letter in mid-January to Delaware's Senator John
Townsend about the administration's nomination to a federal judge-
ship of William H. Holly, whom he claimed was a member of the
"communist" All-American Anti-Imperialist League and the American Civil Liberties Union.[3]

Pierre nonetheless held his public fire, given his position on both
the NRA's Industrial Advisory Board and the National Labor Board.
Doing so helped him maintain his influence with General Johnson,
and he attempted to capitalize on a rising crescendo of criticism of the
General by labor and consumer interests by lending a sympathetic ear
and consoling words to his chief. After showing moral support to
Johnson by attending a mid-December meeting hosted by the Commerce Department on the role of the consumer in the recovery program,
Pierre was solicited in early January to recruit fifteen new members
to various industry code authorities. Relying on the network he had
forged in the repeal fight, Pierre selected names from AAPA director
and activist lists provided by Stayton and Shouse. As a sign of appreciation for his support, Johnson also asked Pierre to become his

deputy administrator in charge of food industry codes. Pierre declined, however, citing his existing NRA labor duties as more vital. When the NRA's code authority pricing hearings, held on January 9, unleashed another Pandora's box of complaints at Johnson's policies (including some from the NRA's own Consumer Advisory Board), Pierre again consoled his boss. He also seized the opportunity to urge the elimination of separate representation for consumer and labor interests within the NRA apparatus. His assertion that the NRA's authorizing legislation required only "that we shall have a labor and consumers' advisor who has no real power except to advise" was readily endorsed by the wounded Johnson.[4]

Having worked his way fully into Johnson's trust, Pierre was confident enough to outline an overall plan for national economic recovery to the General on January 23. He asserted that the federal government should begin by immediately issuing statements (1) in support of the profit system, (2) in opposition to any further depreciation of the dollar, and (3) advocating a mobilization order enlisting three to four million youth in vocational schools. Job training would be focused, in anticipation of the need for skilled labor, on jobs in such industries as leather and shoes. At the same time, Pierre called for less governmental competition with private industry and suggested cutting back civil works spending, ending the Agricultural Adjustment Administration's (AAA) "plow-under" schemes in favor of selling food surpluses to the vocational education camps, and increasing the government's military orders (which would directly benefit the Du Pont Company as a major munitions supplier).[5]

Although he did not directly say so, Pierre's blueprint amounted to a peacetime proposal for World War I–style national military mobilization. As for the NRA's future in this plan, Pierre urged continued efforts to eliminate sweatshop labor conditions, the insistence on improved prospects for business profits before issuance of rulings that would increase operating costs (including labor costs), and short-term reductions in work hours and increases in wages only in industries with "inelastic" demand. He continued to oppose Senator Black's thirty-hour bill, proposed a reduction in building costs of 10 percent, and advocated that the NRA lift prohibitions on corporate price fixing in those instances in which price competition resulted in a waste of resources. Rather than supporting continued PWA construction, which in his view competed with private contractors, he lobbied that PWA funds be used for early mobilization of armed forces to accompany his scheme for increased military requisitions. Opposing the lending of home mortgages by the Home Owners' Loan Corporation (HOLC), he advocated the replacement of government financing with loans tendered by private building associations.[6]

Pierre found, however, that his opportunities to influence the Roosevelt administration's policies through General Johnson were being squeezed out by his time-consuming but equally vital defense of corporate prerogatives on the National Labor Board. Showdowns between unions and employers, and between employers and the NLB, continued to multiply as workers pressed for practical implementation of the vague collective bargaining guarantees of section 7a. Despite the Reading formula, a number of companies, including Weirton Steel and Budd Manufacturing, refused to recognize the NLB's jurisdiction in their labor disputes or to permit government representatives to supervise representation elections. Pierre had already received complaints from GM's Alfred Sloan about the NLB's lack of a "definite line of procedure" and the NRA's "badly worded" labor provisions. Although Sloan admitted that multiple, or minority, representation in plants rather than a single bargaining agent would produce an unmanageable proliferation of wage scales and work rules—a rare admission among industrialists—he nonetheless refused to accept majority representation in the hands of outside industrial unions. In his estimation, the "wrong people" were leading the labor movement and could not be trusted to show restraint in their demands.[7]

In a concession to business concerns, on January 19 the NLB ruled that the major steel companies could execute their collective bargaining agreements with the individual officers elected by the workers rather than the union itself, despite the threat to job security such procedures could trigger for union officers in the plants. Pierre, however, demanded that his colleagues go farther and directly endorse the right of minority worker representation in factories. If they did not, he threatened, employers would have no choice but to follow the policy that "any employee going on strike shall be considered to have resigned" and thereby forfeited his job rights and security. While such disputes festered within the NLB, Pierre continued publicly to sing the NRA's praises before civic and business audiences. On January 25 he heralded it before the American Arbitration Association as a worthy effort to "restore orderly business" and to bring about a structure for industrial cooperation that would eliminate strikes and labor conflict.[8]

The administration's collective bargaining stance only became more muddled in early February. Hoping to clear up the confusion over the meaning of section 7a, on February 1 the President issued Executive Order 6580, which appeared to give Roosevelt's official sanction both to the Reading formula and to the principle of majority plant representation. The next day, however, the NRA's Industrial Advisory Board issued its own interpretation—one which backed minority representation—and on February 3 Johnson and his second-in-command, Donald Richberg, echoed the same line in their "interpretation" of Order 6580. While Pierre and his NLB colleagues wrestled with the conflicting versions of section 7a, and with a mounting load of labor cases, his allies began mobilizing in behalf of traditional business prerogatives. With Du Pont executives participating, the Special Conference Committee, which had not held a general meeting with member company chief executives since 1930, convened on February 8–9. Labor problems were the dominant topic of discussion. The panel took heart from the fact that representatives from all of its member companies had secured appointments to the Industrial Relations Committee of the Commerce Department's Business Advisory and Planning Council. On February 20, on Pierre's prompting, Gerard Swope also extended John Raskob an invitation to join the council, an offer he accepted three weeks later. Attempting to maintain a positive outlook, Alfred Sloan, while fretting over the New Deal's uncertain direction, conceded, "We have certainly been shaken out of the lethargy by which our ideas have heretofore been bound and dominated."[9]

Besides maintaining General Johnson on a course supporting minority labor representation and the open shop, Pierre was also prevailing upon the NRA head, with less success, to resist a new version of a constitutional amendment on child labor. Citing the country's recent experience with prohibition, Pierre claimed, "No Federal law or constitutional amendment will abolish child labor unless the parents in the community are convinced that child labor should not exist." On the whole, however, he remained content with Johnson's views. In a February 12 address, he lauded the NRA for promoting "opportunity for industry, for labor, and for the consumer." The President's decision in February to concede to the wishes of conservative budget director Lewis Douglas and to wind up the Civil Works Administration by May 1 also pleased him.[10]

Soon, however, a series of developments ensued that marked the end of Pierre's already faded honeymoon with the Roosevelt administration. Following a "Field Day" of criticism levelled at the NRA on February 27, on March 1 a majority of the NLB rejected Pierre's arguments in behalf of minority labor representation and instead endorsed majority plant representation in a pivotal group of cases. The hearings, involving the National Lock Company, Kibler Trucking Company, and, most prominently, the Denver Tramway Company, pitted union representatives against firms that had refused to bargain with them following plant elections but had negotiated instead with their own "employee committees." With Pierre personally sensitive about protecting the legality of such company-sponsored bargaining groups, given their similarity to Du Pont's own "Works Council," the majority ruling in behalf of the unions was a staggering blow. Compounding the damage was the fact that on the same day as the announcement of the Denver Tramway decision, NLB chairman Robert Wagner introduced a national labor disputes act in the U.S. Senate. Under the New York senator's proposal, a National Labor Relations Board with subpoena powers and the right to issue rulings enforceable in the federal courts on labor practices complaints would be created. Less than a week later, in response to the litany of protests that had been levelled at corporate domination of NRA code-making and enforcement practices, President Roosevelt by executive order created a National Recovery Review Board, headed by NRA critic and famed defense lawyer Clarence Darrow. The panel was charged to hold a series of twelve public hearings, beginning on March 15, and to issue recommendations for potentially sweeping charges in the agency's structure and procedures.[11]

The immediate implications of the NLB's decision on majority representation were dramatic throughout the du Pont's economic empire. Nowhere were they more so than at General Motors. GM already faced the threat of a strike at the hands of American Federation of Labor locals. Fearing the impact walkouts would have on recovery, President Roosevelt requested NLB intervention. Promises of a hearing by the panel warded off an immediate strike, but demands made by the union on March 14 for implementation of the Reading formula and majority bargaining representation were rejected by GM's William Knudsen the next day. With both sides staring at another confrontation, the White House sponsored mediation efforts on March 21–25 in which the President and Hugh Johnson each met separately with the adversaries. The administration's solution, drafted by Johnson, reflected the higher priority placed on keeping plants open than on upholding collective bargaining rights. It offered proportional representation on a "works council," which retained slots for company unions, and created an Auto Labor Board with the power to decide which bargaining agents would be sanctioned as the workers' chief representatives. Because Johnson's solution apparently yielded to the industry's interpretations of section 7a bargaining rights, including the approval of proportional representation and company unions, du Pont in-law and GM executive Donaldson Brown declared that it made him "tremendously happy." Alfred Sloan similarly concluded, "All's well that ends well."[12]

All, however, was not well, at least not if the du Ponts had assumed that the auto settlement represented a permanent change of heart by the administration on the majority representation issue. The NLB majority, for one, despite the auto accord, remained ready over Pierre's objections to stick with the earlier precedent set in the Denver Tramway case. Faced with such opposition, Pierre, after securing his replacement on the Industrial Advisory Board of NRA with Raskob, now focused his attention on obtaining Roosevelt's personal endorsement of the minority representation principle across the board. While he put his remaining hopes on a personal meeting with the President, other family members, who had soured on Roosevelt well before the automobile settlement and had not been reconciled by it, urged a complete severing of ties to the adminstration and a declaration of political war. With Pierre still counselling "patience" and "practical suggestions for betterment," in-law Ruly Carpenter on March 16 expressed his "great mystery" at FDR's policies to John Raskob. Repeating the family's objections of government competing for labor with industry in the Civilian Conservation Corps and the CWA, Carpenter charged Roosevelt with deliberate, demagogic vote buying. As examples, he cited the cases of a houseboat cook in Fort Myers, Florida, who had quit his private employment for a government job as a painter at one dollar an hour and of South Carolina planter friends who had been unable to get harvest hands because of competition from the CCC. Mystified at the President's use of class rhetoric, he wondered aloud, "Why should a man of Roosevelt's education and birth—campaign on a campaign of labor against capital?" The aim of Carpenter's jeremiad was to goad Raskob into leading a political crusade designed to flush out the administration's "real" purposes and to steer it back on course. "A man like yourself," he wrote, "a supporter of his and *persona grata* in Washington could . . . set many minds at rest."[13]

In his March 20 reply, Raskob sympathized with Carpenter's views but revealed how little remaining influence he had within official Democratic circles. Citing the need of an independent political organization devoted to "encouraging people to work, encouraging people to get rich, showing the fallacy of communism in its efforts to tear down our capital structure, etc.," he urged Carpenter to assume the duty instead. Holding forth Pierre as one who "has set us a fine example," he prodded, "you haven't much to do, and I know of no one that could take the lead in trying to induce the Du Pont and General Motors groups, followed by other big industries, to definitely organize to protect society in the suffering which it is bound to endure if we allow communistic elements to lead the people to believe that all businessmen are crooks, not to be trusted, and that no one should be allowed to get rich." In Raskob's judgment Carpenter was "in a peculiarly good position to do this in that you are young enough to undertake the work, you have the time, you are wealthy enough not to have to depend upon a job or salary for a living, and are in a position to talk directly with a group that controls a larger share of industry through common stock holdings than any other group in the United States. When I say this I mean that I believe there is no group, including the Rockefellers, the Morgans, the Mellons, or anyone else that begins to control and be responsible for as much industrially as is the Du Pont Company."[14]

Although Carpenter was personally unwilling to lead the fight, his martial spirit had not waned a week later, as evidenced by his words to Delaware Senator Daniel Hastings. He blamed the situation in Washington on Roosevelt's actions in turning over emergency powers to "a gang of fanatical and communistic Jew professors," whom he dubbed "Frankfurter and his thirty-eight hot dogs." Carpenter also directed his pleas for action and overheated blasts at the New Deal to Pierre. "I am unable to see," he expressed to the family patriarch, "how they expect to increase employment and at the same time cut production." Citing the growth of government largesse, Carpenter warned that federal spending would even erode the fealty of businessmen to free enterprise, for "as Roosevelt is going to give money away, they might as well get their share." He concluded, "Isn't it time for the better class of the Democratic party to rise up and curb this communistic policy before it is too late?"[15]

The du Pont circle's growing sense of besiegement in the early months of 1934 also was being reinforced by congressional developments. On February 8, Senator Gerald Nye introduced a resolution calling for the creation of an investigating committee that would examine the role of munitions makers in America's entry into World War I as well as other foreign controversies. In mid-April, the Senate, prodded by Nye's speeches, press exposés (including a *Fortune* article), and the publication of a best-selling book entitled *The Merchants of Death*, adopted the resolution. The family emphatically did not want public scrutiny of its international cartel dealings, for they were at an especially sensitive stage in 1934. After years of failure in courting the German company I.G. Farben into mutual market-protection and patent-exchange deals, talks now were moving forward on possible exchanges of information on the production of synthetic rubber with the Third Reich's chief chemical manufacturer. The du Ponts took but cold comfort in the President's unwillingness to comment publicly on the wisdom or folly of Nye's headline-hunting foray. Making matters worse, the 1934 session of Congress had spawned the Fletcher-Rayburn, or Securities and Exchange, Act (creating the Securities and Exchange Commission to regulate stock trading practices); the Air Mail Act (stipulating rigid controls over the awarding of federal contracts that the du Ponts later claimed forced the family-backed General Aviation Corporation to dissolve); the Communications Act, which created the Federal Communications Commission as a broadcasting regulator; the National Housing Act, which established the Federal Housing Authority (perceived by the du Ponts as a competitor to the private housing industry); and the Railroad Retirement Act, which established pensions for interstate railway workers funded from payroll taxes (drawing the ire of railroad directors Pierre and Irénée du Pont, John Raskob, and Donaldson Brown, among others). The Special Conference Committee relayed its objections to the Securities Act directly to Hugh Johnson, as did Pierre, and Irénée complained that the SEC violated human nature, claiming "Men are by nature speculators, and Nature enforces the necessity of speculation on all of us." Also drawing intense fire was the Wagner-Lewis unemployment insurance bill, which Pierre and Irénée claimed sanctioned government payments for striking workers.[16]

In light of these signs of "leftward" drift by both the administration and the Congress, Pierre already had decided to resign his post on the NRA Industrial Advisory Board in favor of Raskob. Anticipating the additional resignation of the board's secretary, C. L. Hunziger, he urged Alfred Sloan to find a reliable substitute to carry on the tasks of analyzing NRA codes and preparing the IAB's daily statement. Pierre himself plunged fully into a last-ditch effort to seek Roosevelt's personal guarantee of minority labor representation and the open shop. As early as March 8 he contacted White House appointments secretary M. H. McIntyre seeking a private session with the President, only to be put on hold for two weeks while Roosevelt embarked on a Florida cruise. Pierre's request for a "little talk" was in fact not fulfilled until a month-and-a-half later, on the morning of April 26. Only two days before the meeting, Du Pont Company economist F. C. Evans reported to the Special Conference Committee in advance of the issuance of its 1933 annual report his firm's intention to bolster plant-by-plant Works Councils rather than accept either outside labor representation or company-wide representation elections. In his session with Roosevelt, then, it came as no surprise that Pierre pressed for a presidential commitment to industrial self-government in labor relations and a formal endorsement of minority representation in plants. The ever-slippery Roosevelt, however, was willing only to pledge himself to a "rule of reason"—one which in most instances appeared to prefer avoiding the unwieldy multiplicity of bargaining agents within factories that Pierre's minority representation view would require.[17]

Pierre, like others in the family network, now concluded that under present political circumstances it was pointless to rely on Roosevelt to defend the family's interests. Only vigorous outside pressure could push the President away from the grip of "anti-business" or "radical" advisors and back on a "sound" path. For Pierre, the "last straw" was his failure to persuade Roosevelt to provide public backing for his view of labor relations. The President's refusal to cooperate also confirmed for Pierre his tentative, earlier decision, following the initial Denver Tramway setback, to leave the National Labor Board. As another signal of his break with the Democratic administration, in mid-May he refused solicitations for any further contributions to defray party debts, citing his opposition to the administration's policies as his reason. At the same time, however, Pierre also had grown weary in the larger sense of his nearly decade-long battles for prohibition repeal and corporate economic stewardship. Having reached the age of sixty-four, he believed that if a new movement was to be formed to exert outside pressure on the administration, leadership would have to pass to younger men—most likely his brother Irénée or John Raskob. Accordingly, he turned down a request from the reconstituted Crusaders to deliver an anti–New Deal speech on CBS radio, as did political ally Al Smith. The Crusaders were forced to settle for a talk by National Industrial Conference Board economist Dr. Virgil Jordan instead.[18]

If Pierre was tiring of the political wars, Irénée sounded increasingly energetic and militant. Citing a speech of Dr. Jordan's of early January, on May 31 he wrote his elder brother an extended discourse on the need to resurrect the nucleus of the AAPA as the basis of a major anti–New Deal pressure group. "If the old AAPA personnel is going to work together for future benefit," he insisted, "this particular problem is well worthwhile and I would gladly join in it." Belittling Repeal Associates, Irénée admitted, "I am not particularly interested in advising different states as to how they should handle their liquor problem. It is entirely artificial and errors will not be serious, but when it comes to the scrapping of the Constitution and starting the U.S. under a state capitalistic system, that is quite different." The drift to "governmental capitalism," he maintained, would "spell lack of progress and lower the scale of living for the future." Irénée's favorite example of nonsensical government policy was the AAA's "absurdities of paying farmers to let land lie fallow and paying them again to plow under the crops, and at the same time financing reclamation projects for greater crops and utilizing an army of 30,000 men in the Department of Agriculture to show how to make greater crops." The motivating source of such follies, he believed, was clear. "Politicians must buy people's votes," he stated, "using funds from the Federal treasury. The greater their sphere of action, the greater the cost to the community." Irénée insisted, however, that he did "not think it is too late to start a campaign of education. I believe that President Roosevelt is sane, competent, and open to conviction. He has been misled by his advisors."[19]

By the beginning of the summer, the du Ponts' fears of a slide into communistic statism were approaching panic. The demogogic Huey Long, who had launched his "Share Our Wealth" redistribution crusade in February, was attracting converts at an alarming pace. In San Francisco, a general strike had paralyzed city services. A burgeoning number of "radical" mayors, governors, and congressmen were threatening higher taxes and greater regulatory controls on "big business." The 1934 revenue measure, rather than adopt the du Ponts' preferred method of a federal sales tax, modestly boosted estate taxes and promised to open up corporate tax and salary information to public inspection. To the orthodox du Ponts, it did not even have the virtue of contributing much to budget balancing, since it collected but a third of a billion dollars in additional revenues. In the meantime, the state of Delaware, which had claimed a budget surplus of over $1 million in fiscal 1933, was estimating its 1934 deficit at $100,000 and rising. With state and national welfare and relief needs stubbornly refusing to abate, the country's unemployment rate hovered at around 12 million, or well over 20 percent of the workforce. Membership in the American Federation of Labor had jumped from 2.2 million in 1933 to over 4 million, and John L. Lewis was leading a series of independent organizing drives.[20]

Given Pierre's long battles on the NLB, the insistence by William Green of the AFL that majority representation was valid if the bargaining agent chosen was an outside union, but not if the workers opted for no representation or for a company union, was doubly infuriating. More outrageous was President Roosevelt's belated endorsement of the Wagner Labor Relations bill. It was now even easier for individual du Ponts to give greater credence to self-proclaimed "Redhunter" Franklin Ralston Welsh's claims of a communist conspiracy, or "Red network," in the country that included economist Stuart Chase, the Roosevelt administration's Rexford Tugwell and Frances Perkins, socialist Norman Thomas, and officials of the AFL, ACLU, and the Industrial Workers of the World. Irénée now claimed that "the entire Administration program since the London Economic Conference was dropped has been out of step with sound procedure." He also characterized the Nye Committee, which had begun to issue sensational public charges at the munitions industry, as a product of the communist Third International, misguided idealists, and yellow journalists. The du Ponts and other corporate leaders were but mildly reassured by the President's acceptance of a watered-down resolution that extended the life of the NLB for another year and renamed it the National Labor Relations Board, instead of replacing it with Wagner's proposed stronger agency. Little else about the direction of national policies, however, seemed comforting.[21]

With the major du Ponts concluding that some vehicle for jolting the administration back on course was required, "talent scouts" Shouse and Stayton began to reopen the channels of organizational contacts and to recruit new loyalists. One such recruit was corporate attorney Raoul Desvernine, who was recommended by Shouse to John Raskob in mid-June on the basis of his lobbying efforts against securities legislation and his Catholic faith. Both Raskob and Pierre attended the June 15 meeting of the Industrial Advisory Board and took additional soundings. On the same day, signalling an impending battle, President Roosevelt apparently jettisoned the labor formula worked out for the automobile industry by Hugh Johnson by stating at a press conference that the issue of minority representation there would have to be "worked out in each individual case." Although he resisted entreaties from his brothers to make the occasion a public forum for an attack on the New Deal, Pierre transmitted his formal resignation from the NLB in late June, leaving his nominal membership in the Commerce Department's Business Advisory and Planning Council as his sole remaining link to the administration.[22]

While Pierre separated from the New Deal, his brothers and John Raskob pursued their recruitment plans with colleagues in Delaware and on Wall Street. On June 15, Irénée received an invitation from the Crusaders to attend a meeting a week later designed to construct "a strong and militant support of our Constitutional form of government and opposition to organized minorities seeking special advantages." He issued a call privately for a drive to "stop the move toward the left" by creating "a 'groundswell' of public opinion." Raskob, within days of formally assuming his duties on the NRA Industrial

Advisory Board on July 1, summoned Shouse to John W. Davis's offices in New York City on a "matter of some urgency." The "urgent matter" consisted of a briefing from Raskob that relayed the Du Pont Company board's unease at the New Deal and demanded concrete responses. Typical of company officials' attitudes were those of vice-president H. G. Haskell, who drew parallels between the New Deal and the "social legislation" planks of William Jennings Bryan's 1896 campaign and wondered "how to get the education across" to the public on the dangers posed by the "Alphabetical Police Force." On July 9 Raskob and Davis lunched with General Motors executives John Pratt, John Smith, Donaldson Brown, Alfred Sloan, and Du Pont insiders Walter Carpenter, Irénée, and Lammot, with Irénée relaying the results of the meeting to Pierre the next day.[23]

The main item of discussion among the executives was the potential value of forming a "stockholders association" that would disseminate information to investors on the dangers of the New Deal. An enthusiastic Davis urged that the proposed organization be broadened to include property owners in general, with the theme of a "return to the Constitution." (Davis had recently given a speech on that topic and had circulated copies to Shouse, Raskob, and Pierre.) He also urged an alliance of like-minded groups, reminiscent of the prohibition-era United Repeal Council, that would include the Crusaders, the American Legion, and others. After the summit, each conferee was to prepare lists of twenty-five potential contacts in order to raise start-up money and recruit an executive committee. Determined to get his influential elder brother on board, Irénée urged Pierre to meet the group "next Tuesday."[24] For their part, the Crusaders had already launched a weekly radio address series, which lasted until mid-August. In addition, on the same day that Davis aired his views to the executives of GM and Du Pont, similar conversations were held in the directors' rooms of the General Foods Company.

Follow-up sessions, which included political veterans Al Smith and James Wadsworth, Jr., continued through July and were held at such various locations as Davis's New York law offices, Smith's Empire State Club, GM's offices off Columbus Circle, and other private clubs and dining establishments in the city. A continuing obstacle to progress in the July planning discussions was the disagreement among participants over the shape and scope of the proposed anti–New Deal organization. While conferees agreed on the new body's role as a political counterweight to insurgent and communistic assaults upon private property and business prerogatives, they quarreled over how broad its own constituency should be and, as a reflection of such differences,

over the appropriate name for the organization. Should it be a stockholder association or an alliance of broader propertyholding interests?
Should it be independent of, or tied to, the Crusaders' similar revitalization push? As an indication of the confusion created by the parallel efforts, industrialist S. W. Colgate, although agreeing on the need
to fight statist totalitarianism, put off Irénée's solicitation by asking,
"What about the Crusaders?"[25]

As early as July 16, John Raskob read to Irénée over the telephone
his own organizational blueprint for a "Committee for the Integrity
of Property." In it he proposed a structure of divisions, each concerned
with a different type of property ownership, overseen by a central executive committee. Raskob's list of proposed officers included Pierre as
chairman of the board, famed aviator Charles Lindbergh as president,
and a board of executive vice-presidents including Shouse, Grayson
Murphy (heading the "securities holders" division); Lewis A. Taber,
representing farm owners; Virgil Jordan as chief of the statistical division; Joseph Choate for legislative matters; Howard Heinz or E. F.
Hutton from the industrial property section; William Graham for insurance policy holders; and "a Consumers' League man" (referring
to a civic organization sponsored by the du Ponts in Delaware) as the
voice of home owners. Slots for vice-presidents for publicity and for
savings banks were left open. Raskob proposed for himself the duties
of treasurer and finance committee chairman and urged the creation
of three additional at-large executive positions for Wadsworth, possibly
Stayton, and a "reliable" member of the American Legion. Wanting
a central role for the du Ponts but wishing, especially given the Nye
investigation, to avoid the public perception that du Ponts dominated
the new organization, he observed, "I think the above list has sufficient
sprinkling of du Pont men—more would be disadvantageous." Pragmatic political considerations also led him to argue privately against
a major position for Al Smith "for fear of stirring up political animosity,
particularly of a religious nature."[26]

Jouett Shouse weighed in with his own ideas four days later. While
wanting a prominent position for himself, he echoed his former boss's
newfound reservations about Al Smith. Referring to "Tuesday's meeting," he claimed that the presence of both himself and Smith would
present an image of the organization as merely a collection of revenge-
minded anti-Roosevelt Democrats. If Smith were considered for the
chairmanship, Shouse insisted, he could not also serve. If Pierre agreed
to be chairman, however, he would be willing to participate actively.
Clearly envisioning the presidency of the organization for himself, the
same position he had held in the AAPA, he called for a "mutually

satisfactory financial arrangement" that would guarantee a two- or three-year post, a three-week vacation before starting the new assignment, a budget of at least $250,000, personal control over the appointment of publicity and research heads, an executive assistant, an immediate cash retainer of $25,000, a yearly salary of $36,000, and a monthly expense account of $1500. After more phone conversations between Shouse and Lammot du Pont, they arranged to meet in late July with Alfred Sloan and Raskob to approve the terms.[27]

While Shouse pursued his private negotiations, Raskob continued to receive advice from General Motors colleagues on broader organizational arrangements. On July 23, the chairman of GM's finance committee, du Pont in-law Donaldson Brown, relayed the written recommendations of research aide Stephen M. DuBrul on Raskob's proposed entity for the "protection of property rights." The DuBrul memorandum, which had actually been drafted almost a month earlier, asserted that any effort publicly seen as "directly interested primarily in the protection of established property rights" would be automatically discounted. In his view, the nation faced an even deeper "condition in which public morality has broken down," and in which "every effort is being made to repudiate obligations," especially those of the federal government. Claiming that the present generation was allowing the erosion of constitutional liberties, limits on governmental powers, and property rights because they had never been called upon to defend them, DuBrul warned that if present trends continued "representative government will become mob government" and such rights as free speech and jury trial could even be lost. "What we really have," he claimed, "is a rapid deterioration in the basic concept by the citizens themselves of the nature of American government," a "deterioration into Communism" accelerated by popular impatience and "sloppy" New Deal thinking. To counter the slide into disaster, the DuBrul memo cautioned the new group's organizers not to focus narrowly on the defense of property alone, but create "a league for the preservation of constitutional liberties" that would be "'aggressive in its opposition to hostile legislation," devoted to constitutional liberties as the organizers defined them, and "educationally defensive of these rights." It called for an organization that would draw its support from the middle class but that would be sponsored by nationally known persons above public reproach, not merely drawn "from the leaders of industry or finance as such." It should be, according to DuBrul, "constructively critical" and committed to the idea that "by preserving the principles of the Constitution, property rights will be thoroughly and adequately protected."[28]

Despite, or perhaps because of, the multitude of suggestions, disagreements over structure and title for the new organization remained unresolved. The day after the meeting between Raskob, the du Ponts, Shouse, Sloan, and others—at which Raskob had formally presented his model, the "Union Asserting the Integrity of Persons and Property"—Sloan proposed an alternative, the "Association Asserting the Rights of Property," and suggested naming George Sloan, president of the Cotton Textile Institute, to the executive committee. Two days later Pierre du Pont countered with his own ideas, preferring the substitution of the word "Rights" for "Integrity" in Raskob's title and proposing a twelve-member executive committee, a fifteen-member board of directors, and daily officers selected by the executive committee. In his judgment, the new forum should limit its policy focus to opposing those popular doctrines which, in his view, were undermining private and personal initiative. His own list of candidates for the executive committee included Al Smith, Charles Lindbergh, Shouse, Davis, and Irénée. For various divisional vice-presidencies, he suggested Pauline Sabin (home owners division), Samuel Harden Church (for a depositors division), and perhaps Columbia University president Nicholas Murray Butler and economist E. R. A. Seligman for other slots. Pierre preferred Smith as general chairman, Lindbergh as his deputy, Shouse as president, Irénée as head of the finance committee, Raskob as treasurer, and John W. Davis as executive secretary.[29]

By month's end, the squabble over a name for the organization still had not been settled. Shouse liked the "National Property League" and E. F. Hutton chipped in with the "American Federation of Business." Raskob, Sloan, and Pierre continued to lobby for their preferences. At least Lammot, Raskob, and Pierre had agreed on Shouse's appointment as president. With the exception of Pierre redefining Shouse's demand for a $25,000 retainer into a salary advance of the same amount, they agreed to his terms. While the new league's prospective leaders continued to bicker over organizational details, Pierre and Irénée directed William Stayton to draft a series of solicitation letters to former executives of the AAPA. As phrased by Stayton, the appeals stressed the New Deal's responsibility for broadening the tax powers of the Sixteenth Amendment beyond recognition into "an instrument to redistribute wealth, to communize the nation, and to confiscate the property of one man and dole it out to others." He cautioned, however, that a direct assault on the tax amendment would both be "misunderstood" and lack popular emotional appeal. Instead he urged his former compatriots to base their appeals on the theme of returning to the Constitution. Stayton asserted, "The public ignorance concerning it is dense and inexcusable, but, nevertheless, there is a mighty—though vague—affection for it."[30]

As the focus of the projected organization broadened from that of a business lobby into a conservative political pressure group, some of the ringleaders began having second thoughts. Alfred Sloan, who in the past had tried to keep GM from partisan entanglements, was willing to support an "economic organization" but not a forum for highly public political activity. On August 3 he indicated to Raskob through intermediary Donaldson Brown his "cold feet" toward another scheduled meeting. Brown himself, although remaining committed to the project, refused to take Sloan's place at the session, insisting "Too many cooks spoil the broth." He took the opportunity, however, to pass on his advice that the new entity be kept separate from the Crusaders, and he strenuously rejected the title "American Federation of Business" on the grounds that it both limited the effort's appeal and implied equal standing for the AFL. In contrast to Sloan, Brown favored a broader-based organization that could speak for a "large body of voters," but he retained the belief that its main purpose was still a self-interested one—to seek the "reversal of the NRA theory of spreading work with compensating increases in hourly wage rates."[31]

While the Crusaders solicited titans in the food processing and agricultural products industries, the founders of the new league found their best hunting within the chemical industry. This was hardly surprising given the Du Pont Company's preeminence. The electric utility industry, frightened at the looming prospect of legislation forcing new regulations and the dismantling of holding companies upon them, was another eager ally. Because the process of organization-building had not gone forward at the desired pace, however, and because of the lingering hope that Roosevelt, as a man of their own economic class, would "see the light" and repudiate his "radical" advisors, the du Pont circle intended to cast its new venture as a voice for "constructive legislation" rather than direct confrontation with the White House. To avoid public charges of an anti-Roosevelt vendetta, Raskob, Shouse, and the du Ponts agreed that the President would be notified before any official unveiling, and that he would even be solicited for an endorsement of the group's aims. With Shouse, the organization's soon-to-be president, tabbed as the emissary to the White House, Raskob impressed upon him the need to indicate a nonconfrontational spirit to Roosevelt.[32]

The league faced an imposing requirement in mobilizing sympathetic conservative elements into an effective political force in time to affect the fall's congressional elections. Given the difficulties of that task, Raskob himself preferred some form of merger with the Crusaders, perhaps by making Fred Clark an executive committee member and designating his group as a subsection of the organization. Even if other sympathetic business and patriotic forces were not to be formally absorbed into the "Defenders of the Constitution" (Raskob's new choice for a title), both he and Irénée continued to court members of the National Industrial Conference Board, "Henry Curran's organization" (the anti-bonus National Economy League), and even the Elks. Their recruitment scheme, designed like a chain letter, centered on attracting prominent supporters who, in turn, would take the lead with their friends and professional colleagues to recruit still more allies. The first targets were chosen so as to provide a nucleus for local chapters in important metropolitan ares, such as Philadelphia, Pittsburgh, New York, Detroit, Chicago, Louisville, St. Louis, and Houston. The core of the new organization—elitist, urban, and centered on the East Coast—bore a striking resemblance to the corporate, "cosmopolitan" membership of the AAPA.[33]

Throughout the planning sessions of July and early August, Pierre du Pont kept himself regularly updated on developments but chose to adopt a more low-key role in this new effort. To his old partner in the repeal fight, William Stayton, he noted that while he had participated in discussions with his brothers, Raskob, Sloan, and others "to accomplish what has been in our minds," he had not attended the planning meetings, "as I did not wish to be involved in anything new." Despite Pierre's modest disavowals, however, he was not able to stay completely out of the action. At his direction, Stayton had been corresponding with 6500 former AAPA directors and the officers of a dozen different patriotic organizations. Pierre also made plans to raise the subject of the new organization at the next executive committee meeting of the AAPA's remnant, the Repeal Associates.[34]

While the du Ponts prepared for the unveiling of their new foray into national politics, Franklin Roosevelt returned from Hawaii to wrap up plans for a round of early fall campaigning. Roosevelt was concerned about the implications of a "back to fundamentals" rumbling among such disaffected Southern and conservative Democrats as Senators Gore of Tennessee, Byrd and Glass of Virginia, and Clark of Missouri. The early Maine state elections, scheduled for September, would present an anti–New Deal challenge led by "Jeffersonian" Democrats Bainbridge Colby, the former Secretary of State; and William R. Pattangall, anti-Klan leader at the 1924 Democratic convention and chief justice of the state's supreme court. Within the du Pont family itself, Republican members, most notably Ruly Carpenter, were now soliciting Pierre to contribute to the Republican National Committee for the first time in several years in order to stem the "tide of Socialism and confiscation of property now running rampant in Washington." On the "left," growing numbers of strikes, including a longshoremen's walkout in San Francisco, prompted Pierre to write Lloyd K. Garrison, the new chief of the NLRB, and urge that unions be required to put strike calls to supervised membership votes. He insisted, "Abuse of the strike privilege has become a national evil."[35]

The du Ponts clearly hoped that the new organization would provide a rallying point for disaffected industrialists, conservative Democrats, and anti-radical groups. It was appropriate, then, that a prominent anti-administration Democrat and corporate lawyer, former presidential nominee John W. Davis, finally gave the cause its formal name. In a letter to Raskob on August 8, he proposed the title "American Liberties League," and next to the typewritten suggestion he penned, as a slight modification, "the Liberty League." Davis's alternative was greeted with wholehearted enthusiasm by GM's Donaldson Brown, who read in the initials ALL a larger significance as to the organization's intended breadth of appeal. A week later, with the group's name finally settled, Shouse filed incorporation papers in Washington, D.C., creating the American Liberty League as a movement to "combat radicalism" and "uphold the Constitution."[36]

August 15 proved a busy day for the du Pont operatives for more reasons than just the Liberty League's incorporation. At GM headquarters, Alfred Sloan issued a statement on labor policies to all the company's employees which asserted, on the one hand, that "no real conflict of interests between employers and employees" existed but, on the other, that it still reserved the prerogatives of hiring and firing completely to management and rejected union demands for nationwide collective bargaining with GM in favor of plant-by-plant negotiations. Most noteworthy, however, was the scheduled White House meeting of Shouse with President Roosevelt to inform him of the Liberty League's existence and purposes. In the late afternoon, following a forty-minute wait in an outer office, Shouse paid his courtesy call in a meeting he described as cordial. He reassured the President of the "non-partisan" and "educational" aims of the League, as well as its wish to cooperate with his administration. After hearing him out, Shouse claimed, Roosevelt even declared, "I can subscribe to that 100% and so can you."[37]

The President did take special pains to defend the Tennessee Valley Authority, a sore point among businessmen as an example of state socialism and competition with private enterprise, as a "yardstick" to see "whether certain things could be done by the Government with benefit to the people and at the same time show a profit." But he held out the olive branch that he might even seek a formal advisory role for the Liberty League's leaders with his administration, as he had done previously with prominent businessmen through Commerce Department and NRA advisory panels. Roosevelt even directed his secretary to respond favorably to press inquiries about the League during the President's absence from Washington for a week of campaigning.[38] Perhaps indeed, as certainly Pierre, Raskob, and Shouse hoped if not expected, Roosevelt's show of courtesy indicated a lingering receptivity to their advice. It did appear to be a promising beginning for a renewed effort to redirect the recovery policy of the nation. Time would tell if the effort could actually count on the administration's continued acquiescence or, even better, its cooperation.

The du Pont inner circle, 1919: seated, left to right, are Henry F., Pierre S., and Lammot du Pont; in the second row, Irénée du Pont and John J. Raskob. (Courtesy of Hagley Museum and Library.)

Alfred E. Smith, ca. 1930. (Courtesy of Hagley Museum and Library.)

Democratic party chairman John Raskob with Governor Franklin D. Roosevelt, ca. 1930. (Courtesy of Franklin D. Roosevelt Library.)

Pierre du Pont presenting Block Aid relief check, 1932. (Courtesy of Hagley Museum and Library.)

Pierre du Pont campaigning in Wilmington for repeal, 1932. (Courtesy of Hagley Museum and Library.)

Jouett Shouse promoting the newly formed American Liberty League, August 28, 1934. (International News Photo, courtesy of University of Kentucky Libraries.)

Naugatuck (Connecticut) *News*, August 27, 1934.
(Copyright by Naugatuck *News*; photo furnished
courtesy of Franklin D. Roosevelt Library.)

New York *Post*, December 14, 1934. (Copyright by
New York *Post*; photo furnished courtesy of Franklin D. Roosevelt Library.)

THE SPIRIT OF '35   —By Jerry Doyle

New York *Post*, January 12, 1935. (Copyright by
New York *Post*; photo furnished courtesy of Franklin D. Roosevelt Library.)

Puzzle: What Is the Little Boy Waiting For?

New York *Times*, January 19, 1936. (Copyright ©
1936 by The New York Times Company. Reprinted by permission; photo furnished courtesy of
Franklin D. Roosevelt Library.)

Washington *Star*, March 16, 1936. (Reprinted with permission from the Washington *Star*; photo furnished courtesy of Franklin D. Roosevelt Library.)

Washington *Post*, April 24, 1936. (Copyright by Washington *Post*; photo furnished courtesy of Franklin D. Roosevelt Library.)

CLEANING UP AFTER THE POLITICAL HALLOWEEN PARTY —By Jerry Doyl

New York *Post*, November 6, 1936. (Copyright by New York *Post*; photo furnished courtesy of Franklin D. Roosevelt Library.)

The "old soldiers" of the du Pont family in 1950: left to right, Irénée, Pierre, and Lammot du Pont. (Courtesy of Hagley Museum and Library.)

chapter 9

Launching the Liberty League

On August 22, 1934, from the office number 1066 of the National Press Club building in Washington, Jouett Shouse publicly proclaimed the du Ponts' new venture in political conquest. According to his prepared statement, the purpose of the American Liberty League was to "defend and uphold the Constitution . . . to teach the necessity of respect for the rights of persons and property as fundamental to every successful form of government . . . to teach the duty of government, to encourage and protect individual and group initiative and enterprise, to foster the right to work, earn, save, and acquire property and to preserve the ownership and lawful use of property when acquired." Shouse insisted that the new organization was not "inimical" to the current administration, nor was it intended as a "stop-Roosevelt" movement. While claiming that the League "would not actually participate in elections," he admitted that it would "take an active interest in and definite position on questions of legislation affecting economic and social problems," issue reports based upon "its research and studies," appear before congressional committees, and "oppose legislation that appeared dangerous and conduct a thorough educational campaign through the press and radio."[1]

As described by Shouse, the new organization in structure remarkably resembled the old AAPA, though with the different avowed aim of becoming "a real factor in assisting toward recovery." The original executive board had a stronger professional political flavor, however, with anti-Roosevelt Democrats Al Smith and John W. Davis, Republicans James Wadsworth and Nathan Miller (a U.S. Steel director and former New York governor), and Irénée du Pont as members. The League did intend to stay out of the pending November elections, but not for the reasons publicly stated. It was not lack of interest but lack of opportunity that would keep the League out of the fray: the du

Ponts and their allies had concluded in their final meetings before the August announcement that they lacked sufficient time and money to be effective in the fall. Shouse specifically had prevailed upon the executive panel to wait until a national fund of a million dollars in pledges (to be gained from forty commitments of $25,000 each) had been raised. By mid-August, only $40,000 actually had been received. Given the League's embarrassingly slow progress in ironing out structural and financial details, in fact, many would have preferred to delay a public announcement of the organization's existence until after the fall elections. Unfortunately, word of the organizational meetings already had been leaked to the New York *World*'s Elliot Thurston. On August 21, Senator Harry Byrd additionally relayed to John Raskob that according to a DNC official privy to the Thurston story, the newspaper would claim that five Senate Democrats, including Byrd and Carter Glass, were actually cooperating in this "anti-Roosevelt" effort. In order to steer off possible political recriminations against the Virginia Senators by the White House, Shouse opted to "go public" the next day and to emphasize the League's nonconfrontational intent.[2]

Even if the desire to protect conservative Democrats had not arisen, the League's leaders were in no immediate position to take on the President openly. The stance they were willing to take publicly at the outset was their constitutional opposition to the growth of decision-making power in the executive branch without specific congressional or judicial authorization. Such a complaint was but an ideological smokescreen, however, given the prior willingness of prominent du Ponts to serve on New Deal boards and agencies as long as executive policies had been shaped by them and had met with their approval. Pierre had seen the growth of federal executive emergency powers as a vehicle to institutionalize industrial self-government by corporate chieftains. His real argument with the administration, which he freely admitted privately, was that while "the original and often repeated statement was to the effect that industry would be permitted to govern itself, . . .this plan has not been carried out and there seems no indication that it will be." On the specific subject of the administration's labor policies, he claimed that while the President privately agreed with his sentiments on minority plant representation (citing Robert Wagner as his confirming source), Roosevelt had never replied to his written inquiry of April 30 following their private White House meeting. Several days after the League's official announcement, Pierre was still trying to influence NRA policy on a variety of fronts, advocating to Donald Richberg, for example, that the agency differentiate between long-term work projects and those intended for immediate unemployment relief.[3]

Given the continuation of such efforts to influence national policy even after the formation of the Liberty League, it seems clear that the organization's original purpose was, as historian Donald R. McCoy has noted, "to influence the Administration and if unsuccessful, to oppose it." Both Pierre and John Raskob, at least, still hoped that Roosevelt could be persuaded to use his immense political clout in their behalf. The League itself actually was but one aspect of a broader strategy to put pressure on the administration through a variety of channels. Du Pont Company executives increased their contributions to the National Association of Manufacturers from $725 to almost $17,000. Irénée du Pont, the family insider most intrinsically hostile to Roosevelt, gave $5000 to the Crusaders and the first of three installments (eventually totalling $1400) to the ultra-conservative Minute Men and Women of Today.[4]

But how would Roosevelt react publicly? Despite the President's perplexing habit of seeming to acquiesce happily to any viewpoint expressed in private, public signs of the administration's impending reaction were less favorable. On August 10, five days before his meeting with Shouse, Roosevelt had told a Green Bay, Wisconsin, audience of two letters of criticism from businessmen and promised that "the people of the United States will not restore that ancient order." It was also not a particularly reassuring indicator that the President had chosen August 18, three days after the Shouse meeting, to accept in writing Pierre du Pont's months-old resignation from the National Labor Board. At best, Roosevelt appeared to be waiting for others to give their reactions to the League before expressing a public judgment himself.[5]

On the occasion of the announcement, Shouse actually hoped to solicit a presidential endorsement. With Roosevelt out of town attending the funeral of Speaker of the House Henry T. Rainey, calls to White House press spokesman Steven Early (despite what Shouse had thought were Roosevelt's prior assurances of a positive statement) received noncommittal replies. When Roosevelt did return to the capital on August 24, his comments were anything but positive. According to the President, the League had indicated its commitment to only "two of the Ten Commandments." He wondered aloud where the League's spirit of charity had been misplaced. Admitting that Shouse had notified him in advance of the League and its aims, he claimed that he had not voiced an opinion at the time because it was "none of my business." As the *Washington Post*'s correspondent noted, the President charged the League with placing "too much stress on property rights, too little on human rights." The reporter concluded, "His tone . . . can only be interpreted as potentially hostile." In the words of another correspondent, Roosevelt "praised" the League "with faint damns." The President gave a far more blunt assessment of the new organization five days later in a private letter to Ambassador William C. Bullitt in Moscow. "All the big guns have started shooting," he observed, referring to them as the " 'I can't take it' club."[6]

Within the President's coterie of advisors, some professed to welcome the coming-out of the conservative opposition. Interior Secretary Harold Ickes expressed delight at having the "enemy" out in the open and predicted that the announcement presaged an impending realignment of American politics. Relief czar Harry Hopkins quipped that the League was full of "right thinking people . . . so far Right that no one will ever find them." Almost everyone with an opinion, in fact, disbelieved the organization's claims to want to "help" the administration. The Pittsburgh *Sun-Telegram*'s John P. Cowens pointedly queried if the League was simply "a major relief project to find a job for Jouett Shouse." *Collier's* and *Commonweal* echoed Ickes's prediction of an emerging conservative versus liberal partisan realignment. *Newsweek* boldly blazoned, "The Tories have come out of ambush." The *New York Times*, expressing sympathy for the League, predicted that its Wall Street leaders would pressure other stockholders to join and claimed, "The financial community sees in the movement the nucleus of a new force for conservatism." Critics challenged the legal credentials of the League to judge constitutional questions of individual rights. Philosopher John Dewey of Columbia University openly contested the claim that the New Deal had confiscated property without due process, and the ACLU's Arthur Garfield Hayes attacked the League's claim by citing its indifference to the liberties of political radicals or the poor. In his weekly radio broadcast from Royal Oak, Michigan, Father Charles Coughlin in turn dismissed the new organization as the "mouthpiece" of greedy bankers.[7]

Supporters of the New Deal in Congress smelled a new and inviting target for political vituperation, a promising opportunity to assume the rhetorical offensive. The "I Can't Take It Club" was quickly adopted as the Liberty League's unofficial title by liberal Democrats. Noting the prominence in it of former Democratic presidential nominees Al Smith and John W. Davis and projected Republican 1936 hopeful James Wadsworth, critics also labelled the League the vehicle of "two has-beens and a would-be." Fearful of political recriminations, even conservative Democrats such as Carter Glass and Harry Byrd hurried to disavow any formal connections with the League. Other Democrats, including even the Louisiana "Kingfish," Senator Huey Long, advocated the creation of a rival organization of pro-administration businessmen, such as West Coast sugar titan Rudolph Spreckels and the Bank of American's A. P. Giannini. Even among many conservative Republicans, memories of how the Raskob-led Democratic party and the du Ponts' AAPA had savaged Herbert Hoover contributed to a less than enthusiastic greeting. To Hoover's former Secretary of War, Patrick J. Hurley, the group was nothing more than the old "smear brigade," and, with a certain bemusement, the former president himself privately noted, "Unbelievable as it may be, Raskob wrote asking me to join." As for Republican insurgents, they looked forward to the occasion, as signalled by Gerald Nye in an August 27 speech at the Chicago World's Fair, when the du Ponts would be grilled by the Senate's munitions inquiry.[8]

League spokesmen did their best to deflect the initial barrage of criticism. Directors Miller and Wadsworth assured the annual meeting of the American Bar Association and a civic audience in New York, respectively, of the group's educational emphasis and lack of ill will toward the administration. At a Wilmington press conference, Irénée insisted that he was "most desirous of being of use to the administration, having voted for Mr. Roosevelt." The League's assertions of the value of having created a principled forum of opposition to specific policies found support in the resignation on August 30 of budget director Lewis Douglas over the administration's spending increases. Less than a week later, while attempting to disabuse Samuel Harden Church's renewed third-party dream, Pierre insisted that while members did "regret and oppose" federal overspending, the League itself would not object publicly to the wisdom of an economic policy if it had been "properly authorized by Congress." Over the radio Jouett Shouse claimed that the League's existence would indirectly aid the administration by restoring business's confidence in it, and that the organization would refrain from casting aspersions on its critics' motives. On the same day, September 7, editorial columnist and League supporter David Lawrence issued a statement which, by citing proposals to confiscate wealth in Minnesota, Louisiana, and California, purported to underscore the need for the new body. Later in the month Lawrence repeated his argument in a *U.S. News* column, entitled "The Tenth Commandment."[9]

Despite public statements to the contrary, the du Ponts and their allies had been stung sharply by the President's overt hostility. Nonetheless Pierre, the family member most hopeful of a positive reaction from the administration, continued to shy away from any prominent leadership role in the Liberty League. Weary of the political fight and citing illness, he preferred to limit his public activity to continuing service on Wilmington's Relief Commission, Incorporated, which met on a weekly basis to allocate municipal, state, and FERA relief funds. Instead of Pierre, Irénée and Raskob took responsibility for stewardship of the League's efforts. For the organization itself, this succession of family political leadership meant the gradual adoption of a more combative, even intemperate, approach toward both the New Deal and its personal leader and symbol in the White House.[10]

Irénée, the heir apparent to Pierre's position as political activist in the family, had maintained his Republican identity and his doubts about the willingness of any Democratic administration to deliver sound policies. He had never staked a claim to insider status within the Roosevelt administration, even in its earliest days, and had been one of the first in the family to advocate the severing of ties with it. Irénée also brought to the political struggle against the New Deal the imprint of his own personality—a more militant, emotional, unguarded style of conservative leadership than that which Pierre had demonstrated in the AAPA. His visceral, even paranoid, fear of incipient radicalism and Bolshevism eventually led to personal contributions to, or consideration of alliances with, some of the most reactionary groups in America, including even such former "dry" enemies as the Ku Klux Klan. To Irénée, however, it was Roosevelt and the New Deal that represented dangerous extremism. Claiming that the administration's "intemperate language leads to intemperate acts," he warned, "When we speak of the government operating railroads, banks, and industries, we really mean that they will be operated by absentee political appointees." He believed a system of this type could constitute a democratic socialism and would degenerate rapidly into communism.[11]

John Raskob, like Irénée, also had soured quickly on the possibility of establishing a "sound" working relationship with the Roosevelt administration. His displeasure with New Deal measures, especially the regulatory crackdown on Wall Street, was magnified by his personal irritation at the Roosevelt-controlled Democratic party's persistent unwillingness to repay the extensive financial commitments he had accumulated on its behalf from 1928 to 1932. Ever since he had grudgingly turned over party reins to James Farley and the rest of the Roosevelt apparatus, he had demanded repayment of his DNC loans, only to be rebuffed. Not until September 4, 1934, did Raskob, after a series of increasingly heated exchanges, receive a $5,000 installment, followed by $10,000 more in October. Even these payments occurred only after Jouett Shouse, in behalf of his old boss, had raised the subject with the President. One understandable reason for Farley's delay, besides the shortness of party funds, was concern over the political wisdom of making payments to a man who might use his influence to help defeat New Deal supporters in November. An angry Raskob insisted that, as one faithful to the League's nonpartisan pledge, he had not contributed money to any candidates in the upcoming elections except to Democrat governors Herbert Lehman of New York and Albert Ritchie of Maryland. "I have done nothing," he insisted, "that has not been open and above board."[12]

Having been forced into a premature public unveiling of their organization, the Liberty League's sponsors plunged into a series of promotional speeches before wealthy audiences. Besides attempting to counter the original barrage of negative publicity, the speakers welcomed new forums for the recruitment and financial solicitation of sympathetic industrialists, bankers, and professionals. In addition to the original directorate of five (which included Irénée) and John Raskob, other prominent promoters included E. F. Hutton (doing double duty for the Crusaders as well), industrialist H. B. Rust, Pauline Sabin, Colby Chester, Ernest T. Weir of Weirton Steel, and J. Howard Pew of Sun Oil. These individuals, who had been among those on the "inside" during the summer's discussions of organizational strategy, comprised an initial twelve-member "executive committee." With seven constituting a quorum, they held informal weekly meetings at New York's Metropolitan Club or the Empire State Club. As persons with extensive networks of social, professional, and industrial contacts, executive committee participants followed informal, direct methods of financial and membership solicitation. In addition, citing pragmatic political and legal grounds, the New York Stock Exchange's Richard Whitney advised Raskob that the members of the exchange also would best be approached by individual Liberty Leaguers rather than through a mass solicitation.[13]

What Whitney's advice signalled, however, was the hesitancy of many businessmen, for fear of either failure or retaliation by the administration, to become visibly identified with the new cause. Alfred Sloan, upon returning from a European vacation, declined to head up a promotional drive in New York. Sloan complained that all of the League's directors save Irénée were career politicians, casting perhaps a nonpartisan, but certainly not a nonpolitical, image. From New Orleans, a contact warned Shouse not to expect much recruiting success in his region, claiming, "The masses in the South regard the Washington administration as a Santa Claus." Attorney Raoul Desvernine, a law partner of League director Nathan Miller, cautioned Raskob about the obstacles presented by the Federal Corrupt Practices Act to lobby-group solicitations. He also related the sobering tale of how H. B. Earhart of Detroit, with objectives in mind similar to the du Ponts', had invited business executives the previous spring to a series of dinners only to become frustrated at the timid response. Although to Irénée the recruitment of wealthy and prestigious men into economic or geographic divisions was essential to the "mass production of members promptly," too few outside the du Ponts' circle (and in the case of Alfred Sloan, even within it), seemed willing to take the risks.[14]

Symptomatic of the emerging difficulties in attracting prominent political figures as well were the refusals of Byrd and Glass to become Virginia state directors and Hoover's rejection of a similar role in California. Parallel efforts to create property divisions, echoing the original intentions of Raskob to have the League become a voice of personalty-owning interests, totally collapsed. The work of Pauline Sabin to form a Liberty League equivalent of the WONPR in the shape of a woman's division also floundered from the outset. Irénée had hoped, and the original $1 million subscription goal illustrated it, to generate an active national League leadership of at least forty, and perhaps from fifty to sixty, wealthy members. Instead, as early as September 20 he was recommending the establishment of a more workable five- or six-member "operating committee" to direct the recruitment effort, for it was becoming more and more difficult even to guarantee a quorum of executive committee members at meetings. Although not adopted immediately, Irénée's recommendations were approved several months later. Although an "advisory" committee of prestigious names was formed and eventually reached over two hundred members, the "advisors" would always have but a small place in the organization. A full month after the league's creation, John Raskob was still being forced because of inadequate operating funds to loan president Shouse $4,000, on top of an earlier $6,000, toward the expenses of the Washington office. Because of the financial squeeze, Shouse did not even receive his formal contract until November, with its terms backdated to September 1.[15]

With Irénée and Raskob hoping to generate parallel interest-group and geographic (state) divisions, comparable to a corporation's product-line and regional divisions, the du Ponts' home state of Delaware served as the "flagship" operation. One week after Shouse's Washington press conference of August 24, the Delaware Liberty League was incorporated. But even in Wilmington, the response was disappointing. Constitution Day ceremonies on September 17 provided a public takeoff, with featured speakers Pierre du Pont and former Pennsylvania Liberal party gubernatorial candidate John M. Hemphill. Pierre predictably took the opportunity to quote freely from George Washington on the "baneful effects of a spirit of party" in American politics. His colleague William Stayton, serving initially both as a membership secretary to the national organization and as president of the state chapter, launched a mail solicitation aimed at former Delaware AAPA members, Du Pont and Hercules Powder employees, prohibition repeal convention delegates, twenty-five "leading citizens of the state," and attendees of the September 24 meeting of the heavily du Pont–influenced Delaware Safety Council. Newspaper advertisements with mail-in membership blanks were placed in Wilmington's dailies. But few individuals outside the family's immediate circle signed up. Even Pierre's wife, Alice Belin du Pont, declined a request to serve as an honorary chairperson of the state division. Responding to concerns from the National Civic Federation's James W. Gerard about the spread of pro-communist sympathies and ideas, a mournful Pierre could only lament, "I am quite at sea as to what remedy is to be applied."[16]

If the glacial pace of progress was not discouraging enough, in September the du Ponts found themselves deflecting charges of war profiteering in public testimony before the Nye Committee. Having begun hearings on September 4, Nye and his allies on the panel were determined to demonstrate that World War I and other lesser conflicts had been inspired by the munitions industry—the "merchants of death." In the first of three series of appearances before the committee, the du Ponts were called upon to testify in Washington from the twelfth to the fifteenth of September. They were grilled over their contacts with political and military officials in Latin American countries, including Argentina and Mexico, their cartel dealings in the 1920's with foreign arms merchants (most notably the British Imperial Chemical Industries and Germany's I.G. Farben), and their sales of munitions to both sides in the Chaco War, which had begun in 1932.[17]

As befitted their varying personalities, each du Pont adopted a different demeanor toward inquisitors. Pierre managed to maintain his usual calm visage. Cousin Felix du Pont occasionally displayed a comically unbelievable naiveté. Lammot, as always, projected an image of cold competence, punctuated by his declaration, "I would rather have a form of democratic government, but the way matters now stand

I think our Constitution is on the verge of going into the scrap basket, and that's why I have joined the Liberty League." But it was Irénée who provided the real sparks. Showing his disdain in front of the committee by blowing smoke rings from his pipe, he displayed a haughty contempt for those he considered point men for communism. Investigations by committee staffers into the du Ponts' lobbying and campaign contribution activities of the previous fifteen years only magnified Irénée's preoccupation with maintaining the secrecy of the Liberty League's files. He pressed Jouett Shouse to exercise vigilance in screening potential employees, fearing the penetration by "a spy intent on distorting everything we do and making trouble." In response to the family's intransigence in turning over records to his panel, chairman Nye thundered, "The world is going to see the need for curbing these merchants of death and their business . . . There is a large effort being made to slow up the investigations."[18]

By September 27, citing the rummaging of investigators in "our personal files in Wilmington," Irénée lamented, "We will be no more free than are the people of Russia today." A day later he complained to Shouse that the contents of a newspaper story, the "Today" column by Raymond Moley, could only mean that information about the League's financing plan had been leaked. He personally had good reason to be fearful of what investigators would find in his political files, for he had already given over $35,000 to various Republican organizations, $5,000 to the Crusaders, a token $25 to the anti-union New York State Economic Council, and had sought out the help of retired General Amos A. Fries in distributing Liberty League membership cards to American Legion members. Further feeding Irénée's paranoia about government snooping and incipient communism were his growing contacts with the Hearst newspaper interests through reporter Earl Reeves. Reeves featured a series of four weekly interviews with Irénée from mid-September through early October, and he relayed to both Irénée and Lammot descriptions from *Pravda* of Joseph Stalin's stated intentions to "lead the proletariat of all countries to socialist revolution throughout the world."[19]

The adverse publicity being generated by the Nye inquiry was complicating the organizational efforts of the League at the very time that it appeared to make their success more imperative. Following the inability to pry Charles Michelson away from the Democratic party, the League hired William Murphy as its publicity chief on September 22. Following his first round of congressional testimony, Irénée, along with other executive committee participants, once more hit the hustings. On October 4, he addressed a luncheon meeting of the Manufacturers and Bankers' Club of Philadelphia on the theme "Why America Needs the Liberty League," and followed it that evening with a dinner meeting of the executive committee in New York. On the eighth, after acknowledging Houstonian Will Clayton's acceptance of a League slot, he commenced engagements in New York, Chicago (with himself, Raskob, and Shouse hosted by corporate attorney Ralph Shaw), and Atlantic City. Industrialist H. B. Earhart headed another fundraising dinner in Detroit on the tenth, and the next day William Stayton, on Pierre's urging, issued an invitation letter to all former executive committee members of the AAPA.[20]

Because of the League's early recruitment difficulties within the corporate world, it was already facing the dilemma posed by the need on the one hand to raise a larger core of ideologically committed activists outside the du Pont circle while avoiding on the other the corresponding danger of overt links with the "lunatic fringe" of the right. The latter risk was constantly being skirted because of Irénée's periodic flirtations with extreme conservative causes. Such concerns helped determine the resolution of the League's relationship with its anti–New Deal ally, the Crusaders. Following the announcement of the League's formation, in late August the Maryland "commander" of the Crusaders, Edgar Allen Poe, Jr., stated that a merger of the two organizations "would be no surprise." The two administrative chiefs, Fred Clark and Jouett Shouse, discussed the possibility many times. In late September, the League's executive committee empowered a three-person group consisting of Raskob, Shouse, and Pauline Sabin to "fix the relations between the two organizations." Merger would avoid the duplication of activities and organizational costs of the two groups and would have the short-term effect of increasing the League's corporate representation, perhaps lessening the urge to look further afield for supporters. On the negative side, however, merger carried with it the danger of lessening the degree of exclusive policy control enjoyed by the du Ponts via an independent Liberty League.[21]

At a crucial October 18 meeting of Raskob and Irénée with Crusader representatives James Bell (president of General Mills), Douglas Stewart, Clark, and Hutton, a compromise of sorts was reached. The conferees agreed that a new Crusaders drive, with a new Voice of the Air radio series, would be launched to replace a previous effort which had been halted at the time of the League's unveiling. The two organizations would remain as separate entities but would share interlocking directorates and contributor lists. Assuming prominent roles in both movements were E. F. Hutton, Colby Chester, John W. Davis, Sewell Avery of Montgomery Ward, and Will Clayton (members of the Crusaders' advisory council and the League's executive committee) and Alfred Sloan, Robert Lund, George M. Moffett, and Elton Hoyt II (members of both organizations' advisory committees). The League formally gave $9000 to the Crusaders for its radio program, since it did not duplicate any similar League activity, and Irénée personally gave another $5000 at the end of the month to the Voice of the Air. Despite attempts to accommodate each others' activities and to divide roles, however, the retention of two separate organizations led to the splintering of contributions to each. Howard Heinz, for example, begged off from a pledge to the League's $1 million subscription fund because of his obligations to the Crusaders as well as his public position as chairman of the National Industrial Conference Board.[22]

Another reason for avoiding complete merger was the lingering, if subsequently debunked, hope of Raskob and Pierre that Roosevelt would come around to their point of view, thereby making unnecessary an immediate and visible consolidation of anti–New Deal corporate forces. Raskob took heart, for example, from the American Federation of Labor's resolution, passed at its San Francisco convention, in opposition to "government competition with private industry." Neither Raskob nor Pierre had yet formally resigned their positions on the Commerce Department's Business Advisory Council, and they took as a conciliatory gesture the President's preelection appointments of the NAM's Robert Lund and the U.S. Chamber of Commerce's Henry I. Harriman to the same panel. As a member of the council, Raskob had been appointed to a subcommittee studying federal unemployment insurance and old-age pension proposals in advance of the 1935 congressional session. In an address to the American Bankers Association on October 24, Roosevelt issued more conciliatory signals, calling for an "all-American recovery team" that would include the business community. Pierre urged Brooks Darlington, publicity director for the League in Delaware, not to issue any blanket condemnations of the New Deal before the elections, and Darlington concurred, citing the need to appeal to the "little fellow." A day before the November vote, Raskob professed his lack of interest in opposing the administration to James Farley. He took the occasion to advocate a balanced budget, the elimination of federal relief, income tax reduction, 20 percent wage cuts paired with maintenance of the forty-hour week, currency stabilization, industrial cooperation, and delays in consideration of any unemployment insurance proposals.[23]

Even Irénée hesitated in coming out forcefully against the administration in advance of the congressional elections. Attempting to convince Baltimore and Ohio Railroad president Daniel Willard to join the Liberty League, he still insisted that the organization had not been designed to "smear" Roosevelt and that its launch had been premature and not unplanned. But despite the outer show of calm, Irénée was becoming rapidly frustrated with the lack of urgency and commitment from fellow business executives. Adding to the sense of crisis were the continuing warnings against the appearance of too many du Ponts or General Motors executives on the league's leadership roster. In order to speed up the accumulation of the $1 million fund, the League's organizational structure was redefined. By early November Shouse and Stayton were empowered by the executive board to select individuals for the advisory committee, with a projected membership of two hundred, without requiring its prior screening. This advisory panel would not have responsibility for setting policy but would lend prestige and money to the cause through its prominent enlistees. In turn, the executive committee, originally projected to reach fifty or sixty members and to provide the bulk of the subscription fund through larger fees, was now to be capped at twenty-five. A more ominous sign of Irénée's desperation, however, was his serious consideration of a November 1 offer of support from Hiram Evans, Imperial Wizard of the Ku Klux Klan. Evans urged a confidential meeting of the two men to discuss organizational collaboration against radicalism. Tempted enough not to reject the solicitation out of hand, Irénée sought Shouse's advice by letter on Election Day on how to respond.[24]

Irénée's fighting instincts already had been roused by the October 30 release by Senator Nye of an extensive list of his and his brothers' political contributions since 1919, a blatant preelection attack on the family's supposedly "corrupt" influence in government. But the du Ponts' mood plunged to new depths as a result of the November 6 election returns. Although their spokesmen were accurate in asserting that the elections had not been a direct test of strength of the League (after all, it had shied away from challenging congressional New Dealers), no heart could be taken from the balloting. Democratic strength rose in the Senate from 60 to 69 and in the House of Representatives from 313 to 322, translating into 70–75 percent control of both houses. For only the second time since the Civil War, a party in power actually gained seats in both houses in a midterm election. The Democrats' margins were also the largest any party had won since Reconstruction. Besides the partisan verdict, analysts agreed that the returns signaled a popular desire for more, not less, government activism to fight the Depression. This interpretation could only embolden more ardent New Dealers such as Harry Hopkins to press for additional relief spending.[25]

At best, Irénée and his cohorts hoped that the dramatic reversals of the election would galvanize their fellow industrialists into action. The League already had planned that following a postelection sendoff rally, full-scale propaganda efforts would begin in earnest. On Election Day itself, Irénée was negotiating with the American Press League for the preparation and circulation to public schools and Liberty League members of copies of the Constitution and the Bill of Rights. He also pledged $1000 to Frank Schoonover for a private mailing of similar materials and contemplated authorizing a calendar, a "liberty bell" emblem, and lapel buttons. On November 7, Jouett Shouse issued a public statement entitled "Why? The American Liberty League," which became the first of a series of addresses and press releases published in pamphlet form for outside distribution. Still, however, as demonstrated by the U.S. Chamber of Commerce's postelection pledge of cooperation with the President and Congress, much of the business community remained timid.[26]

Although the Liberty League had received nearly three-quarters of its required $1 million in pledges by early November, actual receipts were but $64,000 as late as midmonth. As a necessary consequence, Irénée and his partners stepped up their personal moneyraising efforts. Irénée sent brother Lammot a draft letter aimed at Du Pont Company stockholders and postdated for November 21. On November 9, Stayton notified Shouse that the stockholders of General Motors, U.S. Rubber, General Foods, and the Corn Products Refining Company (H. B. Earhart's company), numbering about a half million (two-thirds of them in GM alone), would also be targeted for solicitation. Company approvals were still being awaited for similar appeals to Goodyear, Goodrich, Firestone, Montgomery Ward, Sears, Matheson Alkali, Stanley Works, and North American Corporation stockholders. As part of the general effort to broaden the organization's business base and thereby alter the League's image, Pierre du Pont alone was placed on the expanded advisory committee as "representing the entire group" of Du Pont executives. Donaldson Brown was asked similarly to prepare, and to pare, a sufficient but minimum sampling of GM officers.[27]

With Shouse designated the League's official political spokesman, the du Ponts now prepared to wage open ideological war against the New Deal. In preparation for what Irénée anticipated might be new heights of political invective from the Nye Committee and other enemies, he retained Shouse as his personal attorney. On November 10, Arthur Krock of the *New York Times* wrote that "now that the elections are over, something will soon be heard of the American Liberty League." That "something" consisted of prominent Leaguers fanning the countryside issuing salvos at the New Deal. On November 11, recruiter E. F. Hutton urged a Hot Springs, Arkansas, audience of businessmen to "consolidate their forces" in order to halt government experimentation and truly "help" the President's recovery program. He repeated the message the next day in Houston. Pauline Sabin, who had formally launched the Women's Division on the tenth, echoed Hutton's message in a press release two days later. Speaking before the Bond Club of New York on November 20, Jouett Shouse used the strongest public language yet by a Leaguer against the New Deal. Employing the Volstead Act as an example of dangerous federal experimentation and regulation, he warned that while the dangerous tide of statism "did not begin with this administration," the current regime had demonstrated a similarly alarming "disposition to regiment production."[28]

Between the addresses of November 10–12 and Shouse's remarks over a week later, Hutton, Raskob, and Irénée embarked on a major recruitment effort on the West Coast. The three men, who operated as an informal finance committee for the League, were intent on raising money for the organization's operating fund and building chapters in Los Angeles and San Francisco. At a gathering hosted by Robert A. Milliken, their main backer in Los Angeles, Irénée blasted the NRA for having wasted time and resources on code enforcement while ten million Americans remained unemployed. The most productive result of the Southern California swing, however, was E. F. Hutton's success in securing an immediate $2500 contribution and a subscription pledge of $25,000 from Hollywood producer Hal Roach. In San Francisco, Hutton and Irénée were unable to hold personal meetings with prominent anti-radical leaders Frank Belgrano (the American Legion's national commander) and Leland Cutler. Through the help of banker Asa V. Call, however, telephone contact was made with Eustus Cullinan, head of a nonpartisan conservative movement which had helped defeat gubernatorial candidate Upton Sinclair and his EPIC (End Poverty in California) wealth redistribution plan. After an appearance before the Bohemian Club, they also attempted in a cordial, but frustratingly noncommittal, session to officially enlist William Randolph Hearst in the cause.[29]

The triumvirate's West Coast foray did not escape the notice of Beverly Hills's best-known resident, satirist Will Rogers. On November 15, his syndicated newspaper column poked fun at the recruiters as "three hundred million dollars worth of talent." Although Rogers privately apologized to the extra-sensitive Hutton later by telegram, even then he added, "You must admit Ed that you three boys with your financial standing and background out to save the constitution, it does lend itself to some little touch of humor." Irénée, in a fighting mood upon his return to Wilmington, chose to renew preliminary discussions with the Ku Klux Klan's Hiram Evans. Ten days earlier, following Evans's initial contact, Jouett Shouse had advised Irénée to be cautious. "I think it might be well for you to see him and see what he has to offer," he opined, "but it seems to me his organization has largely passed out of the picture and I do not believe they can be of much service to us or to anyone else." On November 20, a less guarded Irénée relayed to Evans that secret "vigilance committees" had been formed on the West Coast in fear of property confiscation, the "Red menace," and the return of a form of "carpetbagging" in which "patriotic citizens had to organize secretly for their protection against racketeers supported by the U.S. government." He urged Evans, "Your organization is the outgrowth of that original society. Perhaps it is a good time to revive it in a cause commensurate with the one which called it into being." He did maintain, however, that such a new role for the Klan would require "fighting entirely in the open." To plan toward that aim, Irénée suggested an early personal meeting between them.[30]

Irénée's combative spirit carried over into an address to University of Delaware students the next day. Warning of the dangers of "beneficent" dictators, he praised the American system of checks and balances, particularly its sluggishness toward "absurdly wrong legislation," and contrasted the history of American prosperity with the failure of Soviet communism. But while the November returns and the League's frustrations had angered Irénée into action, albeit sometimes of an unwise nature, they had discouraged brother Pierre. The du Pont patriarch received on November 14 a letter from the Delaware Trust Company's J. Ernest Smith which contained a lengthy excerpt of an item of private correspondence written by the English critic Lord Macauley in 1857. Macauley had maintained that "institutions purely democratic must, sooner or later, destroy liberty or civilization, or both." An assenting Pierre passed on to other members of the League's inner circle the complete quotation, which continued:

> On one side is a statesman preaching patience, respect for vested rights, a strict observance of public faith. On the other is a demagogue ranting about tyranny of capitalists and userers and asking why anybody should be permitted to drink champagne and ride in a carriage while thousands of honest people are in want of necessities. Which of the two candidates is likely to be preferred by a workingman who hears his children cry for bread?

Macauley had concluded to his American correspondent that the U.S. Constitution presented an inadequate defense against demagogic tendencies, claiming that it "is all sail and no anchor." In his own desperate search for an "anchor," Pierre now renewed his old arguments to John Raskob for restricting the franchise. A sympathetic Raskob already had suggested to James Farley the requirement of an examination and the subsequent issuance of voter identity cards for eligible citizens. But to Pierre he maintained that while "if there was any practical way of excluding a very large and undesirable population from voting, that would be best . . . failing that it seems to me most desirable to try to make the undesirable population as desirable as possible through education, appeals to patriotism, etc., etc."[31]

While Pierre's circle of du Ponts were assuming a more confrontational approach to the White House, other cousins, ironically, were maintaining a cordial correspondence at least with the First Lady. In large measure the acquaintance owed to the surprising courtship of the President's son, Franklin D. Roosevelt, Jr., and Ethel du Pont, the daughter of Pierre's cousin Eugene. The romance had been spotted by photographers as early as April, and two months later the young Roosevelt had attended Ethel's formal debut at her father's Owl's Nest estate. Eleanor Roosevelt had hosted her on board the presidential yacht *Sequoia* to watch Franklin, Jr., row as a member of a Harvard crew against Yale. Responding to a letter from Ruth du Pont (the wife of another family cousin, Winterthur's Henry F.) complaining about cartoon attacks on that "blameless citizen" J. P. Morgan, the First Lady had related, "I gave the cartoon to the President, and he says that people in prominent positions, such as Mr. Morgan and himself, must expect articles and cartoons of this nature—only that most of them are ten times worse." Subsequently Ethel received an invitation to spend the Christmas holiday as a guest at the White House.[32]

If the courtship was a minor embarrassment to the Liberty Leaguers in the du Pont family, more serious political shocks were soon to occur. In mid-November, Houston businessman and League booster J. S. Cullinan warned du Pont loyalist William Stayton that certain members of Congress intended to "take your organization for a ride, place it on the spot, and keep it there." On Tuesday, November 20, a special House committee on un-American activities, headed by Democrats Samuel Dickstein of New York and John MacCormack of Massachusetts, met in executive session in the upper room of the Association of the Bar in New York City. Their witness, Smedley Darlington Butler, formerly a major general in the Marines, proceeded to unfold a bizarre tale of a fascist plot, sponsored by powerful financial interests, to seize by force the government of the United States. Butler, a two-time recipient of the Medal of Honor for service in Mexico and Haiti, had become a leading gadfly for such causes as the soldiers' bonus, the outlawing of war, and the Veterans of Foreign Wars and an equally harsh critic of both the munitions industry and the American Legion.[33]

According to the general, on August 22, 1934, Gerald MacGuire, a veteran active in the Connecticut American Legion and a lawyer in the offices of Grayson Murphy (an original director of the Legion in 1919), sought his leadership of a "militantly patriotic" super-organization of veterans. The group, similar in nature to the French right-wing Croix de Feu, would conduct a "march on Washington" that would force a change in the government. MacGuire reportedly assured Butler that $3 million was immediately available for the purpose, with $3 million more in reserve. His solicitor's aim, Butler claimed, was to produce through threat of arms a peaceful transfer of power similar to what "Mussolini did to the King of Italy." According to the plan, Roosevelt would obtain the resignations of Secretary of State Hull and Vice President Garner and then appoint one of the organizers as his "acting president." If the President refused to cooperate, he would be forced to resign. Butler said that MacGuire claimed that half the membership of the American Legion and the VFW were prepared to follow the general's lead.[34]

Butler charged that MacGuire was acting in behalf of powerful financial interests, especially the Morgan establishments. His evidence for the accusation was his claim that a year earlier, in July 1933, MacGuire and Massachusetts American Legion official William Doyle had asked him to lead another "rank-and-file" movement to oust the Legion's national leadership at its Chicago convention and to obtain a platform endorsement of the gold standard. According to Butler, he had been shown bank deposits of $42,000 and $64,000 to indicate the seriousness and means of MacGuire's backers, who included Grayson Murphy and the "billionaire Lieutenant" of the Boxer Rebellion, Singer heir Robert Sterling Clark. The general asserted that the plotters had told him that the speech written for his use had been drafted by Morgan attorney John W. Davis. When MacGuire approached Butler for the second time, in August 1934, he had also indicated, according to the general, that the money for the plot would be provided by the Morgan interests through either Davis or W. R. Perkins of National City Bank.[35]

The main assertion of a direct du Pont involvement in the plot came through the claim that guns for the effort would be obtained from

Remington Arms, which the du Ponts had acquired earlier in the year. In addition, Butler claimed that in response to his question, "Is there anything stirring yet?" MacGuire had replied, "In two or three weeks, you will see it come out in the papers. There will be big fellows in it. This is to be the background of it." Was Butler referring to the Liberty League? Others charged by Butler as accomplices to the "Legion plot," as it soon became known, included former governor Joseph B. Ely of Massachustts, American Legion national commander Frank Belgrano, Al Smith, former Legion commander Louis Johnson, Hugh Johnson, and Morgan partner Thomas W. Lamont. To complete the tale, Butler (who claimed that he had been personally slated to head the government if Roosevelt chose not to cooperate) added that in the event he would not participate, the plotters had planned to enlist General Douglas MacArthur or former Legion commander General Hanford MacNider as his replacement.[36]

Wishing to ensure public attention for his charges in spite of the closed nature of the hearing, Butler fed the outlines of his tale to reporter Paul Comly French of the Stern newspapers (the Philadelphia *Record* and New York *Evening Post*). The story appeared in sketchy form on November 20, and French himself testified before the committee the same day to corroborate Butler's charges. According to the reporter, MacGuire had told him the additional detail that as a preliminary step to the formal takeover, Butler was to have been appointed head of the Civilian Conservation Corps, a position from which he was to build up a private army. Gerald MacGuire's rebuttal testimony the same afternoon proved full of holes and faulty memory, and particulars of the Butler and French testimony concerning the 1933 plot to force the Legion to adopt the gold standard were corroborated by the committee. In addition, correspondence obtained by the investigators between MacGuire and Clark in the spring of 1934 indicated that MacGuire had examined personally the strength and characteristics of veterans' movements in Mussolini's Italy, Hitler's Germany, and France. Of the Croix de Feu MacGuire had written admiringly, "Those fellows are interested only in the salvation of France, and I feel sure that the country could not be in better hands."[37]

The parts of Butler's bizarre story which could be immediately tested did not directly implicate the du Ponts in anything. Nonetheless, given the nature of the charges, public airing of the accusations encouraged rabid speculation concerning the possible involvement, either as an organization or as individuals, of the du Pont Liberty Leaguers. Had the League been the organization Butler claimed MacGuire had alluded to on August 22? Had prominent Leaguer John W. Davis been a party to any of the dealings alleged to have occurred in either 1933 or 1934? Had the du Ponts intended to help such a plot through their purchase of Remington Arms? Specific individuals linked to the scheme were quick to refute the charges (Grayson Murphy—"A fantasy"), (Frank Belgrano—"The American Legion is not involved in the slightest degree in any march on Washington"), (Hugh Johnson—"I know nothing about it"). Many in the press, jaded by a constant flow during the Depression years of rumored left-wing or right-wing plots, had difficulty taking the charges seriously. To the *New York Times,* "the whole story sounds like a gigantic hoax." *Time* burlesqued the Butler charges in a rendition depicting the general, astride a white horse, assembling a crowd of veterans at a CCC camp and then marching to the capital, trailed by an ammunition train from Remington Arms and a column which included Hugh Johnson, General MacArthur, and, in a limousine, J. P. Morgan and Thomas Lamont. The investigators, although not so inclined to dismiss the activities of MacGuire, Clark, and perhaps Murphy, issued a preliminary statement on November 26 that announced, "This committee has no evidence before it that would in the slightest degree warrant calling before it such men as John W. Davis, General Hugh Johnson, General James G. Horbord, Thomas W. Lamont, Admiral William S. Sims, or Hanford MacNider. The committee will not take cognizance of names brought into the testimony which constitute mere hearsay."[38]

At their core, the accusations probably consisted of a mixture of actual attempts at influence peddling by a small core of financiers with ties to veterans organizations and the self-serving accusations of Butler against the enemies of his pacifist and populist causes. What was important for the future of the Liberty League, however, was not the fact that little hard evidence could be found of collusion against the government. Instead, what mattered, and was most damning, was that the popular image of the du Ponts as greedy industrialists and "merchants of death" gave the charges immediate credibility. Such perceptions further eroded the already shaky claims of the Liberty League to be a voice of legitimate, respectable, conservative opposition. Nor did the actions of the du Ponts and their political allies in the organization help to dispel the early image of reactionary irresponsibility. Was it wise, for example, even given the League's financial difficulties, to accept and keep a $4900 contribution from Robert Sterling Clark? Was it wise six months later, in view of the charges made against him, for the du Ponts to hire Grayson Murphy as League treasurer? Was it astute to seek, as Irénée had already done, backstage cooperation from American Legion officials in membership drives or to solicit Frank

Belgrano to head up the League's "anti-Red" recruitment in San Francisco? And what was Irénée doing even considering cooperation with Hiram Evans and the Ku Klux Klan? Such actions, if discovered by others, could only further cement an image of the leaders as irresponsible and dangerous "anti–New Deal fascists." Ironically, rather than learning a lesson from the incident, the Wilmington district manager of the Massachusetts Mutual Life Insurance Company, Robert E. Jackson, took a cue from the Butler charges and urged Irénée to launch a covert campaign of "Legion education and membership infiltration" aimed at building "an army drawn up in defense of the common purpose of these two organizations."[39]

The net effect of all the fall's public setbacks was to throw the League's solicitation efforts into total disarray. By November 24 the organization's initial round of financial contributions had been nearly exhausted. Casting doubt on Irénée's hopes that "Chicago, Detroit, Cincinnati, St. Louis, and Houston will give us more cause for optimism," Sewell Avery in the Windy City, H. B. Rust in Pittsburgh, and Earhart in Detroit all were running into insurmountable obstacles in obtaining the hoped-for eight $25,000 contributions per metropolitan area. Attempts to recruit prestigious academic leaders to the advisory committee, such as MIT president Dr. Karl T. Compton, went equally badly. Despite the circulation of a letter from Irénée to all contributing members, with additional membership blanks enclosed, by two weeks later only fourteen individuals had given as much as $1000 apiece to the League's national office. Those larger contributions nonetheless represented over half, or $46,000, of the organization's total of but $82,000 received. Irénée and Lammot du Pont alone were responsible for $20,000. To a business associate Irénée admitted that "the national situation is discouraging." In a spirit of dejection he lamented, "It is curious that in the East they think the Liberty League is too antagonistic to the President. In the West they think we are 'pussyfooters' and lacking in courage. I think California has deferred active participation because we will not come out and demand deportation of Reds and a clean sweep of Reds in Washington."[40]

In the hope of restoring order out of chaos, the League on December 1 hired Dr. A. P. Haake, former managing director of the National Association of Furniture Manufacturers, as Jouett Shouse's assistant for state chapter organization. From his winter home in South Carolina E. F. Hutton pushed ahead with a series of speaking engagements. But in an act of dubious wisdom, Irénée continued his flirtation with the Ku Klux Klan. Following his mid-November return to Atlanta from a California recruitment foray, Hiram Evans had suggested a personal meeting at or about December 8. Despite renewed advice from Shouse that the League had little to gain from such contacts, Irénée countered, "I think he wishes to improve the reputation of the Klan by adopting an objective which will make it more popular and, in any case, has come out for the Constitution." Irénée directed Shouse to make tentative arrangements for him to meet the Imperial Wizard at the League's Washington headquarters on December 18, following an expected second round of verbal combat before the Nye Committee.[41]

To Irénée's embarrassment, only two-and-a-half months into its existence the Liberty League was already in danger of becoming a political laughingstock. At the national press's annual Gridiron Dinner of December 8, the characters "Wallingford" Shouse, "Ponzi" Raskob, "Dynamite" du Pont, and "Polly go Between" Sabin, with the background music of ringing cash registers, were lampooned. Shouse, depicted accepting a dime in contributions from John D. Rockefeller, was quoted as saying, "If anybody's in favor of saving the Constitution, its a sure win he's got at least a million dollars." December certainly was no time for the League to be weakening, however. Shouse and Raskob both warned of the dangers looming in the 1935 session of Congress. As early as November 24, Shouse, anticipating New Deal initiatives, had listed for the executive committee the likely issues of the spring. Expected were an NRA renewal bill, a new NLRB measure with specific prohibitions on company unions and the open shop, a thirty-hour workweek proposal, increases in AAA crop-reduction powers, renewal of the Reconstruction Finance Corporation, boosts in HOLC and Farm Credit Act loan programs, major jumps in public works and relief spending, greater governmental controls on "open-market" banking operations, a permanent bank deposit insurance system, old-age pensions and unemployment insurance, and curbs on utility holding companies.[42]

Shouse steered the League toward adopting a policy platform for the upcoming session similar to that of the U.S. Chamber of Commerce. The chamber had proposed limiting NRA codes to clearly defined interstate businesses, permission for minority labor representation and the open shop, possible repeal of the Bankhead Cotton Control Act, spending reductions aimed at a balanced federal budget, specific cuts in public works and relief, opposition to the soldiers' bonus, and rejection of any new controls on the banking industry. At a meeting of the executive committee on December 6, with advertising executive Edward L. Bernays serving as a consultant, a group of four members, consisting of Shouse, Al Smith, Pauline Sabin, and Colby

Chester, were named to prepare separate proposals on the League's program and organizational restructuring for consideration two weeks hence. Putting his own views on the public record on December 8 in an address before the Beacon Society of Boston, Shouse proposed the transfer of relief administration from the federal executive to the Red Cross. As part of the private debate between League members on the forthcoming "platform," J. S. Cullinan urged Pierre du Pont by letter to move beyond general fealty to the Constitution toward specific attacks on "invisible government," federal tax, currency and credit policy, and banking controls, especially taxation.[43]

A new area of activity briefly considered for the League, but tabled for the near term, was the employment of the organization's lawyers as a legal service to combat New Deal regulation in the courts. William Stayton already had conducted an analysis of the constitutionality of government-owned corporations such as the Shipping Board and the TVA for Pierre, but the results had not been satisfactory. "If the question is closed beyond attack," Pierre wrote, "I do not think that the American Liberty League should concern itself with the utility question. If there is room for attack," he added, "the American Liberty league is certainly doing a public service by opposing unconstitutional acts." Supported by Will Clayton, Stayton maintained that while Supreme Court litigation, conducted solely between plaintiff and defendant, left no room for outside private participation, it would nonetheless be valuable to lobby bar association representatives into giving monthly briefings to the justices on present issues. An uncertain Pierre, however, refused to press for litigation other than that of member lawyers accepting solicitation from firms under New Deal attack. On the specific advice of Philadelphia utility executive John E. Zimmerman that it was "too early" to "take a hand in the utility situation," and that the League should "sufficiently establish itself" first, Pierre replied that he would not urge "an active interest in the power situation unless I hear again from you."[44]

Irénée played what was for him an uncustomarily minor role in the executive committee's yuletide discussions on the forthcoming League platform, for he, like Pierre and Lammot, again was engaged in verbal combat with the Nye investigation. With public hearings resumed on December 4, the du Ponts were called upon once more to defend their Old Hickory plant contract dealings with the federal government during World War I, their links to ICI and I.G. Farben, their covert machinations to undermine the Geneva disarmament conference of 1925, and their knowledge of German rearmament in violation of the Versailles Treaty. Once again, Irénée generated the most headlines of the three for his outspokenness. While admitting that, as a sign of his company's impressive political clout, he had once considered hiring Republican party chairman Henry Fletcher as a lobbying agent, Irénée asserted that the country now had become "pretty near" possessing an absolute monarch in Roosevelt. With the papers once again full of references to and innuendos against war promoters, Father Charles Coughlin took to the airwaves on December 16 to assail the du Ponts as "merchandizers of murder." For its part the Nye committee chose the family's last scheduled day on the witness stand, December 20, to disclose to the press the existence of anti–New Deal correspondence between Raskob and Carpenter of the previous spring. Having seized it, as Irénée had feared, from company files, Senator Nye publicly trumpeted it as the wellspring of the Liberty League. About the only good derived from the December ordeal in Washington was that Irénée's two weeks of testimony forced him to cancel his prearranged private appointment with Hiram Evans.[45]

While Irénée defended the family's honor before congressional inquisitors, his brother Lammot and John Raskob pursued other channels to influence the upcoming congressional session. As a member of the Commerce Department's Business Advisory panel, Raskob was serving on subcommittees to study "decentralization of industry" and, more important, "social legislation"—focusing in particular on federal old-age pensions and unemployment insurance. In addition, both Raskob and Lammot had secured appointment as NAM representatives to the NAM–U.S. Chamber of Commerce Committee for Business Recovery created by the Joint Conference of Business Men. The panel in turn organized a major business summit conference to map industrial strategy, called the "Congress of American Industry," to be held at White Sulphur Springs, West Virginia, on December 17–19. With the gathering designed to impress organized business's policy views squarely upon the administration, Raskob held a prominent position as chairman of the platform and resolutions committee. Nor surprisingly, the product of his panel's labors reflected the views of the du Ponts and the Liberty League on the major issues. It included opposition to federal intervention in "local" labor disputes, endorsement of the open shop, rejection of sympathy strikes or lockouts, support for voluntary business participation in industrial codes but only a temporary renewal of NRA, resistance to federal administration of relief, repudiation of government competition with private industry (such as in the TVA), opposition to "arbitrary" crop restrictions, endorsement of a balanced budget, and calls for lower taxes. With very few differences, the White Sulphur Springs document also served as a blueprint for the platform deliberations of the League's executive committee on December 20.[46]

Besides platform and policy recommendations that called upon the Liberty League to infuse "into the old symbols of America . . . a new life," the executive committee on December 20 entertained a sweeping report on organization. The report provided the hitherto chaotic recruitment effort with its first systematic "road map." As recommended in the plan's "federal" blueprint, the organization's headquarters would be in Washington, D.C., with regional offices in Chicago and New York. The Women's Division nerve center would be in New York, with a second branch immediately in Chicago and another later in San Francisco. Each state would be organized by congressional districts except in the case of large cities, which would have individual chapters. Each state organization would provide five to ten members who also would serve as national directors and representatives on a projected 250-member advisory committee. In keeping with the principle of "decentralized management—centralized control," an executive committee of no more than twenty, meeting at least twice monthly, would maintain "entire" policy jurisdiction. Previous notions of forming divisions on the basis of property ownership classifications were jettisoned, but advisory expert groups were planned, including an "economic council," a research and statistical panel, a historical group, a legal committee, and a public relations panel.[47]

The Washington headquarters, serving as the daily national clearinghouse of activities, was tabbed to receive the lion's share of a monthly budget expected to exceed $60,000. President Shouse would oversee a comptroller, a publicity director, a research director, a legislative liaison, a membership secretary, and a state organization director. Educational activities would be channeled outward from Washington, including dissemination of League material through newspapers, churches, schools, business and professional groups, authors, lecture programs, radio addresses, agricultural and labor allies, movies, and like-minded patriotic organizations. The Washington office would implement policies formulated by the executive committee, prepare the educational material for distribution, serve as the contact with subsidiaries, conduct legislative research, prepare speech materials, and centralize bookkeeping. Although the executive committee was uncertain if the League fell under the restrictions of the Federal Corrupt Practices Act, Shouse indicated that his office would be prepared to file annual reports of financial contributions to the clerk of the House of Representatives, as directed in the law.[48]

With the reports on program and organization safely in executive committee hands awaiting final endorsement, the long-overdue re-structuring might have been expected to bolster the du Ponts' spirits at Christmastime. But Irénée and Raskob, two-thirds of the fundraising nucleus of the organization, already were weary after only four months of accumulated frustration with the enterprise. By year's end, the League had raised only a little over $94,000 and had spent $92,000 just on operating expenses, leaving little to launch a 1935 political offensive with. In Irénée's absence, the executive committee on December 20 "rewarded" him with election as its chairman and named him to subcommittees on finances and legislative policy. But Irénée was not at all certain he wanted the responsibility any longer. Relaying the message that he might be unable to attend the January 7 executive session because of another appearance before the Nye panel, he suggested to Shouse that perhaps he was "really needed there more than in the Liberty League." "To me it seems," he claimed, "the Red network has spread further in Washington than most people suspect." Although further testimony proved not to be required, Irénée still made plans to leave for a winter vaction in Cuba, even cancelling a December 28 parley with Hiram Evans because of his need to rid himself of a "gripping cold." He indicated to the executive committee his initial unwillingness to serve as its chairman, although he promised to maintain his seat on the panel. Urging additional decisionmaking centralization in the form of a smaller "operating committee" within the executive committee, Irénée cautioned his heretofore less-active partners that "simply running up a flag will not bring the huge membership we had hoped for."[49]

E. F. Hutton, the third member of the League's financial triumverate, already felt that Irénée and Raskob had bailed out of the cause. Having made plans to pursue solicitation efforts in Georgia, South Carolina, and Tennessee early in the new year, he became ever more frustrated at his two colleagues' apparent backsliding. Accordingly, he recommended the appointment of Al Smith as executive committee chairman in place of Irénée—a move Raskob successfully blocked. But Hutton otherwise was right in assuming that Raskob's personal enthusiasm had waned as much as Irénée's. The former Democratic party chieftain's frustrations only deepened on December 27 when he learned that a joint securities account he had maintained with Shouse as a "partnership" to record trading results was to be investigated by the Bureau of Internal Revenue. Not coincidentally, on January 2 he wrote a complaint to the DNC that he was still paying interest on $50,000 he had borrowed and loaned to the party and demanded an immediate partial settlement and a payment of the remaining balance by March 1. Like Irénée, however, Raskob also chose to leave his troubles behind by departing the country, in his case on a four-month world cruise scheduled to start on January 10. Having been appointed at the White Sulphur Springs gathering to a National Business Conference Committee, he nonetheless resigned it on January 3 and took an extended leave of absence from the Business Advisory Council as well.[50] Less than half-a-year old, the du Ponts' Liberty League still was lurching from crisis to crisis, impoverished and lacking an effective leadership.

chapter 10

Disintegration and Rebirth

On January 7, 1935, without the vacationing Irénée du Pont, the Liberty League's executive committee met to approve platform and organizational proposals for the coming year. The fifteen-member panel had constructed a better geographic balance of representation, although despite the November efforts no one from the West Coast had as yet been enlisted. But despite the bravado that the executive committee alone represented some "thirty-seven million dollars" of clout, the Liberty League was in financial trouble. Two of the organization's three main fundraisers, Irénée and Raskob, had suspended their efforts and left the country, and the third, E. F. Hutton, increasingly was frustrated at being left to bear the burden alone.[1]

The League's haplessness, in fact, encouraged backbiting from within over both platform and leadership. J. Howard Pew, a doctrinaire free-market conservative, demanded that the League support vigorous anti-trust and pro-competition planks as well as reduced government spending, a viewpoint the du Ponts could not endorse. John W. Davis, upon receiving a copy of Jouett Shouse's new booklet *You Are the Government* on January 3, pondered aloud, "Sometimes I wonder if we are aggressive enough." Three days after the executive committee session, Samuel Harden Church, an expert on political trial balloons, expressed to H. B. Rust, "I am somewhat afraid that the prospect of the League was launched at an inopportune time in coming before the public." Noting that the congressional elections had "discredited" the League "to a certain extent," Church grudgingly gave praise to the enemy, claiming, "Mr. Roosevelt is like Jack Dempsey when Dempsey was at his best." He expressed hope, however, that the President's political clout would erode due to his "spreading it over too wide a base." Despite the bickering, E. F. Hutton's private suggestion that

Al Smith take over as chairman of the executive committee was blocked by Irénée's defenders, and the panel adopted the idea of a five-member "administrative committee" to carry out weekly policymaking duties in lieu of more frequent executive committee meetings.[2]

If the Liberty League scarcely was ready for a tangle with Roosevelt the political heavyweight, the President himself seemed nearly as pacifistic. Congressional liberals deemed his 1935 legislative recommendations mild, even "Tory," with the notable exception of a call for a $4.8 billion emergency appropriation for work relief. Prodded by a Cabinet-level committee on "economic security" chaired by Labor Secretary Perkins, Roosevelt did call for old-age and survivors pensions and unemployment insurance, but the administration bill lacked minimum national standards and allowed the states enormous latitude in setting the scope and level of benefits. Even Roosevelt's work relief bill entailed payment by the government of "security wages" far below prevailing rates for similar jobs in private industry. He also asked Congress for a two-year extension of the NRA, with greater emphasis to be placed on collective bargaining enforcement, workplace conditions, and "fair competition" compliance. Other administration proposals called for amendments to the Agricultural Adjustment Act (AAA) designed to increase executive powers over production levels. The President's tone, however, was restrained, even conciliatory, rather than confrontational.[3]

Following the President's message, the Liberty League's administrative committee, consisting of Shouse, Chester, Sabin, and Smith (with Irénée, the fifth member, still absent), and New York office manager Henry DuBois acting as secretary, on January 11 held the first of what became a regular pattern of Thursday morning meetings. In a procedure that would be followed dozens of times over the next two years, the members received typed proposals for their consideration, revision, and public release as pamphlets a week or so later. Besides pamphlets on New Deal measures prepared by the research department, the speeches given by prominent Leaguers (sometimes aired over radio, given the networks' occasional willingness to provide free air time) were often reprinted for popular distribution as well. Once the committee decided in its initial gathering to focus exclusively on national, or "interstate," policies with constitutional implications, a staccato of anti–New Deal criticisms emanated from the League's Washington office. The committee approved release of the League's policy platform, followed by pamphlets attacking the administration's budget proposal, advocating a more limited NRA extension, and assailing the relief bill. Pointedly ignored in the League's analyses of the constitutional implications of pending legislation, however, were opportunities to show sympathy for individual liberties other than property rights. Despite entreaties from black conservative Joseph V. Baker of Philadelphia, for example, the League refused public comment on the proposed Costigan-Wagner anti-lynching measure.[4]

The League's decision to file year-end financial disclosure reports with the House of Representatives resulted in additional public attention being placed on the heavy financial contributions of the du Ponts. The outcry generated by the disclosures led an otherwise sympathetic Frank Kent of the Baltimore *Sun* to castigate the group anew for its "ineptitude." Hoping to counter such criticisms of its effectiveness, the League's Washington office made sure that its attack on the budget was in the hands of every member of Congress by mid-January. The League scored the administration for a return to unacceptably high levels of regular expenditures, a $2.5 billion increase in the national debt, and dangerously large pools of discretionary public funds for works projects. A week later the NRA and the Emergency Relief Appropriation bill received the same treatment. Pamphlet authors recommended limiting the NRA's renewal to one year and rewriting section 7a of the original NIRA to permit minority plant representation and the open shop. In its attack on the relief bill, the League maintained that such granting of direct discretionary authority over funds to the executive branch represented an unconstitutional delegation of legislative authority, one which could be used as a demagogic political weapon, and invited both a larger federal bureaucracy and a planned economy in place of "the economy of nature and the plan of 'Nature's God.' "[5]

Concerns expressed by the du Ponts and their supporters over a major new expansion of federal relief efforts were far from merely theoretical or ideological. Pierre du Pont had personally served on the board of directors of a private corporation, the Relief Commission, Inc., of Wilmington, which had made decisions regarding allocation of state relief and FERA moneys in Delaware. Although the state's contributions had been exhausted by the end of January, and the state projected a budget shortfall of almost a million dollars for 1935, Pierre did not welcome the Roosevelt proposal, for it carried with it both greater federal spending *and* greater federal administrative and distributive control. Besides the dangers to private "initiative" posed by increased assistance, Pierre opposed relinquishing control of relief to a partisan, patronage-dealing bureaucracy outside his influence. For similar reasons, and facing likely court challenges of the legality of a private corporation dispensing public funds, Governor Buck, a du Pont relative, reconstituted the private entity under public charter in early February, renamed it the Temporary Emergency Relief Commission of New Castle County, and reappointed Pierre to its board of directors.[6]

Even with the launching of the "war of words" against the ongoing New Deal in early 1935, the League continued to flounder. Backbiting continued, much of it directed at Irénée and Raskob by other prominent members on the grounds they were not "pulling their weight." E. F. Hutton, having already addressed Macon businessmen on January 18 and scheduled for early February trips to Columbia, South Carolina, and Memphis, Tennessee, pointedly wrote to Irénée, "We've all got to keep on the job, because the man who has 'the dog by the tail' so to speak [Raskob], has scooted off for four months' rest." He lamented, "We can't get very far passing the buck with the Liberty League." After the death of his daughter Inez Yvonne of pneumonia on January 28, it seemed even less likely that Raskob would cut short his restorative cruise to face the sea of troubles, including those of the League, that awaited him at home.[7]

Even without active leadership by Irénée and Raskob, the propaganda mills of the Washington office continued to turn. With hearings commencing in both the House Ways and Means Committee and the Senate Finance Committee on Senator Robert Wagner and Congressman Robert Doughton's omnibus "social security" bill, on February 4 the League issued *Economic Security*. The pamphlet urged separation of unemployment insurance from the "nonemergency" provisions of old-age pensions and caution toward implementing either. On the same day, Jouett Shouse addressed the Philadelphia County League of Women Voters and an NBC radio audience on "Democracy or Bureaucracy," again attacking the administration's relief proposal. Over the written objections of Irénée (indicating the real danger of his losing control because of his distance from the organization), who did not believe that the issue raised constitutional objections, the administrative committee approved a pamphlet attacking legislation regarding the veterans' bonus. And on February 25, while commending Roosevelt for not having used discretionary powers granted him by Congress to further inflate the currency, the League warned about the dangers of such powers, and of price inflation, in yet another brochure.[8]

Despite these efforts, however, it was not the Liberty League but another conservative organization, the Sentinels of the Republic, that actually claimed an early policy victory. The Sentinels, sporting the motto, "Every citizen a Sentinel! Every home a sentry box!" had originated after World War I as an anti-radical, anti-statist organization. It had fought the Child Labor Amendment, the Sheppard-Towner Maternity Act, and a proposed federal Department of Education, and had amassed a card index fingering some 2000 so-called radicals. At the beginning of 1935, Raymond Pitcairn of the Pittsburgh Plate Glass Company revived the cause, with tax legislation his new special target. In the federal tax measure passed in 1934, which modestly boosted estate taxes and abolished consolidated returns, "pink-slip" provisions opened up income tax information and corporate salary figures to public inspection and exposure. Claiming that such features were a violation of constitutional rights, the Sentinels launched an intensive lobbying campaign to repeal the "pink-slip." Pitcairn, seeking the du Ponts' cooperation in the cause, wrote Irénée and Pierre in early February to blast the "New Inquisition." Pierre and Irénée both agreed to "talk up" the Sentinels movement, but they refused to commit themselves or the League as yet to the "broader question" raised by Pitcairn's solicitation—the repeal of the Sixteenth Amendment. To the surprise of the du Ponts and others, the Sentinels achieved the repeal of the "pink-slip" provisions within weeks.[9]

For its part, the League was still stubbornly trying to lay the groundwork for a national movement. The Washington office announced the formation of college chapters on the campuses of Northwestern University, the University of Nebraska, Princeton University, the University of Wisconsin, and Yale. But the financial recruitment effort abruptly collapsed with E. F. Hutton's decision of February 18, prompted by his growing frustration and the illness of his wife, to abandon fundraising in favor of a lengthy stay in Arizona. At once Pierre arranged for William Stayton to summon Irénée, who had not intended to return until March. Irénée's return temporarily bolstered his elder brother's spirits but did little to calm his own angry, frustrated mood. In his delayed response to Frank Kent's earlier criticism of the League's efforts, he lambasted the New Deal as "a bare-faced redistribution of wealth by Robin Hood methods." Pierre questioned his own previous advice to Shouse in urging that the League's public attacks focus on the relief bill, observing, "Perhaps I have been mistaken in my suggestions as to the attack on the plan of placing large amounts of money in the hands of the President for expenditures without restriction." Citing also an unsuccessful effort to prod greater contributions from Alfred Sloan and other GM associates, Pierre optimistically opined that at least "the flare-up over the political associations of the League has subsided and will not become prominent."[10]

Pierre's prediction soon proved very wrong. On February 15, the MacCormack-Dickstein committee presented its final report on the "Legion plot" to the House of Representatives. The panel noted that while "evidence was obtained showing that certain persons had made an attempt to establish a fascist organization in this country," and that "there is no question but that these attempts were discussed, were planned, and might have been placed in execution when and if the financial backers deemed it expedient," certain "immaterial and incompetent evidence" against a number of prominent individuals had been omitted from the report. In reaction, General Butler, who already had begun issuing broadsides against the munitions industry via Philadelphia radio station WCAU, charged the committee with a whitewash. According to Butler, the report's omissions included his remark following his reference to the conversation with MacGuire in August 1934, "In about two weeks the American Liberty League appeared, which was just about what he [MacGuire] described." Also withheld was reporter French's testimony that MacGuire had indicated financial backing for the coup from League member John W. Davis. Butler called upon the committee to explain why the "big shots" had not been called upon to testify, including Grayson Murphy, Al Smith, Douglas MacArthur, and Hanford MacNider. Representative Dickstein, replying to Butler's charges in a subsequent radio broadcast, defended the panel's decision to protect the reputations of individuals by claiming that the additional charges were "wholly without consequence" and unsupported by corroborating evidence.[11]

Despite Dickstein's rebuttal, the damage to the League had been done by Butler's charges. Trying to reenlist Hutton to the cause, Irénée admitted, "I think we were all misled in thinking how easy it would be." Hutton's reply was at least partially encouraging, for interspersed with blasts at new schemes by FDR advisor Rexford Tugwell as the worst of "Russia and Italy combined" was the willingness to "stage a Paul Revere with you in any part of the country." He continued to criticize Raskob's "cold feet," however, and, referring to Al Smith's limited public promotion of the League to a single New York radio address, added, "I think the population of New York is about seven-and-a-half millions, and Al Smith can not talk to all of them at once." Urging the former governor to take a more vigorous role, he prodded, "Tell him [Smith] to forget the past and read the Hearst editorials." An appeal by Irénée to journalist Frank Kent to join the League was rejected, however, with Kent indicating similar responses to earlier solicitations from the National Economy League and the Crusaders. Adding to Irénée's woes was the growing impression that Stayton's double duties in the Delaware and national offices were hampering both causes. On February 20 Irénée privately indicated to Jouett Shouse that Stayton would be asked to resign his state position. By month's end the national office faced $8000 in unpaid bills, with no money in hand, a monthly payroll to meet, and a reliable weekly income of only $500. Irénée was forced to deposit $20,000 more of his own money in Bankers Trust Company, with the same amount then borrowed from the bank by the Liberty League.[12]

Despite the money problem, the League's printing presses continued to turn. Although president Shouse still insisted, "We are neither for nor against the administration," and claimed, "we shall support it when we can," more attacks on pending legislation followed. Next on the League's "hit list" were the thirty-hour week bill, sponsored by Senator Hugo Black of Alabama; the Public Utilities Holding Company Act, also known as the Wheeler-Rayburn bill because of its chief sponsors, Senate insurgent Burton K. Wheeler of Montana and Representative Sam Rayburn of Texas; and the Banking Act of 1935, which sought to further centralize "open market" control in the hands of the President's appointees on the Federal Reserve Board in Washington, D.C. According to the League's penmen, the banking bill would throw open the nation's monetary policy to the "whims of political influence" and likely produce "disastrous inflation." Hugo Black's bill once again was hammered as an unconstitutional control of intrastate firms. As for the Wheeler-Rayburn measure, which sought to empower the SEC to dissolve utility holding companies unable to provide economic justification for their existence, Pierre du Pont personally collected opinion from Philadelphia utility magnate John Zimmerman on the legislation's constitutionality, as did Jouett Shouse with H. B. Rust and James Wadsworth. Publicly the League scored the measure as a "calamitous blow" if enacted. But despite the public attacks, and a letter from Irénée to Senator John Townsend of Delaware, the utility measure passed the Senate on March 15 anyway. Similar appeals by Irénée to Representative Howard Smith of Virginia to head off the administration's work relief bill also failed.[13]

Rather than such defeats immediately pulling more conservative opponents of the New Deal together behind the League's efforts, the result instead was additional internal bickering and declining morale. H. B. Rust informed Irénée that conservative stalwart J. Howard Pew, among others, was becoming increasingly discouraged. Irénée's own combative reaction was to prod Shouse to quit having the League apologize for its political motives and stop denying that it was a "smear Roosevelt" cause. Angered previously by Shouse's release of a pamphlet criticizing the bonus bill on the instructions of the administrative committee over his objections, Irénée urged that henceforth all drafts be reviewed by the entire executive committee rather than just the smaller panel, an idea colleagues quickly rejected. From Chicago, Sewell Avery reported that confidence in both the League and the Crusaders was at a low ebb. George May, an official of both the Du Pont Company and Delaware Liberty League, cited his dissatisfaction at the organization's inability to reach the "rank and file." As May's comment suggested, general membership solicitation was going as badly as fundraising. By March 12, only Delaware and Pennsylvania claimed complete state chapters. The national organization also was still seven major contributors short of the original goal of forty $25,000 pledge underwriters.[14]

Despite the disappointments, the du Ponts still drew sharp lines in the dirt on the subject of consolidation with other conservative political entities. The refusal to merge reflected their longstanding fear of losing organizational control within a larger, overarching coalition, and it also suggested their persistent distaste for intense political involvement with those considered social unequals. As one example, the du Ponts accepted the Sentinels' Raymond Pitcairn as a one-time contributor to the League, but not as a long-term underwriter in spite of the League's financial difficulties. Similar considerations finally convinced Irénée to abandon the idea of formal cooperation between the League and the Ku Klux Klan. Nonetheless, in noting to Jouett Shouse the Klan's anti–New Deal efforts, including a folder of attached printed materials, Irénée labelled them "very good" and sardonically observed, "It is strange what 'bed fellows' politics make." No similar social qualms applied to the members of the Morgan financial empire. On March 12, Irénée wrote George Whitney requesting the "house of Morgan's" help in underwriting the League. This time, however, it was he who was rebuffed. Even the attempt by Stayton to secure Du Pont Company stockholders' and employee lists from president Lammot was rejected on company policy grounds, although Lammot advised him to obtain the same information through public channels. Jouett Shouse's proposal for a Kiplinger-style newsletter to members similarly had to be tabled. Additionally, Irénée called upon him by month's end to modify the original subscription agreement downward to the already-pledged level of $837,500, so that redemption solicitations could begin to defray the League's first half-year's operating expenses of almost $160,000.[15]

Irénée's return from Cuba in mid-February and his resumption of active leadership once more put him on the League's "hot seat." Executive committee members and contributors alike expected quick results, and he became the target of unsolicited advice at the very time he renewed efforts to place his personal imprint more fully upon the organization. To Earl Babst, the chairman of the American Sugar Refining Company, he reiterated his determination to halt the slide toward "socialism, or perhaps more properly, national capitalism." On occasion he let slip his dissatisfaction with Shouse's Washington lobby operation. John Zimmerman's letter criticizing Shouse and James Beck, while praising Al Smith, brought the less-than-ringing endorsement from Irénée for Shouse that "No one else suggested a better man for the purpose, hence he was elected." Irénée did caution against public airing of the League's internal strife. "I think we'd better hang together rather than be hung separately," he observed, paraphrasing Benjamin Franklin. "Won't you join in the hanging?" Having offered his colleague the advice to hang tough, however, he disregarded his own counsel and returned to Cuba on March 30.[16]

Conservative morale continued to plummet with the signing of the $4.8 billion work relief bill on April 8, which gave Roosevelt even more discretionary spending and wage-setting authority. Liberty League pamphlets blasted the NRA's price-control powers and condemned the relief measure as an abdication of Congress's "proper responsibility." But the attention of the du Ponts, and of the business community generally, now shifted to Senator Robert Wagner's labor relations bill. Wagner's proposal called for the creation of a permanent National Labor Relations Board with the power to conduct labor representation elections and restrain business from such "unfair labor practices" as favoritism toward company unions or firing of union employees. Even before the onset of the 1935 congressional session, the Special Conference Committee had seen in the creation of a temporary NLRB the previous June an omen of new efforts to attack management's traditional prerogatives. Alarm had persisted despite the agency's impotence in the face of resistance from the Justice Department and the NRA. Owing in part to the absence of effective means of resolving disputes, in late 1934 a series of violent strikes over collective bargaining rights had flared up in San Francisco; Butte, Montana; Milwaukee; Indianapolis; Toledo; and New York City. On February 21 Wagner introduced his measure, featuring a three-person

NLRB which would serve, in his words, as a "Supreme Court" of labor relations.[17]

The main public assault on the Wagner bill was led not by the League, but by NAM president James Emery and U.S. Chamber of Commerce head Henry I. Harriman. Behind the scenes, however, Pierre du Pont pressed for the validation of company employer associations, minority bargaining representation, and the open shop and demanded that unions, like businesses, be required to comply with financial disclosure statutes. He further urged that unions be required to allow their members to vote on collective bargaining proposals and on the decision to strike before being led out by their officers. The Liberty League issued a pamphlet echoing Pierre's views in mid-April, and it referred to the NLRB measure as one "which would do violence to the Constitution, stimulate industrial strife, and give one labor organization a monopoly in the representation of workers without regard to the wishes of the latter." Despite the President's lukewarm support for the bill, the League also charged that a presidential signature of the measure would be a corrupt payback for the approximately $6,000,000 received by the Democrats from John L. Lewis's United Mine Workers.[18]

Other Liberty League attacks on pending legislation showed off the organization's fledgling "brain trust" of conservative academics. Neil Carouthers of the Lehigh School of Business Administration attacked what he called "government by experiment" over the NBC Red Network on April 17. According to Carouthers, the Depression represented but a healthy economic cathartic that was eliminating "poisons," and the New Deal, by threatening to interrupt it unnaturally, merely was extending public misery. Yale political scientist Ray Bert Westerfield explained "How Inflation Affects the Average Family" on the same network the next evening, and on the twenty-sixth Walter Spahr of New York University employed the Blue Network to blast "political banking" as a step "toward a thorough socialization of our major economic institutions." In *The AAA Amendments* the League charged the administration with a "trend toward a Fascist control not only of agriculture but also of a major sector of manufacturing and distributing industries." If Leaguers seemed confused as to whether the New Deal was socialistic or fascistic, or both, they did agree with E. T. Weir's charge of April 30 before the University Club of Chicago that the administration had incited class hatred by characterizing businessmen as "selfish obstructionists" to the New Deal's "self-proclaimed multitudinous, altruistic, and celestial plans."[19]

The League's resources, however, were once more at the point of exhaustion at the very time when the legislative danger was greatest. By mid-April E. F. Hutton, who had already been talked out of an "early retirement" from the struggle once by Irénée, now threatened again to quit. William Stayton reported to Pierre that GM executives were bailing out from their subscription commitments. Citing Raskob's earlier plans not to return to the United States until May 20, he pleaded with his mentor to take charge of the organization by attending the April 29 executive committee session. A panicked Pierre hurried a telegram to the absent Raskob on the fifteenth, stating bluntly: RECOMMEND YOU AND IRENEE MEET WITH LEAGUE COMMITTEE EARLYST [*sic*] POSSIBLE DATE. AFFAIRS IN BAD SHAPE—DISSOLUTION THREAT-ENED. The telegram failed to connect with the transitory Raskob, but a longer letter, which described the situation as "at sixes and sevens," did finally reach him when his cruise vessel docked in Honolulu. To both of his colleagues Pierre related the GM news, Pauline Sabin's failures with the Women's Division, Shouse's purported lack of di-rection, and his desperate bailout action with Lammot in advanc-ing portions of their subscription pledges as immediate operating cash.[20]

Once the two men rushed back to their posts, they were informed by Hutton that his services to the League had ended. A disheartened Raskob also seemed more than ready to wash his hands of the effort. In a confidential, retrospective letter to Pierre, he admitted, "It's hard to know what to do about the Liberty League." He recalled that the banking group, "consisting of men close to our crowd," the previous summer "had started a similar movement through the Crusaders which they felt should be merged with our effort. This was done." Nonethe-less, the League had continued to run into difficulties in obtaining sufficient financial support from the same interests. As Raskob saw it, either the League's enlistees had not yet become sufficiently alarmed at the New Deal to dig deeply into their pockets, or else they had counted upon being able to "secure a free ride much as they did with you [Pierre]" in the prohibition repeal fight. Another possibility, he added, was that potential benefactors outside the du Ponts' immediate circle had been intimidated by the fear of retaliation. Irénée, for ex-ample, cited sugar executive Babst's fear of political revenge in the form of White House manipulation of import tariff quotas.[21]

Despite the gloomy outlook for the League, and the continuing costs of duplication of effort, the du Ponts nonetheless continued to reject the alternative of consolidation with other anti–New Deal organiza-tions. On the advice of Du Pont Company executives George Patterson and Ruly Carpenter, Irénée ruled out merger with either the American Legion or the Ku Klux Klan. Total merger with the Crusaders (who were employing the voice of Dr. Preston Bradley to assail New Deal legislation over the radio thrice-weekly) was similarly deemed unwise. The du Ponts grudgingly did concur to reconsider closer coordination of the League's propaganda and lobbying activities with the ultra-conservative Sentinels, National Economy League, Builders of the Republic, and a "sound money" committee headed by Princeton economist Edwin W. Kemmerer. Raymond Pitcairn of the Sentinels, wanting more, urged Pierre a week-and-a-half later to accept "group action, such as we secured in the Anti-Prohibition fight through the United Repeal Council." No such single umbrella organization, however, was forthcoming.[22]

One limited source of consolation for the du Ponts was the fact that Franklin Roosevelt was experiencing his own political troubles. Through the early weeks of the congressional session liberal Democrats and insurgents complained about the President's lethargy in fighting for his own proposals, much less those of Black and Wagner. The national economy stood on a discouraging plateau, with joblessness still hovering at close to 20 percent. Democratic political operatives around the country were registering a rising groundswell of discontent from marginal farmers, blue-collar workers, the indigent, the elderly, and the unemployed. Of a spate of popular rabble-rousers that included Upton Sinclair, Charles Coughlin, and Eugene Talmadge of Georgia, the White House most feared Senator Huey Long, the Louisiana "Kingfish" whose Share Our Wealth crusade had swollen in a matter of months from several thousand to several million. Secret polls taken by the DNC in the spring of 1935 showed the President's popularity at its lowest ebb since taking office.[23]

April's end also saw organized business formally declare political war on the Roosevelt administration. At its national convention in Washington, D.C., the U.S. Chamber of Commerce featured spokesman after spokesman in a series of denunciations of New Deal relief, labor, and fiscal policies. The Liberty League's propaganda assault now blasted the Guffey coal conservation bill, a "little NRA" measure creating a codemaking commission for the bituminous coal industry with excise-tax rebate powers of enforcement, as an unconstitutional extension of federal power, a "program of government ownership," and an arbitrary and capricious infringement on the liberties of producers and employees. Behind the scenes, William Stayton was urging his mentors to undertake a far bolder reorientation of the League's mission. Expecting amid the organization's chaos that Pierre would personally take over the League, Stayton lobbied him to lead it toward a long-term effort to modify or repeal the Sixteenth Amendment. According to the aged veteran of the repeal fight, the "primary evils" of Roosevelt's policies were economic—for him the constitutional issues were only secondary—and were based fundamentally upon expanded notions of the federal tax power.[24]

For the shorter term, Stayton lent his voice to the calls of several corporation lawyers within the League that the organization assume a new role as a pro-business battler in the courts. He urged that the group continue its lobbying against "unconstitutional" legislation, but that it also take the position that anti–New Deal rulings in lower federal courts were binding. The League also should, Stayton maintained, involve itself in litigation and, when appropriate, use legal opinions as campaign information against pro–New Deal legislators. He further suggested to Pierre that in order to counter the AFL as a voice of labor, the League immediately should recruit a labor arm from company unions such as that of Weirton Steel. Pierre took Stayton's advice to Jouett Shouse, who, backed by publicity chief William Murphy, endorsed only the idea that the League should interest itself in court litigation. He cautioned, however, that they should not "set ourselves up as oracles."[25]

In their previous political sparring, Franklin Roosevelt and the du Ponts had found their respective fighting energies wax and wane as if in concert. It was now the du Ponts, feeding off the new public militancy of the New Deal's other organized business foes, whose turn it was to revive first. By early May, despite the reversals of such early subscribers as Hal Roach, the du Ponts' additional investments were accompanied by the return of Irénée to active leadership, the new involvement of Pierre, and renewed pleas for outside assistance to enable the League to secure its $1 million subscription target. The selection of Louis A. Drexler as Delaware's new League president finally freed up Stayton for full-time duty in the Washington office, where he could serve as Pierre's personal eyes and ears. Pauline Sabin's Women's Division, which had only proved a financial millstone, mercifully closed its doors on May 1. In order to secure greater financial cooperation from the house of Morgan and its Wall Street allies, and to free up Irénée from extensive moneyraising duties, Grayson Murphy, despite his prominence in "Legion plot" accusations, was named to the executive committee as the organization's new treasurer. Irénée now accepted the call as the executive committee's active chairman.

And, finally addressing the logistical difficulties of coordinating meetings of twenty or more individuals scattered around the country, at Irénée's urgings the full committee agreed to meet only once monthly on a fixed date, indirectly giving the administrative committee an even freer hand in management.[26]

The belated managerial reforms and financial streamlining revived the du Ponts' spirits and ended their talk of winding down the League. Instead, plans accelerated for a mid-June "coming-out" rally of the reinvigorated cause at a joint gathering of the executive committee and the now approximately 150-member advisory committee in Chicago. At the executive committee's May 7 session, the place and time for the rally were set for the Drake Hotel on June 14. Pierre directly participated in the meeting, substituting for Irénée because of his brother's speaking engagement in Dearborn, Michigan. The younger du Pont's time was not wasted, for before his hosts, the Fords, he took the opportunity to blast "the demagogue's hypocritical cry of 'divide the wealth.' " Chicago attorney Ralph Shaw arranged meetings between Colonel Robert McCormick of the Chicago *Tribune* and Stayton, Murphy, Irénée, and Sewell Avery for May 15 to make additional preparations. James Wadsworth, eagerly anticipating the public event, expressed the sentiments of most in the League when he declared, "I think our League prospects are improving. But I do wish we'd stage a public meeting *somewhere!* We need some dramatizing and publicity. This is a fight!"[27]

The du Ponts were now fully aware that they were engaged in a political fight to the death with Franklin Roosevelt. The intensity of their rhetoric and actions showed it. Pierre displayed his Social Darwinist views of leadership to Amos Pinchot, declaring that "the one fundamental advantage in America in the business world is the determination to let the best man win." Referring to the New Deal's partisan bureaucrats, he insisted, "I can see no reason why men without experience and in a large measure self-appointed or appointed by their ability to talk should be more successful or more reliable." Sentiment within the League for a lawyer's committee to examine New Deal enactments and publish opposition briefs grew stronger after the Supreme Court on May 6 declared the Railroad Retirement Act unconstitutional. Irénée concurred with Du Pont Company executive A. B. Echols on the desirability of such a lawyer's panel launching a court test of the WPA's "four-billion-dollar slush fund." He counseled against action until at least the end of the congressional session, however, citing the danger that the legislators might enact something even worse. Jouett Shouse advised Irénée that the Supreme Court would not entertain a taxpayers' suit. Borrowing from Stayton, however, he did suggest prompting the family's congressional allies to propose a bill making the declaratory judgments of lower federal courts against New Deal measures binding until and unless they were reversed by the Supreme Court.[28]

The Liberty League's propaganda initiatives showed signs of reinvigoration and renewed militancy. Irénée greeted enthusiastically a suggestion of University of Virginia dean Charles G. Maphis that the Liberty League participate in a public "round table" forum on New Deal economic policies. Advised of the $700 price tag for involvement in the encounter, he deemed it a "wise expenditure." Leaguers G. W. Dyer on CBS and Raoul Desvernine on NBC respectively attacked AAA "regimentation" of farmers and general New Deal constitutional violations. A League document of May 13 referred to a substitute NRA bill authored by Senator Bennett Champ Clark which provided only a ten-month renewal as "a recommendation for action to relieve American business from a quicksand of bureaucracy and visionary experimentation." The Clark bill, which also exempted intrastate business from codes and barred price-fixing arrangements except in mineral resource industries, already had been approved by the Senate Finance Committee. On the fourteenth it was endorsed by the full Senate without even a roll call. Two days later League writers blasted the Bankhead farmers' home bill, labelling it an "exercise in socialism" that would cost additional billions, "encourage farmers to contract debts without improving their ability to pay them," subsidize "a particular class of citizens," and encourage "scandal and political favoritism." With some reluctance the League did praise the President's May 22 veto of the Patman veterans' bonus bill. Individual du Ponts, including Pierre but not Irénée, even sent personal congratulations to Roosevelt, which led him to return to Pierre that he had been "particularly gratified to know that you approve the message." But the League immediately returned to the attack with a May 26 pamphlet scoring the TVA as an assault on private enterprise and "a vast experiment in State Socialism."[29]

Given Pierre's experiences in the NRA's National Labor Board, however, the threats posed by the TVA and other measures paled in comparison to those of the Wagner bill before Congress. Already the Special Conference Committee, a third of it representing du Pont interests, had plotted a joint strategy of "information" dissemination to workers intended to head off anticipated union drives. Both Du Pont and General Motors had carried the action through. The Wagner measures had been reported out of the Senate Labor Committee on May 2, and floor debate commenced on the fifteenth. To the further dismay of the du Ponts, Roosevelt refused to intervene to block Senate passage, which followed the next day on a vote of 63 to 12. Four days after that, the House Labor Committee favorably reported the bill to its colleagues, and on May 24 Roosevelt finally endorsed the legislation publicly. A nervous Pierre relayed to the NLRB's Jacob Billikopf his total and unyielding opposition to "forced unionism and denial of right of representation to the individual or to minority groups."[30]

On May 27, the du Ponts finally had reason for celebration. In a case known as the Schechter Brothers poultry, or "sick chicken," decision, the U.S. Supreme Court declared the code enforcement provisions of the National Industrial Recovery Act unconstitutional. Doubling the pleasure was a second decision the same day striking down the Frazier-Lemke Farm Mortgage Act. League spokesman Jouett Shouse hurriedly included references to the high court's actions in his remarks the next day to a Charlotte, North Carolina, audience. A more vigorous exploitation of the news awaited the President's public reaction to the decisions on May 31. In a press conference that extended to an hour-and-a-half, Roosevelt condemned the "horse-and-buggy"-era reasoning of the justices and labelled the pending Wagner Act "must" legislation. A startled but delighted Washington staff of the Liberty League rushed to redraft its planned June 1 press release with the intention of defending the Supreme Court and lampooning the President's statement. Radio companies eager for a conservative response to Roosevelt extended free air time on the twin subjects of the rulings and the presidential reaction. At Irénée's lobbying, former Senator Thomas F. Bayard of Delaware was sounded out, but he declined, recommending that the League reprint the insurgent but anti-NRA Senator William E. Borah's June 2 speech, entitled "How to Meet the Issue." Irénée reluctantly agreed, for while he was hardly an admirer of the Idaho legislator, he conceded that Borah was occasionally "right" on an issue, while Roosevelt "never was."[31]

If Pierre's chief legislative symbol of the New Deal's evils, among many candidates, was the Wagner labor bill, for Irénée it was still the relief spending of the administration. Reasserting his personal control over League policy, Irénée vetoed a more general attack on "inflationary trends" authored in pamphlet form by Shouse, asking "What is unconstitutional with this?" Personally appearing before the Delaware Liberty League's executive committee, he recommended, and the

panel concurred, that a petition be sent to Governor Buck both protesting the constitutionality of the federal relief appropriation and
charging that because of political manipulation the state was not receiving its fair share of the federal moneys. Irénée's plan was to use
the Delaware petition to pressure the national organization into adopting a similar stance. Since the League required that state policy positions harmonize with those of the national organization, Irénée's
action insured that the anti-relief petition would be taken up by the
executive committee, probably at the Chicago meetings.[32]

Although he could not personally attend the Chicago rally, Pierre
also sought to set the policy tone of the meetings by circulating com-
parisons of the 1912 Socialist Party platform of Eugene Debs and the
Roosevelt record. By early June the administrative committee's composition had also shifted slightly, with Nathan Miller's replacement
by Colby Chester and the addition of Stayton. When the officers gathered at the Drake Hotel, the main products of their deliberations were
the formal unveilings of a new membership effort, headed by a National
Recruiting Committee and local Voluntary Recruiting Committees,
and, more significantly, a legal auxiliary called the National Lawyers'
Committee. In keeping with the earlier discussions of the idea, and
emboldened by the recent Supreme Court actions, Jouett Shouse announced that the new committee would examine the constitutional
standing of New Deal legislation and "contribute its services," in the
form of legal briefs and counsel, to test cases. The panel consisted of
some fifty-seven prominent attorneys, most from corporation firms,
and was chaired by League activist Raoul Desvernine.[33]

As the Chicago announcements suggested, the Liberty League was
determined to redouble its membership recruitment, especially of corporate stockholders. Unfortunately, the new effort smacked of the same
misguided notion as the initial League's plans for property divisions.
The push aimed at creating a variant of a security-holders division by
recruiting stockholders, savings depositors, and life insurance policyholders. But once more, major companies balked at providing lists of
names. Even Pierre, although he was a director in the Pennsylvania
Railroad, could not obtain or copy its stockowner roll of some 233,000
names. Ralph Shaw complained that corporate executives in Chicago
were equally uncooperative. With the League unable to do the job
itself, Irénée urged the Committee for the Nation, through its leader
J. H. Read, Jr., to help "stop the move toward the left" by generating
a "ground swell of public opinion." Jouett Shouse, pointing to a recent
scandal in which Western Union had been sued for $3 million over a

similar scheme that turned out to be fraudulent, shot down an alternative suggestion of John Raskob's for a chain-letter solicitation.[34]

With the Liberty League having renewed its energies and prepared for extended warfare with the administration in early May, the White House belatedly mobilized for battle almost a month later. Galvanized into action by the Schechter decision, Roosevelt and his advisors plunged enthusiastically into the legislative offensive for "little NRAs," utility holding company laws, the Wagner measure, and, a special blow at the business opposition, a new tax bill. The new tax offensive found ready allies among senatorial progressives such as James Couzens and Robert La Follette, Jr., who had pushed it as the focal point of a highly symbolic "anti-superrich" program. On June 19, Roosevelt publicly joined the tax insurgents, shifting from support of a more modest measure to another, crafted by Felix Frankfurter, that called for increased tax liabilities for those with incomes over $50,000.[35]

As later scholars have noted, the tax measure was far more sound than fury. When eventually enacted, it actually raised but an additional $45 million as a result of the upper-bracket change, and only $250 million overall. In the three years that followed its passage, only John D. Rockefeller failed to avoid becoming subject to its higher rates. But regardless of its later "toothlessness," businessmen generally and the Liberty League in particular responded immediately to the President's tax message as if they had been mortally wounded. As historian Mark Leff has explained the tax fight in the context of the entire congressional session, "Prior to mid-1935, businessmen saw themselves as defending their prerogatives to define the government's proper role. Now their concern went deeper: that the government would take the lead in imposing an ideology that was decidedly hostile to business." Lawyers' Committee member Ralph Shaw informed Jouett Shouse that the President's remarks of the nineteenth had left him virtually "frothing at the mouth." William Randolph Hearst labelled the proposal "essentially communism" or, more accurately, "demo-communism," a "bastard product of Communism and demagogic democracy." James True, the proto-fascist publisher of *Industrial Control Reports*, injected into his newsletter unsubstantiated rumors of the President's alleged deteriorating mental condition and anti-Semitic references to Frankfurter and White House aides as "that Karl Marx . . . and his legal kikes."[36]

The du Ponts themselves combined personal outrage at Roosevelt with renewed plans to use their fellow businessmen's rising anger to aid their recruitment efforts. As of late June, the Liberty League still claimed but 36,000 members, with less than 10,000 actual financial contributors. Of questionable value was cousin A. Felix du Pont's suggestion to William Stayton that an anti-Roosevelt comic strip, set in a fictitious country, be created and marketed. Attempting to prod American Telephone and Telegraph president Walter S. Gifford to provide a stockholders' list, Irénée claimed that he had disposed of his own AT&T holdings because of "excessive" federal taxes on dividends. Asserting that "the first group of industries to be seized by our Socialistic government would be banks, public service corporations, and means of communication," he said he had opted to sell his stock at a loss "rather than have my interests confiscated." Renewing his entreaties to E. F. Hutton, Irénée laconically predicted, "As I see the New Deal, it is getting more and more underway, and you can probably expect jail sentences before the year is over. The shooting will probably begin next year, when they find that Socialism won't work and want to blame it on somebody." Nonetheless, Hutton held out, as did Alfred Sloan, who still refused to involve GM stockholders on the grounds that the League was a political rather than an economic organization.[37]

The League's published attacks on a range of proposed New Deal measures continued, but the Congress proceeded to approve them anyway. A late June pamphlet lambasted the AAA amendments bill as "new schemes for overcoming laws of nature." Irénée continued to press for an assault of the relief appropriation in the courts, but both Raoul Desvernine and John W. Davis counseled that there was little basis for a constitutional challenge. With the Senate already having passed the Public Utilities Holding Company Act and its "death sentence" provision by a single vote, on July 2 the League blasted it and praised those in the House who voted successfully by a 216-to-146 margin to remove the hated feature. Actually, the House bill was far less than a complete victory for utilities, for it merely shifted the burden of proof from the holding companies, who would have had to justify their existence, to the SEC, now required to defend a dissolution judgment. Wishing to concentrate the League's resources on the lobbying battle, Jouett Shouse brushed aside competing suggestions that a new women's branch be launched. To the du Ponts' great dismay, however, the Wagner Act won final congressional approval on June 27, and the President signed it into law on July 5.[38]

Reeling from another round of policy defeats in Congress, Liberty Leaguers looked with special enthusiasm to taking on the New Dealers directly at the University of Virginia's Institute of Public Affairs Round Table on July 8–13, scheduled to be carried nationally on radio. Once again, Alfred Sloan resisted du Pont entreaties, this time to be a participant in the Virginia debate. Nonetheless, an impressive "brain trust" of critics was collected, including Nicholas Roosevelt of the New York *Herald-Tribune*, Neil Carouthers, J. Howard Pew, Walter Spahr, Raoul Desvernine, William Stayton, James Wadsworth, and journalist Demarest Lloyd. Unfortunately, the League was deprived of a blue-ribbon showdown with the New Deal's best. After Raymond Moley and Internal Revenue commissioner Guy Helvering had already accepted invitations to the debate, the White House, through the DNC's Charles Michelson, passed the word that they should withdraw. As a result a less prominent (and in some cases lukewarm) "second-string" cast of administration defenders was substituted, including Senators Rush Holt of West Virginia and Alben Barkley of Kentucky, Representative Fred Sisson of New York, former NRA administrator Hugh Johnson (who had been deposed the previous September), Mrs. Helen H. Miller of the AAA, and Dr. James Hart of Johns Hopkins University. To no one's surprise, they received an earful from the League-sponsored critics, who charged the New Deal with "meddling with business" (Roosevelt), incorporating a philosophy of "Fabian Socialism" (Lloyd), using the tax power as a "punitive weapon" and "an instrument of social control" (Desvernine), and sponsoring an extension of power over industry and agriculture "which rightfully come within the province of state control" (Wadsworth).[39]

The League's ongoing recruitment and legislative lobbying efforts now showed modest improvement. But in a sign of fatigue and resignation over the legislative session's outcome, on July 15 Jouett Shouse departed Washington for an extended European vacation, leaving daily management to Stayton. Irénée's pleadings to the National Life Insurance Company's Fred Howland to provide lists of policyholders, on the grounds that "90% of the people who have insurance policies are opposed to the New Deal," met an equally discouraging response. Grayson Murphy directed Stayton to appropriate $2000 of League funds to the American Veterans' Association for cooperative recruiting and organizational liaison, but with little if any positive result. Additionally embarrassing to the League's self-appointed lead role in the anti–New Deal effort was the discovery, prompted by a conservative call within the Commerce Department's Business Advisory Council for mass resignations in protest of administration policies (which resulted in the retirements of six members, including Winthrop Aldrich of Chase National Bank and prominent Crusader James F. Bell of General Mills), that Pierre du Pont's name still appeared on BAC official lists as a member and, therefore, as a part of the Roosevelt administration. Pointedly reminded of the fact by H. B. Rust, Pierre, who had not been active in the council for a year, still took no immediate action. A month later, he instead belatedly proposed the complete dismantling of the BAC because of the President's refusal to publish its various dissents from administration policy.[40]

Irénée, grasping at straws, recommended creation of a radio program, to be based on the model of an NBC skit on the Supreme Court which had been aired after the Schechter decision. Liberty League pamphlets prepared before Shouse's departure attacked "expanding bureaucracy," "lawmaking by executive order," and the subversive constitutional effects of New Deal laws as cited in federal court decisions. In response, President Roosevelt chided the wealthy's opposition to his tax bill and lampooned their claim to having been persecuted merely for being "thrifty." What was clear to both the administration and its critics was that a congressional session which had begun with a comparatively modest White House agenda had become a revolutionary "second New Deal"—one with far more dramatic and divisive class overtones. When Congress finally concluded its work in August, the handiwork additionally included the Guffey-Snyder and Connally Acts, which established "little NRAs" in the bituminous coal and oil industries. Despite a second House vote on August 1 which had conclusively defeated the Senate's earlier "mandatory death sentence" provision, the Public Utilities Holding Company Act, with a feature that eliminated all such firms more than twice removed from the operating companies and empowered the SEC to initiate elimination of "first-degree" companies not in the public interest, became law. The new Banking Act of 1935 gave the President appointment power over the Federal Reserve Board of Governors' seven representatives on a Federal Open Market Committee. Roosevelt also signed the Social Security Act, which funded an unprecedented national program of unemployment, disability, and old-age insurance out of employer and employee payroll taxes, on August 14. In the session's last days, the President even got his "soak-the-rich" Wealth Tax Act. Even in an instance in which Roosevelt had not gotten his way—the Neutrality Act of 1935—the congressional product had hardly been to the du Ponts' liking. Fueled by the Nye investigations, an isolationist Congress had imposed in the legislation a mandatory embargo on the sales of "implements of war" to belligerent countries scheduled to last until the end of February 1936.[41]

Outside pundits wondered if the administration's burst of energy after the Schechter decision and its heightened anti-business combativeness represented a permanent switch away from its earlier tendencies toward cooperation with business and toward central planning. The change in orientation was seen as a move toward pro-competitive "atomization" of business or broker-state economic pluralism. Faced with a stagnating economy and rising unrest from the left, Franklin Roosevelt clearly had moved off dead center. But for how long, and for how great a distance, would his "drift to the left" go? With alarm the du Ponts were reminded of the President's quoted remarks during the 1935 session to a congressman regarding the Guffey bill: "I hope your committee will not permit doubts as to the constitutionality, however reasonable, to block the suggested legislation."[42] In the du Ponts' minds, Roosevelt's unprecedented assault on the power and prerogatives of business somehow had to be ended. To do that, they now would direct their main public vehicle, the American Liberty League, toward the dual forums of the federal courts and the pending presidential contest of 1936.

chapter 11

Mobilizing for Armageddon

By the end of the 1935 congressional session, not only had the du Ponts and other anti-administration figures reached the point of complete revulsion for the New Deal, but their personal hatred of "that man in the White House" had become even more open and intense. Within the most scurrilous of the anti-Roosevelt circles, a "whispering campaign" had been instigated questioning his mental faculties. Hostility toward the President on the part of the du Ponts and other like-minded business executives was no doubt fueled by their sense of betrayal at the hands of a man of similar wealth and breeding. It was also stimulated by their specific objections to his administration's policies, which they viewed as arbitrary, self-serving, demagogic, and subversive of business powers and prerogatives. But part of the bitterness of their response stemmed from their need to blame someone for the inability of corporate America to regain the public's trust. The popular heroes of the 1920's had become the villains of the 1930's. How else, without plunging into demoralizing self-recriminations, could the du Ponts explain the stubborn durability of national mistrust—especially in light of their and others' efforts to reinstate their good image— except as the work of a political demagogue fanning the flames of class hatred?

The anti-Roosevelt "thesaurus of hate," well documented by scholar George Wolfskill, painted the President as a "renegade Democrat" who had sold out the party's noble "Jeffersonian" heritage of limited federal power. Vicious letter-writers called him a "cripple," "dupe," or "dictator," surrounded by "radicals," "Reds," "kikes," and "aliens." The gossip-mongering included accounts of Roosevelt's megalomania, mental deterioration, alcohol abuse, and even syphilis. To the du Ponts' credit, Pierre and Lammot never, and Irénée in only his most intemperate moments, stooped to such a level of character assassination privately or publicly, although their private expressions did carry hints of latent anti-Semitism and racial and class prejudices. But while they maintained a level of decorum in their assaults on Roosevelt, their allies in the efforts did not always follow suit.[1]

Amidst the disappointments of the Liberty League's first year of existence, the du Ponts could at least be credited for having helped craft a broad conservative opposition ideology of the political right through their organization's research and propaganda. Thoroughly infused with the du Ponts' Social Darwinist credo that private executives tested in the marketplace made better policy stewards than elected or appointed career politicians, the League's literature set forth a comprehensive, if not always consistent, critique of the New Deal and its dangers. According to the organization's spokesmen, the New Deal threatened the balance of power between the national government and the states. Centralization of power in the executive branch foreshadowed tyranny and dictatorship. Federal policies had abandoned the unifying approach of cooperation with industry for one of confrontation and coercion which had retarded "natural" economic recovery. Governmental regimentation of production and prices had created evils greater than those of overproduction and low farm income. Tax policies were demagogic, socially divisive, and damaging to private investment and recovery. New Deal spending threatened to ignite a disastrous inflation. Roosevelt's work relief programs constituted blatant political patronage that encouraged "boondoggles" and undercut personal initiative at the same time that it damaged private employers. And federal banking and securities policies had hamstrung the investment community and subjected financial markets to improper political influence.[2]

What this critique added up to was the conviction that the Roosevelt administration had abandoned the wisdom of "industrial self-government"—of the corporate state—for the dangers and uncertainties of the "broker state." The broker state, which fixed the central role of arbiter between conflicting national economic interests in a popularly rooted, partisan national government, struck at the heart of the du Pont family's cherished presumptions of hegemony not just over their business empire, but within the national economy. The New Deal threatened to institutionalize a powerful federal executive branch, with an independent electoral base and the prerogatives of patronage, that for its own demagogic and self-interested purposes would elevate to a comparable standing with business the claims of organized labor, agriculture, consumers, even (though to a lesser extent) the unorganized poor and jobless. The broker state, the du Ponts were convinced, was an "unAmerican," anti-republican creed that would lead inevitably from a statist democratic socialism into an outright communistic tyranny. Underscoring their growing perception that the expanding New Deal was part of a broader socialistic plan was the abrupt shift of the American Communist Party in 1935 from hostility toward Western liberals, including the Roosevelt administration, to an "anti-fascist" strategy embracing cooperation with the non-Marxist left in a Popular Front.[3]

Throughout the fall of 1935, the du Ponts employed the Liberty League to carry on their ideological war against the New Deal and the broker state. In the effort Irénée and Pierre were intimately involved, screening pamphlet drafts, steering the topics addressed by the organization's literature, even personally collecting research data. Pierre, for example, paid Du Pont Company researcher F. K. Reybold $450 out of his own pocket for compiling anti-Roosevelt and anti–New Deal quotations that could be recycled by the League in its printed materials. In September, he contributed his personal critique of the constitutionality of the Potato Control Act and, in November, he personally tried to verify claims of vote fraud against the AAA in an Iowa "corn-hog" referendum. While conducting his own examination of the Townsend old-age "revolving pension" plan, Pierre quoted "one of my employees" to the effect that "the result of old-age pensions would be idle children supported by pensions of old parents," and he questioned the soundness of Townsend's funding scheme. Toward both old-age benefits and unemployment insurance Irénée's blunt opinions were conveyed to John Raskob. "To adopt the principle of 'cracking down' on those who do the things which give most to society seems to me nonsensical and couple it with rewarding those who do the least for society is too foolish to be called asinine."[4]

The reinvigorated formal leadership of Irénée, combined with the more active assistance of Pierre, did have one disharmonious effect. Jouett Shouse, who had been frustrated for months at receiving the brunt of criticism and gossip emanating from Irénée's direction about the League's failures, hoped that Pierre's greater interest might signal his willingness to replace Irénée as chairman of the executive committee. Shouse was angered by Irénée's criticism in early September for having drafted a leaflet, entitled "Promises vs. Results," that in the chairman's view strayed from the League's proper purview of constitutional critiques of the administration into the realm of "partisan" controversy. Irénée apparently preferred to toy with the more Utopian notion of working for proposals to bring about the "ultimate limitation of the franchise." Pierre, for his part, agreed with Shouse and E. F. Hutton that the League needed to expand its assault of the Roosevelt administration beyond mere debate over constitutional questions. But Pierre, given both his continuing pessimism of the chances to stop the New Deal soon and his family loyalty, was not inclined to undercut his brother's authority. "Probably there is no hope," he expressed in a sentiment that seemed to underscore Irénée's wish for a more restricted electorate, "in a situation that is based upon the gullibility of the American public." In any event, Pierre was not without his own implausible policy dreams. Later in the year he would reassert to a private correspondent the wisdom of William Stayton's idea for an effort to repeal the Income Tax Amendment.[5]

Despite the internal squabbles, the League's pamphlets, speeches, and press releases continued to hammer away at the New Deal. Printed materials were now available to the Washington, D.C., bureaus of about 350 different newspapers, to all the major press associations, and to prominent editors and columnists. Over 7500 public, college, and university libraries received the League's literature, as did virtually every member of Congress. Beginning in August, a bulletin series, modeled on the Kiplinger letter, was launched. Mimeographed on multicolored paper, the bulletins offered condensed versions of pamphlet attacks, accounts of League activities, anecdotes, and appeals for members and funds. Pamphlets blasted the Potato Control Act ("another step toward Socialism"), and even the President's call in September, intended to reassure business, for a "breathing spell" after the frantic activity of the past session. Jouett Shouse warned that Roosevelt's comment signalled his intent to return at a later date to "every kind of regulatory legislation, . . . fiscal uncertainties that have resulted from going off the gold standard, devaluing the dollar, increasing deficits . . . and an unbalanced budget." Capitalizing on the theme of the occasion, League speakers, including James M. Beck, Albert Ritchie, Bainbridge Colby, and Shouse, chose Constitution Day, September 17, for an additional round of Roosevelt bashing.[6]

By October, hoping to follow up on the "Save the Constitution" theme in preparation for 1936, the League commissioned the production of 10,000 calendars depicting the Framers for distribution to members, with Irénée personally underwriting the cost. The same month, however, the Executive Committee declined participation in the distribution of former Treasury advisor James Warburg's anti-Roosevelt tract, *Hell Bent for Election*, reflecting Irénée's desire not to publicly show his partisan hand too quickly. Meanwhile, League pamphleteers warned Americans in *Your Public Debt* that they would have to assume the duty of reducing government expenditures. In *Dangerous Experi-*

mentation, New Deal measures were ascribed to "half-baked theories." Rexford Tugwell's Resettlement Administration, dubbed "Tugwell's Folly," was said to resemble Soviet-style collectivization. The administration's economic policies were incongruously labelled as similar to both "Mercantilism and Fascism" and as irreconcilable with American democracy. League economists Kemmerer and Carouthers criticized pro-inflationary policies as a "sad irony" in that they would lead the country down a "primrose path to destruction" most harmful to the poor themselves. According to the League's November broadside *Work Relief,* "partisan loyalty has remained an essential in obtaining employment." The following month a pamphlet entitled *Alternatives to the American Form of Government* ostensibly sought to analyze the dictatorships of the USSR, Germany, and Italy, "whose underlying theories bear upon present attempts to regiment industry and agriculture in the United States."[7]

While the Washington office churned out propaganda, the League's leaders, including the du Ponts, occupied themselves with preparing for the 1936 campaign and, in the nearer term, bolstering attempts to challenge the New Deal in the courts. As early as June 1935 consideration of possible candidates to head a stop-Roosevelt effort had begun. Pierre insisted to John Raskob, who had prior experience in such efforts, that any such planning involve conservatives from both parties. He warned, however, that Southern Democrats were unlikely to vote for a Republican alternative to Roosevelt, whereas the Republicans would resist a coalition ticket with a Democrat at the top for fear of destroying the GOP's identity. Reflecting the latter concern, insurance executive Fred Howland lobbied Irénée to align the League behind a Republican presidential candidacy headed by Kansas Governor Alfred M. Landon.[8]

In contrast to Howland's approach, Congressman James Beck hoped to usher in a genuine partisan realignment based on purer conservative and "radical" factions. He favored a conservative coalition against Roosevelt, and in late July, along with Frank Knox, Patrick Hurley, and Governor Harry Nice of Maryland, he consulted with former president Herbert Hoover on the subject. By August he had attempted to coordinate a strategy meeting between himself, Robert McCormick, George Moses, Ritchie, Davis, Ely, and Eugene Talmadge and had visited the anti-Roosevelt newspaper titan Hearst. Pro-League columnist David Lawrence, the recent author of a strident volume entitled *Stumbling into Socialism,* called for a coalition Constitution Party, and H. B. Rust notified Irénée that fellow League loyalist E. T. Weir was in contact with automaker Walter Chrysler on a "definite scheme" to defeat the President in 1936. Even before the Congress adjourned, Bainbridge Colby floated the idea of a separate nominating convention of disaffected Democrats in the spring. Also in August, Pierre, reverting to his earlier dislike of both existing political parties, promoted the idea of a "coalition free from the name Republican or Democrat" to the conservative black leader Joseph V. Baker.[9]

The du Ponts' hopes of an electoral repudiation of Roosevelt in 1936 were boosted by the mid-term congressional election in Rhode Island's First District in mid-August, which saw an open Roosevelt foe, Charles R. Risk, carry a traditionally Democratic district by some 13,000 votes. Emboldened by the outcome, du Pont in-law Ruly Carpenter urged the Liberty League to intervene in subsequent contests by circulating legislative voting records in appropriate districts. Bainbridge Colby reiterated his call for a "Jeffersonian Democratic" convention, and Hearst even indicated a willingness to bury the hatchet of a long-standing political feud and talk up Al Smith as a "Jeffersonian" nominee. In Hearst's words, even a Smith candidacy was preferable to the "imported, aristocratic, Asiatic Socialist Party of Karl Marx and Franklin Delano Roosevelt." Emerging as a likely umbrella organization for a conservative Democratic challenge to the President was the Southern Committee to Uphold the Constitution, headed by John Henry Kirby of Houston, one-time NAM president and backer of innumerable conservative causes, including the Sentinels. On August 20 Irénée received an appeal for support from Kirby's group, on which he commented to Stayton, "I think the more such organizations the better." He concluded, "It will aid in their enthusiasm to assist them, rather than try to convert them to the Liberty League." Stayton's reply, which noted as a positive item Kirby's earlier directorship in the AAPA, concurred with his boss, and he characterized the two organizations' approaches as being like the "Catholic path" and the "Methodist path" to heaven.[10]

Although no specific contact or help had been extended to his candidacy, and although he personally symbolized everything that was distasteful to the du Ponts about American politics, even Huey Long merited at least a rooting interest from the League. The du Ponts were well aware of the damage Long could do Roosevelt through a primary challenge or a third-party candidacy. So was the White House. James Farley confidentially reported to the President that Long was capable of carrying three to four million votes, including as many as 100,000 in Roosevelt's native New York. In short, even if Long could not win himself, he could throw victory to another by eating into the President's normal constituency. Speculations concerning the "Long factor," however, were abruptly and permanently silenced on September 8, when the Kingfish was shot in the rotunda of the Louisiana statehouse and died two days later.[11]

Long's sudden death, combined with Al Smith's continued hesitancy toward coming out of electoral retirement, meant that as the fall season began the du Ponts found themselves limited to acting as private cheerleaders of Kirby's mobilization efforts. The Texas activist opened office space for the Southern Committee in his own Kirby Building, which had been built for him by Jesse Jones, former head of the Reconstruction Finance Corporation (RFC) and which also housed his Texas Taxpayers League, Texas Tax Relief Committee, Texas Election Managers Association, and Order of American Patriots. In mid-September Kirby informed a select circle of 5000 by letter that the Southern Committee was determined to defeat the reelection of Franklin Roosevelt. In Kirby's words, "Every informed American knows that if Mr. Roosevelt is reelected in 1936, the sovereign rights of the states will be completely demolished and power over all their affairs little and big will be consolidated in Washington." As one of the recipients of the appeal, Irénée on September 17 sent the Southern Committee a check for $5000 in support.[12]

The behind-the-scenes involvement of the du Ponts in anti-Roosevelt electoral politics in the early fall was overshadowed, however, by the public activities of the Liberty League's National Lawyers' Committee. On August 15 Raoul Desvernine notified Irénée that a subcommittee was busily drafting a report on the legality of the Wagner Act, and a week later the *New York Times* publicly cited the panel's existence. Although the Lawyers' Committee ostensibly was a voluntary organization of attorneys serving without pay, and not restricted to Liberty League members, claims of detachment from the League were fragile at best. The League served as publisher and distributor of its reports, at least a dozen members of the organization were prominent Leaguers, and the national office of the League had been instructed by Irénée's executive committee to give chairman Desvernine $25,000 in discretionary funding.[13]

On September 29, the Lawyers' Committee released its report on the National Labor Relations Act. Both the drafting subcommittee, chaired by Weirton Steel attorney Earl F. Reed, and the full committee argued that the measure was an improper use of the interstate commerce clause of the Constitution and an intrusion upon the contract rights of both employers and employees. The panel's verdict of "unconstitutional" was hardly surprising, but the section of the report that turned heads was Reed's advice to industrial employers on the

basis of the report. "When a lawyer tells a client that a law is unconstitutional," he maintained, "it is then a nullity and he need no longer
obey that law." Reed's counsel, along with the timing of the release,
indicated the triggering of a wholesale legal assault upon, and defiance
of, the NLRB's collective bargaining machinery. Another shot had
been fired a week earlier, after company attorneys had relayed to plant
managers at Du Pont the need merely to avoid creating proof of employer control of worker-representation plans in order to avoid NLRB
sanctions. The company's representative, in response, had reported to
the Special Conference Committee the distribution of two circulars
"explaining the Wagner Labor Relations Act" to employees. On the
same day that the Lawyers' Committee report was issued, Jouett
Shouse also announced that the Liberty League would provide free
legal services for individuals and corporations unable to afford litigation costs against the NLRB.[14]

From the issuance of the Lawyers' Committee report on the Wagner
Act until the Supreme Court decision upholding the measure in April
1937, the NLRB found itself tied in knots by injunction suits. Besides
court actions, the offensive against collective bargaining also included
dramatic increases in the use of, and spending for, company spies and
police. The Pennsylvania Railroad Company, on whose board of directors Pierre du Pont served, upped its expenditures for industrial
detectives from less than $50,000 the previous year to $80,000 in 1935.
General Motors and its subsidiaries boosted their spending from nearly
$240,000 in 1934 to over $400,000 in 1935, and their purchases of tear
gas climbed from less than $1500 to over $16,000. Owing to the Du
Pont Company's greater long-term success in preventing penetration
of its plants by outside unions, Lammot's segment of the family empire
was the one major exception to these kinds of increases.[15]

The Liberty League found itself plunged once more into public
controversy when the Lawyers' Committee took the New Deal to court.
The *Nation* observed in "A Conspiracy of Lawyers" that the Wagner
Act report reflected only the view of corporation lawyers and that no
constitutional law professors or labor lawyers had even been consulted
as to their views. Reed's advice to business to defy the law also led
the editorialist to warn, "If lawyers turn themselves into an organized
body dedicated to inciting the public to disobey the law . . . that is
conspiracy." The *New Republic* dismissed the report as simply a propaganda ploy by corporation lawyers on behalf of their clients, "not far
above the level of criminal lawyers who try their cases in the newspapers."[16]

With great relish, Interior Secretary Harold Ickes assumed the po-

sition of point man for the administration. Referring to the Lawyers'
Committee as "Chief Justice Shouse and his fifty-seven varieties of
associate justices," he noted in a pointed jab at the Liberty League
president's $54,000 income, "Mr. Shouse beats the Chief Justice of
the Supreme Court in salary; but then, he is a greater constitutional
authority." If the League would go further and double his adversary's
salary, Ickes suggested, Shouse would "probably take on the work of
the executive and legislative branches of the government as well." In
a serious vein, the Secretary charged that the committee's action in
issuing the report before the Supreme Court had even been called upon
to rule on the Wagner Act was "evidence *per se* of disrespect for the
court." Shouse merely dismissed the attack as the product of a "persistent denouncer," and Raoul Desvernine, congratulating his colleagues on October 2 for their initial effort, claimed, "You could not
ask for a better approval than Mr. Ickes' nonsensical remarks." Lammot du Pont attempted to capitalize on the League's renewed notoriety
by urging company stockholders to enlist in the League. H. B. Rust
also informed William Stayton that two "large employers" were now
willing to receive Liberty League literature, so long as the League's
official emblem was not on it, for stuffing into workers' pay envelopes.[17]

Controversy over the appropriateness of the Lawyers' Committee's
activities continued in various forums. An editorial in the October
issue of the *United States Law Review* deemed it "just a little incredulous"
that such a body of lawyers would take it upon themselves to judge
an act of Congress "before it has found its way into the courts or
received judicial interpretation." The journal's editors concluded that
the report's actual purpose could only be to influence the courts themselves, or else to so arouse public opposition to the law so that "confidence in the courts will be impaired should the legislation be held
constitutional . . . Neither purpose has anything to commend it." Supporters of the committee countered that the law journals themselves
through their articles constantly questioned the constitutionality of
legislation, though admittedly not in as widely and publicly dissemi-
nated a fashion. The AFL in its national convention denounced the
Lawyers' Committee action as well, which drew a written response
from Desvernine. In Desvernine's estimation, the exchange proved a
public relations bonus, for while the national press had not published
the actual text of the labor federation's resolution, it had printed extensive excerpts of his reply. In the meanwhile, the 40,000 copies of
the original Lawyers' Committee report were grabbed up so rapidly
that League president Shouse ordered a second printing.

Not all publicity was to the good, however. The Liberty League was not only drawing controversy and occasional praise but also ridicule for its foray into constitutional adjudication. Recognizing that fact, the President rejected advice that the White House sponsor a rival lawyers' organization on the grounds that "that Liberty League crowd only hurt their cause by doing an unethical thing." After a radio address by James Beck in which he warned, "We must defeat the sappers and miners of the New Deal who are insidiously undermining the very foundations of the Constitution," the Hod Carriers' and Common Laborers Union Local 536 in his home state satirically appealed to the Lawyers' Committee for free legal aid. Publicist Charles Michelson of the DNC, having released an exhaustive report on the lawyers' business ties documenting the claim that profit was guiding legal principle, took direct aim in his October 20 "Dispelling the Fog" newspaper column. Ridiculing the "Little Supreme Court" for its fallibility, he cited the records of prominent members in their previous individual efforts at arguing cases before the Supreme Court. John W. Davis stood at 17–15, James Beck at 2–8, and George Wickersham at 3–3. Michelson also accused the Liberty League of improper influence peddling by recruiting sitting judges as members, citing the specific case of Judge John F. Carew, a Roosevelt appointee to the New York Supreme Court. It was also known that a number of prominent jurists, including William H. Ellis of the Florida Supreme Court, U.S. District Judge Merrill E. Otis, Louisville federal judge Charles I. Dawson, and Pennsylvania Supreme Court Justice George W. Maxey, were supporters of the Liberty League. In a roundabout swing both at the League and the conservative majority on the U.S. Supreme Court, Michelson pointedly wondered if his enemy had "ever thought of approaching the members of the national tribunal of last resort."[18]

Nearly a month later, amidst rumors (later proven false) that an individual or organization outside the legal profession had originated the complaint, the committee on professional ethics and grievances of the American Bar Associaton met in Columbus, Ohio, to consider disciplinary action against the National Lawyers' Committee. Despite the language of Canon XX of the ABA's *Canon of Ethics*, which stated, "Newspaper publications by a lawyer as to pending or anticipated litigation may interfere with a fair trial in the courts and otherwise prejudice the due administration of justice" and are "to be condemned," the panel gave the committee a clean bill of health. "The [ABA] Committee," they declared, "is unable to see anything unethical or improper." While Leaguers rejoiced over the finding, it did not alter the fact that the controversy had delayed the preparation and issuance of additional Lawyers' Committee attacks on New Deal laws.

Nor did the verdict clear the Liberty League's legal campaign in the "court of public opinion," as supporters of the President viewed the outcome as another example of a conspiracy among the affluent to "get Roosevelt." With the risk of professional censure lifted, the Lawyers' Committee resumed the offensive and was now joined by others. The Edison Electric Institute widely circulated an anti-TVA opinion, and Commonwealth and Southern utility head Wendell Willkie issued a similarly harsh judgment on the Public Utilities Holding Company Act. The Liberty League found, however, that following the initial hubbub over the Wagner Act critique, subsequent reports paled in comparison. On December 9, the lawyers branded the Guffey-Snyder coal conservation bill unlawful "on four counts," and the Potato Control Act was deemed "flagrantly unconstitutional" on December 30. But save immediate reaction from administration officials directly involved in the programs in question, the reports generated disappointingly few political sparks.[19]

Instead, the thoughts of pundits, politicos, and Leaguers themselves, including the du Ponts, moved back to the pending presidential contest. By November 2, George Creel was still wondering aloud in a *Collier's* column, "Who will lead the anti-Roosevelt forces?" One prominent Roosevelt-hater definitely in search of a candidate was William Randolph Hearst, and in November he appeared to find one in the person of former Kansas governor Alf Landon. As early as September the Hearst press made the tentative decision to build up Landon's national reputation, and Dick Berlin of *Good Housekeeping* dispatched reporter Adela Rogers St. John to interview the candidate. Hearst representative John Lambert also visited the governor in Topeka to sound out the mutual compatibility of the politician and the publisher. State newspaper editors, especially Oscar Stauffer, Arthur Capper, and Roy Roberts, also fueled the Landon boom. The White House was well aware of Hearst's machinations, and the President forced George Peek out of his position as foreign trade advisor for a speech he made before the War Industries Board Association on November 11 that to Roosevelt's ears sounded "like a Hearst editorial." Hearst's Los Angeles *Examiner* issued its own broadside against the administration three days later, declaring, "This band of revolutionary radicals proposes to OVERTHROW THIS GOVERNMENT. AND THEY ARE DOING IT."[20]

Stepping up their own campaign activities were the Crusaders and the Sentinels of the Republic. In early October the Crusaders launched another weekly fifteen-minute radio series, this time over the Mutual System and New England's Yankee Network. Besides the radio messages, which attacked the New Deal and promoted the specific cause of tax reduction, the organization shipped out fourteen-by-twenty-two-inch broadsides in mailing tubes four times a month defending American industry and criticizing government interference. The Sentinels, committed to the elimination of the Constitution's "general welfare" clause as a justification for federal economic intervention, established an editorial service to 1300 small and rural newspapers across the country. In October, they sponsored a New York rally at which James Wadsworth scored the New Deal's "planned economy" schemes before a crowd of 5000, and a month later Raymond Pitcairn sent the organization's new pamphlet, "The Story of the Sentinels," to John Raskob.[21]

The most bizarre tactic of the campaign was an anti-Roosevelt cartoon feature film prepared by the Sentinels and entitled *The Amateur Fire Brigade*. In October Lammot du Pont took his wife Margaret and "some of the children" to a Philadelphia screening of the film. The President was depicted in one scene as a boy astride the Democratic donkey backwards, and in a second as the engineer of a disabled New Deal train. In yet another sequence, from which the movie's title was derived, the administration was pictured as a house built of alphabet blocks which burned while an inept band of amateur New Deal firefighters failed to douse the flames. The dour Lammot came away skeptical of the effort. "I was not particularly impressed with the movie," he noted, questioning whether it would "take with the public." A month later, on November 21, at Raskob's invitation the League's executive committee received a private screening, along with introductory remarks and a speech by anti-Roosevelt Democrat Henry Breckinridge, the Sentinels' preferred candidate for president. Although the Sentinels wanted the League's cooperation in raising $360,000 for national distribution of the film, the executive committee opted not to pursue the matter further.[22]

Since his return from his world cruise in the spring, John Raskob had continued to give financial assistance to the Liberty League and, as the Sentinels' approach indicated, still had received solicitations for help from related movements as well. But rather than take an active part in the League's or the Sentinels' political efforts, he now preferred to employ business channels to pressure the government toward a different course and to "educate" the public of the danger of communism. The previous December the joint NAM–Chamber of Commerce conference at White Sulphur Springs had created a National Business Conference Committee, chaired by Judge C. B. Ames, to coordinate public policy studies and positions. After Ames's sudden death, Raskob had been chosen to replace him. In a major address to the NBCC on October 24 with ally Lammot du Pont in attendance, Raskob counseled that "under no circumstances should business engage in partisan politics." Nonetheless, he still insisted, "Business has made such long, rapid strides that the heads of our institutions have had little time to give proper attention to the matter of organizing some method of enabling our citizens to understand and sympathize with the problems of business, the advantages of so-called 'capitalism' versus communism and the dangers of being misled by irresponsible soap box orators, mostly aliens." He warned, "Communism is stalking through Europe and the progress it is making in our own country is much too serious to long ignore."[23]

Despite his hopes that the NBCC might become the basis for a concerted educational effort by business, Raskob argued successfully against holding a second major rally in December because of its conflict with a scheduled December 9 round-table conference of industrial and labor leaders called by George L. Berry, the President's new "coordinator for industrial cooperation." According to the counsel of the NAM's Robert Lund, the apparent public challenge that would be posed by a rival NBCC conference would only make the organization a "target for demagogic attack." Others within the du Pont circle who had shied away from Pierre's Liberty League efforts, or who had dropped out, now also attempted to work through associational channels to arouse business from its lethargy. Lammot urged Raskob to suggest that the NAM's efforts to organize investors within member companies be consolidated with those of Chicago businessman Hugh S. Magill's American Federation of Investors, Inc. GM's Alfred Sloan, in spite of his reluctance to expose his company to political buffeting, nonetheless personally attacked the administration in an address before the Michigan Chamber of Commerce in late November. In Sloan's words, the nation "must liquidate the panaceas and discard quack theories." Even more bluntly, E. F. Hutton was quoted as telling a business audience that it must form a financial "superlobby" to "gang up" on the administration.[24]

By December, then, various du Ponts and their business colleagues had set many organizational wheels turning in the effort to derail the Roosevelt administration. The Du Pont Company prepared to launch a major "institutional publicity" effort in 1936 to rehabilitate its image, including sponsorship of a radio entertainment program, "The Cavalcade of America." Through their involvement in the NAM and the NBCC, John Raskob and Lammot du Pont were promoting business cooperation in the fight against the New Deal's purportedly foreign ideological "isms." Signalling an even greater NAM political militancy than before, and the likelihood of greater coordination between its activities and those of the Liberty League, Colby Chester "transferred" from the League's executive committee to become the NAM's new president. Replacing him on the League's panel was Raoul Desvernine. Pierre du Pont, while still maintaining the status of a retired elder, nonetheless utilized his personal research and professional contacts to promote business cooperation with the Liberty League's anticipated campaign against the President. And Irénée, while directing the League's anti-administration legal efforts, covertly encouraged the stop-Roosevelt campaign of late 1935 by word of mouth and by check-book. It was because of the growth of this loose network of anti–New Deal organizations that Irénée could claim, "I think the work of the League is nearly finished, for the country is constitutionally minded, yet we must not let up until the menace of the present Administration toward it is removed."[25]

Within the American Liberty League, far more impressive propaganda and financial resources, if not a grass-roots mass membership, had been amassed by the end of 1935 than at any time since its creation. Because of the League's narrow membership base, however, it was still reliant upon the popular mobilization activities of friendly regional and national conservative and superpatriotic organizations. By December the League still had active state chapters in fewer than twenty states, and none save Nebraska, Missouri, and California west of the Mississippi River. By year's end it claimed 75,000 members, a doubling of strength since July but still a tiny base from which to topple an incumbent President. As with the AAPA, however, even those figures were deceiving, for membership consisted merely of sending in one's name and address, with or without dues, to the national office. The renewed efforts to recruit stockholders and insurance policyholders largely had failed, with the Insurance Company of North America the only major insurance firm which had shown a willingness to cooperate. In recognition of the situation, the four available members of the administrative committee—Chester, Shouse, Smith, and Irénée (Stayton was incapacitated with two broken ribs suffered in a fall out of bed)—directed the rechanneling of remaining national recruitment moneys into educational and research purposes. Included were plans for a new information service to rural weekly newspapers, which eventually did assist some 1800 publications at a cost of $30,000. Membership solicitation, in turn, was abandoned to the state chapters.[26]

Although the League's fundraising still reflected a narrow base of givers even within the corporate community, the value of the contributions largely had overcome the lack of volume. Donations and subscription pledges now sustained a national operation which had doubled in expense within a year to over $40,000 a month. Contributions to the national headquarters alone in 1935 totaled over $483,000, with expenses calculated at about $390,000. Of this income, over $270,000 had been raised among the executives of the Du Pont and General Motors corporations. Less than $35,000 had come in gifts of less than $100. Within the Du Pont–GM circle, fully $200,000 had been given by du Pont family members, in-laws, and siblings. The list included Irénée du Pont ($79,000); Pierre, Henry F., S. Hallock, and William du Pont ($15,000 each); Donaldson Brown, Ruly Carpenter, and Charles Copeland (also $15,000 each); Lammot ($10,000); Archibald du Pont ($2500); Walter S. Carpenter, Jr. ($2334.33); and Irénée's wife Irene ($1000). John Raskob chipped in $15,000, and General Motors executives John T. Smith, John L. Pratt, and William Knudsen added $15,000, $15,000, and $5000 more. The Bankers Trust Company, in which Raskob was a director, issued $20,000.[27]

Du Pont family members similarly dominated funding of the Delaware state branch, which in 1935 received $8755, all but $1255 in contributions of over $100. When all the du Pont family contributions to the League at all levels were totalled, the figure stood at over $204,000. Other company executives provided another $152,000 to a total income of over a million dollars. Less than two dozen individuals, most of them members of the Du Pont–GM circle, had given the organization over half its operating moneys. Nearly 30 percent had come from the du Pont family alone. According to figures compiled later by a congressional investigating committee, in 1935 executives of GM and its subsidiaries were responsible for gifts of almost $219,000 to the Liberty League and $23,750 to the Crusaders, although they gave only $100 to the Sentinels. Du Pont management donated nearly $275,000 to the League, $22,825 to the Crusaders, and $16,000 to the NAM (mostly from Lammot), but only $125 to the Sentinels.[28]

Much of the enormous level of du Pont financial investment in the League had gone toward the securing of "high-priced help." Jouett Shouse alone was receiving $54,000 ($36,000 in salary, $18,000 in expenses). Publicity director William C. Murphy drew $14,000, while four other staffers received $10,000 or more and four others were in the $5,000–10,000 range. The salaries, quite generous for their time, added to the League's public image that selfish profit guided its officers' principles and that its financial leaders, the du Ponts, were stuffy, sanctimonious hypocrites. As Stuart Chase of the *Nation* asserted, "Their whole attack has been tight-lipped, long-nosed, fanatically ungenerous and intolerant." Other critics preferred comic ridicule to strenuous denunciation. At the December 14 Gridiron Dinner, a reporters' skit prominently depicted nine supposed Delphic oracles, one bearing a golden box, representing Lawyers' Committee and League members Jouett Shouse, John W. Davis, James M. Beck, David A. Reed, Bainbridge Colby, Frank J. Hogan, Thomas N. McCarter, George Wickersham, and Frederick R. Coudert. When queried by "an Athenian citizen" about the box's contents, the reply was, "The sacred foundation of our being. It tells us what to do and when to do it." "Could I see it?" "Of course not . . . When anyone examines it, it changes color like a chameleon." "How can one tell what it means?" "Once a week, revelation is given when wise persons announce what it means—that week." "Permit me," said one oracle, "to exhibit the historic charter on which our freedom rests. The Contribution List of the Liberty League." The "Chief Justice" of the oracles, "Shouse," then declared, "It is your duty to protect this sacred document with your life and uphold it with your cash."[29]

Although the Liberty League's cash was an object of ridicule, it represented at the same time a financial kitty that the Roosevelt campaign itself could but dream of at the end of 1935. As it looked forward to the 1936 campaign season, the DNC claimed a balance of only $22,710.76. That figure did not even take into account lingering unpaid obligations and pledges, which ironically still included the balance of John Raskob's pre-1933 party loans. Raymond Moley predicted that if an election were held immediately, the President would lose in such key states and regions as New York, Pennsylvania, Ohio, Indiana, Illinois, and New England. A *Literary Digest* poll echoed the Moley assessment, citing figures that 58 percent of respondents opposed the New Deal and only 40 percent backed Roosevelt.[30]

Such public findings gave the du Ponts additional hope of ousting Roosevelt and regaining government influence. Wishing to present a "positive" policy alternative to the New Deal in advance of the 1936 congressional session and to put pressure on both major parties' platform committees, the administrative committee approved and released to the press on December 26 a "twelve-point program." Its main recommendations were to (1) reduce spending to the level of Treasury receipts, (2) limit direct relief to modest temporary programs while phasing out federal grants in favor of state and private funding and federal loans, (3) halt WPA-style work programs immediately and allow only public works that demonstrably did not compete with private industry, (4) broaden the tax base and cut spending while avoiding using the tax system to redistribute wealth, (5) reject currency inflation schemes and political control of banking and consider reestablishing the gold standard, (6) eliminate TVA-style schemes for competition with business and government economic planning, (7) repeal the "death sentence" provisions of federal utility legislation, (8) study Social Security with the aim of transferring its operations to the states, (9) repeal all agricultural restrictions based on a "scarcity theory" of raising farm income, (10) nullify the Canadian reciprocal trade agreement and defend the Senate's treaty ratification power more vigorously, (11) reverse the trend of executive usurpation of legislative functions and abolish New Deal bureaucracy, and (12) reassert Congress's power to protect the Constitution and its separation of powers by opposing any amendments to the contrary.[31]

Of even greater political importance than the League's issuance of a platform, however, was the decision to hold a lavish public "kickoff" dinner in Washington's Mayflower Hotel on January 25, with the featured speaker none other than that most prominent name among anti-Roosevelt Democrats—Al Smith. Announcement of the dinner created a flurry of political excitement, for Smith had refrained from political speeches for two years. His reappearance was interpreted as a clear sign that he would again seek the White House. Certainly that was what longtime Democratic fundraiser Thomas Chadbourne and Pauline Sabin hoped it would mean when they prodded him to accept the speaking engagement. Southern party activist and Lawyers' Committee member Forney Johnston also promoted to Raoul Desvernine and Jouett Shouse the idea of a Smith candidacy backed by an anti-Roosevelt coalition of Republicans and conservative Democrats. Johnston claimed that in its behalf the electric utility industry alone would spend over a billion dollars.[32]

As for the du Ponts, they were certainly receptive to a new Smith campaign, particularly in light of the other choices available. Irénée wrote J. Howard Pew, ostensibly for the purpose of having him take his place at the administrative committee meeting in early January, but more significantly to lobby him to recruit a large group from Pennsylvania to attend the Mayflower dinner. Even though Irénée was scheduled for another six-week hiatus in Cuba, beginning January 3, he made arrangements to return early so as to attend the festivities personally. In preparation for the event, Pierre ordered 26,000 copies of *Hell Bent for Election* for distribution, and he finally tendered his formal resignation from the Business Advisory Council to chairman Henry P. Kendall on December 27. Pierre nonetheless rejected the vituperative label "syphilitic cripple" applied to the President by a private correspondent, as well as the writer's plan of deporting "un-American" aliens.[33]

In a reflective mood at Christmastime, Pierre explained his political odyssey from being an early supporter of the New Deal to a champion of Franklin Roosevelt's demise. "I voted for Mr. Roosevelt," he replied, "spent six months in Washington aiding on the Industrial Advisory Board and the National Labor Board and, together with many others, helped to push along projects that, though of doubtful nature, fundamentally all hoped would be properly worked out." But as time had passed, he had become "less and less pleased with the whole situation." Again he described the administration's shift in labor policy as marking the irrevocable turning point. As he viewed it, the Wagner bill's reversal of the President's acceptance of minority labor representation had been "intended to drive every man into a union whether he is willing or not, otherwise to be deprived of representation."[34] A President who, it had been hoped, would usher in the bright new day of the corporate state within the rubric of a recovery program had instead become the enemy, the leader and symbol of the broker state. Franklin D. Roosevelt—and the changes he had come to represent—would have to be utterly defeated in 1936.

chapter 12

Taking a Walk

As 1936 began, Franklin Roosevelt had good reason to be concerned. According to the first *Literary Digest* poll of the year, the President was opposed by 60 percent of those questioned in a survey of thirty-six states. As he wrote to longtime political friend and diplomat Breckinridge Long, "We are facing a very formidable opposition on the part of a very powerful group among the extremely wealthy and the centralized industries." Chief among Roosevelt's most dangerous potential adversaries were the du Ponts and their allies, but as yet it was unclear how—and in behalf of whom—their resources would be employed. Some of them were advocating fusion of anti-Roosevelt Democrats with Republicans as part of a genuine ideological realignment of national politics. Others favored attempting to deny Roosevelt the Democratic nomination and, failing that, launching a third-party bid—perhaps a "constitutional Democratic" ticket with Al Smith at its head.[1]

It was with such possibilities in mind that the du Ponts had urged Smith to keynote the Liberty League's January 25 dinner at the Mayflower Hotel. Although the "unhappy warrior" had finally consented, he had discouragingly little enthusiasm for the fight. Making the former New York governor even more sullen was the kind of political trap the President reveled in springing. After Christmas the *New York Times* revealed that the First Lady had extended an invitation to Smith to stay overnight at the White House when in Washington for the banquet. According to presidential sources, not only had Smith turned down the gracious offer but he had on a number of other occasions similarly "snubbed" the Roosevelts' hospitality. Actually, as Smith accurately claimed, he had only once before been invited to the White House, when in November 1933 he, his personal physician, and John Raskob had taken tea with the First Family. Nonetheless, newspaper allies of Roosevelt had a field day attacking "Al's snub," and the

President had flushed out an indirect confirmation that the dinner would feature open attacks upon him.[2]

The leaking of the invitation to Smith and his refusal was but the first of a carefully orchestrated series of attacks by the administration on the League and its political bedfellows. The White House tendered a similar offer of hospitality to Governor and Mrs. Eugene Talmadge prior to the Democrats' annual Jackson Day festivities of January 8. The Georgia anti-Roosevelt leader, preparing for his own presidential sendoff in the form of a "Grass Roots Convention" in Macon, similarly was forced by the need to avoid open discourtesy and hypocrisy to decline the invitation. More damaging to the du Ponts was the action taken by the Senate Lobby Investigation Committee, which had been created the previous summer to look into charges of arm-twisting by stockholders during the debate over the Public Utilities Holding Company bill and which was chaired by an ally of Roosevelt, Hugo Black of Alabama. On January 2, the Black Committee released its findings on the amount of du Pont contributions to the Liberty League. Newspaper headlines trumpeted, "Liberty League Controlled by Owners of $37,000,000."[3]

All of the White House machinations merely set the stage for the fireworks unleashed by the President the evening of January 3. With Roosevelt arranging the first nighttime State of the Union address, scheduled for national radio coverage, Republican party chairman Henry P. Fletcher charged that the speech would be purely "undisguised politics" but failed to acquire equal time for a GOP radio response. His prediction was borne out. Shortly after 8:00 E.S.T., Roosevelt launched into a sharp attack, replete with veiled references to the Liberty League, that to press observers sounded like a "party rally." "We have returned the control of the Federal Government to the city of Washington," he proclaimed, but "we have earned the hatred of entrenched greed." In his most direct allusion to the League, he charged his opponents with stealing "the livery of great national constitutional ideals to serve discredited special interests." If they were sincere, the President insisted, they would openly demand the total repeal of the New Deal. But they were not. "They realize that in thirty-four months we have built up new instruments of public power. In the hands of a people's government this power is wholesome and proper. But in the hands of political puppets of an economic autocracy such power would provide shackles for the liberties of the people." In pursuing their selfish aims, he maintained, they "engage in vast propaganda to spread fear and discord among the people . . . But such fear as they instill today is not natural fear, a normal fear; it is synthetic, manufactured, poisonous fear that is being spread subtly, expensively and cleverly by the same people who cried in those older days—'Save us, save us, else we perish!' "[4]

Making it doubly hard for the League to counterattack effectively was the fact that the President's rhetoric was accompanied by mild election-year legislative proposals. His request for but $1.5 billion in fiscal 1937 relief spending punctured the League's arguments on the rising federal budget and deficit. Jouett Shouse nonetheless assailed the administration for sponsoring a "riot of extravagance" and "the greatest orgy of peacetime spending by any nation in the history of the world." An examination of the budget published by the League decried Roosevelt's repudiation of pledges he made in 1932 to restrain federal spending and balance the budget. A more inviting target was the political maneuvering of Jim Farley to send federal employees solicitations to the Democrats' $50-a-plate Jackson Day dinner.[5]

More stinging to the Democrats was the U.S. Supreme Court's January 6 ruling against the Agricultural Adjustment Act. In the "Butler decision," a majority of the justices ruled that Congress unconstitutionally had employed the tax power to regulate agricultural production. The action threatened not only to throw the farm program into chaos, but also exposed the Treasury Department to a multitude of tax recovery suits, necessitating likely new taxes to offset an expected, but uncertain, level of revenue losses. The Butler decision prompted William Stayton to predict to Pierre that the President would now seek a constitutional amendment broadening the commerce clause so as to allow taxation and regulation of products in intrastate commerce. Although he professed to be less concerned about the likelihood of such an amendment than his colleague, Pierre nonetheless authorized the preparation of a list of the thirteen states most likely to provide the margin to block any such ratification effort.[6]

The administration and its allies, however, were determined to maintain the political offensive despite the AAA setback. The President himself publicly acknowledged the Butler decision with disarming calm. On January 7, the Nye Committee resumed its public hearings, this time focusing on the Morgan interests for a month and a half. Senator Joseph Robinson of Arkansas, the administration's legislative point man, replied sharply to the League's attack upon the State of the Union message. "Had Mr. Roosevelt recited the Ten Commandments," he insisted, "they would just have accused him of plagiarism, and second, found some ulterior motive for his quoting the Decalogue." Party boss James Farley charged that the League's intent was to restore economic control to the "same crowd that wrecked it before," and he repeated the President's challenge to opponents to be honest enough to call openly for congressional repeal of the New Deal.[7]

Roosevelt personally continued the attack on Jackson Day, January 8. At the Mayflower Hotel at 10:00 E.S.T., some two-and-a-half weeks before the Liberty League's festivities, the President openly compared himself to another public symbol of expanded popular democracy, Andrew Jackson. "Haughty and sterile intellectualism opposed him," he proclaimed. "Musty reaction disapproved him. Hollow and outworn traditionalism shook a trembling finger at him. It seemed that sometimes all were against him—all but the people of the United States." Besides proving a rhetorical success, the dinner raised an immediate $100,000 for the Democrats. By the time of the League's dinner, contributions stood at $275,000. Speaking before a New York audience the following day, Farley accused the President's opponents of plotting a "campaign of defamation" for the sake of "getting back inordinate privileges."[8]

On January 10, in a more direct personal blow at the du Ponts, Commissioner of Internal Revenue Guy Helvering charged before the Board of Tax Appeals that John Raskob and Pierre du Pont still owed over $600,000 in federal taxes on their stock-swapping transaction of 1929–30. In a choice bit of irony, Raskob the same day repeated his demand for immediate payment from the DNC of $25,000 in past loans. A week later that amount in revenues received from the Jackson Day dinner was issued to him. On January 12, the *New York Times* carried claims from the White House that Roosevelt had personally taken steps to insure an honest, apolitical investigation of the tax case and that he had not purposely targeted the du Ponts for prosecution. It was curious, however, that within a month after Helvering made his charges the New York *Herald-Tribune* reported that the administration had filed huge income tax claims against seven prominent Liberty Leaguers. Charging publicly that the investigations were intended to intimidate the League in advance of its upcoming rally, Raskob insisted, "What better evidence could be offered to support a charge of tyranny and cheap politics against high administration officials?" At the same time, he took the occasion to defend Pierre as "a really great and fine character and a citizen whose integrity, honor, and love of country have become firmly established in the hearts and minds of his fellow citizens through nearly fifty years of active life in industry, philanthropy, and political and social welfare of his state and country."[9]

The administration was not wholly without its own troubles. Within the Treasury Department, Undersecretary T. Jefferson Coolidge and

Assistant Secretary L. W. "Chip" Roberts, Jr., broke ranks with the President over his emergency budget recommendations. Coolidge's resignation, accompanied by disharmonious public exchanges, created new unease within the business community. On January 20, the Liberty League issued a new broadside, entitled *Professors and the New Deal*. The pamphlet purported to survey 150 "leading educators" (many of whom happened to be Leaguers) and reached the scarcely astounding conclusion that the New Deal was opposed by "the overwhelming majority of the academic profession." Pierre du Pont also was now in a more aggressively anti-Roosevelt mood. Stung by the new round of tax charges, he increasingly referred to his antagonist as corrupt and dishonest. He repeated to friends his growing opinion that he should have launched a direct frontal assault upon the Sixteenth Amendment in the 1920's rather than upon its "younger brother," prohibition. To a private correspondent he added to his list the Seventeenth Amendment, which provided for the direct election of senators, as "likewise ill-advised." Even the Nineteenth, or Women's Suffrage, Amendment, he insisted, "however beneficial in purpose, does not seem to have made a material difference in the quality of government." While Pierre waxed constitutional, others debated anti-Roosevelt electoral strategy. New Deal adversary Joseph Ely offered his opinion to the press that the Liberty League would not sponsor a third-party effort. Du Pont executive George H. May privately urged a spring campaign to make Al Smith the Democratic nominee.[10]

With the banquet but two days away, on January 23 the administration's "hatchet-man," Senator Lewis Schwellenbach of Washington, delivered a vicious attack on the Liberty League and the du Ponts on the Senate floor. Citing the Raskob–du Pont tax charges, he accused the former DNC chairman of passing a "rubber check" for over $4 million, backed by League benefactor Bankers Trust Company. Actually, the bank's "contribution" had been a loan secured with the necessary collateral and later repaid. Turning his venom toward Al Smith, Schwellenbach noted numerous instances of FDR's loyalty to his old mentor and claimed that Smith had been duped into his opposition course by "leeches, rascals, crooks, and bloodsucking lawyers who control the American Liberty League." Although Interior Secretary Ickes "champed at the bit" for the opportunity to give his own public denunciation of the League, administration strategists deemed it wise for the moment for the President and his Cabinet to leave the "low road" to their congressional allies.[11]

The Liberty League's much-publicized meetings in Washington began on January 24 with sessions of the Lawyers' Committee, accompanied by a new pamphlet version of John W. Davis's speech before the New York State Bar Association, *The Redistribution of Power*. The next day the executive council and advisory committee gathered in joint session, hearing president Shouse's report on "Seventeen Months of the Liberty League." However, all of the business sessions were but a prelude for the evening's banquet and speechmaking. Tables had to be placed in the Mayflower's main corridor to handle an overflow crowd of two thousand invited guests. Four thousand others requesting tickets had been turned away for lack of space, but as late as the twenty-fifth the volume of requests still stood at seven hundred a day. Those unable to attend the "dinner with the du Ponts" nonetheless could listen to the proceedings on radio. Besides an "even dozen du Ponts," those in attendance included two former Democratic nominees for President (Smith and Davis), former governors Joseph B. Ely and Albert Ritchie, at least a dozen current or former members of Congress, former administration officials James Warburg, Dean Acheson, and Lewis Douglas, and, as one reporter dubbed it, "the greatest collection of millionaires ever assembled under the same roof."[12]

By general agreement afterward, the preliminary speeches by Dr. Neil Carouthers and Judge Charles I. Dawson dragged on far too long. At one point, presiding officer Shouse tugged so forcibly at Dawson's jacket that, according to an observer, rubber coattails should have been provided Dawson beforehand. Actually, Dawson's remarks did include the prophetic passage, "Does any man or woman within the sound of my voice doubt that the President hopes, if reelected, he will have the opportunity within the next four years to place upon the Supreme Court enough judges holding his own constitutional views to change the whole current constitutional construction in this country?" The words were lost, however, in the rustle of anticipation for the "unhappy warrior." Stepping to the microphone to deliver his first openly political speech in two years, a Smith resplendent in white tie and tails launched into a biting, sarcastic diatribe against the Roosevelt administration.[13]

Without ever mentioning his adversary by name, Smith recited the familiar litany of charges against Roosevelt—of setting class against class, ignoring the 1932 Democratic platform, wasting resources and creating bureaucracy, and erecting a socialist state. He asserted, "The young brain-trusters caught the Socialists in swimming and they ran away with their clothes." Claiming communistic overtones to the New Deal, Smith proclaimed, "There can be only one capital, Washington or Moscow. There can be only the clean, pure, fresh air of free America, or the foul breath of communistic Russia. There can be only one flag, the Stars and Stripes, or the flag of the godless Union of the Soviets. There can be only one national anthem, the Star Spangled Banner or the Internationale." He drew the most applause, however, when he issued the political warning that at the upcoming Democratic convention, he and his allies could "either take on the mantle of hypocrisy or we can take a walk, and we will probably do the latter."[14]

Immediate reaction to the speech was—as expected—mixed. Smith himself managed to avoid postmortems in the press by leaving immediately for Palm Beach with his wife. In Pierre's judgment, the address was "perfect." John Raskob echoed his friend, saying, "He gave a splendid definition of democracy." The League's opponents, in contrast, returned constantly to the theme of Smith as betrayer of his party and of his own working-class heritage. In the words of South Carolina's James Byrnes, "It was the voice of Oliver Street, but the thought of Wall Street." Even dispassionate observers questioned the political wisdom of Smith delivering his attack before an audience of millionaires. Nonetheless, the League moved immediately to capitalize on the publicity generated by the address. The national headquarters received over a thousand telegrams—95 percent of them favorable—the next day. Within a week, over 9000 requests for copies of the speech had been counted, with 2000 more inquiries addressed to Smith himself. Contributions included with the letters came to over $2300, mostly in amounts of ten dollars or less.[15]

John Raskob took the opportunity to issue a membership appeal to 150,000 individuals, including Du Pont and GM stockholders and upper-grade employees. In his written solicitation, Raskob cited his personal "rags to riches" story, which he claimed would have been impossible "under a socialistic, communistic or other form of government which fails to encourage initiative." He urged his listeners to contribute to the League's battle to "root out the vicious radical element that threatens the destruction of our government." Within a month's time, the appeal generated 1703 new members and over $30,000 in additional contributions. By the end of the month, the League was claiming a voluntary membership of about 75,000, 151 college chapters, and an information service to 1363 weekly papers, and a state headquarters in Massachusetts finally opened. Pierre declined a request from the Patriots of America to distribute its literature in the Midwest, but he did send $100 and a membership card to the Minute Men and Women of Today and ordered 30,000 copies of James Warburg's *Hell Bent for Election*. Pierre's latter action suggested at least some degree of coordination with the GOP, for the Republican National Committee ordered 200,000 copies at the same time.[16]

Administration and congressional counterattacks were not long in coming. On the same day as Smith's speech, a press release from the Senate Lobby Investigation Committee headed by Hugo Black announced the issuance of questionnaires to prominent businessmen concerning their contributions to the Liberty League. Although the League in 1935 had been a forceful opponent of the Wheeler-Rayburn bill, Pierre was convinced that Black's real interest in his organization's lobbying activities stemmed from its role in defeating his cherished Thirty-Hour bill. Given the timing of the announcement, it was generally assumed, as the *New York Times* noted, that the Black Committee would attempt to discredit the League by parading its contributors' list and probing its financial connections with other right-wing groups. The League's lawyers advised the members of the executive committee that they were not required, in their judgment, to answer the questionnaires. While the Black Committee maneuvered, the President privately instructed party publicist Frank Walker to "get someone in Pennsylvania to run this down, and he will find that three-fourths of these people are 'fat cats' and then prove it to the public."[17]

Within a matter of days after the Smith speech, administration spokesmen took to the airwaves. On January 27 Interior Secretary Ickes, fielding a prearranged question from Senator Alben Barkley at a Town Hall public forum, used Smith's own words against him. Ickes noted that in February 1933 Smith had stated that in an economic emergency, as in war, a democracy must "become a tyrant, a despot, a real monarch" and place the Constitution "on the shelf." During the 1928 campaign the former New York governor had also insisted, "The cry of socialism has always been raised by powerful interests that desired to put a damper upon progressive legislation." The main response, however, came over nationwide radio the next day by Senate Democratic leader Joseph Robinson. Although Roosevelt had originally preferred Indiana Governor Paul V. McNutt, at aide Steven Early's advice Robinson—the former 1928 running mate of Smith—received the assignment. The senator's address displayed all the earmarks of a political sermon, including as its central passage Genesis 27:22—"The voice is Jacob's voice, but the hands are the hands of Esau." Although the draft had been finalized before Secretary of State Cordell Hull could insert additional jabs, it still contained plentiful references to Smith's turnabout from his earlier progressive days. "It was strange," Robinson intoned, "to see you in such company, Governor Smith. Within a few feet of the table at which you sat were members of the power trust, some of whom you denounced by name in 1928." He lamented that "the brown derby," the symbol of Smith's common origins in 1928, had been exchanged for "the high hat."[18]

Leaguers immediately claimed that not only had the Robinson speech not damaged their cause, it actually had publicized Smith's "coming-out party" even more widely. In the New York municipal office, Henry DuBois cited polls a week later which indicated sentiment running 60 percent to 40 percent in favor of Smith in the city, with an even split in a Chicago survey. Ironically, Smith's charges of "socialism" received a stronger, albeit backhanded, rebuttal from none other than Socialist party leader Norman Thomas. Smith's call of January 25 to Democrats to "take a walk" from their party, however, did receive the unsurprising endorsement of Republican James Beck, who urged Raskob to call upon other "patriotic Democrats" to nominate a second ticket. Beck maintained that such an effort would aid the GOP's chances by taking general election votes away from the President.[19]

Whatever momentum the administration's opponents enjoyed, however, soon evaporated in the controversy surrounding the political gathering scheduled for January 29. Backers of Georgia's Eugene Talmadge had organized a "Grass Roots Convention" of self-proclaimed Jeffersonian Democrats from seventeen Southern and Southwestern states, to be held in Macon. The organizers claimed that the purpose of the gathering was to counter "the appearance in government of theories and actions which are alien, foreign, and inimical to America and Americanism." With Talmadge hoping to use the meeting as a springboard for his own presidential challenge, allies John Henry Kirby, Jesse Jones, and anti-Semitic preacher Gerald L. K. Smith issued the invitations. When the two-day convention began, despite heated and overtly racist rhetoric from such speakers as Smith and author Thomas Dixon, less than half the 7000 auditorium seats were filled. Of the attendees, only about 150 had travelled from outside Georgia itself. Even worse, in their zeal to boost the Talmadge challenge to Roosevelt, his backers distributed copies of the *Georgia Woman's World* to delegates. The racist publication contained a photograph of the First Lady in the company of two Howard University ROTC officers that was contemptuously referred to as "the nigger picture." Of special embarrassment to the du Ponts was the discovery several weeks later that Pierre, Irénée, Lammot, and Raskob all had contributed money to underwrite the meeting in Macon, although in ignorance that racist literature would be distributed. Complicating the family's position further were the actions of Henry F. du Pont and Alfred Sloan, who gave the Talmadge effort additional funds even after the bigoted nature of the convention had been disclosed.[20]

The fiasco was but one striking indication of the political ineptness of the du Pont–sponsored "stop-Roosevelt" movement. By early February the idea that one or more regional candidates could deny the President renomination already was collapsing. Talmadge's claim on the loyalties of voters even in the Deep South was highly doubtful. Mirroring the weakness of the Liberty League west of the Mississippi, no rival candidacy had emerged there save the ranting spectacle of Missouri's James A. Reed. Al Smith's evacuation to Florida for almost a month following his Washington speech did little to promote his or others' chances of unseating the incumbent. The New Yorker's limited political schedule in Palm Beach did include a private viewing of the Sentinels' *Amateur Fire Brigade* film at contractor William F. Kenny's home. Other than its amusement value to Smith, however, the movie proved of no real worth. Following its censure by the Ohio State Division of Film Censorship on the grounds that it encouraged disrespect for the presidential office, attempts by Smith benefactor Thomas Chadbourne to raise funds for national distribution collapsed. Given Smith's continuing diffidence, about the only rival to Roosevelt for Northeastern delegates was an old party warhorse, Colonel Henry Breckinridge, who made at best a poor replacement.[21]

The du Ponts themselves appeared scarcely more dedicated to assuming public leadership of the stop-Roosevelt campaign. Following Smith, in early February Raskob and Irénée left for winter vacations— Raskob to Florida to join his New York friend, Irénée to his Xanadu. Administration informer George Creel reported to the White House that a rabbi friend of his had seen the "former walking deficit of the Democratic party" in Palm Beach and had commented unflatteringly, "He looked as queer in shorts as Al Smith must have felt at the Dupont [*sic*] Liberty League dinner." Pierre, in contrast, stayed behind in Wilmington, but even his efforts were limited to making financial contributions to state anti-Roosevelt efforts, including $500 to a New Hampshire organization and $500 more to the favorite-son campaign of Governor Ely.[22]

The du Ponts' ineffectiveness reflected not merely fatigue, but also an almost pathological inability, given their distaste for politicians and electioneering, to anoint any one candidate who might possess the necessary skills to lead the electoral parade. It demonstrated both Pierre's elitism and his naiveté toward the electoral process, for example, when he privately pointed to GM's Sloan as "the kind of man I should select." After all, he maintained, "When one is ill, does he call upon his Congressman to prescribe, or does he go to a doctor trained to care for the ailment in question?" On the basis of his disillusioning New Deal experience, he had concluded that to achieve effective, professional government, federal authority in anti-trust and other economic areas, if it could not be coopted, must be shrunken and centralized private control must be legitimized. As a consequence, he now sounded a more "Jeffersonian" note. "I have always believed," he insisted, "that a partial division of our government into forty-eight state governments, together with one limited Federal head, is the best plan for development."[23]

The very elitism of the du Ponts—reflected in anti-democratic notions and their ignorance of grass-roots electioneering—played directly into the hands of the Roosevelt campaign. The Liberty League, even more than the GOP, became a favorite public whipping boy. DNC propaganda trumpeted the "ingratitude" of the du Ponts and other industrialists for failing to acknowledge the administration's role in "saving" American capitalism. Du Pont Company profits, admittedly, had risen 18 percent above 1929 levels, and $15 million more than in 1934, to $55 million by 1935. Adding to the public perception of the family as tax cheats, on February 8 the Associated Press carried a story setting the unpaid tax liability of Raskob and Pierre from 1929–30 at better than a million dollars. And even when the administration experienced a political defeat, it still seemed capable of garnering political mileage from it. When the Congress overrode the President's veto of the Patman veterans' bonus bill, with good grace Roosevelt promised to accelerate the date of initial payments to June 15—only one week before the Democratic convention. Crude attempts at verbal retaliation such as Raskob's charge that the President had borrowed tens of thousands of Warm Springs Foundation funds in 1928 without ever repaying them were smilingly rebuffed by White House spokesmen.[24]

As James Farley later observed, the "gaping hole" in the battle lines of the opposition—whether it be Republicans or conservative Democrats—was its sustenance from the hands of the Liberty League. The Liberty League could all too easily be lampooned as a tool of the wealthy intended to further its own, rather than the national, interest. Toward that end Farley's operatives led the assault. Coordinating the barrage of propaganda from the DNC, ironically, was an assistant of Charles Michelson in the publicity bureau who had been a former Hearst reporter in New York State, and International News Service correspondent from 1933 to 1936, Edward L. Roddan. Roddan planted stories, provided material and quotations for pro-administration speakers, and coined the Liberty League's new label—the "Millionaires Union." From the standpoint of the President's campaign advisors, the strategy could hardly have been simpler. Best of all, Roosevelt himself could leave much of the invective to others until he chose the proper moment to appear. As Roddan explained it, the basic technique was to "parade their [the Liberty League's] directorate before the people" and "blame them for everything." Farley aptly demonstrated the approach before a Washington Day banquet in Wichita, Kansas, stating that the League "ought to be called the American Cellophane League," since "first, it's a du Pont product, and second, you can see right through it."[25]

While Democratic supporters of the President rejoiced at the League's availability as a foil, Republicans already were learning the painful lesson of needing to keep their distance from the organization. Republican party chairman Henry Fletcher denied reports that the GOP would join forces with the League. In order to protect the Republicans, the League's executive committee also issued a statement insisting that it would officially pursue a "non-partisan opposition to Franklin D. Roosevelt." The GOP's public statements, however, left open a window of support from individual Jeffersonian Democrats backed by prominent Leaguers. Presidential hopeful Arthur Vandenburg of Michigan told a Lincoln Day audience in New York City that he welcomed "Jeffersonian cooperation—not only in the battle line, but subsequently in the council chamber after next November's victory is won." The next morning Fletcher confessed that consideration had been given to offering Cabinet posts to anti–New Dealers Lewis Douglas and Joseph Ely in the event of a Republican triumph. Both Vandenburg and Senator David Reed of Pennsylvania, another erstwhile contender, even suggested the possibility of a conservative Democrat as a running mate. Such "trial balloons" also were promoted by New York Liberty Leaguer Henry DuBois, who urged the GOP to fully incorporate dissident Democrats in decisionmaking positions.[26]

The League itself, however, continued to vacillate between the courses of immediate aid to the GOP, an anti-Roosevelt challenge for the Democratic nomination, a third-party effort in the fall, or some mixture of the above. Henry Breckinridge, hoping for active assistance from the League, announced his intention to challenge the President in the Ohio Democratic primary and expanded his regional candidacy to include the states of Illinois, New York, New Jersey, Massachusetts, Florida, and Pennsylvania. Joseph Ely spearheaded a similar delegate-contesting exercise in Massachusetts. But Liberty League backer and publicist David Lawrence argued that the organization should either dissolve or transform itself into a serious third party. A contrary view was held by Jouett Shouse, who confided to the Delaware office's Ernest

May that in his judgment a third-party effort would be a "waste of time and a waste of money." The Republicans, he insisted, offered the only real hope of unseating Roosevelt. While Shouse admitted that the League already had become a target of the administration, he still maintained that it served as a rallying point for disaffected Democrats and independents, and for that reason he urged the Republicans not to nominate a moderate, "straddling candidate." Although May disagreed, Shouse still foresaw a public role for the organization in the upcoming national campaign.[27]

The League's national office did attempt to counterattack with new pamphlet literature, but not all the pamphlets were well received. *The Story of an Honest Man* protested the administration's firing of Major General Johnson Hapgood following his criticism of WPA "boondoggling" before a House Appropriations subcommittee. *Dangerous Experimentation*, which criticized a federally funded shoe-repairing project in Mineola, New York, drew fire from an angry Joseph Robinson. "I think you people read the accounts of the severe winter through which we have just passed," he declared. Praising the government's efforts to provide funds to "repair the damaged shoes of children" who went to school in "ten degrees below zero" temperatures, Robinson sarcastically concluded, "The du Pont brothers must have been shocked when Shouse showed them that classic example of undermining the moral fiber of children on relief." Of more direct political damage to the anti-Roosevelt campaign were developments in Maryland. The sudden death of ex-Governor Albert Ritchie deprived the state's stop-Roosevelt forces of their most prominent figure, and the endorsement of the President by conservative Senator Millard Tydings on March 6 locked up that state's delegate contest.[28]

Causing greater frustration was the efficient political "hatchet job" being done on the Liberty League and its associates by the Black Committee. By mid-February the panel had received responses to its questionnaires to businessmen concerning their contributions to the League or to other anti-administration efforts. Despite official League protests at the information-gathering tactics, even Irénée had dutifully provided data on his lobbying contributions. On March 6 it was learned that Federal Communications Commission agents had made copies of some 13,000 messages which had been sent through the capital offices of Western Union and had turned them over to the Black inquiry in response to a blanket subpoena covering the period from February 1 to December 1, 1935. The committee's justification came from evidence it had unearthed that various anti–New Deal groups had lifted names from telephone directories and sent some

100,000 unauthorized telegrams in their attempt to defeat the Wheeler-Rayburn bill. Calling the congressional action a "fishing expedition," Jouett Shouse took to the airwaves on NBC radio to defend the League's conduct and to accuse the committee of unconstitutional search and seizure. Nonetheless, Black and his associates also obtained the long-distance telephone records of leading anti-administration figures. On March 21, the panel, while naming no names, leaked information that the same small group of wealthy individuals had funded the anti–New Deal lobbying campaigns of the Liberty League, the Southern Committee to Uphold the Constitution, the Sentinels, and the Crusaders, among others.[29]

First to challenge the legality of the Black Committee's tactics was newspaper mogul William Randolph Hearst, who filed suit in the District of Columbia Supreme Court for an injunction against both Western Union and the congressional panel in order to halt additional seizures. Although Western Union opted not to contest the action, the Black Committee remained a party to the suit. Providing Hearst's legal defense and, by extension, the defense of other administration adversaries was the Chicago law firm of Winston, Strawn, and Shaw, whose chief partners were prominent Liberty Leaguers and whose own 1935 telegrams had been purchased by the congressional inquiry from Western Union for $100. On March 11, Judge Alfred Wheat granted a temporary injunction blocking Western Union from releasing additional messages. With Wheat's action followed by a permanent injunction, Shouse issued a public congratulation to the courts for preventing "the opening wedge to censorship of the press," and he urged a Senate inquiry into the Black Committee's methods. A Senate majority, however, rebuffed Shouse by authorizing an additional $12,500 to continue the lobbying investigation. Even the passage of a new Lobbyist Registration Act in early April, requiring regular, detailed reports of lobbyists' contributions and expenditures, did not halt the Black inquiry. Instead, juxtaposed alongside headlines reporting GM's 1935 profits of $167 million (up $72 million from the year before), the committee announced its plans to hold public hearings later in the month.[30]

Despite the growing list of political discouragements, the du Ponts plugged on. They continued to evaluate requests for donations from anti-Roosevelt causes, including some of questionable standing. Pierre fielded solicitations from the Taxpayers Association, headed by former Governor W. H. "Alfalfa Bill" Murray, and from the obscure Defenders of the Constitution. Upon his return from Cuba in late March, Irénée received a new request for aid from the KKK's Hiram Evans.

The Imperial Wizard argued that "the same group, closely allied for twelve years, must be personally contacted throughout the nation" before it was too late. Irénée did have the sense to reject formal co-operation with the Klan, but he encouraged Evans's separate efforts, saying, "I think your organization could do a great deal and it would be well worth while for you to attempt something of that kind."[31]

Both brothers, nonetheless, were despairing of the prospects of un-seating Roosevelt. Smith's speech had drawn $46,000 in contributions within a month, and student memberships had climbed by over 5300 since the beginning of the year. But overall membership levels re-mained low, and the League was forced to retain a professional solicitor to augment the efforts of William Stayton. Attempting to find a silver lining, Irénée informed E. F. Hutton on April 10, "We passed the 100,000 mark (few enough, God knows), but consider [referring to the British army at the start of World War I] the contemptible little army of 100,000 in 1914." His pride, however, prevented him from heeding the pleas of Stayton to counter the Black Committee's insinuations by releasing not just the details of his political contributions but also his patriotic and charitable gifts. Citing the folly of chasing "every red herring," Irénée also vetoed underwriting a second Virginia round-table debate. Irritated at the Republicans' retreat from public iden-tification with the League, he sarcastically observed, "Our august leaders of the Republican party have just appointed a new Brain Trust for their own instruction."[32]

Although he adopted a more philosophical mien, Pierre similarly was discouraged. "I despair," he wrote, "of any reasonable coalition between Democrats and Republicans." To Frank Atwood he lobbied for the need for a genuine ideological realignment of national partisan politics. He maintained, "Instead of the old-time relation, which for years has been based on contentions between protectionists and their adversaries or fighting over the Civil War, we must have a new line-up which needs a conservative party based on defense of the Consti-tution . . . and perhaps a communistic party based upon radicalism and abandonment of the Constitution and also of our economic sys-tem." To Pierre the main point of contention "between the capitalistic system and the communist system is largely a question of who shall have the responsibility of management." With that belief in mind, he yearned for the Republicans to nominate "a man of well-known ability in the industrial field," since "practice has shown that politicians are not fitted for this kind of job."[33]

The du Ponts' "old guard" of political allies was passing, the most literal examples being the deaths in the spring of 1936 of Albert Ritchie and James Beck. The assault of the Black Committee, however, gave little time for mourning or reflection. Following a conclusive court victory against the telegram seizures, Jouett Shouse employed NBC radio to launch an attack on the committee's continuing "abuses of power." Unintimidated, the panel began taking testimony on April 8 from organizations linked to the Liberty League, starting with the American Taxpayers League and the Crusaders. On April 10, the Farmers Independence Council took its turn, succeeded five days later by the Southern Committee to Uphold the Constitution. By April 17, the Sentinels were under the microscope. What the series of hearings succeeded in demonstrating was that a network of anti-Roosevelt organizations had received well over a million dollars from the same small group of wealthy industrialists and financiers, with the du Ponts at the top of the list.[34]

The disclosure of significant du Pont contributions to a network of anti-administration causes was scarcely earthshaking, but particular details of the family's activities proved embarrassing for their display of either ineptness or deception. The Farmers Independence Council, for example, claimed to be a legitimate representative of opponents of New Deal agriculture policies, and League spokesman Shouse denied any Liberty League role in developing or funding the organization. But the council's president, Kansas cattleman Daniel I. Casement, was a Liberty League advisory council member, and Stanley Morse, self-described as an agricultural engineering consultant to the Liberty League, was the council's first vice-president and general manager. The organization first shared Washington office space with the Liberty League, then with the League's Chicago office. And as the Philadelphia *Record* gleefully pointed out, the FIC's largest benefactor was "that old hayseed Lammot du Pont, who kicked in $5000 (crops pretty good this year, ain't they, Lammot?)" Most of the remaining backing came not from farmers but from Chicago packing interests intent on killing the AAA in 1935. The Black Committee could not find a single working farmer in the entire organization, and Pierre's defense of his brother's role on the grounds that his ownership of a 4000-acre estate qualified him as a farmer was hardly convincing.[35]

The hearings exposed to public view the Sentinels' *Amateur Fire Brigade* campaign, as well as the du Pont circle's contributions to the Macon "Grass Roots" Convention that had displayed the "nigger picture." To Pierre's credit, when an anti-Roosevelt correspondent suggested additional circulation of the photograph in the South on the grounds that "There are some things they [Southern white voters] understand," he emphatically refused to recommend that the Liberty

League assist the effort. He also declined to make an additional $2000 contribution to the Macon meeting's sponsor, the Southern Committee, in early May. But the damage had been done to the du Ponts', and the League's, reputations. Black Committee investigators unearthed and released a list of questionable family contributions in 1935 that included the following:[36]

Southern Committee to Uphold the Constitution		Farmers Independence Council	
John Raskob	$5,000	Lammot du Pont	$5,000
Alfred Sloan	$1,000	Alfred Sloan	$1,000
(after Macon)			
Pierre du Pont	$5,000	*Sentinels*	
Lammot du Pont	$3,000		
Irénée du Pont	$100	Irénée du Pont	$100
Henry F. du Pont	$500	A. B. Echols	$75
Economists National Committee		*American Federation of Utility Investors*	
Walter Carpenter, Jr.	$100	A. B. Echols	$25
Lammot du Pont	$1,000		
Crusaders		*New York State Economic Council*	
Irénée du Pont	$10,000	Lammot du Pont	$1,000
Lammot du Pont	$1,000		
Alfred Sloan	$10,000	*Minute Men and Women of Today*	
A. B. Echols	$75	Irénée du Pont	$1,400

A particularly sensational aspect of the hearings, and one which damaged further the League's public reputation, was the hunt by committee investigators for evidence of sporadic or consistent anti-Semitism by Leaguers or their allies. In the examination of the Sentinels, anti-Semitic statements by president Alexander Lincoln were aired, as well as similar comments by the League's Mrs. Henry Bourne Joy. Jewish organizations quickly demanded public apologies from both organizations and the resignations from them of prominent Jewish members such as Joseph Proskauer, a longtime ally of Al Smith. Amidst such charges of fraud and prejudice, it came as no surprise that prominent industrialists who might have otherwise contributed to the League's election-year efforts, such as automaker Walter Chrysler, declined on the grounds that the League had been misrepresented to them.[37]

As if the buffeting at the hands of the Black Committee was not enough, in mid-April other charges against the Liberty League surfaced. Heber Blankenhorn of the NLRB reported to a Senate subcommittee studying enforcement of the Wagner Act, headed by Senator Robert La Follette, Jr., of Wisconsin, the existence of a wholesale campaign by industrial employers to defy the law. The origin of the La Follette panel was a resolution of March 23 calling for the creation of a subcommittee of the Senate Education and Labor Committee to study "violations of the right of free speech and assembly" in the collective bargaining process. According to the NLRB spokesman's information, firms had spent some $80 million dollars for the use of labor spies, gunmen, tear gas stockpiles, and strikebreakers. Blankenhorn's testimony, given on April 15 (the same day that the Black investigation was interrogating officers of the FIC), included a chart tracking nearly 200 agencies employed in strikebreaking or labor espionage. The testimony implicated the Liberty League in the effort to obstruct the Wagner Act when it noted, "Public records show the close organizational connections between professional spy and strikebreaking agencies, plant munitioning concerns, and a league of lawyers sponsoring concerted obstructiveness in the courts." Few who heard the report doubted that the "league of lawyers" cited as central to the effort to frustrate the law was the Liberty League's National Lawyers' Committee. Although in his initial report Blankenhorn named no names, as one example he cited an instance in which a member of the National Lawyers' Committee had appeared before the NLRB "defending a steel company which is buying tear gas from [a] chemical company and spies from [a] detective agency, whose offices interlock with the Liberty League lawyer." Joined with the embarrassing revelations of the Black investigation, the La Follette panel's preliminary accusations led a *New York Times* writer to conclude that the du Ponts "must now find very little satisfaction in what they got for their money."[38]

As damaging as the congressional inquiries of April were, they could have been worse. The du Ponts themselves were never officially called to appear as witnesses. Additional organizational allies, such as Women Investors in America and the American Federation of Investors, successfully defied committee requests for their complete files, sparing the family the possibility of more embarrassing headlines. The hearings, however, drove the public wedge between the GOP and the Liberty League even deeper. As James Farley gleefully noted, "The Liberty League is making it more embarrassing for the Republicans every day. They can't repudiate it because they need the money; they can't absorb it, otherwise they make the Liberty League out a liar; they can't ignore it, because they need American Liberty League ideas and brains." While the administration continued to lampoon the League, it took steps to line up its own cadre of business supporters. With Lammot du Pont, Colby Chester, Ernest T. Weir, Robert Lund, and John Raskob plotting anti–New Deal strategy at a gathering of twenty-five industrial leaders in New York on April 13 under the aegis of the National Business Conference Committee, the administration laid its own plans for a Good Neighbor League, to be headed by columnist Stanley High, as a counterpoint. By early May, the President had resumed his practice of inviting leading businessmen to White House "stag dinners," with the roster including Bernard Baruch, Walter Chrysler, Owen Young, and even fading Liberty Leaguer Will Clayton.[39]

The steady stream of attacks by presidential surrogates, combined with Roosevelt's deft courtship of businessmen, infuriated the du Pont circle. But there was little they could do about it save lash out privately against the President to each other. Alfred Sloan, noting a particularly irritating address Roosevelt made to a young audience in Baltimore, grumbled to John Raskob, "I have always thought the President was not intellectually honest, but after reading this speech I have come to the conclusion that he is not even intellectual." Upon his return from Florida, Raskob found a challenge from Senator James Couzens of Michigan to his earlier claim that a "vicious radical element" existed within the administration. He now engaged in an extended debate with the senator via published letters, and transmitted copies of his replies to the directors of Du Pont, General Motors, Bankers Trust, and the Lawyers Trust Company. Declining to give Roosevelt any share of credit for the partial economic recovery, Raskob proclaimed that industry itself "has perhaps gone 75% of the way in taking care of its unemployed." If unencumbered by high taxes, he maintained, industry would finish the recovery job by itself.[40]

While the du Ponts and their allies fumed, the stop-Roosevelt movement fizzled. On the Republican side, a James Wadsworth boomlet completely flopped, and a correspondent lamented to Raskob that the GOP remained "confused as between five or six candidates" (including Alf Landon, Senators Arthur Vandenburg and William E. Borah, Frank Knox, and ex-president Herbert Hoover), "no one of whom seems to be quite the right fellow." The conservative Democrats' picture was even worse. Despite the prior assumptions that Ely would be able to hold his own in New England, Reed likewise in the Midwest, and Talmadge in the Deep South, such hopes had disintegrated. In New Hampshire, a fight for an uninstructed delegation—a struggle led by lawyer John S. Hurley and assisted financially by Pierre du

Pont—collapsed in the face of the administration's patronage power. Similarly, Connecticut's delegates lined up with the President. In Louisiana, the White House entered into a "Second Louisiana Purchase" with the remnant of the Long machine, receiving delegate pledges in exchange for the restoration of state patronage and the dropping of tax evasion charges against machine leader Seymour Weiss.[41]

Following the failure in New Hampshire, Ely's campaign to keep his home state's delegates from the clutches of Governor James M. Curley and the Roosevelt forces evaporated, causing him to lament, "One lone Democrat can't lick four billion dollars [the federal relief spending] and he is foolish to try." On the heels of a Roosevelt victory in New York City's delegate contest on April 2, Henry Breckinridge had been similarly overwhelmed in Pennsylvania, Maryland, New Jersey, and Ohio. Al Smith's favorite-son presence proved of little clout in New York, and the President's popular vote ratios over Breckinridge were eighteen-to-one in Pennsylvania's late-April primary and six-to-one in Maryland's May 4 balloting. By the end of May, Eugene Talmadge had opted to pull out of even the Georgia primary rather than risk humiliation in his home state.[42]

Although the League tried to fight back, it had little fighting spirit left. On May 5 the national office issued a broad assault on the administration's record, entitled "Twenty-eight Facts about the New Deal." Five days later, Jouett Shouse transmitted signed petitions to the Senate in protest of the Black Committee's telegram seizures and demanded disciplinary action, without effect. In midmonth, Shouse appeared on NBC radio to remind the public that "You Owe Thirty-One Billion Dollars." But even with the help of a Supreme Court ruling on May 18 striking down the Guffey Coal Conservation Act, the National Lawyers' Committee, already scarred by the attacks of the fall and the La Follette committee's accusations, suspended further legal opinions until after the Court's scheduled adjournment. Although Al Smith, in recognition of his past leadership, had been selected as a national Democratic convention delegate from New York, reports were already circulating in the press that he would not even attend the Philadelphia gathering.[43]

Raoul Desvernine, leader of the National Lawyers' Committee and now president of Crucible Steel as well (leading to speculation that he had been the lawyer referred to in the Blankenhorn report), had abandoned for the moment his organization's publications denouncing the New Deal in favor of his own book-length diatribe, entitled *Democratic Despotism*. Almost immediately after its publication on May 8, Secretary of Agriculture Henry Wallace assailed the volume, which purported to describe the roots and dangers of the New Deal, for its illustration of a swastika-like banner as a symbol for the Roosevelt administration. Desvernine's literary effort was not even that well received by the du Ponts, who saw it contributing little to the electoral battle at hand. Pierre, while he praised its content, added, "Being a lawyer, Desvernine is a little bit legalistic at times." Irénée directly rebuked the author, stating, "We must win the election by getting the votes of the common people, who can hardly be reached by your book."[44]

What kept the du Ponts going was not any realistic hope of blocking the renomination of Franklin Roosevelt, but instead the notion that he remained vulnerable in a general election. Private polling buttressed that belief. In a confidential report to Pierre, Du Pont public relations researcher Edmond E. Lincoln claimed that 80–85 percent of the country's newspapers opposed the New Deal. He also cited the *Literary Digest's* claims that 63 percent of its respondents did not favor the President, and that Roosevelt could count on only twelve states (eleven of them in the South) as safe. Injecting his own emphasis, Lincoln asserted, "*No Digest poll with so strong a margin has ever been wrong in the past.*" Even the Gallup Poll claimed that 56 percent of its respondents did not favor the New Deal, including 70 percent of the nation's clergy, business groups such as the Chamber of Commerce and the NAM, the American Bankers Association, and even large numbers of farmers, urbanites, industrial workers, the young, and women. The key for Roosevelt's enemies, Pierre was told, was to generate a high voter turnout, for in the previous four presidential contests only an average of 53 percent of eligible voters had participated. With that advice in mind, the Liberty League's executive committee on May 14 issued a call for members to undertake a chain-letter "get-out-the-vote" drive. Each member was instructed to secure ten voter pledges, with each of them expected to obtain ten more, and so on. The League set a goal of ten million voter registrations with the aim of outweighing the President's expected "patronage vote" of relief beneficiaries.[45]

Few among the League's leaders could be absolutely certain that Roosevelt could be beaten. They nonetheless were convinced that he *must* be. Pierre declared to the Southern Committee's John Henry Kirby, "A vote for Mr. Roosevelt is a vote for the socialist ticket." To another writer, he again castigated himself for "not having undertaken the repeal of the 16th Amendment . . . instead of the 18th Amendment." In retrospect he concluded that repeal of the income tax could have been secured "quite as easily," with "much greater" benefits. Jouett Shouse, one of the few political professionals in the du Ponts' entourage, was less confident in the poll figures. Telling a private correspondent that he did not believe that the President could be defeated, Shouse still added, "I am going to do everything I can to try to defeat him." In a grudging concession to those within the administration he considered his chief ideological enemies, he noted, "Frankfurter is very able but he has some extremely radical views." Shouse's personal survey of the Republican field in advance of their Cleveland convention led him to conclude that either Vandenburg or Landon— probably Landon—would be the GOP nominee. "Either of them," he indicated, "would be entirely satisfactory to me."[46]

The beginning of June brought some favorable omens, but they again were soon drowned out by the bad. On June 1, in a 5–4 decision, the Supreme Court struck down New York State's minimum wage law as a violation of the right of private contract. The du Ponts also took heart from rumors in New York newspapers that the Republican convention might produce a Landon-Wadsworth ticket. But as if the League were being followed by a black cloud, the next day its president found himself the object of a $15,000 lawsuit from a pedestrian who claimed that Shouse had run a stop sign and hit him. On June 6, the La Follette subcommittee received an additional Senate appropriation of $15,000 for its probe into employers' obstructions of labor rights. According to information just received from Heber Blankenhorn, General Motors had reported in SEC documents paying over $167,000 to the Pinkerton Agency for labor spies. Left-wing publications, including the New York *Daily Worker*, charged that the Liberty League and the Hearst press were sponsoring the Klan-style Black Legion, which had been accused of anti-union violence and murder in Michigan against the United Auto Workers.[47]

Well after the 1936 election, such charges of anti-labor brutality garnered additional headlines. When the La Follette panel months later obtained the 1936 minutes of the Special Conference Committee, it learned that in its June meeting Du Pont and General Motors representatives openly considered utilizing such right-wing organizations as the Men of America and the Sentinels for anti-union activity. Du Pont member F. C. Evans informed his colleagues that his company had decided not even to distribute literature from the Men of America because "sooner or later" they would find themselves " 'on the carpet' before some congressional committee from which it would logically develop that the Du Pont company was helping the movement and this, from a public-relations standpoint, would be undesirable." In response to a written inquiry of June 1 from Special Conference Committee secretary Edward S. Cowdrick on the usefulness of the Sentinels, however, GM's labor-relations director Harry Anderson had replied,

"I have never heard of that organization . . . Maybe you could use a little Black Legion down in your country. It might help." It was clear to the La Follette subcommittee that attempts to organize workers into unions for collective bargaining purposes had been tied up by legal obstruction and the threat and use of violence against workers—moves that had been orchestrated by the Special Conference Committee. The NLRB reported that in the first six months following passage of the Wagner Act, the number of unfair labor practices cases had outweighed representation complaints by a four-to-one margin, and only thirty-one NLRB-supervised employee representation elections had been successfully held.[48]

While their companies fought the encroachments of industrial unionism, the du Ponts themselves focused on the upcoming party conventions and the general election to follow. With at least four Liberty Leaguers on the fifty-three-member Republican platform committee (although James Wadsworth and Ogden Mills had failed to secure such appointments), and others exerting influence within the GOP hierarchy, a receptive hearing could be counted on for the League's policy proposals. Of greater significance was the fact that one-third of the twenty-one-member GOP national finance committee consisted of prominent Liberty Leaguers, including Sewell Avery, Herbert L. Pratt, Joseph Pew (brother of J. Howard Pew), Hal H. Smith, E. T. Weir, Silas Strawn, and chairman William B. Bell. Disagreements within the League again surfaced over such issues as an anti-monopoly free-enterprise plank, with the Pews' support of such a stance opposed by Irénée on substantive grounds and because it was not "strictly" a constitutional question. Pierre sustained his brother, arguing that "so-called monopolies" were only innocent "large businesses."[49]

Although he similarly advocated that the Republicans avoid tariff issues, Pierre pointedly endorsed the denunciation of "Governmental monopolies" other than those sanctioned in the Constitution. The postal service, for example, he had no quarrel with, even though he believed it was "inefficiently handled." Regarding other issues, Irénée regretted the League's earlier public opposition to the soldiers' bonus on the grounds that it had been an unpopular position and one which had not even involved a constitutional question. In reaction to the recent Guffey decision, William Stayton floated the idea that Fourteenth Amendment "due process" and "contract clause" protections be extended by constitutional amendment to the individual states. Pierre appeared to concur, responding, "Personally I am not keen about giving this power [of contract] to any save the individuals affected."[50]

By the time the GOP convention opened in Cleveland on June 9, the Liberty League had already spent $265,000 for the year and was $60,000 in the red. Despite the expenditures, however, the organization had done little to influence the Republicans' choice of a presidential nominee. None of the prospective nominees particularly excited the du Ponts, although all were preferable to Roosevelt. Borah and Hoover were the most unacceptable; Borah because of his insurgent and isolationist record in the Senate, Hoover because of past clashes over prohibition and his unelectability. Knox seemed slightly too much a progressive. Vandenburg's otherwise impeccable ideological credentials were marred by his isolationism and his service on the Nye Committee, and Landon remained a largely unknown quantity. Any suspense, however, dissipated on the afternoon before the first roll call when the New York and Pennsylvania delegations announced for Landon. The action nipped in the bud a belated stop-Landon movement which had been orchestrated by supporters of Borah and Hoover. Vandenburg and Knox, recognizing the inevitable, proceeded to second the nomination of the former Kansas governor, with only Borah refusing to concede. On the first ballot, all but nineteen delegates (eighteen of them from Wisconsin) cast their votes for Landon, and Wisconsin soon moved to make the nomination unanimous.[51]

The du Ponts and their allies in the League devoted less energy to the choice of a GOP standard-bearer than to attempting to influence the choice of a running mate. Even there, the League's hopes of the convention choosing a Jeffersonian Democrat for vice-president as part of a coalition ticket came up empty. John Raskob lobbied Delaware Republican delegate and du Pont in-law C. Douglas Buck to push for Joseph Ely, indicating that Al Smith would campaign in his behalf in cities with large Catholic populations such as Chicago, New York, Philadelphia, and Boston. Buck reported back, however, "I could find but little sentiment at the convention for a coalition ticket." What GOP leaders he consulted wanted, Buck maintained, was not a coalition campaign with either a disaffected Democrat or a Liberty Leaguer, but a League-supported third-party effort to siphon votes away from Roosevelt, featuring perhaps Ely, Lewis Douglas, Breckinridge, Smith, or Newton Baker. Whatever the postconvention strategy, Raskob concurred, "everything must be done to keep from losing New York and Illinois, and of course, Pennsylvania." Other Northeastern states, particularly those in New England, were deemed safely Republican. In the immediate aftermath of the GOP convention, another offer of help came from Texan J. S. Cullinan, who indicated to the du Ponts his willingness to head a Democrats for Landon state chapter which would be coordinated with similar efforts elsewhere.[52]

About a week after the Republicans concluded their business in

Cleveland, the Congress did likewise in Washington. Among the comparatively few noteworthy actions in an otherwise desultory election-year session were the Walsh-Healy Public Contracts Act (giving the federal government the power to set minimum wage and maximum hour and price levels for firms under federal contract), the Robinson-Patman Act (barring discriminatory manufacturers' discounts to large chain-store clients), a $2 billion veterans' bonus bill, a soil conservation act intended to replace the defunct AAA, and a tax bill, including an undistributed profits tax, designed to raise about $800 million in new revenues. A new Neutrality Act extended previous congressional arms embargoes toward belligerent nations to prohibit financial loans. While these measures pained the du Ponts, most embarrassing was the Black Committee's decision on June 20, the last day of the session, to release to the press its composite figures on du Pont and Liberty League contributions to a panoply of right-wing organizations since mid-1934.[53]

With the end of the legislative session as a backdrop, the Democrats gathered in Philadelphia for their coronation of the incumbent President. In a last-ditch effort to disrupt the proceedings, on the Saturday preceding the opening gavel Al Smith, Bainbridge Colby, James A. Reed, Joseph Ely, and Daniel F. Cohalan sent an open telegram to all convention delegates. The message had been prepared earlier in the week during a Liberty League executive committee meeting held in Smith's Empire State Building offices and transmitted from John Raskob's summer home in Maryland. Reciting the familiar litany of conservative complaints against the President and urging a return to traditional party principles, the telegram's authors called upon delegates to undertake the "putting aside of Franklin D. Roosevelt." Failing that, they continued, "you should put aside the name of the party." The message concluded, "If you fail, then patriotic voters of all parties will know unhesitatingly to what standard they must rally in order to preserve the America of the great leaders of the past." Smith and other conservative Democrats were urging their fellow partisans to abandon openly a Democratic party led by Franklin Roosevelt. In his own preconvention address Jouett Shouse issued a call to Democrats to "take a walk" in the general election.[54]

Undercutting the impact of the appeal, however, was the fact that not even all anti-Roosevelt Democrats were in support of "taking a walk." A day after the story first broke on June 21, newspapers reported that among others, John W. Davis, Lewis Douglas, and Bernard Baruch had refused to sign the telegram and had urged that it not be sent. After some confusion in their ranks, the President's campaign strategists, fearing an embarrassing pro-Smith floor demonstration, gave orders to block any efforts from the floor to have the telegram read publicly. Even an administration reply to the appeal, in the form of remarks by pro-Roosevelt speakers at the William Jennings Bryan Memorial Breakfast scheduled for the Penn Athletic Club, was vetoed. Setting the tone from the top, the President himself rejected the idea of a personal counterattack on Smith, advising instead that he be ignored and "see if he breaks out again."[55]

He did not. The Philadelphia convention unfolded as the President's handlers had envisioned—as a smoothly flowing paean of praise to the leadership of Franklin D. Roosevelt. A nominating speech by former New York Supreme Court Justice John E. Mack was followed by fifty-seven seconding speeches in an eight-hour eulogy. With only one brief incident—a minuscule demonstration on Thursday by young Republican infiltrators who unfurled Smith banners and chanted, "We want Al"—the Roosevelt coronation played itself out fully. Adding a dramatic exclamation point to the festivities, on Saturday night, June 27, the President personally accepted his party's renomination with a fiery address fine-tuned by aides Tom Corcoran and Stanley High. Underscoring the themes he had set at the beginning of the year, Roosevelt compared the struggle of American patriots over political tyranny some 160 years earlier to his contemporary fight to resist the modern tyranny of "economic royalists." He proclaimed, "The economic royalists complain that we seek to overthrow the institutions of America. What they really complain of is that we seek to take away their power . . . In vain they seek to hide behind the flag and the Constitution." He concluded with a ringing call: "To some generations much is given. Of others much is expected. This generation of Americans has a rendezvous with destiny."[56] If they agreed with little else in the President's address, the du Ponts concurred that the 1936 election was a rendezvous with destiny, both for the nation's, and for their own, political fortunes.

chapter 13

A Rout and a Valley Forge

Once the nominations of Alf Landon and Franklin D. Roosevelt were settled, the du Ponts and their Liberty League allies knew that their mission was to provide as much assistance, directly or indirectly, to the GOP as it would allow. The partnership between the League and the Landon campaign, however, proved an unusual one. As individuals, the du Ponts and other wealthy Leaguers supported the Republican ticket with speeches, behind-the-scenes policy and organizational advice, and hefty financial contributions. As an organization, the League kept up the fiction of its nonpartisan stance, fearing that a more overt linkage to the GOP would hurt rather than help Landon's chances. In turn the Republicans eagerly accepted every bit of covert aid provided by the League while insisting publicly that they were not its captive.

As a consequence of the need to avoid any public hint of collusion, the GOP and the Liberty League occasionally found themselves engaged in unknowing and inefficient duplications of effort. In one narrow escape, Jouett Shouse urged both Raskob and Irénée to fund and create a series of fifteen-minute radio programs featuring folksy Midwestern characters, songs, and anti–New Deal homilies in order to reach the "common man." Shouse envisioned a featured character similar to the "Seth Parker" radio personality, and scriptwriter Frank Chase crafted one, named "Goodwyn" or "Good" Hollister, who sat in a village store dispensing verbal sallies at AAA, Share-Our-Wealth, and other "crackpot" schemes. Unfortunately for Shouse, the price tag for such a show was estimated at $100,000—money that the League's backers could not afford to divert from direct contributions to the GOP campaign. At the same time, the Republicans were proposing their own series of skits, written by Henry Frank Carlton and entitled "Liberty at the Crossroads." In the GOP version, various characters, including the Founding Fathers, farmers, and a young couple supposedly delaying marriage because of high taxes, took turns criticizing Roosevelt's policies. Although NBC and CBS rejected the Republicans' programming, the series was carried by the Mutual Network—including WGN, the flagship station of the publisher of the conservative Chicago *Tribune*, Colonel Robert McCormick.[1]

The Liberty League issued public disclaimers of organizational cooperation with the GOP. Irénée, at the advice of prominent League Republicans Howard Heinz and James Wadsworth, repudiated claims by Democratic campaign director James Farley that a "sinister coupling" of the two causes existed. Only a common commitment to the Constitution bound them, he insisted, and he called upon the new Republican party chairman, John D. M. Hamilton, to issue his own denials. Following the statement, however, Wadsworth advised Irénée to avoid any further focus on the issue through even another public denial, insisting that Landon's own statement to the same effect on June 28 was sufficient. Wadsworth confidently reassured Irénée, "I have never believed that the smearing of the League will become a potent feature in the campaign." Covertly, Heinz, Wadsworth, and the du Ponts were still determined to do their utmost for Landon. Heinz insisted to Irénée, "We must do everything in our power to put Landon over." Wadsworth, certain that Eastern farmers would repudiate the President, maintained that in spite of public embarrassments, "Our Liberty League is still doing good work." Although the Nye Committee's release of its final report on July 18, 1936, generated another round of adverse headlines, the New York Republican insisted that "already it is apparent that its [the Liberty League's] continued existence cannot be injurious to Landon. I am mightily glad we didn't quit."[2]

As the League's most powerful leaders, the du Ponts set the tone for their colleagues' involvement in the presidential contest. In their case, the primary method of participation was through the pocketbook. On July 28 alone, Pierre du Pont issued $5000 each to eleven different local, state, and national Republican campaign organizations. A day later Irénée gave $5100 apiece to twelve more such bodies, and, supplementing an earlier $5000 to the Republican National Finance Committee and the Delaware Republican party, extended another $100 to each of them. Besides doing his brother one (hundred) better, Irénée believed that by giving contributions in excess of $5000 he could report them on his gift tax deduction statement. As illustration that the du Ponts' individual contributions to the GOP were but one facet of the larger struggle against the broker state, upon urgings by the Special

Conference Committee the Du Pont Company also on July 28 upped its contribution to the anti-union American Management Association to $1000.[3]

At the same time that they aided the Republicans, the du Ponts viewed with favor any political developments which might erode the President's political constituency. They eagerly approved even the efforts of Roosevelt's critics on the left to organize a third-party challenge, although they did not give direct aid to the plan. Since the death of Huey Long the previous September, the followers of Share-Our-Wealth, the Townsend old-age pension movement, and other economic redistribution schemes had searched for a standard-bearer. Gerald L. K. Smith had assumed control of the Long movement, and had even tried to divert attention from Eugene Talmadge at the Macon Grass Roots Convention. By May 1936 Smith had joined ranks with Townsend in a political alliance, accompanied by the demagogic radio priest from Royal Oak, Michigan, Father Charles Coughlin. With Coughlin, head of his own National Union for Social Justice, leading the way, the trio and their supporters gathered in Cleveland. Although the meeting was originally planned as a convention to nominate Townsend for president, the gathering instead endorsed the candidacy of North Dakota Non-Partisan League crusader William Lemke on a "Union Party" slate.[4]

Lemke was forced continually to deny lingering charges that he was a "paid agent" of the Liberty League in his stop-Roosevelt crusade. League spokesmen similarly rejected the accusations, but there was little doubt that the League wished nothing but the best for Lemke's cause. The North Dakotan hoped to hold together a motley collection of Townsendites, Coughlinites, and the Farmer-Labor Party behind a platform calling for the confiscation of incomes over $500,000, currency inflation schemes, and farm relief. Coughlin bragged that he could woo ten million Eastern Catholic voters from the Democrats, while Townsend's support was counted upon to coax similar gains among the elderly. Lemke, in turn, claimed that he would personally pull in the farm vote of the upper Great Plains. Given such grandiose private predictions, the Lemke campaign publicly declared the comparatively modest goal of diverting three million votes from Roosevelt. However, the Union party was able to secure places on only thirty-five of the forty-eight state general election ballots. Smith and Townsend urged their backers in the remaining states to cast their votes for Landon.[5]

Although the du Ponts welcomed whatever help Lemke could provide, they felt a far greater ideological affinity for the efforts of Jeffersonian Democrats to pull votes away from Roosevelt. The urge to help them grew as the League continued to receive advice not to give a formal endorsement to the GOP ticket. The Baltimore *Sun*'s Frank Kent warned that any endorsement of Landon by the League would backfire, and Lammot du Pont seconded the opinion, adding, "I hope the American Liberty League will not 'come out' for Landon because that was not the original purpose of the American Liberty League." By early August, Arthur Krock of the *New York Times* was reporting that "Republicans, feeling that its [the Liberty League's] implied endorsement and support are very hurtful, have made plain their wish that the League as a unit take a position outside the party breastworks." The League's public relations damage to the GOP was so great, he maintained, that at the GOP convention in Cleveland Republican chairman Hamilton "would have walked a mile out of his way rather than be seen in the company of a Leaguer." Krock's advice to the League to disband, however, sparked an angry denial from James Wadsworth that the GOP had "shied away" from the organization's help.[6]

Tired of the League's being cast as the Republicans' publicly shunned relative, Irénée blasted both sides in the race for being "suckers" for accepting Roosevelt's "hooey" regarding the League's unpopularity; words he claimed had been designed just to "make a split" in the opposition. "I think," Irénée insisted, "the Liberty League is doing the only job that is really worthwhile, but the cause is aided by some of the other organizations like the Crusaders." He pointedly added, "If the Liberty League is not wanted by the Republican party, it is because they too do not believe in Constitutional government." Although he continued to be bitter over what he viewed as the Republicans' failure to press the attack on Roosevelt's "anti-Constitutional" actions, Irénée was forced to bow to the inevitability of a covert campaign role for the League. Reacting to continuing rumors of an impending League endorsement of Landon, Jouett Shouse disingenuously declared that the organization "will endorse no party. It will endorse no candidate. It has not contributed and will not contribute to any campaign fund."[7]

With the League forced into a noncommittal posture toward Landon, the du Ponts' earlier hesitance toward making direct financial offerings to the Jeffersonian Democrats began to dissipate. In early July, the Independent Coalition of American Women, created at a Toledo, Ohio, convention, endorsed the Landon ticket and established the goal of recruiting a million anti–New Deal Democrats and inactive Republican women. The cause's national director, Mrs. Mabel Jacques Eichel of Connecticut, was a veteran of both the fight against prohibition and the Liberty League's ill-fated women's division. The Independent Coalition took on all the aspects of a distaff version of the Jeffersonian Democrats, with Mrs. Edwin T. Meredith (wife of Wilson's former Secretary of Agriculture) as national chairman and Mrs. James A. Reed and Mrs. Joseph B. Ely as additional officers. Spouses of Liberty League advisory committee members prominent in the organization included Fleishmann heiress Mrs. Christian R. Holmes and Mrs. William T. Healey of Atlanta. In mid-July, however, Jouett Shouse disavowed any connection with the women's group, the Jeffersonian Democratic presidential efforts of Henry Breckinridge, or the Sentinels. At month's end, with individual du Ponts funneling thousands of dollars to Landon, and prior to Shouse's firm disapproval of a formal endorsement of Landon by the League, Irénée du Pont declined to contribute to a Jeffersonian Democrat radio fund or even to give $25,000 for a pro-Landon effort by Texas Democrats. Part of the reason was the lingering public relations damage to the du Ponts from their earlier subsidization of the Sentinels, the Southern Committee, and the Macon Grass Roots Convention of January. When solicited by a correspondent with clearly racist and anti-Semitic attitudes to contribute further to such causes, Irénée combatively countered, "I am not at all in accord with Jew-baiting, negro-baiting, or any other crusade against groups, for these groups are not homogeneous. There are many good Jews, and I know plenty of good darkies."[8]

By early August, however, as avenues of formal assistance to the GOP closed, others to the Jeffersonian Democrats and similar efforts gradually opened. On August 6, Pierre ordered 200 copies of the anti-Roosevelt diatribe "And Satan Came Also," by League publicist William C. Murphy, for personal distribution. Over the next two days, the Jeffersonian Democrats, headed by James Reed, Sterling Edmunds (of the Southern Committee to Uphold the Constitution), Bainbridge Colby, and Joseph B. Ely, held their own nominating convention in Detroit. Other prominent figures among the forty-two conservative Democrats in attendance were Henry Breckinridge, John Henry Kirby, and ex-congressman Joseph W. Bailey, Jr., of Texas. The convention chose Reed as national chairman, Edmunds as secretary, and Ely to head up the finance committee, with the national headquarters to be located in St. Louis. Although a third-party effort was already too late, over the objections of Ely the delegates, unlike the Independent Coalition of American Women, opted against a formal endorsement of Landon. Instead, they agreed to act as political coordinators of the national anti-Roosevelt effort outside the GOP, with the precise methods and organizational ties left to the discretion of each state's leaders.

Henry Breckinridge, in turn, served as the personal liaison between his group, the Liberty League, and the Landon campaign.[9]

With Breckinridge's active assistance, Landon solicited the financial help of additional Liberty Leaguers. A special target was the recently remarried Pauline Sabin Davis. The Kansan's earlier "dry" history on the prohibition question, however, kept her from active support or contributions to him. Breckinridge also utilized his position as covert consultant to the GOP presidential nominee to urge Landon's cultivation of New York Mayor Fiorello LaGuardia and Commissioner Robert Moses and to avoid employing the unpopular Herbert Hoover as a spokesman. The du Ponts' own itchiness to contribute more to the stop-Roosevelt effort, and the continuing optimism purveyed by pollster E. E. Lincoln, led them to seek out new forms of assistance. In late August, Lincoln relayed to Pierre du Pont the results of a *Farm Journal* rural "straw poll" that claimed, despite an overall equal division of votes between Landon and Roosevelt, that Landon held a majority or plurality in sixteen states with 256 electoral votes—only ten short of victory. An emboldened Irénée agreed to co-sponsor with J. Howard Pew, in the form of a $1000 gift, a short anti-Roosevelt movie or stereopticon exhibit for distribution and display in churches by Congregationalist clergyman Ernest A. Reese.[10]

As late as the first week of September, however, both Pierre and Irénée were still refusing all overtures to aid directly the Jeffersonian Democrats' fall offensive. Irénée refused to distribute anti-Roosevelt literature for Democrats offered by John Henry Kirby on the grounds that "I, of course, have a reputation of being a Republican." Pierre privately cited the previous embarrassments at the hands of the Southern Committee and similarly declined to underwrite distribution of Kirby's pamphlet. Jouett Shouse urged others to do likewise, observing, "I like Mr. Kirby very much, but I think the Grass Roots Conference held by his group not only did no good but did real harm." What both Irénée and Pierre would have preferred, clearly, was an overt, bipartisan stop-Roosevelt coalition spearheaded not by the Jeffersonian Democrats but by the "right kind" of people—namely the Liberty League. Such a role had been already foreclosed, but Pierre and Irénée continued to finance the Landon campaign on their own. In August, Pierre gave $5000 to the Iowa GOP and a token $150 to the Independent Coalition of American Women. Irénée extended $5100 and $2500, respectively, to Utah and South Dakota Republican chapters and $500 more to New York City's National Republican Club.[11]

The du Ponts continued to take heart from every encouraging indicator they could find. Even though the state of Maine was traditionally a Republican bulwark, the news of Landon's victory over Roosevelt in that state's early September elections gave rise to the slogan, "As goes Maine, so goes the nation." In support of the Landon effort in Maine, Irénée and Pierre each had contributed over $10,000 to the state GOP, Lammot, A. Felix du Pont, and Alfred Sloan had chipped in $5000 each, and Henry du Pont $2500 more, according to reports filed in early October. Similarly encouraging were the primary election results from Michigan, where du Pont adversary James Couzens had been defeated in his renomination race for the U.S. Senate. On the negative side of the ledger was the outcome of the Georgia senatorial primary, in which Eugene Talmadge was trounced by the administration's endorsee, Richard Russell, by a two-to-one margin.[12]

It was clear, however, that while contributions from various du Ponts were still very useful for the campaign ahead, the Liberty League as an organization no longer was. The League's public activities in September were limited to the usual round of Constitution Day addresses on the seventeenth and the sale of twenty-five-cent license-plate emblems bearing the Liberty Bell insignia and legend, "Uphold the Constitution." Besides its bad press, a less publicized, but equally limiting, damper on the organization was the arrival of the due dates on the original 1934 subscription loan notes of $25,000 per subscriber per year. Unless the League could reimburse their pledges before year's end, the Internal Revenue Bureau would likely view the agreements as taxable gifts to the organization and not as loans. Irénée ominously predicted that "a good many of the original backers" would not be willing to extend their commitments any longer. Although he agreed to approach the "Wilson men" and the "GM men," even he was preparing to reduce his own support from a level of $160,000 in 1936 down to $25,000 for the coming year. Pierre, while conceding the "lack of financial backing," called upon Shouse and others not to dissolve the League, pleading, "*Don't do it!*" Judge Charles Dawson echoed his sentiment, but H. B. Earhart of Detroit indicated a desire to continue the League only through the elections and then to "restudy our situation." Taking on the visage of a personal symbol of the League's crippled status was John Raskob, who had been forced to don crutches because of a knee infection.[13]

As a consequence of the League's troubles, the Washington office prepared to go into hibernation until spring. A number of staffers were laid off. The pamphlet series, having distributed 135 issues and 24 smaller leaflets, now ceased except for those remaining projects already "in the hopper." Rather than continue to publish their own attacks upon Roosevelt, Shouse and William Murphy now steered ideas and submissions to Republican party radio spokesman William Hard, who was delivering four or five talks per week for the Landon campaign. In August, Secretary of Agriculture Henry Wallace's forward to Irving Brant's book, *Storm Over the Court*—which stressed the importance of "presidents who will nominate the right men to the Supreme Court"— was assailed by the League's Raoul Desvernine. The League issued the rebuttal in a pamphlet entitled *A Reply to Secretary Wallace's Question—Whose Constitution? The Dominant Issue of the Campaign*, which decried the administration's resort to the excuse of emergency conditions in an attempt to subvert the Constitution. But even before the end of August, Desvernine's own National Lawyers' Committee packed up until after the election. Its final preelection broadside, *The Dual Form of Government and the New Deal*, which accused the President of subverting local self-government, appeared in early September.[14]

At a special meeting of the Liberty League's executive committee on September 30, the organization's formal operations were suspended for the duration of the election campaign. Chairman Irénée opted to avoid the pain of the occasion by attending a happier event instead— his youngest daughter's twenty-first birthday. Only now, at the pleading of John Raskob and as a favor to his conservative Democrat friends, the du Ponts agreed to channel some of their moneys to help finance a $1 million, twice-weekly radio speech campaign organized by the Jeffersonian Democrats that had begun two days earlier. Like Irénée, Raskob had been solicited to contribute to the anti-Roosevelt Democrats' radio fund almost a month earlier. Until the League's official demise, however, the du Ponts had been unwilling by word or deed to give the go-ahead to support it. Knowing of the pending executive committee decision, however, Raskob gave an initial installment of $33,000 on September 24 and urged Irénée to join in, which he did in the form of a $5100 contribution. In-law Ruly Carpenter gave $5000, as did Pierre and A. Felix du Pont.[15]

Demonstrating an admirable, if somewhat unexpected, sense of chivalry toward the presidential office, Al Smith on the twenty-fourth notified the White House of his upcoming anti-Roosevelt radio speech of October 31, and indicated a willingness to move it later into the evening so as to avoid a conflict in coverage with the President's own scheduled national broadcast. In order to augment the funding for Smith's and others' addresses, Raskob arranged with the Lawyers Trust Company to loan the National Jeffersonian Democrats up to $200,000 on September 29. The NAM's Robert Lund declined to contribute directly to the radio fund because of his public position, but he confidentially relayed, "The few letters we wrote brought in considerably more than half of the money needed." Less helpful was John W. Davis, who took a full month to respond to Raskob's repeated entreaties with a $2500 contribution at the end of October. Despite Raskob's secured loan from Lawyers Trust, the absence of sufficient matching contributions created a shortfall of nearly $100,000 that necessitated a postelection scheme for six individuals, including Lammot and Pierre, each to contribute an additional $16,000 to cover the costs.[16]

The Liberty League's demise had cleared the way for the expansion of the du Ponts' other financial campaigns against Franklin Roosevelt. A preliminary report to the Senate Special Committee to Investigate Campaign Expenditures, chaired by Augustine Lonergan of Connecticut, indicated that up to the end of September the du Ponts had given $383,000 to the Republican party, including $105,000 from the otherwise discreet Lammot. Irénée had offered nearly $100,000, and Pierre had provided over $85,000. In addition, Pierre had sent $5000 each to the "Mr. Kelley Movement" and the Crusaders, and $1200 to the Minute Men and Women of Today. In the month of October, Irénée added another $17,300 to the GOP, $5100 to a Walter T. Collins for "radio work," $2780 to F. Trabee Davison for more radio time, and $5100 to underwrite the distribution of campaign literature, called "Granitegrams," from an obscure Bucks County anti–New Deal organization. Pierre added $2500 each to two Republican congressional campaign organizations in Virginia, $1120 twice to Publicity Associates for anti-Roosevelt literature, and $200 to his own local Kennett Square Republican chapter.[17]

Despite the League's hibernation, the du Ponts and their allies did not hesitate to offer advice to the struggling Landon campaign. Communicating through an intermediary, Kansas City *Star* publisher Roy Roberts, Jouett Shouse urged the GOP candidate to emphasize the administration's betrayal of traditional Democratic beliefs, its desertion of the 1932 party platform, and its backing of independent progressives from the Farmer-Labor and La Follette factions in order to entice conservative crossover voting. Shouse also advocated hitting the specific issues of New Deal waste, deficits, and "boondoggling" relief. Irénée, through Shouse, pressed the Landon campaign to publish an open letter from Gifford Pinchot to Interior Secretary Ickes on the same matters, claiming that it could help the GOP in "the coal districts of Pennsylvania." The League's leadership similarly extended its good offices to the National Jeffersonian Democrats' radio campaign, with Shouse helping to coordinate the speaking schedule. Win or lose, many within the du Ponts' circle believed that the 1936 contest was the seedling of a fundamental political realignment. Shouse, in agreement, relayed a letter to the rest of the executive committee from South Carolina's George L. Buist predicting the emergence of a new "Communist-fascist" versus "Americanist" two-party system.[18]

From the end of September until election eve, with the League's unofficial help the National Jeffersonian Democrats took to the airwaves to plead for Franklin Roosevelt's defeat. In the last ten days of the campaign alone, the speech schedule included remarks on October 23 by Colby and Ely from New England, Colby again the next day from Philadelphia, Breckinridge and Al Smith from Pittsburgh, and James Reed on the twenty-sixth and twenty-seventh from St. Louis and Chicago, respectively. On October 28, Ely and Joseph W. Bailey spoke separately from Providence, Rhode Island, and Topeka, Kansas. The next day, Ely continued from Syracuse, joined by "Alfalfa Bill" Murray from Tulsa. Al Smith culminated the campaign with a 9:30 P.M. address from Albany, a speech personally underwritten by old friend John Raskob to the tune of $7000. Raskob also labored without success to coax the unenthusiastic John W. Davis into giving more than one perfunctory talk and thereby showing that his "heart was in the campaign." A range of individual stations and regional and national networks, including KDKA in Pittsburgh, WGN in Chicago, WOR in New York, WBZ in Boston, the Mutual System, NBC's Basic Blue, Blue Mountain, and Blue Coast networks, and CBS, carried the speeches. The most diligent performers proved to be Ely and Reed, each of whom made six addresses blasting Roosevelt's "radical" tendencies during the six-week effort.[19]

The main attention-getter of the anti-Roosevelt radio campaign, however, was Al Smith. Although the Landon organization had known of Smith's willingness to campaign for the GOP ticket as early as the end of August, Smith only announced it publicly on September 20. Beginning with a New York City address on October 1, he gave a total of five speeches in cities including Boston, Chicago, Pittsburgh, and Albany. At Carnegie Hall he disclaimed wanting revenge against the President, but pronounced, "I firmly believe that the remedy for all the ills that we are suffering from today is the election of Alfred M. Landon." In his concluding address, held at the Harmanus Bleeker Hall in Albany on October 31, he denied that he had charged Roosevelt with being either a "Communist or a Socialist." Nonetheless, he insisted, "there is some certain kind of foreign 'ism' crawling over the country . . . and the sin about it is that he [Roosevelt] doesn't seem to know it." In a rasping voice he urged, "There is nothing you can do if you love America except change from the present administration to Governor Landon of Kansas."[20]

If in the fall it seemed that Liberty Leaguers and Jeffersonian Democrats were carrying an unusually large burden of campaigning for the GOP ticket, it owed partly to the lackluster oratory of the Republican nominee. Hoping that League speakers could help close the oratorical gap between Landon and Roosevelt, GOP party chairman John Hamilton "saw a lot" of Jeffersonian Democrats and even accompanied Al Smith on the train ride to his Chicago speech. Although Landon personally welcomed any aid, he had already reached the conclusion that his cause was doomed. At first glance, it was hard to understand why. Of the nation's 150 largest newspapers, he was supported by 80, to only 55 for Roosevelt. The *Literary Digest* predicted a Landon victory. But as early as the week of the GOP convention, he had been told by Benjamin F. Anderson of the Chase National Bank and Colonel Leonard P. Ayres of the Cleveland Trust Company that business conditions were steadily improving in 1936. "I knew then," Landon later claimed, "that I was beaten. I always had my feet on the ground the rest of the campaign."[21]

Even that previous dispenser of optimism, Du Pont pollster E. E. Lincoln, now recognized the likelihood of defeat. On October 28, he postscripted his own predictions with advice for the future of the Liberty League. Henceforth, he advised, "the du Pont name and the names of former political leaders should be kept as much as possible in the background." Resembling a boy sticking his finger in a dike to hold off an impending flood, Pierre du Pont gave orders to his secretary to give their "colored janitor" copies of the GOP's *National Watchman* to distribute to friends and thereby win over a few last-minute votes for Landon. But the GOP message simply offered nothing to working-class Americans. As pundits noted, the Landon campaign's chief irony was that it attacked various New Deal programs as "government-protected monopolies," but its chief backers did not want a real free-enterprise economy but instead private central cartelization. One observer said that "Landon's supporters want to control by themselves the machinery of stabilization, and they are trying to beguile the voters into agreeing with them by asserting that 'private enterprise' in economic control is the 'American way of life.' "[22]

Franklin Roosevelt, for his part, hit the campaign trail in late September, beginning with an address in Syracuse. He knew, and the shadow campaign of the Jefferson Democrats illustrated it, that he was the focal point, the central issue of the election. But rather than accept passively the League's picture of him as a knowing or ignorant subverter of the Constitution and a purveyor of alien "isms," Roosevelt turned the tables on his critics. While he repudiated charges of radicalism, he continually returned to the personal theme of savior of capitalism. In 1933, he claimed, the captains of industry had come "pleading to be saved." Having saved them, the President asserted, he was now being assailed by the same men for his methods. In St. Paul, Omaha, Denver, Wichita, Kansas City, and Chicago, the President harped on the ingratitude of the rich. "Some of these people really forget how sick they were," he proclaimed. "But I know how sick they were. I have their fever charts . . . Washington did not look like a dangerous bureaucracy to them then. Oh, no! It looked like an emergency hospital." His "distinguished patients," he continued, had insisted on two things—"a quick hypodermic to end the pain and a course of treatment to cure the disease." The official "Dr. New Deal" now claimed that "most of the patients seem to be doing very nicely. Some of them are even well enough to throw their crutches at the doctor."[23]

The campaign trends, combined with improving economic news, enabled Roosevelt to win over business converts even among previous deserters. Roosevelt's list of campaign "fat cats" included Joseph E. Davies of General Foods, Henry Doherty of Cities Service, C. E. McCann of F. W. Woolworth, the Straus family of R. H. Macy, tobacco titans R. J. Reynolds and Mrs. Doris Duke Cromwell, Harold McCormick of International Harvester, Herbert Swope of RKO, and Sosthenes Behn of IT&T. In a stinging rebuke of the du Ponts, even the major brewers—Pabst, Ruppert, Busch, and Feigenspan—backed the President. Chase National Bank, Manufacturers' Trust, and the United Mine Workers alone loaned over $250,000. Among other major contributors were millionaires Cornelius Vanderbilt Whitney of New York, Mary and Margaret Biddle of Philadelphia, Joseph P. Kennedy of Boston, A. P. Giannini of San Francisco, and even Jesse Jones of Houston. James Warburg rejoined the Roosevelt fold on October 18, and Liberty Leaguer Will Clayton, forsaking his leadership of anti-Roosevelt activities in Texas, did likewise.[24]

Having succeeded in isolating his opponents, Roosevelt in late October launched a final campaign swing through Pennsylvania, Maryland, and Delaware. The symbolism of the visits was not lost on the President, who remarked to Joseph Robinson his desire "just to assure myself that the du Ponts are not broke." The last round of the campaign, however, was a "gloves-off" political speech at the scene of many a good prizefight—and many a mismatch—Madison Square

Garden. Roosevelt clearly sought a knockout. "For twelve years," he intoned, "this Nation was afflicted with hear-nothing, see-nothing, do-nothing government. The Nation looked to Government but the Government looked away." One verbal jab followed quickly after another. "Nine mocking years with the golden calf, and three long years of the scourge! Nine crazy years at the ticker, and three long years in the breadlines! Nine mad years of mirage, and three long years of despair." Defiant, confident, he proclaimed, "Powerful influences strive today to restore that kind of government with its doctrine that Government is best which is most indifferent . . . Never before in all history have these forces been so united against one candidate as they stand today. They are unanimous in their hatred of me—and I welcome their hatred!"[25]

Only the voters' verdict remained. Each camp had its own predictions of the outcome, with the Roosevelt forces displaying considerably more optimism. Jouett Shouse privately opined to a St. Louis correspondent on November 2, "My own guess is that Roosevelt will win though I think it will be very close and there is a real chance for Landon." Although he professed "great faith" in the *Literary Digest* polls, he less encouragingly added, "everything depends upon the attitude of those who have swelled the registration lists to unheard of proportions." Roosevelt's campaign boss, James Farley, had scribbled out his own predictions at New York Democratic headquarters the day before the election. "Landon," Farley had judged, "will carry Maine and Vermont. Seven electoral votes."[26]

James Farley's only mistake was his statement that Maine and Vermont had seven electoral votes—they actually had eight. On November 3, Franklin Roosevelt, polling eleven million more votes than Alf Landon, won an electoral landslide with a 523-to-8 margin in the electoral college. Roosevelt's performance was especially impressive in the cities. He carried 104 urban areas of more than 100,000 people, to Landon's two. New York City, the home of General Motors' offices and the citadel of Al Smith, gave the incumbent a plurality of 1.3 million votes. Rather than illustrating the Liberty League's September rallying cry, "As goes Maine, so goes the nation," the electorate had merely declared, along with Farley, a new axiom—"As goes Maine, so goes Vermont." The Liberty League's effort to prevent the reelection of Franklin D. Roosevelt—an effort that had seen the League on the front pages of the *New York Times* on some thirty-five different occasions in 1936—had failed miserably. The League's national headquarters had spent almost $520,000 in the year, and the du Ponts as individuals had given over $850,000 more to the stop-Roosevelt effort. Company president Lammot had extended $190,000, Irénée had chipped in $121,000, and Pierre had added another $111,000. The Du Pont Company's executives had provided $30,000 to the NAM and almost $40,000 to the Crusaders; their counterparts at GM had donated $35,000 more to the Crusaders. All of that money irretrievably had been spent—and all for naught. With understandable irritation, a little over a week after the election Pierre and Irénée found themselves forced to contribute an extra $17,500 to pay off the nearly $100,000 in debts of the fruitless Jeffersonian Democrats' radio fund.[27]

With an understandable, however irrational, need to seek reasons or scapegoats for their repudiation, the du Ponts and their allies tried to interpret the election. Raoul Desvernine maintained that "emotionalism triumphed over reason." Jouett Shouse still insisted that the *Literary Digest*'s September poll had been accurate, but had been based upon June and July data, and he blamed Landon's lackluster campaign style for the outcome. With more than a touch of bravado, Joseph Ely said of the Roosevelt campaign, "I don't think they did very well. They only got five or six million votes that weren't on the payroll against our seventeen million." A bitter Al Smith, still disparaging the President for not having served in World War I, nonetheless implicitly indicted Landon for the failure by claiming that he had cast his own vote solely "on a negative basis." Displaying a kind of grudging admiration for the President was Pennsylvania's David Reed, who attributed Landon's loss to "the most expert demagogue that has ever appeared in American politics." Expressing a viewpoint shared by the du Ponts, he added, "I suppose that when we gave the vote to everything on two legs, we should have anticipated that every now and then the electorate would go haywire over a demagogue." The GOP's John Hamilton did extend his personal thanks to those such as John Raskob who had offered "splendid assistance" to the campaign, but such words only added to the sting of defeat. A bitter Pierre charged of Roosevelt, "With him are all the elements that pertain to dictator." The announcement of niece Ethel du Pont's engagement to Franklin D. Roosevelt, Jr., shortly after the elections only rubbed more salt into fresh wounds.[28]

Why had the du Ponts and their views been so completely rejected by the American people? Part of the answer clearly lay in Franklin Roosevelt's acknowledged superiority as a campaigner—an attribute the du Ponts both admitted and scorned at the same time. In addition, it was certainly true that the du Ponts and their Liberty League supporters made their share of tactical mistakes along the way. Among other errors, they placed too much faith in Al Smith's presumed appeal to the "common man," a personal appeal already years out of date and, with its bearer, saddled with the burden of an unappetizing economic message. In a deeper sense, the du Ponts misread the attraction of Franklin Roosevelt not just as a skilled electoral tactician but as a symbol of the new role of the federal government in the lives of Americans. The du Ponts actually succeeded in making the 1936 election what they had wanted it to be—a referendum on Franklin D. Roosevelt. What they had not understood was that the popularity of Roosevelt the man could not be separated from that of Roosevelt the policymaker. To the public, the two strands of Roosevelt's image were a seamless web.

The du Ponts were also victims of their own ignorance about how mass-based partisan politics actually worked. Horrified for years at the messiness, earthiness, and demagoguery of the electoral game, they tried to circumvent it through the Liberty League, their own version of merchandized, top-down politics. An ideology, even an anti-democratic one, they believed, could be "sold" to a national mass market if only it was "packaged" correctly. While always lacking a strong membership base, or even a consensus of support from within the business community, the du Ponts and their allies tried to sell themselves as disinterested, conscientious objectors to the federal government's accumulation of broker-state power, and they reduced their ideological objections to a simple, and misleading, popular slogan, "Save the Constitution." On the basis of their experience with the AAPA, they believed that such a merchandizing approach would work in a broader political campaign.

What they never understood, even about the repeal fight, was that it had not been they who had created the popular opposition to prohibition. They had merely ridden it. Their greatest asset had never been their ability to move masses, but instead their capacity to map legislative strategy and to pressure politicians in the manner of a traditional political lobby. They were, above all, business managers and fundraisers, not politicians or even ideological "salesmen." The supreme irony of 1936 was their mistaken belief, based upon the supposed malleability of an untrained electorate that they constantly disparaged, that the "demagogue" Roosevelt could be thwarted through their own well-financed, rival "marketing" campaign. After their defeat, they concluded that their message had not been at fault—they had simply been outdone by a more masterful salesman. They could even take a strange kind of personal solace in that.

The du Ponts violated the first rule of any effective salesmanship— to know your "customer," his needs, and his buying psychology. They never grasped that to a majority of voters they stood for an outmoded set of economic and social ideals, regardless of the new "industrial self-government" structures they proposed to defend those ideals. To all too many Americans, big business had had its chance at self-regulation and governance, at disinterested public stewardship. It had failed because of its propensity for narrow self-interest and greed. Besides the debilitating blows to business's image caused by the stock market crash and the Depression, as well as those delivered by the President's campaign rhetoric, congressional investigations such as those of Nye, Black, and La Follette had discredited the du Ponts' claims of disinterested concern for the nation. Completing the demolition job was the growing plausibility in 1936 of the argument that the very policies the du Ponts assailed had helped them as much as or more than they had helped less affluent Americans. As the *New Republic*'s Hamilton Basso wrote of this emerging image of business "ingratitude," "it is as if a band of men joined together to assassinate their best friend." Taking but one example from within the du Ponts' own economic empire, General Motors' sales from 1932 to 1936 had tripled; in 1936 the company logged a record stockholder dividend of over $200 million.[29]

Such figures largely were irrelevant to the du Ponts, because what was fundamentally at stake to them was not mere profits but the reins of economic *power*. Although their ideas were wrapped in different campaign packaging, they were still selling the idea of the concentration of American industrial policymaking power in their, and like-minded corporate conservatives', hands. Popular sentiment and partisan politics, however, were nudging national leaders in a more pluralistic direction—toward recognizing labor, farmers, and consumers as partners to business, with the federal government acting as a broker of national economic interests. Roosevelt had become the personal symbol in 1936 of that emerging broker state. The du Ponts, as a result of their proudly maintained elitism, had lost touch with the shifting ideological currents of the American political economy.

Could—should—the fight go on? Answering that question was not easy for the du Ponts. The immediate need for a Liberty League or some other organization to act as a check on the further acquisition of power by Roosevelt seemed greater than ever after the election. Equally obvious, however, was the Liberty League's less-than-sterling record of accomplishment. And what of the longer term? Should the League be used as a springboard, given the GOP's embarrassing showing and renewed predictions of its demise, for a new conservative party in America? Such a plan would require months and years of commitment, and Pierre du Pont, for one, was unwilling to take on another exhausting challenge. Since his so-called retirement from active leadership of the Du Pont Company, he had already been serving as Delaware's chief tax collector for eleven years and was the sole member of the state's liquor commission.

In a series of agonizing sessions of the administrative committee, the du Ponts gave their backing to the continuation of the Liberty League. The organization's electioneering and public relations operations, however, were eliminated and the Washington office readied to "go into winter quarters at Valley Forge." A skeleton staff prepared for a scaled-down role as a legislative reference and lobbying service for congressional conservatives in the upcoming 1937 session. With subscription notes overdue, the decision to continue meant both a hurried refinancing of the organization and major budget cuts. By December the League claimed less than 21,000 contributing members. Treasurer Grayson Murphy informed Pierre that the major noteholders would have to be pleaded with to extend their commitments another four years, to 1940. Irénée, having returned late in the month from a recuperative trip to Cuba, helped sell the financing scheme, telling cousin and noteholder William F. du Pont, "It is the only way one can hope to get anything back." On December 30, Shouse's salary was cut, over his objections, to $12,000. All branch offices and state divisions were instructed to discontinue activities. Shouse, Stayton, research director Crawford, Ewing Laporte, and a handful of stenographers remained in the Washington office, while dozens more telephone operators, message boys, and secretaries were dismissed.[30]

Left on the shelf for further discussion, but no immediate action, was the idea of generating a new political party. Many Jeffersonian Democrats, including J. S. Cullinan and Henry Breckinridge, were enthusiastic. Informal discussions on the subject between the GOP's John Hamilton and John Raskob had already begun. According to Hamilton, GM's Alfred Sloan conveyed in December the feeling within the du Pont–GM circle that a new party was needed to replace the moribund Republicans. If such a course of action was not pursued, the du Ponts would consider withholding any further financial support to the GOP. Such were the flickering embers in December of the dreams that had blazed the previous January. In place of the dream was the reality of a humbled Liberty League. Jouett Shouse, notifying Lawyers' Committee member Ralph Shaw of the decision not to publish their final report on the Social Security Act and instead to shut down the Chicago office, bravely pointed to the immediate agenda. "There is," he wrote, "a field of extremely useful activity for the League but it does not lie at this time along the lines of public relations . . . It is rather a field of research and of personal contact with members of Congress."[31]

The du Ponts anticipated new attacks upon their family's interests in the aftermath of November, perhaps in the form of anti-trust action or additional labor and tax legislation. Reflecting that sensitivity, Irénée chided Herbert Hoover for his failure to defend big business during the campaign. "I do not understand your fear," he interjected, "that trusts which tend to prevent the dissipation of accumulated fortune are a great evil." To another correspondent, Pierre demanded that the Congress regulate unions "even more strictly than are the corporations," for he claimed that "the labor union assumes to dictate a man's right to occupation and the earning of a livelihood."[32] Having undertaken a disastrous election-year assault on the New Deal and Franklin Roosevelt, the family now quietly prepared for what they anticipated would be a protracted siege of their remaining economic prerogatives.

chapter 14

A Last Hurrah

In the aftermath of the 1936 debacle, the du Ponts grimly prepared to employ the Liberty League in a guerrilla war of survival against the New Deal. Only a handful of salaried research assistants, clerks, and stenographers were left to carry on the legislative battle in Washington. Even Jouett Shouse went off the formal payroll at the beginning of 1937, to be sustained in future by direct personal contributions from Irénée du Pont. Public appearances ceased entirely, and the number of League pamphlets and leaflets dropped from 135 in 1934–1936 to only 13 in 1937. Even they were but brief four-page assessments of pending congressional bills. In marked contrast to the hundreds of thousands raised by the League before the election, only $76,000 was amassed for 1937, and even that amount was overspent by some $16,000 by the national office. All state divisions had closed by the beginning of the year save for those in Pennsylvania and Delaware, which had been incorporated separately from the national organization. When the Pennsylvania headquarters closed its doors in January, only the du Ponts' own home-state chapter still remained. Instead of further publication of pamphlets and other mass-circulation literature, the Washington headquarters now limited itself to the distribution of typed confidential lobbying memoranda from Shouse to the former members of the executive committee, on an average of two or three per week (137 in the year).[1]

Even before the close of the old year, the du Ponts had witnessed the stirrings of an ominous new challenge to their economic interests. General Motors, the Depression-era crown jewel of the family empire, now faced sit-down strikes led by the recently consolidated United Auto Workers union. Within GM, du Ponts were still heavily represented on the company's board of directors, executive committee, finance committee, and bonus and salary committee. In a long-standing effort to forestall unionization at GM (in which the du Ponts held the largest stock holdings at ten million shares, or 23 percent), officials had sponsored an extensive array of "welfare capitalism" measures, including employee housing, stock-option plans, and savings and group insurance schemes. At the same time, the company had employed industrial spies from sixty-four different firms to infiltrate and disrupt the union's efforts. Barely a week after the November election, GM had awarded its employees an "Appreciation Fund Bonus" of $10 million, or $35–60 per worker, paired with wage increases. Nonetheless, UAW sit-down strikes had begun in late December with the aim of forcing the company's recognition of the union as the auto workers' official bargaining agent nationwide.[2]

The du Ponts feared an imminent offensive by their political and economic enemies in 1937. The Special Conference Committee's year-end reprise of 1936 had commented, "In the years since 1929 business leadership in the past has been under more persistent and more aggressive attack than in any previous period." Du Pont moneys were redirected to lobbying organizations in anticipation of renewed assaults. Lammot, for example, upped his company's contribution to the NAM from $30,000 to $55,000, and he enlisted as a vice-president of the association. Nonetheless, the choice of GM as strike target took many in the family by surprise. Given the raw economic power of the company, and the willingness of rival Ford to resort to brutal anti-labor violence to prevent unionization, it had been speculated that Chrysler would be the UAW's first postelection target. From the union's standpoint, however, GM's very dominance of the auto industry was its main attraction, for a victory over the leading company would place inexorable pressure on the others to extend similar recognition. GM included 110 plants in fourteen states and eighteen foreign countries and controlled 45 percent of the American car market. By a broad range of measures—sales volume, profits, or the number of employees (a quarter of a million)—it was the largest manufacturing corporation in the world. Its gross 1937 budget of $1.6 billion was equal to the combined totals of the state governments of Michigan, Minnesota, California, Pennsylvania, and New York, and its earnings accounted for 78 percent of the earnings of the entire auto industry. GM also was the largest customer of another du Pont–controlled business, the U.S. Rubber Company, in which the family held a 17 percent stock interest. The Du Pont Company itself, of course, was the auto giant's chief supplier of car finishes and fabrics.[3]

Beginning on December 28, following small-scale incidents of labor unrest at other facilities, workers struck the GM plant in Cleveland.

Two days later, a major work stoppage ensued at the Fisher Body Plant No. 1 in Flint, Michigan, and spread to other factories. During the first six weeks of 1937, GM purchased over $6000 in tear gas (compared to but $500 worth the previous year) after the UAW defied a court injunction to halt the sit-down and Michigan Governor Frank Murphy refused to send in state troops to break the strike forcibly. On February 11, however, GM finally gave in. In exchange for the union's agreement to evacuate company plants, the automaker was forced to accept the UAW as the official bargaining representative in the striking plants within six months and to rehire striking workers. By year's end the rest of the auto industry save Ford had followed suit. Within a month after GM's capitulation, U.S. Steel similarly signed a contract with the CIO-affiliated Steel Workers Organizing Committee. After an eight-week confrontation in March and April, Firestone gave in to the United Rubber Workers. At the end of 1937, General Electric, RCA-Victor, and Philco struck bargains with the United Electrical and Radio Workers. During the year the membership of the Textile Workers Organizing Committee swelled to over 450,000, and the UAW mushroomed from 30,000 to 400,000 strong.[4]

Given GM's defeat at the hands of the UAW, the du Ponts took only meager solace from their own company's success in rebuffing outside union attempts to organize the workers at the Belle, West Virginia, rayon plant. Four days after the end of the GM strike, the family again was buffeted indirectly by damaging headlines from a congressional investigating committee. The La Follette Senate inquiry had turned to an examination of antiunion measures during the Flint strike, and it revealed that GM had infiltrated the upper echelons of the union with at least fifty-two Pinkerton spies from 1934 through early 1937. Similar hearings were held later in the spring on the bloody Harlan County, Kentucky, coal strike and, from June 30 to July 2, on strikebreakers' violence at Republic Steel on Memorial Day. Perceiving in the rise of industrial unionism an irretrievable break with past prerogatives, still sensitive to continuing public scrutiny, and unhappy with the specific settlement at GM, within three months Lammot du Pont resigned as GM's chairman of the board and turned over the post to president Alfred Sloan. Although considerable family influence remained in GM, with Donaldson Brown retaining a vice-presidency and Lammot and Walter Carpenter both named to a new administrative policy committee (replacing the executive and finance committees), a generational changing of the guard had begun. Those now departing from active management at GM included Pierre, Irénée, and John Raskob.[5]

The du Ponts could take a certain satisfaction in the fact that the core of their empire, the Du Pont Company itself, had been able to withstand encroachment by the unions. Irénée confidently assured the nervous governor of Delaware, Richard C. McMullen, of his family's ability to control its employees. He did offer the faint disclaimer that "in the case of Delaware, if anything should transpire, it will certainly be by outsiders coming in to force it on us." In an attempt to take the public relations offensive, the family authorized the printing and distribution of a pamphlet by R. C. Schroeder of the National Publicity Bureau in Washington, D.C., entitled *The "Du Ponts" or the "Roosevelts"?* Printed by the same company that had handled the Liberty League's material, with the same typeface and format but minus the trademark Liberty Bell emblem, the pamphlet urged, "Let's have more du Ponts." Spreading scurrilous charges concerning the President's various private business dealings, it contrasted him with the du Ponts, which it described as "a type which must be developed and multiplied if American labor is to have full-time employment and if the nation's purchasing power is to be restored, without which basic recovery cannot be obtained." Castigating "demagoguery and Du Pont denunciation," the author concluded that the "real friend" of labor was not Roosevelt, but the du Ponts.[6]

The Liberty League itself, particularly with a mothballed Lawyers' Committee, was of no real use in combatting the rise of industrial unionism in 1937. It was of some value, however, in heading off legislative threats from the White House. The du Ponts were led to expect the worst in new welfare legislation when, in his second inaugural address on January 20, Roosevelt cited the continuing challenge of "one-third of a nation ill-housed, ill-clad, ill-nourished." The President's boldest act floored even the now supposedly shock-proof du Ponts. Rather than push vigorously for new social legislation, Roosevelt opted on February 5 to submit a radical restructuring of the Supreme Court. The administration's "court reorganization" bill, citing the grounds of judicial work overload, called for the retirement of sitting federal judges over the age of seventy within six months of their birthdays, or else their supplementation with additional new judges up to a maximum of six new Supreme Court justices and forty-four lower-court members. Even though the Liberty League in 1936 had proclaimed that a victorious Roosevelt might become an even greater usurper of legislative or judicial powers, the plan was astonishing. To League veterans the proposal fit a consistent and dangerous pattern of expediency in the New Deal. As Jouett Shouse relayed to Grayson Murphy, "In the present situation, not merely with reference to the

Supreme Court, but with reference to the whole economic and social set-up, the attempt at undue haste and immediate action by those who would seek to better conditions is apt to do more harm than good."[7]

What Roosevelt's "court-packing" plan did, above all else, was legitimize his political opposition's claims that he aimed at unprecedented personal power. The argument that an age problem on the federal judiciary justified packing it with New Deal supporters was countered embarrassingly by the example of Louis Brandeis as an effective, nonreactionary, yet aged Justice. Nor could hints that advanced age made judges unable to keep up with their workload have had much appeal in the Congress, many of whose most powerful members had already witnessed their seventieth birthdays. Legislative allies of the President had been given precious little warning of the proposal. Most important, the Supreme Court was venerated as a symbol of institutional stability and of the supremacy of law and principle over political expediency, despite (or perhaps because of) its unpopular rulings of the previous several years. Even some congressional liberals questioned the long-term wisdom of undercutting the independence of the Supreme Court, given its not-infrequent role of defender of civil liberties. The divisiveness of the issue also encouraged rival Democratic factions to take up sides and weakened party harmony, which was needed for other objectives. Hugh Johnson and Donald Richberg, former partners in the NRA and now bitter foes, hurled verbal brickbats at each other, with Johnson claiming that Richberg had been the originator of the court-packing scheme.[8]

Even though in hindsight the court plan was a politically unwise gamble, and one that eroded the President's new-won electoral mandate, it was not immediately perceived that way. Many of Roosevelt's opponents, including the du Ponts, were so pessimistic about their own strength and that of the GOP that they doubted the measure could be defeated. Given the Republicans' depleted numbers in Congress, the court fight's early rounds only fed the movement for a new party of opposition to the New Deal. In late February, Alf Landon attended a private meeting in the home of two-time GOP gubernatorial candidate William J. Howey, at Howey-in-the-Hills, Florida, with Jouett Shouse and oilman Thomas Phillips to discuss the prospects of a third party. In addition, the proven unpopularity of the GOP and the Liberty League meant that neither could effectively assume public leadership for defeating the court plan. On the advice of Shouse, Roy Roberts arranged for Landon to avoid making direct reference to the court plan in his Lincoln Day address in Chicago. Instead, conservative congressional Democrats were assigned to take on Roosevelt. A Liberty

League memorandum, entitled "Packing the Supreme Court," was sent to Pierre du Pont for his information, but William Stayton informed him that not only would it not be published but even its internal distribution would be restricted, so as to prevent its leaking to the press. The Delaware state chapter sent postcards urging bankers and lawyers to relay their opposition to their congressmen. But in reply to inquiries from Delaware as to why the national office was not active, Ewing Laporte could only respond, "We have been trying to keep out of the public eye as much as possible."[9]

In the months after the court plan's defeat, Stayton insisted that the Liberty League played a major role in the outcome. But Stayton's claims were exaggerated and self-serving, as the old veteran of the repeal fight tried to use the victory as a catalyst for a League revival. The League did distribute copies of *The Supreme Court Crisis,* by Senator Edward Burke of Nebraska and Merlo Pusey, and, according to Stayton, did "a great deal of work of which the general public did not know." Jouett Shouse lobbied legislators and gave strategic advice to anti-administration Democrats in Congress. Years later, Stayton informed Pierre concerning Senator Joseph O'Mahoney of Wyoming, "He led our fight against the 'Court Packing' bill, we preparing the historical data." But the League's role in the court fight was prone to exaggeration both by its supporters and even by the administration, which sought a convenient political whipping-boy to rally its forces against once more. Both the President, in an August 18 speech at Roanoke Island, and James Farley, in Indianapolis three days later, tried to revive the Liberty League "bogeyman" in the aftermath of their setback. Aiding the cause, columnists Drew Pearson and Robert S. Allen similarly assailed the League in their "Nine Old Men" pamphlet.[10]

In actuality, the League remained in the background throughout the fight. More public efforts were spearheaded by a network of organizations that included the "Defenders of Democracy" (Citizens' National Supreme Court Protective Committee of the National Defenders, Inc.); the Non-Partisan League of Women, Inc., to Uphold the Constitution and Form of Government (headed by Mrs. Catherine Curtis); the Women's National Committee (sponsored by Women Investors in America, Inc.); and publisher Frank Gannett's National Committee to Uphold Constitutional Government. Headed by L. M. Bailey, the Defenders of Democracy sponsored a day of anti-administration speeches by Senators Harry Byrd of Virginia, Royal Copeland of New York, Peter Gerry of Rhode Island, and Patrick McCarran of Nevada on May 10. Gannett's group, however, was by far the most visible and powerful of the lobbyists. Pierre du Pont, reflecting the stance of the family in general, gave the same response to each group that solicited his help as he gave to Senator Townsend of Delaware, "I have been advised that it is more constructive for me to take no part in the political situation, as my efforts might tend to consolidate the Democratic party." He pointedly added, "The course that I am following is not one of my choice."[11]

With Pierre and Irénée both chafing at the bit, as late as the end of March it still seemed quite possible that the court reorganization bill would pass. On March 29, Senator Townsend confided to Irénée, "I feel that, if it were to go to a vote now, we do not have enough votes to stop it, however, we hope to keep it from coming to a vote." The key actor in the drama, nonetheless, was not the Liberty League or even the President, but the Supreme Court itself. On the same day as Townsend's communication, the high court reversed its position of only a year before and upheld the constitutionality of Washington State's minimum wage law. Also sustained were the Frazier-Lemke Farm Mortgage Act, with Justice Owen Roberts switching to provide the 5-to-4 margin on both measures. Two weeks later, the Supreme Court validated the Wagner Act. In a rapid-fire sequence of apparently orchestrated events, on May 18 Justice Willis Van Devanter announced his retirement, providing the President with an opportunity to augment his newfound majority on the Court. Chief Justice Charles Evans Hughes, replying by letter to a request from an opponent of the plan, Burton Wheeler, demolished the assertions that delays and court inefficiency were due to age and maintained that additional judges would only produce more inefficiency, not less. On May 24, the Supreme Court completed its curious transformation when, in a 5-to-4 decision, it upheld the unemployment insurance provisions of the Social Security Act and, by a 7-to-2 vote, its old-age pensions.[12]

With the Supreme Court now repudiating its "horse-buggy" image and showing a more moderate face, the President's attempt to pack it collapsed. While some Senators pressed the administration to compromise, other supporters claimed a larger victory by arguing that through the threat of legislation the President had won the policy war. Vice-President Garner, a critic of the court plan, signalled his lack of support for it by leaving the capital for Texas in mid-June. The Senate Judiciary Committee, chaired by Senator O'Mahoney, proceeded to give the bill an unfavorable report. Raoul Desvernine gleefully claimed to spot the "fine Italian [Machiavellian] hand" of Jouett Shouse in the report's language. In a strange interlude in the midst of last-ditch efforts to save the measure, on June 30 the President and the First Lady traveled to Delaware for the wedding of their son to Ethel du Pont—a public "hatchet-burying" between the two families which was attended by Irénée and Lammot, but not Pierre. Whatever hopes the plan had evaporated for good when the President's Senate floor manager, Majority Leader Joseph Robinson, collapsed and died in mid-July. Yet another blow followed when New York Governor Herbert Lehman's made a public announcement of his oppostition. On July 22, accompanied by shouts of "Glory be to God" from California's Hiram Johnson, Senator Marvel Logan of Kentucky moved to recommit the bill, thereby ending the 168-day battle. A discouraged Logan attributed the outcome to the Liberty League, proclaiming, "The Liberty League lost the election last November, but it appears that it is in a fair way to win it in the Congress." A substitute bill introduced by Garner so as not to "bloody Mr. Roosevelt's nose," called the Judicial Procedures Reform Act, omitted provisions to enlarge the federal judiciary and was enacted in August.[13]

The fight over the court reorganization bill was a draining one, and the administration found itself losing battles on many other legislative fronts as well. A fair labor standards proposal, regulating wages and hours for interstate businesses, met stiff opposition from the NAM and the Chamber of Commerce and stalled in the House Rules Committee. Presidential requests for authority to reorganize executive agencies and to enact a "little-TVAs" regional economic planning bill both went nowhere. Blaming a shortfall of half a billion dollars in tax revenues on tax avoidance by the rich, the administration called for legislation that purposed to tighten the definition of personal holding companies and impose new penalties for tax violations. The measure approved by the Congress, however, generated but $50–100 million in additional revenue. On the heels of the GM strike and the Supreme Court ruling upholding the Wagner Act, Senators Burke and Vandenburg launched a campaign to amend it so as to "equalize" (restrict) union strike powers, outlaw the closed shop, tighten union certification requirements, and investigate claims of communist influence on the NLRB. Even when the President won a narrow victory in beating back a specific Senate condemnation of labor's sit-down technique, he still incurred the wrath of John L. Lewis for his blast at the CIO and "Little Steel" calling for a "plague on both your houses." The combined effect of the plan to tamper with the Supreme Court, other congressional reverses, and public fears of labor militancy and violence was to lend new credence to the warnings of well-to-do-Americans that

Franklin Roosevelt was a power-hungry usurper of constitutional prerogatives who was willing to sanction continued assaults on property
rights.[14]

A series of presidential meetings with congressional Democrats at
Jefferson Island on Chesapeake Bay, meant to mend fences, failed.
Among the consequences of dissension within the Democratic party
in 1937 were several legislative casualties, including child labor legislation, an anti-lynching bill, crop insurance proposals, a call to make
the Civilian Conservation Corps a permanent agency, a bill extending
the Interstate Commerce Commission's control to air transportation,
new food and drug legislation, and a ship safety measure. Given the
President's desire for discretionary embargo powers against "aggres-
sor" nations, the new neutrality legislation handed him was especially
odious, for it mandated that belligerents purchase American goods
only on a "cash and carry" basis, extended the reach of embargoes to
cover both arms and loans, and forbade travel on belligerents' ships.
The President enjoyed a few legislative victories, such as the Bankhead
Farm Tenancy Act, which replaced the Resettlement Administration
with the Farm Security Administration, extended long-term loans to
tenant farmers, and established government-operated migratory labor
camps; and the Wagner-Steagall Act, which provided $1/2 billion in
low-cost housing loans through the new U.S. Housing Authority.[15]

The success of Roosevelt's bipartisan congressional opposition revived notions of regenerating the Liberty League or forging a new
conservative political party. Raoul Desvernine lobbied the du Ponts
to sponsor an "educational" drive and revival in the early fall, claiming
that John Raskob agreed with his assessment. The former leader of
the Lawyers' Committee broke his postelection silence with an address
in July at Wellesley College. Raskob had been privy to meetings in
March and April between Sterling Edmunds (now heading a group
fighting legislation that would restrict child labor, called the National
Association for the Protection of Child, Family, School, and Church)
and fellow Jeffersonian Democrats Colby, Breckinridge, Ely, Reed,
and Bailey regarding a third party. Joseph Ely, however, reminded
the group of the advice given by the defeated Alf Landon as early as
the summer of 1936. "The Constitution," he had noted, "had not
proven to be a popular issue in the 1934 campaign—I doubted if it
were a winning issue in 1936." Quoting Senator Borah, Landon had
concluded, "You can't eat the Constitution." Despite Ely's and Landon's skepticism, however, Edmunds lobbied for the recruitment of
delegates "out of which a new party might be born." Among du Pont
insiders Jouett Shouse seemed most receptive to the idea. With the

court fight as backdrop, Shouse credited Roosevelt unwittingly with forging a "natural coalition" in Congress. But to him the GOP remained unable to serve as the primary unifying vehicle, and he charged the Republicans with being "leaderless and as a party, hopeless." Despite his assertion that the GOP's "old guard" were refusing for the sake of prestige and nostalgia to yield to more vigorous conservative leadership, Shouse nonetheless urged Edmunds that "for the time being things should be allowed to drift." He claimed, "Next March or April [1938] there is apt to be the opportunity for a clarification of views."[16]

The du Ponts themselves remained as opposed to Roosevelt and the New Deal as any of the Jeffersonian Democrats. Personal attacks on their wealth deepened their resentment. In early May, the U.S. Board of Tax Appeals belatedly began a series of hearings against Pierre. Irénée, now so alarmed about the centralization of executive powers in Washington that he opposed even the creation of a National Cancer Center within the National Institute of Health, insisted that "democracy ends in dictatorship" and "this country has gradually gotten away from the form of a Republic to a Democracy." Once again, to friends Pierre agreed that any assault against federal income tax power "had best be deferred indefinitely," but he lamented that tax repeal "could have been readily accomplished fifteen years ago." Both men were still shopping around for conservative "education" groups to back, as evidenced by a June 11 report on the Constitutional Education League by F. C. Evans, a Du Pont executive, Special Conference Committee officer, and NAM member. According to Evans, the organization—headed by the New Haven businessman F. R. Stevens—had proclaimed the laudable goal of raising money for anti-CIO publicity, including a booklet entitled *Join the CIO and Help Build a Soviet America.* In light of the group's tiny twenty-member roster, however, he urged that it not be backed "at this time." It was not surprising, given the apparent impotence of the family to take advantage of Roosevelt's political troubles, that Irénée relayed to Shouse the sentiments of Alfred Sloan that "he is not feeling any too good about the future."[17]

What did the future hold for the family's political prospects? Despite Shouse's disparaging words about the Republicans, the President's series of setbacks had lifted the spirits of many GOP regulars concerning their party's prospects for survival. Other opponents of the New Deal concluded that even if a new party was necessary and possible, the 1936 election had demonstrated the need to keep the du Ponts, and other vestiges of the Liberty League, strictly at arm's length. In other words, even in conservative circles the du Ponts had become "prophets without honor." Du Pont money was still solicited, but few solicitees wanted any visible ties to the du Pont family. Bainbridge Colby urged that the "American Coalition," a loose association of some 120 "anti-Red" patriotic and fraternal organizations created in 1929, lead a new conservative crusade—albeit with only a $15,000 budget. Raoul Desvernine, drawing hope from claims of the diminishing popularity of the CIO on the "strike battlefront," urged revival of the League or some other such organization no later than the fall of 1938. In contrast, E. F. Hutton, already burned by the frustrations of fundraising and mobilization for the Liberty League, counseled Irénée to do nothing and let the Roosevelt administration "hang itself by its own deeds."[18]

Among the brothers, Irénée was especially torn. For while the events of the first half of 1937, particularly the President's court-packing folly, had underscored Hutton's wisdom, he nonetheless feared, as he told Desvernine, that "the Red network has become sufficiently powerful and has enough officials in both high and low positions that it is going to be extremely difficult to get back to the American form of government." But what value was there for the family to subsidize modestly one, or several, organizations over which they would be allowed to exercise little strategic control? Irénée still had the hibernating Liberty League, and given the desertions of outside contributors he had no worries about any challenges to du Pont authority within it. At the year's start, the organization had but $55,000, but by mid-May it had received only an additional $38,000 ($28,000 from Pierre and Irénée alone). The du Ponts continued to pay the remaining staff from their own pockets. Illustrating the absence of a popular base, only about $6000 had been received in the form of contributions of less than $100. But the general consensus of those outside the family who had remained in the League was expressed by GM's William Knudsen, who had given $500 for 1937. In Knudsen's judgment, the League should be allowed "to pass out quietly so as not to be a constant public irritant."[19]

In the second half of the year, while the du Ponts pondered their political future, the administration continued to be buffeted by unfavorable political winds. Roosevelt's recess appointment in August of du Pont nemesis Hugo Black of Alabama to the Supreme Court (replacing Van Devanter) generated a furor over the appointee's lack of judicial experience and his earlier membership in the Ku Klux Klan. Worse yet for the White House was a major economic downturn in the fall, which before it ended destroyed half of the employment gains made in the first term. One effect of the events was to dampen even further any prospects for the replacement of the GOP. Instead, the lasting legacy of the final months of 1937 was an informal ideological alliance in Congress between conservative Democrats and the revitalized Republicans, a formidable legislative bloc the du Ponts now cheered and encouraged. Already anticipating as of late August that the President would attempt the next spring to purge uncooperative incumbents of his own party, employing a half-million-dollar "slush fund of relief money" to mobilize votes against his foes, Irénée urged Republican chairman Hamilton not to oppose those Democrats who had helped block the move to pack the Supreme Court.[20]

It was an irony of Roosevelt's predicament that the 1937 recession had been triggered by—in addition to $2 billion in new Social Security taxes—an essentially conservative decision to cut relief expenditures. Nonetheless, a gleeful Irénée wrote to Senator James H. Hughes, "The trouble with planned economy is that the planners are utterly incompetent to perform the job they have undertaken." Hoping to salvage a few congressional victories and lay the ideological groundwork for the 1938 elections, Roosevelt called Congress back into special session in mid-November for five weeks. Not only did the session prove to be fruitless, but it became a sounding board for growing attacks on the administration's economic policy and calls for tax cuts. By December, the *New York Times* Business Index had fallen from 110 to 85, wiping out the gains made since 1935 in but three months.[21]

Pierre du Pont perceived in the clamor a new opportunity for inaugurating his anti-tax crusade. Following his resignation as Delaware's tax commissioner in October after a dozen years in the post, he was briefed by staffer E. E. Lincoln that while the state of Delaware had paid out over $160 million in federal taxes from 1933 to the middle of 1937, it had received back only $28.4 million in federal relief expenditures from a $16 billion national outlay. In November he urged friends to back William Stayton's plans to form a group opposed to "tax duplication" at local, state, and federal levels. In December, J. A. Arnold of the American Taxpayers League solicited help from Irénée, saying, "You and your associates did well with the 18th amendent. Why not try a real job and one that will bring happiness and propserity to all the people as well as perpetuate the Republic." Irénée passed the message on to Pierre with the note, "This may interest you." Although he continued to display his disgust at the GOP by declining to head up a chemists' subgroup of the party's Division of Business and Professional Men, Pierre now launched exploratory tax-crusade talks with Stayton, Arnold, and Desvernine. While he did so, he continued his scaled-down subsidization of the Liberty League, giving $2500 in October, $3000 in November, and $5000 in December.[22]

Lammot lent his voice to the campaign for lower taxes in late 1937 through his increasingly visible presence in the NAM. Addressing the organization's Congress of American Industry in early December, he called for the removal of "uncertainty" in the tax situation, labor relations, and monetary policy. With tax policy the centerpiece of his program, he called for tax simplification and the leveling of income tax rates and surtaxes on business profits in favor of a single, across-the-board rate for each. Looking to stablized labor relations, he called for the outlawing of the sit-down strike in order to "protect" private property and to reduce the likely number and duration of strikes. If such policies were followed, Lammot insisted, business could launch a $25 billion program of capital investment that would reduce unemployment, lower production costs, and broaden markets, while "maintaining a rule of fair return for all effort." The day after his address, the Brookings Institution endorsed a modification of the federal levy on undistributed corporate profits. When Lammot was called to testify before a Senate committee considering tax changes, however, he backpedalled from his earlier claims, admitting that he had "not thought through" the pros and cons of taxing business profits.[23]

If the elderly Pierre was contemplating yet another policy crusade, and Lammot was assisting it in his own fashion, Irénée and John Raskob were less enthusiastic. They, more than the others, had been scarred deeply by the Liberty League debacle. Without question they endorsed the objective of reduced taxes on business and the wealthy, but they were less easily reinvigorated by the conservative political breezes of 1937. Having traveled to Cuba in November, Irénée returned at the beginning of the next month, but while urging Senator Townsend to work for exemptions for residential real estate (of which he owned a considerable amount) from the inheritance tax, he insisted that he not be mentioned as the idea's source. Only a day later, on December 3, he insisted to Stayton that the nation's problems went deeper than just unwise tax policies. "We have," he wrote, "been breeding stupid and anti-social people faster than we have good citizens." He claimed, "The average person today will accept a bribe if it is only approximately 'sugar-coated,' " and added that they never seemed to object to " 'lawful' confiscation of funds from the very wealthy." Adding to Irénée and Raskob's gloom, despite the President's misfortunes, were the deaths of previous political allies Grayson Murphy in October and Newton Baker on Christmas Day. Attempting to laugh at their recent misfortunes, John Raskob offered his season's greetings to Jouett Shouse in the guise of Santa Claus: "I am sending this note to tell you that the New Deal has taken away the things that I really needed— my workshop, my reindeer, my sleigh. Now I am making my rounds on a donkey. He is old, he is slow, so you will know that if you do not see me Christmas that I will be out on my ass in the snow." Irénée sent Shouse a gift of a pair of scissors—a reminder both of the League's painful cuts and an encouragement to keep "snipping away" at the New Deal.[24]

Opponents and liberal allies of the New Deal alike anticipated a presidential counterattack against concentrated wealth in 1938. Robert Jackson, chief of the Justice Department's anti-trust divison, and Harold Ickes hurled verbal broadsides at "monopolists who have simply priced themselves out of the market, and . . . into a slump." On December 26 Jackson claimed that business was engaged in a "strike of capital" against the administration. A day later Ickes warned that monopoly power again threatened the nation with "big business fascism." But although Roosevelt promised a special section on monopolies in his State of the Union address scheduled for January 3, 1938, and he privately approved of continued examination of the charge of tax avoidance against Pierre du Pont and John Raskob, his program drifted for another three months. Indicating the President's reluctance for an immediate political bloodbath was the fact that his son and private secretary, James Roosevelt, stayed as an overnight guest of Irénée du Pont at Xanadu in early February. Continuing the du Ponts' own "tax offensive," Pierre relayed E. E. Lincoln's findings on Delaware's inequitable treatment to Senator Townsend, and cousin Eugene filed suit to contest an order to him to repay over $63,000 in back taxes from 1933 to 1935 on his children's trusts. Following an exchange of letters between Lammot and Raoul Desvernine in early February, the latter informed Irénée that a conference of opponents to the administration had been held in Washington. While he cautioned, "The nature of the matter is such that I would prefer not writing," he added, "it concerns certain anticipated steps to be politically taken in the near future."[25]

It was not until early April 1938 that the President, following a sojourn to Warm Springs, launched his counterattack in earnest. The triggering event was the unexpected congressional rejection of a proposal to give the administration greater powers to reorganize executive departments. Amidst accusations of presidential usurpation by Frank Gannett's National Committee to Uphold Constitutional Government, the House rejected the bill by a 204-to-196, vote on April 8. Even

Vice-President Garner deserted the administration on the measure, leading to rumors of an alliance between Garner and Shouse. The next day, Roosevelt signalled a new combativeness by going out of his way to needle former Liberty Leaguers Shouse, Frederick H. Stinchfield, and Sewell Avery. On the fourteenth he called upon Congress to resume large-scale relief spending with a $3.75 billion omnibus measure, which was enacted within two months. At month's end, the President gave his blessing to the creation of an intergovernmental committee to investigate the concentration of economic power in America.[26]

The panel, entitled the Temporary National Economic Committee, consisted half of members of federal agencies and half of members of Congress and was chaired by Senator O'Mahoney of Wyoming. In its three-year run, however, the committee produced more smoke than fire. Of greater immediate impact was the energy injected into the adminstration's crusade against monopolies with the appointment of Thurman Arnold as head of the Justice Department's anti-trust division. Over the next five years, Arnold initiated 44 percent of all the anti-trust suits undertaken by the federal government since the passge of the Sherman Anti-Trust Act, although the actual impact of such suits was questionable. Nonetheless, the new assault on wealth, however much limited to rhetoric and symbolic action, sparked an equally vocal reply, including one from the du Ponts. Hugh Johnson, a former advocate of government-business partnership, blasted "semi-Socialistic, anti-business experimenters" for the continuing recession. On May 21, Lammot du Pont called for the release of business venture capital from taxation and regulation in a speech before American representatives to the International Chamber of Commerce. And during a presidential visit to Wilmington to celebrate the tercentenary of the arrival of the Swedes in America, Eugene du Pont privately relayed his concerns to Roosevelt.[27]

The renewed class rhetoric of 1938 generated far more rhetoric than action, and, more to the point, it failed to recapture for the President the political magic of 1936. The administration achieved but minor legislative successes—the attention of all involved was more firmly fixed on upcoming congressional races than on bills. In response to White House "soak-the-rick" oratory, Congress served up a measure which retained at a lower level a token levy on capital gains and kept the undistributed profits tax in name only. (It would be completely stricken the following year.) Despite the opposition of industrialists such as Irénée du Pont, the Congress did enact a national wages and hours law, the Fair Labor Standards Act. The measure, however, was a "tissue of compromises" that covered only a limited number of categories of interstate-business workers. Besides applying to only one-quarter of the workforce, the bill allowed two years for the standards of a forty cents per hour minimum wage and a forty-hour maximum workweek to be reached, although the use of child labor in interstate firms was barred.[28]

Fearful of more extreme attacks on the family's economic interests, Pierre directed William Stayton to gather political ammunition on the administration's spending policies since 1933 and to research charges of irregularities in the private business dealings of the President and his son James. Stayton, still seeking a full-blown revival of the Liberty League, claimed credit to Pierre for helping kill a proposal by George Norris to lower the constitutional amendment ratification requirement from three-quarters of the states to a two-thirds majority in a popular referendum. Pierre also remained acutely sensitive to shifts in federal labor policy in the 1938 session. Insisting that "labor conditions are perhaps more obstructive to business recovery than any other item," he blamed "legislative interference," such as the labor standards bill, as the "root of most of our troubles." Actually, though often Congress's deliberations did not produce the actual results Pierre would have preferred, labor unrest nonetheless showed clear signs of lessening in 1938. A major factor was the recession, which dampened labor's ardor for "voluntary" work stoppages via strikes. In addition, however, the La Follette committee discovered that in the aftermath of the strikes of 1937 and the Supreme Court's upholding of the Wagner Act, the machinery of labor resolution was working more smoothly. Indicating both the economic downturn and a decline in the effectiveness of attempts by the NAM and the Special Conference Committee to tie the NLRB in knots, in 1938 only half as many strikes took place as in the previous year, involving but one-third the number of workers and less than one-third the work time lost.[29]

With their eyes on the upcoming congressional contests, diehard Jeffersonian Democrats attempted to coax the du Ponts from their political hibernation. Following a March conference with James Reed, Ely, Colby, and Breckinridge, Sterling Edmunds complained to Raskob that only a limited amount of preparatory election activity was being done on an individual basis. Raskob nonetheless counseled in late April that "our best program for the minute is one of 'watchful waiting' as things seem to be coming around our way very fast." On others' advice, Irénée and Lammot both refrained from donating to anti–New Deal crusaders John Waters of Wisconsin or Vance Muse, who was now editing the right-wing *Christian American*. From his position of access in Washington, Jouett Shouse did feed Roosevelt opponents information on the "Iowa incident," in which the WPA's Harry Hopkins publicly endorsed the opponent of conservative Senator Guy Gillette of North Dakota (and implied that the state's relief appropriation might be curtailed if Gillette won). But in spite of the President's futile 1938 attempts at a "purge" of congressional opponents, the du Ponts and their allies could claim little credit for his failure. With minimal outside help, Gillette, Senator Walter George of Georgia, South Carolina's "Cotton Ed" Smith, and Maryland's Millard Tydings all gained renomination and reelection. Ironically, one of the few candidates that a prominent du Pont man—John Raskob— tried to help via a $2000 contribution, House Rules Committee chairman John O'Connor of New York, was beaten. Irénée did not even remain in the country during the campaign's final weeks, and only in May 1939 did he belatedly give $5000 to the Tydings campaign to defray lingering costs.[30]

Besides their self-imposed limitations upon political activities, which reflected a hard-earned humility toward the possible, the du Ponts also were chastened by the Liberty League's economic disintegration. The League published but one leaflet in 1938. Shouse's and Stayton's lobbying efforts were funded solely out of the pockets of Irénée and Pierre to the tune of between $6000 and $10,000 a month. In August the Mellon and Weir financial groups agreed to give $5000, and the Pews $2500, for the current year and the next, but all warned of the likely chilling effect that pending federal litigation would have on their donations. Many other contributors, even from the du Pont–GM circle, either avoided being reached or declined requests to give $5000 for the coming year. The du Ponts themselves scarcely were immune from the threat of legal suits. In September, Pierre and Raskob were convicted of illegal stock trading and ordered to pay $2.1 million in back taxes. Lammot sued the next month to recover $5 million in 1934 federal taxes.[31]

Partly in order to rejuvenate backers' enthusiasm for the organization, and also to keep his job, William Stayton prepared an optimistic-sounding history of the League's accomplishments. He prominently cited its achievements in the Court fight and the congressional rejection of executive reorganization, and distributed the report to approximately seventy-five former principal contributors in the hopes of triggering a revival. Attempting to underscore their value in Washington to the du Ponts, both Stayton and Shouse even relayed tips on stock investments gathered from official insider gossip. In November, Shouse interpreted the information that James Farley would be leaving the administration, purportedly to become president of

Baldwin Locomotive, as a sign that that company would soon benefit from additional government contracts. Despite the salesmanship of Shouse and Stayton, however, the organization still failed by early December to line up even the necessary twelve or fifteen individuals to contribute $5000 each toward the $6000-a-month Washington office expenses. Pierre and Raskob settled their tax liability case out of court, but at the loss of $586,369 and $1,473,202, respectively. Irénée, who wanted to maintain the organization at a low level in hopes of a revival in the presidential election of 1940, conceded to Frank Phillips of Phillips Petroleum, "If there are not more than three who think the work worthwhile, it is probably not worthwhile."[32]

The economic picture began to brighten once more for both the du Ponts individually and the Du Pont Company in 1939, despite the termination of patent and market-protection agreements with I.G. Farben triggered by the outbreak of war in Europe. The improved outlook, however, owing to improving domestic sales, did nothing to spur a rebirth of the Liberty League. As for the company, benefits were now being seen from Lammot's long-term reemphasis on new product research. Neoprene, which had been introduced in 1931, enjoyed increasing sales as a sealant. Most significantly, nylon, patented by the company in 1937 and marketed the following year in toothbrushes, electrical wire insulators, and violin strings, now was finding even more uses. In 1940, the company sold its first nylon hosiery for women. The tax fortunes of individual du Ponts also began to improve, suggesting a modest cooling-off of the political war with the Roosevelt administration. Lammot received a full refund from his tax case in March, and Irénée garnered nearly $28,000 in reimbursement in May. The next month Lammot sued to recover another $223,000 in 1935 claims levied against Wilmington Trust. In November the Board of Tax Appeals concurred, citing an out-of-court agreement between the family and government attorneys. Pierre, for his part, admitted in June mistakes in stock reports to the SEC, but was exonerated of any willful wrongdoing.[33]

The winding down of the recession by the fall of 1938, and the successes of the du Pont family and company that followed led to a continued disinclination to favor a revival of the Liberty League. Potential givers to a 1940 "stop-Roosevelt" effort, for example, worried that contributions to the League would have to be disclosed under the Federal Corrupt Practices Act and that they might lead to a new round of tax recriminations. Pierre's efforts to assure friends that disclosure was not required often were not successful. GM's William Knudsen, one of the original $25,000 subscribers to the League, had sought to avoid

paying his final installment of $5,000 since 1937, only to comply grudg-
ingly in May 1939. Coming to the du Ponts' partial rescue in March
was Wendell Willkie, who indicated his willingness to provide one
subscription and to attempt raising two others. Nonetheless, even
among the du Ponts themselves the growing preference was for providing the maximum possible financial help to individual 1940 campaigns rather than siphoning off resources into the Liberty League.[34]

The du Ponts did continue to try to influence legislation through
lobbying channels. In January, Lammot and Raoul Desvernine huddled with Senator Burke in the drafting of debilitating amendments
to the Wagner Act. As an expression of his persistent fears of federal
spending, taxation, and "internal subversion," Irénée pondered contributions to the Association for Interstate Tax Agreement (on which
Raskob was a director), the one-man American Good Government
Society (dedicated to the gold standard and tight monetary policy),
and the Committee of Americans (formed by former Harvard law dean
Roscoe Pound to lobby for lower income taxes). Pierre provided an
additional $500 on top of earlier contributions to the Women Investors
in America, but despite his commitment to the issue, he pragmatically
rejected William Stayton's advice to back the Committee of Americans
or Vance Muse's Coalition of Christian Democrats and Republicans
in a crusade against the Sixteenth Amendment, on grounds that the
timing was "not right." Pierre instead concurred in Shouse's counsel
that he "cooperate in bringing about permanent recovery" in order to
rebuild the family's public prestige. Congress could continue to do the
same for itself by resisting the temptation to "hand out more money
to Roosevelt." Insisting that "today business is doing all that it can
under the handicaps imposed upon it," he conceded proudly, "I am
in no sense a politican and do not understand practical politics, nor
do I care to do so. However, those who are interested tell me that little
can come from a division of political forces, and it is better to get along
with two parties in the hope that either one of them may try to better
conditions."[35]

Above all else, Pierre's lack of enthusiasm for spearheading a new
anti-Roosevelt campaign stemmed from his fatalistic belief that despite
the President's setbacks, he could not be beaten in 1940. Hoping to
raise his mentor's hopes, Jouett Shouse cited an anti–third term article
by Oswald Garrison Villard in the *Nation*, as well as a study of North
Central states suggesting that Roosevelt could not win reelection. John
Raskob personally lobbied for the nomination of John Nance Garner.
Pierre continued to hold out for the possibility that the Republicans
would make themselves palatable by nominating a candidate from

"non-political sources" with proven administrative ability. In the aftermath of the German invasion of Poland and the formal outbreak of World War II in Europe, however, even Al Smith began a limited rapprochement with the White House by supporting presidential efforts to lift the arms embargo to the Allies. The du Ponts' attitudes toward the war in Europe were divided, for while they supported for obvious reasons efforts to lift restrictions on American aid, they also feared that in the drive for national preparedness Roosevelt would accumulate even more power.[36]

It was with such ambiguities about the political impact of World War II on the family's fortunes and on the 1940 election that Pierre endorsed continuing the Liberty League at a skeletal level for a while longer. By October, he had given $18,700 in 1939 to the Washington office. Irénée, for whom the organization had been even more of a personal challenge, had extended an additional $9,300 despite an extended absence in Cuba. Stayton, again trying to stoke the political fires of his benefactors, warned Pierre in December about so-called wealth confiscation schemes in the upcoming Congress, most notably the "Lee Bill" (which would give the President emergency powers to require sworn declarations of personal wealth on which to base the proposed volume of mandatory war bond sales). Also feared were proposals to levy profits taxes on such war materials as airplanes, oil, steel, and possibly cars and trucks, which threatened GM interests. Stayton pushed for a new financial recruitment drive which would contact anyone who had given as little as $25 to the organization in the past. In pleading his case, he quoted J. Howard Pew that "Mr. Roosevelt is capable of trying to embroil this country in war for the purpose of having himself made dictator by force because he has come to fear that he cannot be reelected."[37]

Business's concern over the President's willingness to assume increasing discretionary power over mobilization deepened following the demise of the War Resources Board, which had been created in August 1939 and modelled after the World War I–era War Industries Board. Spurred by criticism of the WRB from liberals and labor groups, the administration then spawned the Office of Emergency Management, resurrected the National Defense Advisory Committee, and established the Office of Production Management, all of which signalled a shift in mobilization authority from private industrialists to the federal executive. Rejected were calls from J. Howard Pew for a six-member Civilian Central Committee, to be created by Congress with full administrative powers and chaired by Lammot du Pont. Even after the shocking German invasion of the Low Countries and France in the spring of 1940, the administration's suggestions to incorporate National Guard units into active Army duty were questioned as another step toward dictatorship by Irénée in a letter to the governor of Pennsylvania. Feuding also continued over Thurman Arnold's reluctance, despite the emergency, to exempt war industries from possible anti-trust actions.[38]

To the du Ponts, threats of growing presidential prerogatives in the war emergency were ample reason to concentrate their financial resources in an attempt to deny the President a third term, rather than channel more funds into a Liberty League in which their faith had evaporated. But which alternative to Roosevelt should they support? As they had done since 1937, they continued to put off attempts by Sterling Edmunds to enlist them in another Jeffersonian Democratic campaign because they thought it fruitless and possibly even counterproductive. In December, Daniel Hastings pressed Irénée to meet a former law partner of Senator Robert Taft of Ohio in order to discuss endorsing Taft for the GOP nomination. With other rumors floating of a possible campaign by Frank Gannett, Pierre, perhaps remembering Gannett's stance in favor of prohibition—and envious of his public role in blocking the plan to pack the Court—opined to James Wadsworth, "Confidentially, I have not been well impressed with Mr. Gannett."[39]

With no small amount of prodding from Jouett Shouse, the du Ponts' search for a presidential candidate increasingly shifted toward Wendell Willkie, the "boy wonder of Wall Street." As head of the Commonwealth and Southern electrical utility, Willkie had aided the League in its fights against the TVA and holding company legislation of the New Deal, and more recently he had aided the family in its time of financial need. At John Raskob's request, Shouse enlisted an old warhorse on agricultural policy, George Peek, as advisor to the candidate on farm issues. Above all, the Willkie effort appealed to the du Ponts because the candidate himself seemed to fit their prescription for a man with business administrative experience; a man outside the corrupting, demagogic mainstream of partisan electoral politics. They also assumed, given Willkie's business background, that his policy views would be congenial to their own preferences. Beginning in April of 1940, the du Ponts threw their private economic weight behind the Willkie GOP nomination drive. On April 8, Lammot notified Alfred Sloan that he had retained Donald Despain at $400 per month for ten months to perform "certain educational work." Part of the work was to distribute circulars to employees comparing the 1940 contest to the 1896 McKinley-Bryan battle, with the GOP the defender of the "full dinner pail." Sloan and Irénée both were solicited to contribute, and Raskob recruited Lammot in turn to have a Willkie pamphlet handed out to Du Pont and GM workers.[40]

Throughout the preconvention period, Jouett Shouse provided issues memoranda for Willkie on such varied subjects as preparedness and farm policy. On the pretext of attending banking conventions, he provided strategy memos on the Midwestern political situation. He urged the candidate to attack Roosevelt specifically for exaggerating America's readiness for war. In order to devote their private energies to the cause without bringing attention to the family empire, Pierre and Irénée resigned as chairman and vice-chairman of the Du Pont Company board of directors, and Lammot quit as company president, on May 20, 1940. Because he still held lingering doubts about Willkie's "soundness," Pierre prepared a private memorandum questioning the candidate on various matters. Was he too reliant on Jewish support, and would that cause him to push for rapid entry into the war? Did he accept some of the New Deal's policies and larger objectives? Did he generally endorse the administration's foreign policy, perhaps too much so? Was he too accepting of New Deal farm policy? And should Pierre dread Willkie's sudden switch from being a lifelong Democrat to running for president as a Republican? Following reassurances to Pierre and Lammot from Henry Carter Patterson on Willkie's "fundamental safeness," Pierre cast aside his reticence. By sending an endorsement telegram on June 27 to Delaware's GOP delegates at the party's Philadelphia convention, Pierre contributed modestly to the stampede that brought Willkie the nomination.[41]

Following the Republican convention, the du Ponts endeavored to help Willkie as much as was allowed. Rejecting a national third-party effort by a Jefferson Democratic ticket, John Raskob and Jouett Shouse helped coordinate Democrats for Willkie efforts in individual states. Special emphasis was placed on winning over Southern and border-state Democrats for Willkie without them having to vote for lesser GOP candidates. Senator Ed Burke spearheaded the Nebraska Democrats for Willkie effort, while Houston attorney Stephen L. Pinckney and James M. Carson did the same in Texas and Florida. Along with Al Smith, Raskob lobbied Pauline Morton Davis to recruit female veterans of the prohibition repeal fight in a "button campaign" for the GOP standard-bearer. Raskob also pressed the candidate himself to court the Morton Salt heiress for her active backing.[42]

Although Shouse and Raskob both declined invitations to give public statements in Willkie's behalf, Al Smith agreed to do so "at the proper time." The "proper time" proved to be a radio address on October

23. In advance of his remarks, Smith employed Shouse to document charges made by David Lawrence of the *U.S. News* that Roosevelt was the "Communist" candidate for president, which he asserted on the basis of Communist voting patterns in previous elections. Shouse could not find such a pattern of Communist voting for FDR, but he claimed that the Socialist and "uncommitted radical" vote had done so. Shouse urged Smith to pin the "bigotry label" on Roosevelt for having purveyed "class hatred, prejudice, and bigotry." In order to counter any anti-Wall Street rhetoric by the administration, Irénée in turn urged the GOP's John Hamilton to publicize the President's own history of speculations in stocks and German currency. Irénée personally arranged the reprinting of 100,000 copies of a 1936 Chicago *Tribune* article on Roosevelt's financial maneuverings. The overriding importance of the Willkie campaign to the du Ponts was best captured in a strategy letter from William Stayton to Pierre and Irénée in late September. "The mere nomination of Willkie," he wrote, "was a great and favorable political event in this country, for it definitely showed that the people could take political matters out of the hands of the politicians."[43]

Wanting to provide the utmost financial help to Willkie, and concerned by the Hatch Act's amended limits on individual campaign contributions of $5000 per party organization or chapter, the du Ponts took steps to shut down the Liberty League. Having already given $15,000 to the organization in the first six months of 1940, on August 15 Irénée proposed its disbanding to Shouse. Eleven days later, Shouse, Wadsworth, Stayton, and Pierre (who had also provided $15,000) agreed to recommend that course of action to the remaining directors and noteholders. In order to ease the pain of the process, Irénée volunteered to pay off the salaries of the League's remaining employees, amounting to $1900, out of his pocket. On September 3, directors Smith, Davis, Chester, Shouse, Stayton, and Irénée gave formal endorsement to the course of action. In spite of the decision, however, Pierre and Irénée opted to continue their regular out-of-pocket contributions to the Washington office through year's end, both to pay off rent on the office lease and to pay the salaries of Shouse and Stayton as they wound up their record-keeping and legal responsibilities.[44]

During the last six weeks of the 1940 presidential campaign, the du Ponts instead channeled massive amounts of money into states in the hopes of boosting Willkie over the top. On October 7, Irénée gave $4000 each to Delaware and Tennessee GOP efforts. On October 31, he transmitted another $4000 to the West Virginia Republican organization. Pierre, now proudly telling friends that he was "an ardent supporter of Mr. Wendell Willkie," found his ardor intensified by a judgment in the fall of $172,000 issued against him for 1931 tax delinquencies. According to later accountings, in the general election the du Ponts gave some $68,350 to the Willkie campaign, with fully $40,000 of it coming from Lammot. According to Representative Chet Holifield of California in a subsequent investigation, however, if one counted the amounts that the du Ponts contributed to independent and incorporated associations not covered by Hatch Act restrictions, the family's actual donations in the 1940 contest stood at $186,780. Allies Alfred Sloan, Raymond Pitcairn, and the Pews provided another $36,000, $29,000, and $108,000, respectively. But despite the time, money, and exertion, Pierre's deepest fears that Franklin Roosevelt could not be defeated were again realized. With a popular vote margin of 27 million to 22 million, and an Electoral College verdict of 449 to 82, the President was winner and still political champion, albeit by the narrowest plurality of any winner since 1916.[45]

Some die-hards remained ready to carry on the fight. E. F. Hutton, for one, urged the defeated Willkie to form a pro-capitalist political crusade and take to the airwaves. He cautioned on the basis of experience, however, not to use the words "Liberty" or "League" in its title, preferring something on the order of "We the People." All the du Ponts, and almost all of their allies and loyal political operatives, recognized that the Liberty League was dead as a vehicle for conservative assault on the broker state and for du Pont–style corporate-state revival. By December 3, the once-proud League faced a final debt burden of some $808,000 in unreimbursed notes to some forty investors. Those owed money by the organization included the "Wilmington group" of du Ponts (over $475,000), the General Motors circle ($84,000), a Pennsylvania group headed by Pew, Weir, and Joseph Widener ($108,000), sixteen non-GM supporters in New York ($107,000), and half-a-dozen others scattered across the country ($31,625). With the noteholders' consent, the remaining financial burden was cleared by the relinquishing of repayment claims, an action which allowed the organization to avoid the indignity of bankruptcy court. A wistful but resigned Irénée spoke for the brothers when he concluded, "It is my opinion that we ought not to give up trying to bring about constitutional government, but when we are led into war, it will of course have to be fought under the jurisdiction of a dictator and for that reason we will have to take a respite. Perhaps I am seeing ghosts—I hope so."[46]

chapter 15

Old Soldiers

In the aftermath of the 1940 elections, as the nation nervously edged toward intervention in World War II, public hostilities between the du Ponts and the Roosevelt administration perceptibly eased. One major source of the change was the new "commonality of interests" of the two longtime adversaries in mobilization for war. Having suspended patent-exchange and market-protection agreements with I.G. Farben for plastics, plexiglas, nylon, and synthetic rubber the previous fall, in 1940 the Du Pont Company had begun constructing smokeless powder plants for the American and British governments on a fixed-fee basis, as well as providing royalty-free licenses for company patents to Washington. Over the next four years, Du Pont built twenty-one powder plants, assisted in nineteen others, and produced over two million pounds, or 55 percent of total American production, of powder for the military. Company improvements in neoprene contributed to the country's crash program in synthetic rubber, and rayon yarn now went into tires and nylon into parachutes. Du Pont paints coated ship hulls. Dyes provided the color for uniforms, and anti-freeze kept Army vehicles running in winter. DDT became a staple of the war in the Pacific. General Motors grossed some $14 billion in contracts during the war, and its stock dividends soared. In 1941 alone, Du Pont received $37 million in GM annual dividends. Du Pont Company sales themselves climbed from $400 million in 1940 to $962 million in 1944, with sales to the U.S. government making up 22 percent of the total. The most spectacular sign of the new partnership with government began a year after Pearl Harbor, when the company agreed to construct a pilot plant at Oak Ridge, Tennessee, followed by a larger complex near Hanford, Washington, to produce plutonium for the Manhattan Project.[1]

Besides their mutual interest in military preparedness, the seeming "mellowing " of the du Ponts' attitudes toward the government in Washington owed to the effects of Father Time on Pierre's generation of family leaders. By the time of the Japanese attack on Hawaii on December 7, 1941, Pierre was approaching age seventy-two, Irénée was but two weeks from his sixty-fifth birthday, John Raskob was nearing sixty-three and Lammot had reached sixty-one. Pierre chose the day after Pearl Harbor to resign his position on the company's finance committee, a key seat of his power in the family for many years. In-law Walter S. Carpenter already had succeeded Lammot as company president, and the younger du Pont had shifted over to Pierre's place a year earlier as chairman of the board. Although they remained personally interested in political issues and trends, the du Ponts' involvement continued to wind down to occasional financial contributions for specific causes and candidates. As one sign of du Pont "mellowing," John Raskob wrote the President on January 30, 1942, that the nation ought to "buckle down" together "under your able leadership." Both Raskob and Al Smith were tendered invitations for private meetings at the White House. In the meantime, the national economy continued to climb out of its Depression doldrums, with unemployment falling in 1941 below 10 percent for the first time in over a decade. War administration also contributed, if not a single decisionmaking chain of industrial self-government on the du Pont model, at least a system, as Ellis Hawley has described it, of "two interlocking structures of economic government, one grounded in political institutions and processes, the other in economic organizations."[2]

As early as January 1941, Pierre gave the order that the final dissolution of the Liberty League be carried out. But the old captain, William Stayton, despite admitting that the President seemed to be displaying a partial "change of heart," successfully put off complying with the order on the grounds he needed more time to sort and classify records. Pierre consented to the request and continued to pay Stayton and an assistant a salary—which constituted a kind of old-age pension for his longtime ally. In biweekly installments Stayton received $1900 in January, $1725 each in February and March, $1600 in April, and a comparable amount in May. Pierre sent $4800 more for the June–August period, ostensibly to prepare an index to the Liberty League's pamphlet series. What Stayton actually had in mind, unbeknown to Pierre, was not an orderly disposition of the League's files but the quixotic dream of staging a League revival; one that he would personally trigger by recontacting the organization's approximately 125,000 members and 27,000 contributors from 1936. Stayton openly lobbied his mentor to lead a new crusade directed at repealing the

Sixteenth Amendment, citing the administration's intentions to extend the income tax to lower brackets and an editorial by David Lawrence calling for a GOP "fight on the home front" against New Deal bureaucracy in 1942.[3]

By September of 1941, with infusions of money still being provided by the unknowing Pierre, Stayton began his covert solicitation of former Leaguers. When Pierre found him out, Stayton pleaded that he be allowed to continue in order to "tie the group together" for the occasion when "the next great constitutional question arises." He even claimed to have the backing of Al Smith and James Wadsworth. Irénée, however, threw cold water on the idea, informing him that not only should the League be ended, but also that he would provide no more funds for cataloging. He added that the aged Stayton should designate someone to act as caretaker of the organization's records in case of his own death. Irénée's coldness did not prevent the Captain from continuing to solicit Pierre for an additional $1000 at the end of 1941 and $500 a month for 1942. Only Stayton's death on July 12, 1942, following a lengthy illness, halted the payments. Ewing Laporte, formerly Shouse's assistant, completed the sorting of records, destroying all files except incorporation records, account books, card files, underwriting documents, minutes, publications, and employee records.[4]

Irénée, despite his opposition to any immediate League revival, was the family member most insistent upoon saving its membership and financial records. In particular, he wanted to preserve the lists of contributors "so that if something should happen by which the League should be resurrected, or its objectives undertaken by a new organization, friends of the movement and their addresses would be known." Demonstrating just how hard it was proving to get the League to die a natural death, the family discovered that despite years-old orders to do so, Stayton had never even filed the necessary legal papers for the organization's proper dissolution. Accordingly, it now appeared that the League could not be legally dissolved except on the embarrassing grounds of insolvency. To guard against even that prospect, Stayton had managed before his death to create a bank account for the Liberty League which, when discovered only on November 25, 1942, still held $563. After weeks more of legal wrangling, Laporte finally secured the "cancellation" of the organization. In contrast, the long-moribund Repeal Associates (the retitled AAPA predecessor of the League), because it had been originally incorporated by Stayton well before the du Ponts' involvement and had never been dissolved during his lifetime, could not be similarly ended. All Pierre could do was remove his name from its directorate.[5]

With the final end of the Liberty League, the du Ponts now found themselves even more in the role of bystanders during the 1942 congressional elections. They did retain a strong personal desire to see the New Deal cut down to size, not least of all because of higher wartime taxes and aggravating anti-trust actions filed by the Justice Department. In 1941, Congress had raised the tax rates on both "normal" business profits (defined as 95 percent of average net income in 1936–38 plus 8 percent net capital addition) from 24 to 31 percent and on "excess" profits from 50 to 60 percent. The next year, Congress raised the excess profits level again to 90 percent. On the anti-trust front, Thurman Arnold's division had been compiling evidence against international cartel arrangements in the chemical industry since 1939. Although a consent decree settled a nitrogen cartel case involving the du Ponts in 1942, the Du Pont Company, ICI, and six other firms were charged with conspiracy to monopolize the world dye industry. Two other suits also were launched against Du Pont patent exchanges in the acrylics and methyl methylacrylate fields.[6]

These concerns were not enough to lead the du Ponts toward a revival of a League-style organization. They did, however, produce private rooting and financial support for GOP congressional candidates. Pierre remained fatalistic about the chances for major Republican successes, stating, "I belong to a past generation that is accorded small attention in these days." Jouett Shouse, however, relayed a preelection prediction that the GOP would win thirty to forty seats, adding that in 1940 Wendell Willkie would have prevailed save for the "bought votes" of "labor and negroes." Pierre replied by suggesting that in the long run it might be better if Roosevelt's party retained control of the Congress, albeit by reduced margins. Then blame could be squarely fixed, paving the way for a more genuine and complete conservative resurgence and realignment. As things stood, he lamented, "the spending of money for so-called legitimate purposes in the national campaign has become practically a buying of votes."[7]

On November 4, Pierre got his wish, for while the Democrats retained control of the Congress, the GOP captured forty-four additional seats in the House and nine in the Senate. Raoul Desvernine wired Shouse, "I have been gloating ever since late Tuesday night." Even these results, however, were not enough to obliterate a decade of hard-earned pessimism. Irénée, although confessing that the results made him feel "somewhat better," still insisted, "I will not feel comfortable until Congress shows clearly a disposition to shear off unnecessary arbitrary powers given to the President." In a memorandum to the family assessing the meaning of the returns, Shouse proclaimed that the verdict was less pro-Republican than anti–New Deal. A receptive Pierre concurred, but he still saw no reason to celebrate. "I am very gloomy on the political situation," he wrote to Shouse, "and will doubtless remain so until the New Deal is thrown out lock, stock, and barrel by a free vote of the American people."[8]

In some respects, Pierre's gloom was justified. Despite the election returns, tax burdens continued to increase throughout the war, and anti-trust threats did not cease. In 1943 Congress again hiked the excess profits tax to 95 percent. Although the law later was amended to allow application for a postwar credit of up to 10 percent of taxes paid, the changes were paired with requirements upon business to renegotiate war contracts after cancellation in order to recover the estimated value of their capital expansion. The Du Pont Company created a special reserve fund of $3.3 million in anticipation of repayment requirements, and, remembering the haggling over the Old Hickory project, moved with marked caution into the Manhattan Project. The company negotiated a contract which required the government to underwrite all construction and operational costs (totalling some $390 million) plus a fee of $1. During the war years, the tax rate on gross revenues doubled from prewar levels to an average of 14 percent from 1942 to 1945. According to company spokesmen, the increased taxes amounted to almost twice the level of company net income in 1943–44 and 1.5 times net income in 1945, despite increased wartime earnings. Furthermore, the Justice Department's anti-trust action against the National Lead Company for manipulation of patent laws returned the du Pont family to court. And in January 1944, yet another suit was filed against Du Pont, ICI, and Remington Arms, in spite of appeals to the Navy and War Departments to intervene in order to avoid disruption of war production.[9]

In view of continued governmental intrusions, as early as March 1943 Jouett Shouse began lobbying the family to support a second Willkie presidential campaign. The former candidate was clearly aware of Shouse's labors, for on March 5 he was provided a copy of the appeal letter with the notation that it was being sent "to a rather important list of whom you have some personal knowledge." Throughout the remainder of 1943 and into 1944 Shouse acted as a political set of "eyes and ears" for Willkie in the Midwest, South, and border states, as he had done four years earlier. This time, however, the du Ponts were more difficult to coax out of political hibernation. Upon receiving the appeal, Pierre again responded that a Roosevelt victory would be preferable, particularly if he were to face a Congress opposed to him. Claiming that as far back as 1934 he had believed that "the president could not extract himself from the difficulties that he was building up unless he attempted the assistance of war to mask his plight," he argued that a fourth term for Roosevelt would force the long-awaited day of political reckoning. Referring specifically to the possibility of yet another term, Pierre stated, "I have never believed that he could be deterred from making the attempt." After all, he concluded, belief in one's own infallibility and indefatigability "is the fate of all dictators or all of dictatorial mind." Sounding even more fatalistic was Irénée, who claimed of the New Dealers, "They have woven too complete a web." Questioning the electability of Willkie in a rematch, he surmised, "Personally, I have a feeling that the country is too late, and no matter what happens, we cannot get the New Deal out of power."[10]

Willkie's withdrawal from the GOP nomination race prior to the 1944 conventions, the nomination of Governor Thomas E. Dewey of New York, and Willkie's subsequent death combined to put an end to any thoughts of a duplication in 1944 of the family's personal efforts in the 1940 campaign. Roosevelt again prevailed in November, though by his narrowest margin yet. Although the du Ponts gave slightly over $100,000 in the anti-Roosevelt cause—with the largest sums again from GOP stalwart Lammot—the elder statesmen of the family remained relatively detached from the contest. They were not enthusiastic about Dewey, and the death of Al Smith in early October was a sobering reminder of more than just their political mortality. As a sign of growing detachment from national political involvements, Pierre du Pont in May resumed duties as Delaware's tax commissioner after a seven-year hiatus (a position he retained until the fall of 1949). Also limiting the family's involvement in 1944 was Irénée's reading of the Hatch Act that only a total of $5000 could be given to the GOP campaign in all its various permutations, rather than $5000 for each separate campaign committee.[11]

Seeking to maximize its financial leverage in politics, the family now once more diverted moneys away from the GOP to other organizations outside the formal Republican hierarchy. Besides continuing contributions to the NAM, Irénée followed Lammot's example and channeled funds into Merwin Hart's new anti-radical political vehicle, the National Economic Council. Hart had a long track record of such causes, including the New York State Economic Council and the pro-Franco American Union of Nationalist Spain. As early as May 1943, Lammot had donated $3000 to him for "economic education." In Lammot's words, "It took the country twelve years to throw out prohibition . . . It took eight years for a reaction by vote to set in against the New Deal, but national polls show that now is a favorable time to begin educating the public in the need for free enterprise." Learning that his brother had been extending Hart $3000 a year in loans "for some years," Irénée was likewise persuaded to give a similar amount in April 1944.[12]

Despite the politically satisfying news of Franklin D. Roosevelt's death at Warm Springs, Georgia, in April 1945, Irénée and Lammot at the end of the war still felt besieged by government restrictions, taxes, and lawsuits. Expressing something less than a wholeheartedly patriotic sentiment, Irénée opined to E. F. Hutton, "God bless the 'black market,' it is the only honest one we have." The family became a vocal part of the chorus of opposition to wartime controls that led to their rapid dismantling by Congress in peacetime. Toward that aim, Irénée extended new contributions to the National Economic Council in the form of fifty shares of Phillips Petroleum stock. But as demobilization and reconversion contributed to a surge of inflation and a wave of strikes, in 1946 the du Ponts directed even more aid to the NEC and its anti-CIO political action committee, American Action (headed by former American Legion commander Edward A. Hayes). In July and November 1945, Irénée transmitted a total of $5000 to underwrite American Action's projected 1946 political expenses. In addition, while Pierre rebuffed solicitations from E. T. Weir, who pleaded with him to aid GOP congressional candidates as "our only medium for carrying on the fight against radicalism," Irénée and allies Lammot and John Raskob plunged in. While giving thousands to the GOP, Irénée, once assured by Lammot that offerings to American Action would not come under Hatch Act limitations, provided the group with $3000 more in May 1946.[13]

Part of Irénée's newfound enthusiasm for American Action stemmed from the fact that in addition to its aims to "fight communism, defeat communist-backed candidates for Congress, and rally to this job anti-communist voters all over the country," its sponsoring organization backed a long litany of other conservative causes. They included reducing federal taxes, the recall of liberal Supreme Court judges, voiding of Wagner Act collective bargaining requirements, the return of tidelands oil to the states, opposition to federal housing and educational aid, and rejection of the United Nations. Such views dovetailed nicely with Irénée's own convictions. "The UN," he asserted as one example, "should be eased out by making it a debating society with no powers except recommendations." As a sign of American Action's, and the du Ponts', hard-right credentials in 1946, on October 28 the organization received the endorsement of the anti-Semitic demagogue Gerald

L. K. Smith and the remnant of his America First followers. Among those GOP candidates receiving American Action support were ultra-conservative senatorial candidates Joseph R. McCarthy of Wisconsin and Senator Harlan J. Bushfield of South Dakota. For good measure, Bushfield received an additional $4000 directly from Lammot du Pont.[14]

The 1946 congressional contest continued the conservative and Republican trends and gave the GOP control of Congress for the first time in sixteen years. It also led to intensified political warfare between the du Ponts and the Democratic administration of Harry Truman. With the Republicans having gained another eleven Senate seats and fifty-four House seats, a celebratory post-election American Action dinner at the Waldorf-Astoria Hotel in New York not only featured the Red-baiting radio commentator Upton Close, but displayed Lammot and John Raskob prominently at the head table. Despite ally John W. Davis's professed hope that the 1946 verdict meant that "we are done with the planned economy boys," the Truman administration counterattacked in 1947 with anti-trust actions against the Du Pont–Sylvania cellophane production partnership and, more significantly, the beginning of an investigation into the family's extensive stock ownership in General Motors. Ironically, in January, some nine months before learning of the Justice Department's inquiry, Du Pont president Walter Carpenter had proposed to the board of directors that preferred stock be issued, convertible to GM shares, as a first step toward disengagement of the two companies. But Pierre du Pont, the founder of the Du Pont–GM alliance, had been determined to preserve the greatest monument to the empire he had built and had scuttled the proposal.[15]

While the family wrestled with the question of the Du Pont Company's future relationship to GM, Irénée gave $3000 to the NEC in January and another $1000 in May to its new research branch, the Foundation for Freedom. In June, he arranged to have NEC newsletters distributed to the members of the National Industrial Conference Board. The NEC's, and others', lobbying efforts led to the passage the same month of the Taft-Hartley Act, which banned the closed shop, industry-wide union bargaining, jurisdictional strikes, and strikes by government employees. In addition, the new measure mandated "cooling-off" periods before union strike activities could be implemented and withheld a union's rights to federal mediation if its officers refused to sign pledges that they renounced communism. As part of the ever-more paranoid national hysteria over internal subversion, Irénée endorsed the NEC's drive to limit immigration quotas, even those applying to refugees from Soviet-occupied Eastern Europe, on the grounds that "under the auspices of the present bureaucracy, preference will be given to communists, and they will be educated in all the plans for revolution that corresponding infiltration has produced in countries adjoining Russia." He concluded, "The only way to keep out 'goons' is not to let anyone in."[16]

As a sign of personal gratitude for the NEC's successes, Irénée sent $2000 more to the Foundation for Freedom's educational service in September 1947. During the entirety of 1947, the Du Pont and General Motors companies' officers contributed $1250 to the American Fair Trade Council for lobbying and "economic education," $20,000 to the American Heritage Association, and substantial sums to the American Tariff League, the Economists' National Committee on Monetary Policy, and the Foundation for Economic Freedom (in which Donaldson Brown served as a trustee and to which he had loaned $40,000 the previous September). In behalf of the latter, Lammot co-hosted a fundraising dinner with J. Howard Pew at the Philadelphia Union League. By the end of 1947, Lammot had given the NEC some $16,000, and Irénée had offered $8000 more, not including his stock gifts. Having entered into joint political lobbying activites with Irénée, Lammot now also took the opportunity to try coaxing Pierre back into giving to the Republican party for 1948. Citing the increase in federal spending over the past eight years from $8.8 billion in 1939 to over $35 billion in 1947, he pressed his oldest brother to return to the GOP fold after many years of self-imposed ostracism. Pierre admitted that it was "very interesting and also encouraging to learn of your continued interest in the Republican party. In a choice of evils, I admit that it has preference over the passing New Deal and its supporters. Perhaps I should accept your advice and go along with you."[17]

As the conservative campaign against the Truman administration and its New Deal legacy entered 1948, the ideological battles again ignited. Aided by du Pont contributions and a $1000 loan from John Raskob, the NEC extended its "educational" activities to college and public libraries throughout the Midwest. Du Pont and GM officers continued their donations to the Foundation for Economic Freedom, the American Heritage Association, the American Economic Foundation (created by former Crusaders chief Fred Clark), and the NAM. In April, Irénée contributed funds to former Gannett operative Samuel Pettengill for his Sunday radio broadcasts in behalf of America's Future, Inc. In the ten months leading up to the November election, he also dispatched $5000, plus fifty more shares of Phillips stock, to the NEC. Besides dispersing funds to conservative allies, the du Ponts also continued to offer policy advice. Irénée, for example, vehemently rejected all arguments in behalf of public housing, even those offered by conservative Republican hopeful Robert Taft of Ohio.[18]

With the creation of a presidential committee on civil rights the previous year and the issuance of its policy recommendations, the family even ventured forth its opinions on racial issues. With a growing number of communities beginning to face the moral and political implications of fair employment statutes, Raymond Pitcairn wrote Pierre to complain about a Philadelphia measure, insisting that "the citizen who desires—and is willing and able—to provide fellow citizens with work, is entitled to choose his employees without dictation." Pierre concurred, calling such ordinances "outrageous interference with personal rights." Citing as proof of his racial enlightenment his effort in behalf of black public schools in Delaware, he nonetheless confessed, "I am not 'hipped' on the race question as no opinion or law could convince me that negroes, as a race, are equal to the whites. The latter have had at least a thousand years' start toward what we call civilization." He concluded that "it was a mistake to give negroes a vote, and it is also a mistake to give all white men and women a vote; that is, if we are to have good government." Irénée was even less temperate in his assertions to in-law, and former governor, C. Douglas Buck. Besides attacking rent control and anti-lynching legislation (calling it an "enlarging the FBI bill"), he assailed school integration on the grounds, "Would you like to have the Government require you to send your daughter to a school where 60% or 80% of the children were "darkies' of a very low and ignorant class?"[19]

The du Ponts' intense dislike of the emerging Fair Deal of Harry Truman, as with their prior hatred of the New Deal, once more illustrated that at the core of their political militancy was not simply a desire to protect profits, but a fundamental drive to preserve their economic power, their social beliefs, and their business and personal prerogatives. As in the war years and even the New Deal's heyday, and in spite of constant complaints about high taxes and incipient communism, the postwar period was a prosperous time for the du Ponts. During the war Du Pont's net income had been $76 million per year. In the 1946–1950 interval preceding the Korean War, it leaped to $182 million per year, driven by booming sales in the synthetic fibers area. But in the du Ponts' view, the federal government continued to attempt to dictate the size, labor policies, and market decisions of business, and now statist intervention threatened to extend into matters of social choice as well.[20]

Adding to the immediate sense of alarm during that campaign summer of 1948, with Harry Truman leveling broadsides at the "good-for-nothing 80th Congress," was the fact that the Justice Department's Anti-Trust Division had resumed its suit filings. The litigation list now included action directly targeted at the Du Pont–General Motors relationship. Ironically, participants in the Justice Department later confessed that their decision to file was based on the understandable assumption, which was later proven erroneous, that Truman would be beaten in November and that his defeat would end hopes for any later anti-trust action. It was also believed within the administration that lodging the suit would appeal to organized labor in the election campaign by projecting a "get-tough" image toward "anti-labor" companies. The Justice Department at the same time pressed ahead with its suit against the Du Pont–ICI patent exchanges and joint ventures in Canada and South America.[21]

Despite the optimism generated by polls showing Truman far behind Dewey, a cautious Pierre still professed long-term pessimism. His old friend John Raskob agreed. "I think," he stated, "we are bound to drift into a Democracy where we will have majority rule instead of continuing our Republic where man is largely protected from injuring himself by reason of the Bill of Rights and the time it takes to amend the Constitution." Hoping to reverse his expectations, Raskob plunged into the NEC's pre-election activities, including another fundraising dinner in September. But to the du Ponts' shock and dismay, following a "give 'em Hell" campaign that displayed what was to them the worst example yet of demogoguery and partisan tastelessness, Harry Truman performed a political miracle and retained the White House on November 2. Within weeks, Lammot was called to appear before a federal hearing on Du Pont's investments in GM and other firms. The usually prepared Lammot confessed afterward to reporters, "I made a bad showing at the end of the session." With Truman's victory now clearing the way, Attorney General Thomas Clark filed suit six months later in federal district court in Chicago to break apart "the largest single concentration of power in the United States."[22]

More convinced than ever that only a complete reeducation of the American public in the virtues of free enterprise and the dangers of "radicalism" could halt the drift toward democratic, anti-business socialism, Irénée and Lammot made additional contributions to the NEC. In a letter accompanying a request for the organization's literature, Irénée lauded Merwin Hart for informing Americans "what the real, basic, underlying trouble is in Washington—an alliance of 'pinks' with some undesirable Jewish people who seem to have seized control of the government." By May of 1950, Irénée had given $17,700 in direct gifts and over $26,000 in underwriting loans for the distribution of the NEC's literature. Other family insiders followed similar paths. Pierre remained on the mailing list of the Gannett remnant, the Committee for Constitutional Government. John Raskob, more fearful of a government "takeover" of public education through federal aid programs, donated $4845 to the same organization to distribute *The Road Ahead*, a tract by John T. Flynn which employed the example of postwar England to show the disastrous consequences of trade union power, government confiscation, taxation, and socialism. In a related effort, in early 1950 Raskob launched a letter solicitation drive that raised $32,500 in contributions for the Committee for Constitutional Government.[23]

As early as the end of 1949, the du Ponts already had provided $10,000 over the previous two years to the American Economic Foundation, $3500 in 1949 alone to the American Fair Trade Council, $5000 in 1948–49 to the Committee for Economic Development, $6000 in 1949 to the Citizens Committee for Reorganization of the Executive Branch of the Government, $5000 to America's Future, Inc., and $4000 to the Economists' National Committee on Monetary Policy. During the period of June 1946 to March 1950, Du Pont executives gave $40,000, and GM officials $50,000, to the Foundation for Economic Education, headed by West Coast businessman and former National Industrial Conference Board executive vice-president Leonard E. Read. Lammot du Pont personally had provided nearly $20,000 to the organization from mid-1941 to 1949, and Irénée as of April 1950 had extended $6000 more. Helping to loosen their wallets was the fact that Du Pont Company stalwarts Jasper Crane and Donaldson Brown both served as trustees of the Foundation for Economic Education, with Crane a vice-president in 1950–51.[24]

Pierre du Pont did not invest as heavily in "economic education" and lobbying ventures as his collegues, but even he toyed one last time with the idea of a nonpartisan crusade to restore pro-corporate conservative ideals. Informed in the fall of 1949 of a fledgling effort launched by college president Theodore A. Distler and Curtin Winsor that "may turn out to be what we are looking for," he tried to enlist former ally E. F. Hutton in early November. To George Wharton Pepper he opined, "If a movement could be organized along the lines that we recently discussed I might find it possible to back the movement and to withdraw support for the [Republican] Party." He asserted, "A non-political effort is the only thing that can save us." Pierre, however, could find no takers for the cause. Most, like former GOP chairman John Hamilton, were only interested in securing du Pont funds for their particular issues and protégés. In Hamilton's case, the objective was to persuade Pierre to coax his cousin Nicholas into heading a finance committee for the reelection to the Senate of Robert Taft as a prelude for another attempt by Taft to win the White House.[25]

Despite the continuing presence of a du Pont on the Republican National Committee in the person of Delaware member Francis V. du Pont (the late Coleman's son), Pierre remained convinced that the GOP merely blocked the way for the emergence of a better, more thoroughly pro-corporate, party. He chided the Republicans for not "coming out squarely for reform measures" rather than just a "modification" of the New Deal. He admitted that his views would lead to defeat for "two or three elections," but "when the crash comes" the party would then be strategically placed to "take up the reins of government." A more fatalistic, and reflective, Pierre resurfaced on his eightieth birthday in response to greetings from Jouett Shouse. "Looking back over the years," he wrote, "it seems that my activites did not contribute very much to the fundamental problems of our country." Confessing "perhaps we were born too soon," he nonetheless sighed, "We lived in the golden age, and for that have much to be thankful for."[26]

The "golden age" of Pierre's generation of du Ponts was fast disappearing. Rather than exiting the stage in a blaze of conservative fanfare and public tributes, however, they were, like the old soldiers they had become, merely fading away into obscurity. What headlines their names generated were not caused by their own actions but by the actions of the federal government in whittling away at their edifice of power. In June 1950, in a manner reminiscent of the Black Committee's investigations of 1935–1936, a House Select Committee on Lobbying Activities chaired by Representative Frank Buchanan of Pennsylvania began looking into the lobbying activities of a multitude of right-wing organizations since 1946. As a product of their inquiries, the various causes to which the du Ponts had contributed, and their amounts, were disclosed to the press. Revelation of the correspondence between Irénée and Merwin Hart also led, as before, to direct accusations of anti-Semitism against the family. Pierre, for his part, clumsily tried again to deflect such accusations by personally claiming one-eight Jewish ancestry.[27]

The outbreak of the Korean War in June 1950, though it raised demand for the products of the du Pont economic empire, once again led to new imposition of excess profits taxes. By comparison to World War II, the terms of the legislation could be seen as generous, for a substantial tax credit was allowed on 1946–1949 earnings and the maximum tax rate on excess profits was set at "only" 62 percent. Nonetheless, the new taxes created new resentments that contracts for a nuclear fuel plant on the Savannah River in South Carolina—part of the thermonuclear, or H-bomb, weapon project—only partly eased. And on October 15, 1950, John Raskob became the first member of the du Pont "big four" to pass away, at the age of seventy-one. Only four months earlier, he had agreed to join the board of trustees of the Committee for Constitutional Government and had entered into a five-year loan subscription agreement reminiscent of the Liberty League's funding plan.[28]

The remaining giants of the interwar generation could only fight holding actions to preserve the symbols of the power they had once held. The Du Pont–ICI anti-trust case, which had finally come to trial in April 1950, concluded over a year later with a decree ordering the termination of the two companies' patent exchanges and the dissolution of joint ventures in Canada, Argentina, and Brazil, sparing only operations in Chile. Despite—or perhaps, in a spirit of vengeance, because of—the Buchanan Committee's disclosures, Irénée continued his contributions to the NEC. Pierre persisted in issuing quixotic calls for a privately led, nonpartisan political crusade to "protect us from the totalitarian spirit of the time." He now suggested a constitutional amendment campaign directed at some "similar definite objective" as a 25 percent cap on all individual and corporate income taxes. Given Pierre's preference for presidential candidates from outside the mainstream of professional politics, he was receptive when friend Raymond Pitcairn in November 1951 recommended his support for General Dwight D. Eisenhower. As the 1952 campaign season approached, the du Ponts also took some satisfaction from the Congress's actions in both 1951 and 1952 in defeating proposals from the Truman administration to increase tax rates.[29]

By early 1952, the secretary of the Committee for Constitutional Government, Edward Rumely, had already received $20,000 from Lammot du Pont, owing in part to Lammot's desire to honor Raskob's commitment. Rumely now proposed to Irénée and Pierre that a fund be established to pay the legal costs of a court challenge of the Buchanan Committee and its methods. In a scenario of events eerily reminiscent of the Black Committee's history, the Buchanan panel had sought the names of the puchasers of 750,000 copies of *The Road Ahead*. The committee charged that the book's "sales" were but a cover for contributions to fund the organization's lobbying activities. Upon Rumely's refusal to reveal the names on First Amendment grounds, the Committee for Constitutional Government was cited with contempt of Congress. Because of the legal expenses of an appeal, Rumely needed additional contributions to fund other ongoing activites, including the publication and distribution of the *Spotlight* newsletter. Of particular appeal to the du Ponts was Rumely's intention to push for a federal tax limitation amendment during the 1952 session. But while the two brothers still weighed the wisdom of additional contributions to the organization, their younger sibling Lammot died following a series of heart attacks. As a tribute to their departed brother, each of them now offered $10,000 to cover his obligation.[30]

A major reason that Irénée and Pierre hesitated to donate to Rumely's cause at first, besides questions about its effectiveness, was the brothers' desire to insure their donating flexibility for the 1952 election season. The more traditionally Republican Irénée professed to GOP committeeman Frank du Pont in late April, as the delegate contest heated up, that he preferred Taft to Eisenhower, lamenting "I wish I knew what the latter really stands for." As late as June 12, the ever-fatalistic Pierre still was insisting that the Democrats would renominate Truman and that he would be elected. During the Eisenhower-Stevenson general election campaign, Jouett Shouse once more eagerly signed up for GOP politicking duty. The du Ponts themselves, however, played a subdued electoral role. Given Eisenhower's image as a non-traditional politican and his stances against internal subversion and for returning tidelands oil to the states, they nonetheless were quite pleased at his November victory. Even more satisfying was the GOP's acquisition of a working majority in the U.S. Senate.[31]

Eisenhower's early success in ending the Korean conflict and removing wartime taxes and wage and price controls won great acclaim from the family. Further cheer emanated from the Committee for Constitutional Government's court victory on March 9, 1953, against the Buchanan Committee. Emboldened by the success, Rumely's group, with du Pont backing, then pressed for passage of the Bricker Amendment (designed to limit presidential power to make agreements with foreign powers without congressional consent) and the Reed-Dirksen Amendment (limiting the top income tax rate to 25 percent unless three-quarters of both houses of Congress agreed to lift the ceiling, even then limiting any increase to 15 percent more than the bottom rate, and eliminating federal death and gift taxes). After new appeals from the Committee's treasurer, Sumner Gerard, that not only had the late Lammot given $20,000 but had, like Raskob, brought in undersigned pledges for $40,000 more, Irénée issued another $3000 in November 1953, $10,000 at year's end to underwrite the distribution of literature, and yet $12,000 more in July 1954 to fund a pro–Bricker

Amendment pamphlet. With the Committee for Constitutional Government's legislative campaigns consistently resulting in failure, however, in September 1954 the brothers finally severed their financial links to the organization.[32]

The du Ponts were learning that even the presence of a friendlier Republican administration in Washington was no guarantee that their policy beliefs would be followed. Nor was it any insurance against the continuation of anti-trust dangers. In February 1953, Irénée, who had resisted any and all suggestions by younger company officers that Du Pont divest itself of GM holdings, personally testified in the federal anti-trust suit against the combination. Having reached the age of seventy-six, the still-combative Irénée nonetheless apologized to his inquisitors for his failing hearing. Pierre, now eighty-three, followed his brother on the stand and insisted that despite Du Pont's longstanding and substantial stock interest in GM (23 percent held by the Du Pont Company and more shares in family hands through Christiana Securities and Delaware Realty Company), the company's ability to dominate paint, fabric, and other sales to GM owed not to Du Pont ownership penetration but to the superiortiy of its products as shown by sales levels to other automakers. Initially the du Ponts believed that they were winning their "days in court" on both the GM suit and the cellophane cartel case. In the latter suit, Delaware federal district court judge Paul Leahy ruled that although the Du Pont Company controlled 67 percent of market capacity, it had achieved that position through the rightful control of cellophane patents rather than illegal means, and therefore the government had not proven the company guilty of monopolistic practices. Nonetheless, rather than accept the lower court's verdict, the Justice Department appealed to the U.S. Supreme Court.[33]

Pierre, the patriarch of the clan, would not live to witness the final resolution of either case. On April 5, 1954, after being stricken with severe abdominal pains from a ruptured blood vessel, the family's guiding force for nearly half a century died. With him, too, seemed to die the chances that the full power and the glory that had been Du Pont would be preserved. Following his severance of aid to the Committee for Constitutional Government, Irénée turned down overtures to join in a purchase bid for the New York *Herald-Tribune*, the voice of "Eastern Establishment" Republicanism. In December 1954, in a temporary victory for the family, federal district judge Walter La Buy did order the government's GM lawsuit dismissed. In 1956 the Supreme Court upheld Leahy's ruling in the cellophane case. Eisenhower's reelection was also received as favorable news by Irénée, the surviving old lion. But within a year the Supreme Court, with three justices disassociating themselves from the case because of prior legal involvements with the company, ruled four-to-two to override the GM ruling of Judge La Buy, and ordered Du Pont to dispose of its sixty-three million shares of General Motors stock.[34]

It was an especially cruel irony that Irénée, the most passionate—to the point of intemperateness—of the brothers, was the one left to rage at the hand dealt the family empire by fate. The Justice Department demanded that the Du Pont Company's GM shares be disposed of by sale and that GM stockholders with no ties to Du Pont be given first option. In 1958 the Internal Revenue Service maintained that the undistributed stock would be regarded by it as taxable dividends to Du Pont shareholders rather than as capital gains. As if the parcelling out of GM stock was not humiliating enough to Irénée, in 1959 the victory of the Castro insurrection in Cuba over the Batista dictatorship resulted in the confiscation of his beloved Xanadu. The vacation estate was turned by Castro into a public museum and restaurant dedicated to the memory of the Marxist revolution and was dubbed the "Casa du Pont."[35]

Even a second federal court ruling by Judge La Buy to allow the Du Pont Company to "pass through" to shareholders only those GM holdings which carried voting privileges, while enjoining Delaware Realty and Christiana Securities from exercising such rights, proved of little relief. The decision, intended to end company control of GM without subjecting Du Pont stockholders to additional taxation and plunges in the value of their portfolios, was overturned on appeal of the Justice Department by the Supreme Court in May 1961. Fortunately for the family, a sympathetic Kennedy administration supported a bill authored by Delaware Senator Allen Frear to allow GM shares distributed to Du Pont stockholders to be treated as tax-exempt capital gains until their resale. Following the bill's passage in 1962, final agreement was reached on the sale of Du Pont, Christiana Securities, and Delaware Realty holdings in GM within three years.[36]

Appropriately enough, the Du Pont–General Motors connection—the great testament to the du Pont family's economic power—barely outlived its remaining founder. Irénée du Pont, the last and most defiant of the old inner circle, died at the age of eighty-six on December 19, 1963. Less than two years later, and some eight years after the initial Supreme Court directive, the Du Pont–GM stock divestiture finally was completed. That same year, Repeal Associates, which under its original title of the Association Against the Prohibition Amendment had been the vehicle for Pierre and Irénée's first major foray into national politics, also expired, having outlived all of its creators.[37]

The family, the company, and the politics of the country would not be quite the same after the passing of the du Pont titans. Although Du Pont's sales continued to climb in the mid-1960's, the company never regained the relative clout it had enjoyed from its GM earnings. Fluctuations in the national economy, poor management decisions, and increasing competiton in the fibers, plastics, and petrochemicals field from Dow and Monsanto, among other factors, added to the breakdown of prior international cartel arrangements to produce declines in return on investment. The need for "new blood" at the top and fresh ideas caused the company to turn to Irving Shapiro—a former Justice Department attorney who became a Du Pont lawyer during the GM litigation, and a Jew—as board chairman, chief executive officer, and "Mister Outside" in the firm's dealings with the federal government and the public. Christiana Securities, the family holding company whose 28 percent equity in Du Pont had insured family control of the enterprise for decades, was liquidated. Under Shapiro, the company moved away from its post-Depression reliance on synthetic fibers—the product legacy of Lammot du Pont—and redirected its efforts into specialized investment areas such as precision medical instruments, X-ray film, agricultural chemicals, and specialty plastics. In order to secure increasingly costly petroleum supplies for its own needs, in 1981 the company acquired Conoco. On the electoral front, William Roth, married to a family in-law, was sent by Delaware to the U.S. Senate in 1970, and Pierre S. ("Pete") du Pont IV, Lammot's grandson, served two terms as the state's governor. But a Pete du Pont GOP presidential nomination bid in 1988 was scuttled after single-digit showings in the primaries in Iowa and New Hampshire, once more illustrating that the family's continued statewide political clout did not translate readily into national success. That same year, amidst embarrassing public disclosures of three decades of safety violations at the Du Pont Company's nuclear weapons processing plant in South Carolina, the federal government ordered its shutdown for an indefinite period.[38]

Pierre, Irénée, and Lammot du Pont, along with John Raskob, presided over the building of an empire, and to varying degrees they witnessed its decline. They sought to use the power of that empire to fundamentally transform American national politics and government. They longed for the restoration in modern garb of a form of early American republican, elitist politics, free of the democratizing impulses and partisan demogoguery of their era—a new "gentry" politics based on the contemporary public virtue of the technocratic business manager rather than the prestige of the landed aristocrat. They meant to bring about the fusion, into a single chain of national economic command, of the dual structures of public and private economic prerogatives—one legitimized by the popular ballot box, the other by the balance sheet and the stockholder election. Like latter-day Federalists, they tried to use the methods of partisan politics to bring about the demise of that same politics, but the processes of popular government proved more durable than their power to change them.

As products of an exclusive world of privilege, education, and business power which they subsequently expanded upon, the du Ponts judged themselves particularly equipped to offer enlightened and disinterested stewardship of public affairs. Although to outsiders their claims of disinterestedness appeared outlandish, they sincerely believed that their enormous fortunes and their record of managerial successes prepared them to provide administrative leadership free of the graft and special-interest favoritism of "professional politics." It was a peculiar outgrowth of the du Ponts' closely guarded social isolation, as well as a measure of their hubris, that they did not perceive their own policy agenda as "special," class-biased, and self-interested. As a result of their myopia, they were able to discount the legitmacy of rival claims offered by other, often weaker, social interests. Having done so, they then concluded that honest and efficient government—the art of "public administration"—consisted in the modern age simply of applying the tested principles of business management. Certain of their own virtue and ability, they doubted virtually all others' capacities in these matters.

Although the du Ponts' private rationalizations revealed a nostalgia for a lost, mythical past somehow untainted by democratic contentiousness, partisanship, and disrespect for hierarchy, their beliefs also fit comfortably within the centralizing, bureaucratic traditions of social control of the Progressive Era—the period which had marked their personal ascendancy. Their image of the masses—unintelligent, irrational, and manipulatable—resembled many progressives' fears of bossism and political corruption. Their alarm at working-class unrest, labor militancy, and radical, foreign "isms" was shared by those very progressives who saw modest government regulation of the marketplace as a necessary alternative to radicalism. As corporate executives who had expanded the international reach of their empire in search of raw materials, new processes, and markets, they abetted the efforts of imperialist-minded progressives like Theodore Roosevelt to override parochial traditions and to expand America's global power and influence. As corporatists, as cosmopolitans, and as conservatives, they endorsed willingly that side of the progressive personality marked by a search for centralized managerial expertise, material comfort, and social order within American industrial society.

What their privileged isolation also bequeathed them, however, was the inability to understand or accept the other side of progressivism—the notion that in order to expand national greatness by preserving avenues of opportunity, government must function independently of powerful private interests and act to promote the political, moral, and material assimilation, empowerment, and uplift of those less advantaged. The New Deal built upon that progressive foundation by expanding the federal government's role in economic welfare and market stabilization, as well as by sponsoring the counterorganization of labor, farmer, and consumer interests. The du Ponts were never able to conceive that private paternalism and philanthropy might be inadequate to meet human needs in times of distress or to acknowledge the short-sightedness and selfishness in their opposition to "broker-state" liberalism. Their unwillingness to entrust anyone but themselves, or men of comparable position and beliefs, with the prerogatives of economic production, representation, and allocation insured their declaration of war upon the Roosevelt administration once it challenged them, even though many New Deal policies proved beneficial to the financial health of their enterprises.

In championing their particular vision of the corporate state so rigidly and exclusively, the du Ponts also made the frequent mistake of shutting themselves off from potential allies of different social backgrounds, ideological nuances, and views on political tactics. Ultimately the family's unshakable faith in its own exceptional virtues—and the corresponding repudiation of people and ideas deemed alien or inferior—paralyzed it at the very times it needed most to build a broader-based conservative coalition. Nothing demonstrated the du Ponts' vulnerability as neophytes in national politics more clearly than this inability to be sufficiently "pragmatic," but their enormous triumphs in the business world had not instilled in them an appreciation of their limitations in the foreign environment of partisan maneuverings and electoral strategy. As a result, they were never able to gain a clear field as the "official spokesmen" of conservatism, or of the oft-misnamed "business community," or even of the largest corporate interests alone. By the demise of the Liberty League, their core of supporters had dwindled to little more than their immediate family. Even within that sanctum, solidarity was often in short supply because of frictions over party allegiances, relative rank and responsibilities, and tactics. In retrospect, despite the success of prohibition repeal that they had championed, despite the temporary ascendancy of John Raskob within Democratic party councils in 1928–1932, and despite early hopes of controlling the direction of New Deal economic policies, the du Ponts never really came close to reversing the long-term political trends they opposed, or to instituting, in its various electoral and administrative features, the corporate state.

Instead of ushering in a corporate state in which private industrial managers could, without fear of challenge, exercise central control over national economic and social policy, the du Ponts witnessed the emergence of a broker state. New national client groups—industrial unions, farm organizations, consumer forums—had become part of a public decisionmaking process in which the federal state, with its distinct electoral power base and its own burgeoning bureaucracy of experts, exercised final choice. The evolution of political brokering did not mean, of course, that corporate America could not adapt to the "mixed" system of public and private managerial power, or even learn how to have it serve its general purposes. But the new strategies of exerting *influence*—which required continual corporate adjustment to shifting political and ideological currents rather than simple dictation of commands—were a far cry from the kind of complete *control* that the du Ponts had dared to dream of. As Pierre, Irénée, Lammot, and Raskob's generation of family leaders passed from national economic and political power, their successors learned, and applied, the methods of influence, as other corporate leaders had begun to do much earlier. The du Ponts' utopian vision of conservative corporatism died along with its architects. In its place, corporate liberalism—or perhaps more accurately, corporate "pragmatism"—assumed center stage in the ongoing drama between big business and the broker state.[39]

Notes

Abbreviations

Beck Papers	James M. Beck Papers, Princeton University Library, Princeton, New Jersey
FDR Papers as President	Franklin D. Roosevelt Papers as President, Franklin D. Roosevelt Library, Hyde Park, New York
Hoard Papers	Halbert Hoard Papers, State Historical Society of Wisconsin, Madison, Wisconsin
IDP	Irénée du Pont Papers, Hagley Library, Wilmington, Delaware
Landon Papers	Alfred M. Landon Papers, Kansas State Historical Society, Topeka, Kansas
PSDP	Pierre S. du Pont Papers, Hagley Library, Wilmington, Delaware
Raskob Papers	John J. Raskob Papers, Hagley Library, Wilmington, Delaware
Shouse Papers	Jouett Shouse Papers, University of Kentucky Library, Lexington, Kentucky
Smith Papers	Alfred E. Smith Papers, New York State Library, Albany, New York
Wadsworth Papers	James W. Wadsworth, Jr., Papers, Library of Congress, Washington, D.C.

A Note on Manuscript Collections. In addition to the manuscript sources appearing in the list of abbreviations, researchers will find valuable materials in the following collections: the Newton D. Baker Papers, Library of Congress, Washington, D.C.; the Bruce Barton Papers, State Historical Society of Wisconsin, Madison, Wisconsin; the John W. Davis Papers, Yale University Library, New Haven, Connecticut; the Papers of the National Committee of the Democratic Party, 1928–1948, Franklin D. Roosevelt Library, Hyde Park, New York; the Lammot du Pont Papers, Hagley Library, Wilmington, Delaware; the Herbert C. Hoover Papers as President, Herbert Hoover Presidential Library, West Branch, Iowa; the Henry Bourne Joy Papers, Michigan Historical Collections, University of Michigan, Ann Arbor, Michigan; the National Broadcasting Company Papers, State Historical Society of Wisconsin, Madison, Wisconsin; the Albert C. Ritchie Papers, Maryland Historical Society, Baltimore, Maryland; the Franklin D. Roosevelt Papers, 1920–1928, and the Franklin D. Roosevelt Papers as Governor, Franklin D. Roosevelt Library, Hyde Park, New York; the

Roosevelt Papers as Governor, Franklin D. Roosevelt Library, Hyde Park, New York; the Alfred E. Smith Records, New York State Archives, Albany, New York; the Papers of the Voluntary Committee of Lawyers, Inc., Collection on Legal Change, Wesleyan University, Middletown, Connecticut.

1. Barons of the Brandywine

1. Irving Bernstein, *The Lean Years* (Baltimore: Penguin Books, 1966), pp. 54, 65.
2. Ibid., p. 54; Harry Jerome, *Mechanization in Industry* (New York: National Bureau of Research, 1934), pp. 122–125.
3. Bernstein, *The Lean Years,* pp. 63–64.
4. Gerard Colby, *Du Pont Dynasty* (Secaucus, N.J.: Lyle Stuart, 1984), pp. 207–209; William S. Dutton, *Du Pont: One Hundred and Forty Years* (New York: Charles Scribner's Sons, 1942), p. 278.
5. For a reliable overview of the development of the du Pont economic empire, see Graham D. Taylor and Patricia E. Sudnik, *Du Pont and the International Chemical Industy* (Boston: Twayne Publishers, 1984). See also the more partisan view of James Phelan and Robert Pozen, *The Company State: Ralph Nader's Study Group Report on Du Pont in Delaware* (New York: Grossman Publishers, 1973).
6. Alfred D. Chandler, Jr., and Stephen Salsbury, *Pierre S. du Pont and the Making of the Modern Corporation* (New York: Harper and Row, 1971), pp. 4–13; John K. Winkler, *The Du Pont Dynasty* (Baltimore: Reynal and Hitchcock, 1935), p. 21.
7. Taylor and Sudnik, *Du Pont,* pp. 24, 27–30.
8. Chandler and Salsbury, *Pierre S. Du Pont,* pp. 321–356, 457, 536; Taylor and Sudnik, *Du Pont,* pp. 62–66, 71–79; Dutton, *Du Pont,* pp. 200–213.
9. Chandler and Salsbury, *Pierre S. du Pont,* pp. 14–49, 104; Max Dorian, *The Du Ponts: From Gunpowder to Nylon* (Boston: Little, Brown, 1961), pp. 260–264.
10. Taylor and Sudnik, *Du Pont,* pp. 76–77, 88–89; Dutton, *Du Pont,* p. 213; Dorian, *The Du Ponts,* p. 264; Colby, *Du Pont Dynasty,* p. 227.
11. In view of his ascetic manner, Lammot's personal life was surprisingly eventful; he was married four times and sired ten children. Taylor and Sudnik, *Du Pont,* pp. 69, 76, 86, 133, 143–145, 151; Dutton, *Du Pont,* pp. 213–214; Dorian, *The Du Ponts,* p. 264; Colby, *Du Pont Dynasty,* p. 279.
12. Dutton, *Du Pont,* p. 214; Taylor and Sudnik, *Du Pont,* pp. 64, 72–73. The best biography of Raskob is in Roy H. Lopata, "John J. Raskob: A Conservative Businessman in the Age of Roosevelt" (Ph.D. diss., University of Delaware, 1975). See also Henry F. Pringle, "John J. Raskob: A Portrait," *Outlook,* August 22, 1928, pp. 645–649, 678; and Chandler and Salsbury, *Pierre S. du Pont,* pp. 39, 313, 435–437, 455–456, 460, 491, 508, 536.
13. By 1921 Raskob already had thirteen children. Dorian, *The Du Ponts,* p. 196; Taylor and Sudnik, *Du Pont,* p. 146.
14. Colby, *Du Pont Dynasty,* pp. 189, 278.
15. Ibid., pp. 265, 277–278.
16. Dutton, *Du Pont,* pp. 365–367.
17. See Ernest Dale and Charles Meloy, "Hamilton M. Barksdale and the Du Pont Contributions to Systematic Management," *Business History Review* 36

(Summer 1962), pp. 127–152. Dutton, *Du Pont*, p. 367; Chandler and Salsbury, *Pierre S. du Pont*, p. 127; Taylor and Sudnik, *Du Pont*, pp. 23, 28–29; Sidney Fine, *Sit Down: The General Motors Strike of 1936–37* (Ann Arbor: University of Michigan Press, 1969), p. 19.

18. Peter F. Drucker, *The Concept of the Corporation* (New York: Mentor Executive Library Books, 1964), pp. 31, 36–45, 49.

19. Colby, *Du Pont Dynasty*, pp. 315–316; B. C. Forbes, "The Salaries That Are Paid in Various Lines," *American Magazine* 89 (January 1920).

20. Colby, *Du Pont Dynasty*, p. 317; Fine, *Sit-Down*, p. 23.

21. Dutton, *Du Pont*, pp. 364, 370; Fine, *Sit-Down*, pp. 23–24.

22. Fine, *Sit-Down*, pp. 24–25.

23. Ibid.

24. E. I. du Pont Company, "The Chemical Industry" (New York: E. I. du Pont Co., 1935), p. 14; Fine, *Sit-Down*, p. 23; Chandler and Salsbury, *Pierre S. du Pont*, p. 136; Colby, *Du Pont Dynasty*, p. 200.

25. "Chemistry's Tremendous Tomorrows," *Literary Digest*, November 3, 1923, p. 23.

2. Anti-Insurgent Politics

1. The originator of the community-society, or *Gemeinschaft* and *Gesellschaft*, dichotomy was Ferdinand Tönnies, in *Community and Society*, trans, and ed. Charles P. Loomis (East Lansing, Mich: Michigan State University Press, 1957), originally published in German in 1887. The sociologist Robert K. Merton elaborated similar concepts in "Patterns of Influence: Local and Cosmopolitan Influentials," *Social Theory and Social Structure* (Glencoe, N.Y.: The Free Press, 1949), pp. 387–420. Recent historians who have applied these constructs include Samuel P. Hays, "Political Parties and the Community-Society Continuum," in *The American Party Systems: Stages of Political Development*, ed. William Nisbet Chambers and Walter Dean Burnham (New York: Oxford University Press, 1975), pp. 152–181, and Jackson Turner Main, who has employed "cosmopolitan-localist" divisions to account for the emergence of the Federalists and Anti-Federalists in *Political Parties before the Constitution* (Chapel Hill, N.C.: University of North Carolina Press, 1972). Robert H. Wiebe's description of the breakdown of "island communities" in *The Search for Order, 1877–1920* (New York: Hill and Wang, 1967) brings a similar explanation to the public controversies of the Populist and Progressive eras; he extends the analyses forward in "Modernizing the Republic, 1920 to the Present," in Bernard Bailyn et al., *The Great Republic: A History of the American People* (Lexington, Mass.: Little, Brown, 1977), pp. 1056–1061, 1126–1133. A variant of the model has also been applied profitably to 1930's politics by Alan Brinkley in *Voices of Protest: Huey Long, Father Coughlin, and the Great Depression* (New York: Alfred A. Knopf, 1984), esp. pp. xi–xiii, 143–168. Finally, Charles W. Eagles, in "Urban-Rural Conflict in the 1920s: A Historiographical Assessment," *The Historian* 49 (November 1986), pp. 26–48, has praised the search for a subtler alternative to earlier "urban-rural" dichotomies, but has warned against continued anti-rural bias and adherence to rigid, exclusive periodizations such as "the Twenties" in its application.

2. For a discussion of the different models of government-business relations in the early twentieth century, see Ellis W. Hawley, "The New Deal and Business," in *The New Deal*, vol. I, *The National Level*, ed. John Braeman, Robert H. Bremner, and David Brody (Columbus: Ohio State University Press, 1975), pp. 51–54. Hawley has been a leader in the exploration of twentieth-century corporate "liberalism" and "conservatism"; for a brief discussion of other works in this area by Hawley, Kim McQuaid, and Louis Galambos, among others, see note 39 to Chapter 15.

3. P. S. du Pont to N. N. Nicholson, December 2, 1919, Pierre S. du Pont Papers (henceforth referred to as PSDP), Series A, File 765.

4. Josiah Marvel to P. S. du Pont, December 3, 1919, P. S. du Pont to Hugh L. Cooper, April 20, 1920, Cooper to P. S. du Pont, April 30, 1920, PSDP, Series A, File 765.

5. P. S. du Pont to Seaver Woods, April 9, 1924, PSDP, Series A, File 765.

6. Ibid.

7. Taylor and Sudnik, *Du Pont*, pp. 18–19. For an account of the earliest du Ponts in America, see William H. Carr, *The Du Ponts of Delaware* (New York: Dodd, Mead, 1964).

8. Dorian, *The Du Ponts*, pp. 158–159. See also Marquis James, *Alfred I. Du Pont: The Family Rebel* (Indianapolis: Bobbs Merrill, 1941).

9. Dorian, *The Du Ponts*, pp. 158–159; James, *Alfred I. Du Pont*, pp. 292–296.

10. James, *Alfred I. Du Pont*, pp. 299–344.

11. Taylor and Sudnik, *Du Pont*, pp. 30–34; Chandler and Salsbury, *Pierre S. du Pont*, pp. 259–300; Colby, *Du Pont Dynasty*, pp. 183–184.

12. Taylor and Sudnik, *Du Pont*, pp. 69–71; Chandler and Salsbury, *Pierre S. du Pont*, pp. 359–368, 400–427; U.S. Congress, House, *Report No. 998*, 66th Congress, 2d sess. (Washington, D.C.: Government Printing Office, 1921).

13. Dorian, *The Du Ponts*, p. 214; Taylor and Sudnik, *Du Pont*, p. 113.

14. Dorian, *The Du Ponts*, p. 196; Fletcher Dobyns, *The Amazing Story of Repeal: An Exposé of the Power of Propaganda* (Chicago: Willett, Clark, 1940), p. 19; Chandler and Salsbury, *Pierre S. du Pont*, pp. 396–397; Taylor and Sudnik, *Du Pont*, pp. 111–113.

15. Dobyns, *Amazing Story*, p. 19; Mark H. Leff, *The Limits of Symbolic Reform: The New Deal and Taxation, 1933–39* (London: Cambridge Univ. Press, 1984), p. 16.

16. Colby, *Du Pont Dynasty*, pp. 252–253.

17. Chandler and Salsbury, *Pierre S. du Pont*, p. 561; Colby, *Du Pont Dynasty*, p. 253; *New York Times*, April 17, 1924, p. 20, May 11, 1924, Sec. IX, p. 11.

18. David E. Kyvig, *Repealing National Prohibition* (Chicago: University of Chicago Press, 1979), p. 200.

19. An excellent discussion of the continuing impact of the insurgents upon 1920's politics is in Arthur S. Link, "What Happened to the Progressive Movement in the 1920's?," *American Historical Review* 64 (July, 1959), pp. 833–851.

20. Colby, *Du Pont Dynasty*, pp. 166–169, 179–180, 185–186.

21. Chandler and Salsbury, *Pierre S. du Pont*, p. 260; Colby, *Du Pont Dynasty*, pp. 221–228, 239, 252, 287–289.

22. Colby, *Du Pont Dynasty*, pp. 216–217.

23. Lopata, "John J. Raskob," pp. 26–27; Chandler and Salsbury, *Pierre S. du Pont*, p. 560.

24. Chandler and Salsbury, *Pierre S. du Pont*, pp. 459, 560, 563–564. A new study of Pierre's educational reform efforts is Robert J. Taggart, *Private Philanthropy and Public Education: Pierre S. du Pont and the Delaware Schools, 1890–1940* (Newark: University of Delaware Press, 1988).
25. Chandler and Salsbury, pp. 459, 560–564; *Outlook*, October 14, 1925.

3. The Opening Wedge of Tyranny

1. Among the many fine studies in recent years of the movement to enact prohibition are Kyvig, *Repealing National Prohibition;* Joseph P. Gusfield, *Symbolic Crusade: Status Politics and the American Temperance Movement* (Urbana: University of Illinois Press, 1963); James H. Timberlane, *Prohibition and the Progressive Movement, 1900–1920* (Cambridge: Harvard University Press, 1963); and Norman H. Clark, *Deliver Us from Evil: An Interpretation of American Prohibition* (New York: W. W. Norton, 1976).
2. See Kyvig, *Repealing National Prohibition*, pp. 36–43, and Nuala McGann Drescher, "The Opposition to Prohibition, 1900–1919: A Social and Institutional Study" (Ph.D. diss., University of Delaware, 1964). On Stayton's background, see "William H. Stayton," *Repeal Review* 7 (July–September 1942), p. 3; and H. L. Mencken, "Man Who Really Busted Prohibition Gives All Credit to Opposite Sex," Baltimore *Sun*, October 30, 1932.
3. Mencken, "Man Who Busted Prohibition."
4. Dayton E. Heckman, "Prohibition Passes: The Story of the Association Against the Prohibition Amendment" (Ph.D. diss., Ohio State University, 1939), pp. 11–14; U.S. Congress, Senate, Committee on the Judiciary, *Lobby Investigation: Hearings before a Subcommittee*, 71st Cong., 2d sess, 4 vols. (Washington, D.C.: Government Printing Office, 1931), p. 4131; Senate, Special Committee Investigating Expenditures in Senatorial Primary and General Elections, *Senatorial Campaign Expenditures: Hearings*, pt. 1, June 9 to July 7, 1926, 69th Cong., 1st sess. (Washington, D.C.: Government Printing Office, 1926), p. 1231.
5. Kyvig, *Repealing National Prohibition*, pp. 46–47; Senate Special Committee, *Campaign Expenditures*, pp. 1234, 1504.
6. Kyvig, *Repealing National Prohibition*, pp. 46–47.
7. Ibid., p. 47; Senate Special Committee, *Campaign Expenditures*, pp. 1235–1237, 1269, 1476–1477, 1480–1481; Gilman M. Ostrander, *The Prohibition Movement in California, 1848–1933* (Berkeley: University of California Press, 1957), p. 184; Heckman, "Prohibition Passes," p. 42.
8. Heckman, "Prohibition Pases," pp. 36–37, 280–281; Kyvig, pp. 47–48; Senate Special Committee, *Campaign Expenditures*, p. 1484.
9. *New York Times*, April 7, 1922, pp. 1–2.
10. Kyvig, *Repealing National Prohibition*, p. 56; Pringle, *Alfred E. Smith: A Critical Study* (New York: Macy-Masius, 1927), pp. 320–328; Matthew and Hannah Josephson, *Al Smith: Hero of the Cities* (Boston: Houghton Mifflin, 1969), pp. 292–295.
11. Kyvig, *Repealing National Prohibition*, pp. 59–65.
12. William H. Stayton to T. Coleman du Pont, September 27, 1925, Irénée du Pont Papers (henceforth referred to as IDP), Series C; "Final Returns in the

Digest's Prohibition Poll," *Literary Digest*, September 9, 1922, pp. 11–13; *New York Times*, November 9, 1922, p. 3, and November 11, 1922, p. 1; "Booze Is the Victor," *Colliers*, October 10, 1925, pp. 8–9.

13. Senate Committee on the Judiciary, *Lobby Investigation*, p. 4170.

14. Stayton to Halbert L. Hoard, May 8, 1926, Hoard Papers.

15. Stayton to Raskob, October 2, 1919, June 5, 1920, Raskob AAPA membership cards, June 26, 1922, April 3, 1924, Raskob Papers, File 102; I. du Pont to G. C. Hinckley, November 27, 1922, August 22, 1924, I. du Pont to Stayton, September 26, December 2, 1925, IDP, Series C.

16. P. S. du Pont to Isabel Darlington, April 27, 1926, P. S du Pont to Stuyvesant Fish, May 24, 1922, PSDP, Series A, File 1023.

17. Kyvig, *Repealing National Prohibition*, p. 81; P. S. du Pont to Stayton, November 16, 1925, PSDP, Series A, File 1023.

18. I. du Pont to G. T. Barnhill, February 26, April 6, 1926, I. du Pont to William S. Prichett, February 9, 1926, I. du Pont to H. G. Haskell, February 18, 1926, "Minutes, 'mass meeting' committee," February 16, 1926, IDP, Series C; Stayton to P. S. du Pont, November 11, 1926, PSDP, Series A, File 1023; unsigned memorandum by Raskob on AAPA contributions, February 1926–1930, Raskob Papers, File 102.

19. P. S. du Pont to Stayton, April 2, 1926, P. S du Pont to William P. Smith, March 19, 1928, PSDP, Series A, File 1023; Raskob to R. N. Holsaple, November 14, 1928, Raskob Papers, File 102.

20. I. du Pont to William Allen White, unsent letter, July 3, 1926, I. du Pont to T. Coleman du Pont, October 19, 1926, IDP, Series J, File 261; P. S. du Pont to Stayton, April 2, 1926, PSDP, Series A, File 1023.

21. P. S. du Pont to Claude A. Buckley, August 23, 1926, PSDP, Series A, File 1023; P. S. du Pont to Arthur W. Little, October 27, 1926, PSDP, Series A, File 765; I. du Pont to William S. Hilles, August 30, 1926, IDP, Series J, File 261.

22. Kyvig, *Repealing National Prohibition*, pp. 89–90.

23. Ibid., pp. 68–69; P. S. du Pont to Stayton, May 27, 1926, PSDP, Series A, File 1023.

24. Quoted in George Wolfskill, *The Revolt of the Conservatives: A History of the American Liberty League, 1934–40* (Boston: Houghton Mifflin, 1962), pp. 46–48.

25. Kyvig, *Repealing National Prohibition*, pp. 88–89, 95; "Reports of Price, Waterhouse & Co.—AAPA," July 1–December 31, 1926, January 1–June 30, 1927, July 1–December 31, 1927, PSDP, Series A, File 1023.

26. According to a private accounting of Pierre du Pont's AAPA subscriptions from 1925 to 1930, his totals dropped from $5250 to the national office in 1926 to but $500 in 1927, then soared to over $43,000 in 1928. "Pierre S. du Pont Subscriptions to AAPA, 1925–1930," P. S. du Pont to Stayton, "Some Attractive Features of the Quebec Plan of Drink Control," October 26, 1926, George W. Abberger to P. S du Pont, December 4, 1926, P. S. du Pont to H. Fletcher Brown, June 17, 1927, PSDP, Series A, File 1023.

27. Colby, *Du Pont Dynasty*, p. 263; P. S. du Pont to Charles N. Fowler, January 28, 1927, P. S du Pont to Arthur W. Little, January 7, 27, 1927, PSDP, Series A, File 765.

28. Raskob to P. S. du Pont, February 19, 1927, Stayton to Raskob, July 22, 1927,

Raskob to Stayton, July 25, 1927, Raskob Papers, File 102; Raskob to George A. Elliot, October 20, 1924, Cornelius Bliss to Raskob, December 27, 1927, Raskob Papers, File 1947; Lopata, "John J. Raskob," p. 40.

29. Lopata, "John J. Raskob," pp. 36–41; Kenneth S. Davis, *FDR: The Beckoning of Destiny, 1882–1928* (New York: G. P. Putnam's Sons, 1971), p. 807.

30. Stayton to P. S du Pont, November 1, 1927, Hinckley to P. S. du Pont, November 2, 1927, PSDP, Series A, File 1023.

31. Grayson Murphy to James W. Wadsworth, Jr., April 28, 1926, Wadsworth to Murphy, May 12, 1926, Wadsworth Papers; Hickman, "Prohibition Passes," p. 13; Kyvig, *Repealing National Prohibition,* pp. 75–78.

32. Kyvig, *Repealing National Prohibition,* p. 91; Stayton to P. S. du Pont, November 1, 1927, P. S. du Pont to Charles A. Meade, December 21, 1927, PSDP, Series A, File 1023; Wadsworth to Murphy, December 2, 1927, Wadsworth Papers; Martin L. Fausold, *James W. Wadsworth, Jr: The Gentleman from New York* (Syracuse: Syracuse University Press, 1975), pp. 221–222.

4. A State of Revolution

1. The conference attendees included AAPA officials Stayton and Hinckley, corporate sponsors Sabin, Murphy, and Harkness, state leaders Codman, William Bell Wait of New York, E. Clemens Horst of San Francisco, Sidney Miller of Michigan, and Austin G. Fox of the New York Modification League, U.S. Senators Walter Edge of New Jersey and William Cabell Bruce of Maryland, Representatives H. S. White of Colorado and Charles Linthicum of Maryland, former congressman Thomas W. Phillips of Pennsylvania, former Assistant Secretary of War Benedict Crowell, and Pierre du Pont. The invitees who were unable to attend were Henry B. Joy, former Secretary of War Elihu Root, and former Solicitor General James M. Beck. Kyvig, *Repealing National Prohibition,* p. 91.

2. P. S. du Pont to Samuel Rea, February 1, 1928, "Draft Report of Subcommittee on Program," Julian Codman to P. S. du Pont, December 27, 1927, PSDP, Series A, File 1023; Fausold, *Wadsworth,* p. 223.

3. "Report to Meeting of January 6, 1928," P. S. du Pont to Rea, February 1, 1928, PSDP, Series A, File 1023.

4. Henry H. Curran, *Pillar to Post* (New York: Scribner's, 1941), pp. 285–286; AAPA Executive Committee to I. du Pont, February 10, 1928, Stayton to I. du Pont, March 20, April 25, 1928, I. du Pont to Henry H. Westinghouse and Paul W. Litchfield, March 22, 1928, Westinghouse to I. du Pont, March 28, 1928, Litchfield to I. du Pont, March 26, 1928, AAPA Executive Committee, "Minutes," April 17, 1928, IDP, Series C.

5. P. S. du Pont to Curran, March 19, 1928, I. du Pont to Curran, March 20, 1928, P. S. du Pont to Curran, May 31, 1928, I. du Pont to Curran, June 29, 1928, IDP, Series C; Raskob to Curran, May 29, 1928, Raskob to Charles H. Sabin, March 22, 1928, Raskob Papers, File 102; Senate Committee on the Judiciary, *Lobby Investigation,* p. 4140; AAPA, "Corrupt Practices Act Reports," PSDP, Series A, File 1023.

6. AAPA, "Cash Receipts and Expenditures, 1928–33," PSDP, Series A, File 1023; Peter H. Odegard, *Pressure Politics: The Story of the Anti-Saloon League*

(New York: Columbia University Press, 1928), p. 181; AAPA, "Corrupt Practices Act Reports," PSDP, Series A, File 1023.

7. AAPA, "Corrupt Practices Act Reports," Finance Department schedule–1929, "Cash Receipts and Expenditures, 1930–33," PSDP, Series A, File 1023; Senate Committee on the Judiciary, *Lobby Investigation*, p. 3957; U.S. Congress, Senate, Committee on the Judiciary, *Modification or Repeal of National Prohibition: Hearings*, 72nd Cong., 1st sess. (Washington, D.C.: Government Printing Office, 1932), pt. 1, pp. 12–13.

8. I. du Pont to George H. May, August 20, 1928, IDP, Series J, File 261; "Resolution Offered by the Executive Committee of the AAPA to the Board of Directors," April 17, 1928, Raskob Papers, File 102.

9. P. S. du Pont to Rea, February 1, 1928, P. S. du Pont to William P. Smith, March 19, 1928, PSDP, Series A, File 1023; P. S. du Pont, "Eighteenth Amendment Not a Remedy for the Drink Evil," *Current History* 28 (April 1928) pp. 17–22; P. S. du Pont to A. J. Martyn, May 10, 1928, PSDP, Series A, File 1023; I. du Pont to P. S. du Pont, February 25, 1929, PSDP, Series A, File 1068.

10. P. S. du Pont to Martyn, May 10, 1928, P. S. du Pont to J. R. Raw, June 21, 1928, PSDP, Series A, File 1023.

11. Kyvig, *Repealing National Prohibition*, p. 105.

12. P. S. du Pont, "To Those Living at Longwood and Interested in Its Welfare," February 10, 1928, PSDP, Series A, File 628; Kyvig, *Repealing National Prohibition*, pp. 98–99.

13. I. du Pont to John T. Adams, February 18, 1928, IDP, Series J, File 261; Raskob to P. H. Callahan, May 25, 1928, Raskob to John E. Wretman, June 7, 1928, Raskob to D. F. Sibley, June 21, 1928, John C. Gebhard to Raskob, July 13, 1928, Raskob to Curran, July 31, 1928, Raskob Papers, File 102; Kyvig, *Repealing National Prohibition*, pp. 99–100. For insights into Hoover's background on prohibition and other issues, see Joan Hoff Wilson, *Herbert Hoover, Forgotten Progressive* (Boston: Little, Brown, 1975).

14. Raskob to Ogden L. Mills, July 2, 1928, T. Coleman du Pont to Raskob, June 14, August 18, 1928, Raskob Papers, File 602; P. S. du Pont to Herbert N. Straus, June 26, 1928, PSDP, Series A, File 765.

15. Lopata, "John J. Raskob," pp. 61–62.

16. Ibid.

17. Pringle, "Raskob," p. 646; Alfred E. Smith, *Up to Now*, (New York: Viking, 1929), p. 382; *New Republic*, July 25, 1928.

18. Raskob, "Acceptance Speech," July 11, 1928, Raskob to I. du Pont, July 19, 1928, Raskob Papers, File 602; I. du Pont private memorandum, August 15, 1928, IDP, Series J, File 261.

19. Lopata, "John J. Raskob," pp. 87–89; Raskob to Curran, July 31, 1928, Raskob Papers, File 602. The best concise biography of FDR in the years preceding his presidency remains James MacGregor Burns, *Roosevelt: The Lion and the Fox* (New York: Harcourt, Brace and World, 1956).

20. Hugh S. Johnson, *The Blue Eagle from Egg to Earth* (New York: Greenwood Press, 1968), p. 117; Lopata, "John J. Raskob," pp. 70–71, 79–86.

21. *New Republic*, July 25 1928; "Democratic National Committee—Summary of Contributions by Denomination," July 19–October 27, 1928, Raskob loan

notes, October 11, 24, 1928, Raskob Papers, File 602; Lopata, "John J. Raskob," p. 73.

22. Raskob to Thomas F. Ryan and Bernard Baruch, October 17, 1928, Raskob Papers, File 602; Curran press release, August 27, 1928, Stayton to I. du Pont, November 1, 1928, I. du Pont to Henry B. Joy, December 24, 1928, IDP, Series C; Colby, *Du Pont Dynasty*, p. 275; *New York Times*, August 28, 1928, p. 2.

23. Chandler and Salsbury, *Pierre S. du Pont*, p. 585.

24. Ibid., p. 586; *New York Times*, August 10, 1928, p.2.

25. Chandler and Salsbury, *Pierre S. du Pont*, pp. 586–587; P. S. du Pont to T. Coleman du Pont, August 22, 1928, PSDP, Series A, File 765.

26. P. S. du Pont to Frank G. Atwood, July 19, 1928, PSDP, Series A, File 1023; James C. Young, "Raskob of General Motors," *World's Work* 56, no. 5 (September 1928); Kyvig, *Repealing National Prohibition*, pp. 104–105.

27. Lopata, "John J. Raskob," pp. 73–74; Colby, *Du Pont Dynasty*, p. 274; Ferdinand Lundberg, *America's Sixty Families* (New York: Vanguard Press, 1937), pp. 179–182. For the most comprehensive analysis of the 1928 election, see Allan J. Lichtman, *Prejudice and the Old Politics: The Presidential Election of 1928* (Chapel Hill: University of North Carolina Press, 1979).

28. David Burner, *The Politics of Provincialism: The Democratic Party in Transition, 1918–1932* (New York: Alfred A. Knopf, 1968), pp. 217–242; "Protestant Press Call it a Dry Victory," *Literary Digest*, December 8, 1928, pp. 28–29; Kyvig, *Repealing National Prohibition*, pp. 103–104; Lopata, "John J. Raskob," p. 92; Jouett Shouse to Francis G. Caffrey, November 13, 1928, Shouse Papers; *New York Times*, November 9, 1928, p. 2.

29. Kyvig, *Repealing National Prohibition*, pp. 116–117.

30. AAPA, "Summary of Cash Receipts and Disbursements, 1929," "P. S. du Pont Subscriptions to AAPA, 1929," PSDP, Series A, File 1023; Stayton to Raskob, July 3, 1929, Raskob Papers, File 102.

31. Kyvig, *Repealing National Prohibition*, p. 127–129.

32. Ibid., pp. 118–121.

33. Ibid., pp. 122–123.

34. Ibid., pp. 129–130.

35. Stayton to P. S. du Pont, September 11, 1928, AAPA, "Board of Directors Meeting," May 14, 1929, AAPA Executive Committee, "Minutes," June 30, 1929, PSDP, Series A, File 1023.

36. AAPA, *Scandals of Prohibition Enforcement* (March 1, 1929); Stayton to Henry B. Joy, T. W. Phillips, and AAPA Executive Committee, September 10, 1928, Phillips to Stayton, August 29, 1928, IDP, Series C; *New York Times*, May 13, 1929, p. 1; AAPA, *Cost of Prohibition and Your Income Tax*. 2nd ed. (July 1930). The pamphlets were issued from the Washington, D.C., office.

37. See AAPA, *Canada Liquor Crossing the Border* (Washington, D.C., July 1929); *Measuring the Liquor Tide*, 1st ed. (August 1929), 2d ed. (June 1930); *Reforming America with a Shotgun: A Study of Prohibition Killings* (November 1929); *Prohibition Enforcement: Its Effect on Courts and Prisons* (December 1930). Issued from the AAPA's Washington, D.C., office.

38. AAPA, *The Quebec System: A Study of Liquor Control* (November 1928); *Government Liquor Control in Canada* (October 1929); *The Last Outpost of Prohibition in Canada:*

Nova Scotia and Prince Edward Island (December 1929); *The Bratt System of Liquor Control in Sweden* (January 1930); *England's Solution of the Liquor Problem* (September 1930); *Temperance by Taxation: How Denmark Does It* (March 1932); *Finland's Prohibition: An Echo of Volsteadism* (June 1930); *Norway's Noble Experiment* (April 1931). For Pierre's own plan, see "Memorandum of Mr. du Pont's remarks on a plan for state control of liquor manufacture and sale," March 8, 1929, and P. S. du Pont, "Plan for Distribution and Control of Intoxicating Liquors in the United States" (n.p., September 1930), PSDP, Series A, File 1023.

39. For a sampling of such sentiments, consult P. S. du Pont to Raw, June 21, 1928, PSDP, Series A, File 1023.

40. Lopata, "John J. Raskob," pp. 63, 102–103; "DNC-Deficit as of Close of Business," November 10, 1928, "Memorandum *re* underwriting agreement," December 17, 1928, Raskob Papers, File 602.

41. Raskob as told to James C. Derieux, "Rich Men in Politics," *Collier's*, March 5, 1932, p. 54; Raskob to Al Smith, December 2, 1930, Raskob Papers, File 2112; Raskob to R. H. Holsaple, November 14, 1928, Raskob Papers, File 602.

42. In attendance at Raskob's dinner summit were Senators Millard Tydings of Maryland, Key Pittman of Nevada, Pat Harrison of Mississippi, Harry Hawes of Missouri, and Robert Wagner of New York, along with former Smith operatives Peter Gerry, Herbert Lehman, and James Hoey and Raskob aide Jouett Shouse. Lopata, "John J. Raskob," pp. 100–105; Raskob to Shouse, May 14, 1929, Raskob Papers, File 602.

43. Kyvig, *Repealing National Prohibition*, pp. 143–144; Lopata, "John J. Raskob," pp. 105–106, 114.

44. Shouse speech, June 10, 1929, Raskob Papers, File 602; Lopata, "John J. Raskob," pp. 106–107.

45. Lopata, "John J. Raskob," pp. 107–108.

46. Ibid., pp. 110–112.

47. Ibid., pp. 124–127; *Commonweal*, May 29, 1929, p. 90; Samuel Crowther, "Everybody Ought to Be Rich: An Interview with John J. Raskob," *Ladies' Home Journal*, August 29, 1929, pp. 9, 36.

48. P. S. du Pont to Raskob, March 25, 1929, Raskob to P. S. du Pont, April 16, 1929, Raskob to 1928 Democratic Campaign Fund Contributors, November 30, 1929, Raskob Papers, File 102.

49. P. S. du Pont to AAPA Directors, June 7, 1929, AAPA Executive Committee, "Minutes," June 20, 1929, P. S. du Pont to Wadsworth, December 10, 1929, PSDP, Series A, File 1023.

5. Depression and New Opportunities

1. Colby, *Du Pont Dynasty*, pp. 286–287, 291; *New York Times*, October 30, 1929; Herbert Hoover to P. S. du Pont, November 8, 1929, PSDP, Series A, File 765; Raskob, "What Next in America?," *North American Review* 228 (November 1929), pp. 513–518.

2. Colby, *Du Pont Dynasty*, p. 287; *New York Times*, January 10, 1936; Lopata, "John J. Raskob," p. 135.

3. Kyvig, *Repealing National Prohibition,* pp. 130–131.

4. Raskob to Curran, October 9, 1929, Raskob Papers, File 102; Wadsworth to P. S. du Pont, December 1, 1929, P. S. du Pont to Wadsworth, December 10, 1929, PSDP, Series A, File 1023.

5. AAPA Board of Directors, "Minutes," February 4, 1930, PSDP, Series A, File 1023.

6. P. S. du Pont to Raskob, December 30, 1930, Raskob Papers, File 102; Kyvig, *Repealing National Prohibition,* pp. 94–96, 123, 128–129; AAPA, "Summary of Cash Receipts and Disbursements, 1930," PSDP, Series A, File 1023.

7. Kyvig, *Repealing National Prohibition,* pp. 137–139; AAPA Executive Committee, "Minutes," April 1, 1930, IDP, Series C.

8. Kyvig, *Repealing National Prohibition,* p. 130; Atwood to George S. Graham, March 22, 1930, P. S. du Pont to Atwood, August 27, 1928, P. S. du Pont to George G. Mead, March 26, 1930, PSDP, Series A, File 1023.

9. P. S. du Pont to Eldridge R. Johnson, July 23, August 19, 1930, PSDP, Series A, File 1023; *New York Times,* April 14, 1930, p. 2.

10. *New York Times,* April 14, 1930, p. 2; *Literary Digest,* April 26, 1930, p. 7; Kyvig, *Repealing National Prohibition,* pp. 144–145.

11. "The Huge Poll's Final Report: All Records Outdone," *Literary Digest,* May 24, 1930, p. 7; New York *Herald-Tribune,* April 7, 1930.

12. AAPA, *Cost of Prohibition and Your Income Tax,* 2d ed.; P. S. du Pont to Mrs. William S. Hilles, November 23, 1929, Raskob Papers, File 602; Kyvig, *Repealing National Prohibition,* pp. 141–142; Morton Keller, *In Defense of Yesterday; James M. Beck and the Politics of Conservatism* (New York: Coward-McCann, 1958), pp. 207–208; *Congressional Record,* February 7, 1930, pp. 3257–3262.

13. Kyvig, *Repealing National Prohibition,* p. 142; AAPA Board of Directors, "Meeting," February 4, 1930, P. S. du Pont to Samuel H. Church, February 7, 14, 1930, PSDP, Series A, File 1023.

14. P. S. du Pont to Church, April 28, 1930, PSDP, Series A, File 1023; Kyvig, *Repealing National Prohibition,* p. 142.

15. AAPA Executive Committee, *AAPA Report for 1930,* p. 6; Lopata, "John J. Raskob," pp. 136–140; *New York Times,* September 3, November 3, 1930.

16. Lopata, "John J. Raskob," pp. 117–123.

17. Ibid., 111–113, 122.

18. "An Analysis of the Publication and Information Service of the AAPA, March 19, 1931," IDP, Series C; AAPA, *Does Prohibition Pay?* (Washington, D.C., October 1930); Kyvig, *Repealing National Prohibition,* p. 129; P. S. du Pont to Ralph Lockwood Hoffman, August 19, 1930, "AAPA–Summary of Cash Receipts and Disbursements, 1930," PSDP, Series A, File 1023.

19. P. S. du Pont to Stayton, September 9, 1930, Raskob to Stayton, October 20, 1930, Raskob Papers, File 102; P. S. du Pont radio address, November 3, 1930, PSDP, Series A, File 1023; Lopata, "John J. Raskob," pp. 123, 140.

20. Curran to Raskob, January 3, 1931, Raskob Papers, File 102; P. S. du Pont to Church, December 29, 1930, Church to P. S. du Pont, January 2, 1931, PSDP, Series A, File 1023.

21. Kyvig, *Repealing National Prohibition,* pp. 139–140, 143.

22. Ibid., pp. 111–115.

23. P. S. du Pont to Curran, January 21, 1931, PSDP, Series A, File 1023; National

Commission on Law Observance and Enforcement, *Report on the Enforcement of the Prohibition Laws of the United States,* 71st Cong., 3d sess., House Doc. 722 (Washington, D.C.: Government Printing Office, 1931).

24. Quoted by Kyvig, *Repealing National Prohibition,* p. 114.

25. Bernstein, *The Lean Years,* p. 252; Colby, *Du Pont Dynasty,* pp. 292–293. For an overview of Hoover's recovery efforts, see Albert U. Romasco, *The Poverty of Abundance: Hoover, the Nation, the Depression* (New York: Oxford University Press, 1965).

26. Lopata, "John J. Raskob," p. 141.

27. C. Douglas Buck to P. S. du Pont, November 10, 1930, P. S. du Pont to F. V. du Pont, November 12, 1930, PSDP, Series A, File 765; Contributors' list, Mayor's Emergency Unemployment Relief Committee, May 29, 1931, PSDP, Series A, File 1164.

28. Lopata, "John J. Raskob," pp. 149–150; Lammot du Pont to Al Smith, June 13, December 30, PSDP, Series A, File 765.

29. Lopata, "John J. Raskob," pp. 141–143; Colby, *Du Pont Dynasty,* p. 294; P. S. du Pont to Buck, December 15, 1930, PSDP, Series A, File 765.

30. James, *Alfred I. Du Pont,* pp. 474–478; Raskob to P. S. du Pont, September 4, 1930, Buck to P. S. du Pont, September 18, 1930, PSDP, Series A, File 1171; P. S. du Pont to Robert G. Houston, January 19, 1931, PSDP, Series A, File 765; Amos A. Fries to P. S. du Pont, March 2, 23, 1931, PSDP, Series A, File 1023; I. du Pont, "Miscellaneous Contributions," n.d., IDP, Series J, File 261.

31. Kyvig, *Repealing National Prohibition,* pp. 134–135; AAPA, *The Need of a New Source of Government Revenue* (Washington, D.C., 1931).

32. P. S. du Pont to Alfred Sloan, May 6, 1931, Sloan to P. S. du Pont, May 8, 1931, PSDP, Series A, File 1023; I. du Pont to H. Lawton Blanchard, October 27, 1930, I. du Pont to Ruter W. Springer, December 17, 1930, IDP, Series C; Kyvig, *Repealing National Prohibition,* pp. 135–136.

33. Kyvig, *Repealing National Prohibition,* pp. 96, 123; AAPA Finance Committee, "Minutes," December 23, 1930, Stayton to Raskob, April 24, 1931, Raskob Papers, File 102; AAPA, "Summary of Cash Receipts and Disbursements, 1931," PSDP, Series A, File 1023.

34. P. S. du Pont to Stayton, January 16, 1931, PSDP, Series A, File 1125; Raskob to Scott Ferris, December 24, 1930, Shouse to Raskob, January 21, 1931, Raskob Papers, File 602; Lopata, "John J. Raskob," pp. 157–160. For a detailed examination of the Raskob-Roosevelt struggle, see David E. Kyvig, "Raskob, Roosevelt, and Repeal," *The Historian* 37 (1975), pp. 469–487.

35. Kyvig, *Repealing National Prohibition,* pp. 146–148; Lopata, "John J. Raskob," pp. 158–159.

36. Raskob speech, March 5, 1931, in *Official Report of the Proceedings of the Democratic National Convention, 1932* (n.p., n.d.), pp. 406–411; Raskob to Franklin D. Roosevelt, March 31, 1931, Raskob to Frederic R. Coudert, March 9, 1931, Raskob to Church, March 9, 1931, Raskob Papers, File 602.

37. Raskob to DNC members, April 4, 1931, Raskob Papers, File 2112; *New York Times,* September 31, 1931, p. 3.

38. "Mr. Raskob's Suggestions," *Commonweal,* April 15, 1931, p. 647; "Chairman

Raskob's Convictions," *Review of Reviews* 83 (May 1931), p. 28; Colby, *Du Pont Dynasty,* p. 296; Lopata, "John J. Raskob," pp. 175–176.

39. Raskob to Joseph Robinson, July 10, 1931, Raskob Papers, File 602; P. S. du Pont to Church, August 25, 1931, Gebhart to P. S. du Pont, October 15, 1931, PSDP, Series A, File 1023.

40. Raskob, "Questionnaire," n.d., P. S. du Pont to Raskob, November 13, 1931, I. du Pont to Raskob, November 27, 1931, Raskob Papers, File 602; *Washington Post,* November 23, 24, 1931. Pierre defended Raskob against the claim that Roosevelt had opposed his original appointment as DNC chairman in 1928. P. S. du Pont to the Editor, *New York Times,* November 24, 1931, p. 1.

41. P. S. du Pont to Shouse, September 9, October 16, 1931, PSDP, Series A, File 765; P. S. du Pont to Church, November 19, December 7, 1931, PSDP, Series A, File 1023; Lopata, "John J. Raskob," pp. 178–180.

42. Walter S. Gifford to P. S. du Pont, August 27, 1931, I. du Pont to Gifford, October 6, 1931, P. S. du Pont to Gifford, October 14, 1931, PSDP, Series A, File 1164.

43. New York *World-Telegram,* October 17, 1931.

6. Uncertain Victory

1. Lopata, "John J. Raskob," p. 186.

2. Ibid., pp. 186–187; Raskob to Albert Ritchie, November 5, 1931, Raskob Papers, File 602.

3. Shouse, "Suggested Program of Publicity for Mr. Raskob," December 11, 1931, Raskob Papers, File 602.

4. Ibid.

5. Lopata, "John J. Raskob," pp. 168–169, 187; Raskob to Norman Mack, January 3, 1932, "Minutes of Victory Chairmen's Meeting," December 12, 1931, Raskob Papers, File 602.

6. "DNC Annual Meeting," January 9, 1932, Raskob Papers, File 602; Lopata, "John J. Raskob," pp. 182–187.

7. Lopata, "John J. Raskob," pp. 169, 179–180.

8. "DNC Annual Meeting," January 9, 1932, Shouse to Raskob, March 12, 1932, Raskob Papers, File 602; Lopata, "John J. Raskob," pp. 180–181.

9. Shouse to Arthur Seligman, February 1, 1932, Raskob Papers, File 602; Lopata, "John J. Raskob," p. 188; *New Republic,* March 2, 1932.

10. William du Pont to I. du Pont, January 9, 1932, I. du Pont to William du Pont, January 29, 1932, IDP, Series J, File 189; Unemployment Relief Commission of the State of Delaware, "Report," September 9, 1932, PSDP, Series A, File 1164.

11. I. du Pont to Fred. I. Kent, April 7, 1932, I. du Pont to Owen Young, June 24, 1932, IDP, Series J, File 189; Lammot du Pont to Raskob, April 11, 1932, Raskob Papers, File 602; P. S. du Pont to John G. Townsend, March 25, 1932, E. E. Lincoln to Lammot du Pont, W. S. Carpenter, A. B. Echols, "Analysis of Glass Bill," March 24, 1932, P. S. du Pont to Charles Sabin, May 9, 1932, PSDP, Series A, File 765.

12. P. S. du Pont to Raskob, January 4, 1932, P. S. du Pont to Shouse, April 12,

1932, Raskob Papers, File 602; Church to P. S. du Pont, January 6, 1932, P. S. du Pont to Church, February 16, 1932, P. S. du Pont to Lammot du Pont, April 20, 28, 1932, Lammot du Pont to P. S. du Pont, April 26, 1932, PSDP, Series A, File 1023.

13. Kyvig, *Repealing National Prohibition,* pp. 151–152; "The Great Prohibition Poll's Final Week," *Literary Digest,* April 30, 1932, pp. 6–7.

14. Kyvig, *Repealing National Prohibition,* pp. 152–153; Raskob to C. Edgar Anderson, April 6, 1932, Raskob Papers, File 102.

15. Lopata, "John J. Raskob," pp. 188, 190; P. S. du Pont to John Garland Pollard, March 21, 1932, PSDP, Series A, File 765; Shouse to G. E. Wilson, personal and confidential, March 7, 1932, Shouse Papers.

16. FDR to Raskob, April 13, 1932, Shouse Papers; Lopata, "John J. Raskob," p. 190; "Confidential-Report on Conference with Governor Franklin D. Roosevelt," April 29, 1932, Raskob Papers, File 602.

17. Lopata, "John J. Raskob," pp. 190–191.

18. Raskob to Edwin R.A. Seligman, May 3, 1932, PSDP, Series A, File 765.

19. I. du Pont to Sloan, June 16, 1932, IDP, Series J, File 189; Harriman quoted in Colby, *Du Pont Dynasty,* p. 297; Raskob to Robinson, May 27, 1932, Raskob Papers, File 1978; I. du Pont to C. Willard Young, June 1, 1932, IDP, Series J. File 189.

20. P. S. du Pont to Sloan, May 9, 1932, PSDP, Series A, File 1173; P. S. du Pont to Gilbert Montague, May 19, 1932, P. S. du Pont to S. C. Bond, May 19, 1932, PSDP, Series A, File 765; P. S. du Pont to Charles Warner, June 3, 1932, PSDP, Series A, File 1134.

21. P. S. du Pont to Lee Warren, May 21, 1932, P. S. du Pont to James Farley, May 24, 1932, PSDP, Series A, File 765; P. S. du Pont to C. H. Geist, June 9, 1932, PSDP, Series A, File 1023; P. S. du Pont to Chairman, Democratic City Committee, Wilmington, Delaware and Democratic State Committee, New York, May 26, 1932, Raskob Papers, File 602; Kyvig, *Repealing National Prohibition,* p. 153; P. S. du Pont to J. J. Seelman, January 22, 1932, P. S. du Pont to Matthew Wohl, June 11, 1932, PSDP, Series A, File 1023.

22. United Repeal Council, "Minutes," June 7, 1932, PSDP, Series A, File 1023; Kyvig, *Repealing National Prohibition,* pp. 153–154.

23. Kyvig, *Repealing National Prohibition,* pp. 154–156.

24. P. S. du Pont to Ralph Shaw, June 20, 1932, PSDP, Series A, File 765; P. S. du Pont to Geist, June 9, 1932, PSDP, Series A, File 1023; Kyvig, *Repealing National Prohibition,* p. 156.

25. Kyvig, *Repealing National Prohibition,* p. 156.

26. Ibid., pp. 156–157.

27. Ibid., pp. 157–158; Lopata, "John J. Raskob," pp. 191–194.

28. Wolfskill, *Revolt of the Conservatives,* p. 15.

29. Kyvig, *Repealing National Prohibition,* p. 158; Lopata, "John J. Raskob," pp. 195–196.

30. Kyvig, *Repealing National Prohibition,* pp. 158, 166; Stayton to Raskob, July 6, 1932, Raskob to Stayton, July 7, 1932, Raskob Papers, File 102; *New York Times,* July 3, 1932, p. 10. Smith quoted in Colby, *Du Pont Dynasty,* p. 305.

31. Raskob to Harry Byrd, July 5, 1932, Raskob to Shouse, July 7, 1932, Byrd

to Raskob, July 27, 1932, Raskob to Byrd, July 28, 1932, Raskob Papers, File 602; Shouse to FDR, July 5, 1932, Shouse Papers.

32. P. S. du Pont to Church, July 8, 1932, P. S. du Pont to Shouse, August 25, 1932, PSDP, Series A, File 1023; Lopata, "John J. Raskob," p. 198; Colby, *Du Pont Dynasty*, p. 306. Curran became head of the anti-bonus National Economy League, formed in July 1932. Al Smith and Newton Baker also signed up for its advisory council.

33. William E. Leuchtenburg, *Franklin D. Roosevelt and the New Deal, 1932–1940* (New York: Harper and Row, 1963), pp. 10–13; New York *Daily News*, August 15, 1932.

34. Colby, *Du Pont Dynasty*, p. 307; P. S. du Pont contribution to Block Aid, August 15, 1932, PSDP, Series A, File 1164.

35. Colby, *Du Pont Dynasty*, pp. 296, 308. Among the financial contributors to the Roosevelt campaign were W. N. Reynolds (R. J. Reynolds Tobacco), William K. Vanderbilt, Cyrus McCormick, Edward Guggenheim, Harry Warner (Warner Brothers), and Mrs. Harry Payne Whitney.

36. Kyvig, *Repealing National Prohibition*, pp. 161, 166; "Ladies at Roslyn," *Time*, July 18, 1932, pp. 9–10; Fred G. Clark to P. S. du Pont, July 22, 1932, P. S. du Pont to Joseph H. Leib, September 23, 1932, P. S. du Pont press release, July 22, 1932, P. S. du Pont to Robert K. Cassatt, September 27, 1932, P. S. du Pont to Mrs. Marguerite du Pont Lee, October 15, 1932, PSDP, Series A, File 1023. According to a later accounting Pierre, besides giving $25,000 to the DNC, also contributed another $2,000 toward meeting the party's debt, $132 for funding a last-minute FDR radio address, $500 to a state Victory Fund committee, and $100 toward the Democrat's Victory Dinner. G. C. Geesey to P. S. du Pont, March 15, 1933, PSDP, Series A, File 765.

37. U.S. Congress, Senate, Special Committee Investigating the Munitions Industry, *Report*, 74th Cong, 2d sess. (Washington, D.C.: Government Printing Office, 1936), pp. 1403–1408; "Irénée du Pont—Political Contributions, January 1, 1919–September 1, 1934," IDP, Series J, File 203; I. du Pont to E. C. Stokes, September 29, 1932, IDP, Series J, File 261; Shouse to P. S. du Pont, October 19, 1932, I. du Pont to P. S. du Pont, October 23, 24, 1932, PSDP, Series A, File 1023.

38. P. S. du Pont to Raskob, August 25, 1932, AAPA, "Summary of Cash Receipts and Disbursements, 1932," PSDP, Series A, File 1023; Kyvig, *Repealing National Prohibition*, pp. 166–167; Dobyns, *Amazing Story of Repeal*, p. 124.

39. P. S. du Pont to August A. Busch, July 8, October 28, December 19, 1932, PSDP, Series A, File 1023.

40. P. S. du Pont to Shouse, Lammot du Pont, Raskob, and Al Smith, November 4, 1932, PSDP, Series A, File 1023; Lopata, "John J. Raskob," p. 199; Kyvig, *Repealing National Prohibition*, pp. 167–168.

41. P. S. du Pont to Eldridge Johnson, November 9, 1932, P. S. du Pont to Matthew Wohl, November 7, 1932, PSDP, Series A, File 1023.

7. A Brief Honeymoon

1. Colby, *Du Pont Dynasty*, p. 295; Fine, *Sit-Down*, p. 21.

2. Colby, *Du Pont Dynasty*, p. 307; Irving Bernstein, *A Caring Society: The New*

Deal, the Worker, and the Great Depression (Boston: Houghton Mifflin, 1985), pp. 17, 86–87, 90.

3. Unemployment Relief Commission of the State of Delaware, "Report," Sepember 30, 1932, PSDP, Series A, File 1164.

4. P. S. du Pont to Mayor's Employment and Relief Committee, November 15, 1932, PSDP, Series A, File 1164.

5. P. S. du Pont, January 16, 1933, PSDP, Series A, File 1173.

6. R. R. M. Carpenter to Raskob, December 8, 1932, P. S. du Pont to Raskob, December 17, 1932, Raskob to P. S. du Pont, December 19, 1932, Raskob Papers, File 602; Shouse to P. S. du Pont, January 16, 25, 1933, P. S. du Pont to Shouse, January 17, 27, 1933, PSDP, Series A, File 1023.

7. Kyvig, *Repealing National Prohibition*, pp. 93, 95; P. S. du Pont to Woll, November 7, 1932, PSDP, Series A, File 1023; Stayton and Shouse to Raskob, November 30, 1932, Raskob Papers, File 102.

8. Kyvig, *Repealing National Prohibition*, p. 169.

9. Ibid., pp. 169–172.

10. Ibid., pp. 173–174.

11. P. S. du Pont to Busch, January 3, 1933, Busch to P. S. du Pont, February 1, March 1, 1933, Busch to R. A. Huber, January 26, 1933, PSDP, Series A, File 1023.

12. Leuchtenburg, *FDR and the New Deal*, pp. 38–40.

13. Ibid., pp. 41–48; Kyvig, *Repealing National Prohibition*, p. 177; J. Joseph Huthmacher, *Senator Robert F. Wagner and the Rise of Urban Liberalism* (New York: Atheneum, 1971), pp. 138–139. A thorough treatment of the first Hundred Days is provided by Frank Freidel, *Franklin D. Roosevelt: Launching the New Deal* (Boston: Little, Brown, 1973).

14. Leuchtenburg, *FDR and the New Deal*, pp. 48–49; Huthmacher, *Wagner*, p. 140.

15. Leuchtenburg, *FDR and the New Deal*, pp. 50–62; Huthmacher, *Wagner*, pp. 142–148; Bernstein, *A Caring Society*, p. 92.

16. P. S. du Pont to S. D. Townsend, March 13, 1933, P. S. du Pont to John Townsend, May 23, 1933, PSDP, Series A, File 765; Raskob to Pat Harrison, March 15, 1933, Raskob to James Couzens, March 17, 1933, Raskob to FDR, April 4, 1933, Raskob to G. Cunningham, May 29, 1933 Raskob Papers, File 602.

17. Kyvig, *Repealing National Prohibition*, pp. 177–178; Huthmacher, *Wagner*, pp. 145–148; Bernstein, *A Caring Society*, pp. 87–88; Irving Bernstein, *Turbulent Years: A History of the American Worker, 1933–1941* (Boston: Houghton Mifflin, 1961), pp. 19–34.

18. Bernstein, *Turbulent Years*, pp. 32–35; Hawley, "The New Deal and Business," pp. 60–61.

19. P. S. du Pont to John Townsend, June 9, July 6, 1933, PSDP, Series A, File 765; P. S. du Pont to Daniel Roper, June 14, 1933, PSDP, Series A, File 1173.

20. Bernard Bellush, *The Failure of the NRA* (New York: W. W. Norton, 1975), pp. 34–49.

21. H. H. Heilman to P. S. du Pont, July 19, 1933, P. S. du Pont to Andrew Mellon, July 20, 1933, P. S. du Pont to Heilman, July 21, 1933, PSDP, Series

A, File 1173; Bellush, *Failure of the NRA*, pp. 48–53; Colby, *Du Pont Dynasty*, p. 317.

22. Huthmacher, *Wagner*, p. 153; Bernstein, *A Caring Society*, pp. 117–120; Colby, *Du Pont Dynasty*, p. 317; Fine, *The Automobile under the Blue Eagle: Labor, Management, and the Automobile Manufacturing Code* (Ann Arbor: University of Michigan Press, 1963), p. 46; Fine, *Sit-Down*, pp. 29–30.

23. Bellush, *Failure of the NRA*, p. 95; Fine, *Automobile under the Blue Eagle*, pp. 159–160.

24. Bernstein, *Turbulent Years*, pp. 172–173; Huthmacher, *Wagner*, p. 160; Bellush, *Failure of the NRA*, p. 100.

25. Bernstein, *Turbulent Years*, pp. 42–60, 96–97, 174.

26. Bernstein, *A Caring Society*, pp. 92–93; George Wolfskill and John A. Hudson, *All But the People: Franklin D. Roosevelt and His Critics, 1933–39* (London: Macmillan, 1969), p. 144; Raskob to A. H. Geuting, September 12, 1933, Raskob Papers, File 602; P. S. du Pont to Leib, September 7, 28, 1933, PSDP, Series A, File 765.

27. Kyvig, *Repealing National Prohibition*, pp. 173–174.

28. Johnson, *Blue Eagle*, p. 343; Bellush, *Failure of the NRA*, p. 94; Ellis W. Hawley, *The New Deal and the Problem of Monopoly: A Study in Economic Ambivalence* (Princeton: Princeton University Press, 1966), p. 78; P. S. du Pont to Leib, December 1, 1933, P. S. du Pont to FDR, November 13, 1933, FDR to P. S. du Pont, November 20, 1933, PSDP, Series A, File 765.

29. FDR to P. S. du Pont, November 24, 1933, PSDP, Series A, File 1173; Bernstein, *Turbulent Years*, pp. 38–39, 177; P. S. du Pont to Hugh Johnson, November 28, 1933, "Memorandum *re* membership of Code Authority," November 20, 28, 1933, P. S. du Pont to FDR, November 29, 1933, PSDP, Series A, File 1173.

30. Bernstein, *A Caring Society*, pp. 35–38, 92–93; Huthmacher, *Wagner*, p. 155; Bellush, *Failure of the NRA*, p. 60.

31. Bellush, *Failure of the NRA*, p. 62; Hawley, *New Deal and the Problem of Monopoly*, p. 151; Raskob to Cunningham, November 21, 1933, Raskob Papers, File 602; P. S. du Pont to George B. May, November 28, 1933, PSDP, Series A, File 765; Sloan to P. S. du Pont, December 15, 1933, PSDP, Series A, File 1173. As early as August, Stayton had assured James Beck that Pierre shared his own growing misgivings about the New Deal. Stayton to Beck, August 28, 1933, Beck Papers.

32. Kyvig, *Repealing National Prohibition*, pp. 184, 187.

33. Ibid., pp. 189–190.

34. Ibid., pp. 181–185; Shouse to P. S. du Pont, September 9, November 9, 1933, Shouse Papers.

35. Kyvig, *Repealing National Prohibition*, pp. 190–191; P. S. du Pont to Grayson Murphy, November 15, 1933, PSDP, Series A, File 1023. James Beck suggested to Stayton that the AAPA be continued as a "committee of safety," a suggestion Stayton agreed with, but he added Pierre and Irénée's belief that such a nonpartisan effort would depend on the continued support of the "conservative Republican wing" represented by Beck and Wadsworth. Beck to E. Parmalee Prentice, November 6, 1933, Stayton to Beck, October 4, 1933, Beck Papers.

8. Deserting the Ship of State

1. Bernstein, *A Caring Society*, pp. 64, 88–89; Bellush, *Failure of the NRA*, p. 62.
2. Hawley, *New Deal and the Problem of Monopoly*, p. 151; Lopata, "John J. Raskob," p. 239; Wolfskill and Hudson, *All But the People*, pp. 153, 163–64; Sloan to Irwin L. House, November 8, 1933, House to Al Smith, November 13, 1933, Smith Papers. Smith's November 24 letter appeared as an editorial in the *New Outlook*. A copy is in the FDR Papers as President, President's Personal Files, File 676.
3. Shouse to Raskob, December 18, 1933, Raskob Papers, File 602; *New York Times*, January 31, 1934, p. 25; Raskob to FDR, November 28, December 15, 1933, FDR Papers as President, PPF File 226; P. S. du Pont to Townsend, January 16, 1934, PSDP, Series A, File 765.
4. Hawley, *New Deal and the Problem of Monopoly*, p. 79; Hugh S. Johnson to P. S. du Pont, January 13, 1934, P. S. du Pont solicitation letter of January 2, 1934, "Memorandum of Meeting with General Johnson," January 17, 1934, P. S. du Pont to Johnson, January 23, 27, 1934, Johnson to P. S. du Pont, February 3. 1934, PSDP, Series A, File 1173.
5. P. S. du Pont, "Plans for Economic Recovery," January 23, 1934, PSDP, Series A, File 1173.
6. Ibid.
7. Huthmacher, *Wagner*, pp. 160–163; Bernstein, *Turbulent Years*, pp. 177–180; P. S. du Pont to Sloan, January 4, 1934, PSDP, Series A, File 1173.
8. P. S. du Pont, "Memorandum *re* National Labor Board on the Question of Strikes," January 27, 1934, P. S. du Pont speech, "Industrial Self-Government," January 25, 1934, PSDP, Series A, File 1173; *New York Times*, January 26, 1934, p. 6.
9. FDR, "Executive Order No. 6580," February 1, 1934, PSDP, Series A, File 1173; Huthmacher, *Wagner*, p. 162; Bernstein, *Turbulent Years*, p. 180; NRA, "Press Release No. 3078," February 1, 1934, PSDP, Series A, File 1173; Special Conference Committee, "Minutes of Meeting, February 8–9, 1934," in U.S. Congress, Senate, Committee on Education and Labor, *Violations of Free Speech and Rights of Labor: Hearings of a Subcommittee*, pt. 45, "Supplemental Exhibits— Goodyear Tire and Rubber Co., Special Conference Committee" (Washington, D.C.: Government Printing Office, 1939), p. 16782 (documents pertaining to this committee henceforth are refered to as La Follette Committee); Lopata, "John J. Raskob," p. 218; Sloan to P. S. du Pont, February 20, 1934, PSDP, Series A, File 1173.
10. P. S. du Pont to Hugh Johnson, February 28, 1934, P. S. du Pont address, February 12, 1934, PSDP, Series A, File 1173; Huthmacher, *Wagner*, p. 155.
11. Bellush, *Failure of the NRA*, pp. 70, 142; P. S. du Pont to National Labor Board, February 9, 1934, PSDP, Series A, File 1173; Bernstein, *Turbulent Years*, p. 181; Huthmacher, *Wagner*, p. 163.
12. Bernstein, *Turbulent Years*, pp. 182–185; Fine, *Auto under the Blue Eagle*, pp. 159–160; Huthmacher, *Wagner*, pp. 163–166.
13. P. S. du Pont to Roper, March 6, 1934, P. S. du Pont to Robert Wagner, March 7, 1934, Roper to P. S. du Pont, March 12, 1934, P. S. du Pont to

Victor B. Woolley, March 20, 1934, R. R. M. Carpenter to Raskob, March 16, 1934, PSDP, Series A, File 1173.

14. Raskob to Carpenter, March 20, 1934, PSDP, Series A, File 1173.

15. Carpenter to Daniel Hastings, March 27, 1934, Carpenter to P. S. du Pont, March 27, April 5, 1934, PSDP, Series A, File 1173.

16. Wolfskill, *Revolt of the Conservatives,* p. 23; Colby, *Du Pont Dynasty,* pp. 319–320; Lopata, "John J. Raskob," pp. 215, 225; Huthmacher, *Wagner,* pp. 171–174; P. S. du Pont to Sterling Edmunds, March 20, 1934, P. S. du Pont to Townsend, March 20 1934, PSDP, Series A, File 765; Lammot du Pont to P. S. du Pont, April 4, 1934, P. S. du Pont, "Statement on Fletcher-Rayburn Bill for Regulation of Stock Exchanges," March 3, 1934, Lincoln to P. S. du Pont, "Comments on the Fletcher-Rayburn Bill," March 27, 1934, PSDP, Series A, File 1068; Lincoln to P. S. du Pont, April 2, 1934, PSDP, Series A, File 1173; I. du Pont to Townsend, April 2, 1934, IDP, Series J, File 261.

17. P. S. du Pont to Sloan, April 13, 1934, PSDP, Series A, File 1173; M. H. McIntyre to P. S. du Pont, March 8, 27, 1834, P. S. du Pont to McIntyre, March 27, 1934, PSDP, Series A, File 765; F. C. Evans to E. S. Cowdrick, April 24, 1934, in La Follette Committee, *Hearings,* "Supplemental Exhibits," p. 16959; P. S. du Pont to FDR, April 30, 1934, PSDP, Series A, File 765.

18. P. S. du Pont to James Gerard, May 15, 1934, Frederic R. Harris to P. S. du Pont, May 23, 1934, P. S. du Pont to Harris, May 28, 1934, PSDP, Series A, File 765.

19. I. du Pont to P. S. du Pont, May 31, 1934, PSDP, Series A, File 1068.

20. Huthmacher, *Wagner,* p. 158; Leff, *Limits of Symbolic Reform,* pp. 64–65; Bernstein, *A Caring Society,* p. 93; Bernstein, *Turbulent Years,* p. 217. Delaware state general fund estimates are in "Unemployment and Relief," PSDP, Series A. File 1164.

21. P. S. du Pont to Bernard Finucane, May 23, 1934, P. S. du Pont to David Walsh, May 25, 1934, PSDP, Series A, File 1173; P. S. du Pont to Wagner, June 4, 1934, Franklin Ralston Welsh to P. S. du Pont, July 9, 1934, PSDP, Series A, File 765; I. du Pont to Paul Harris, May 22, 1934, IDP, Series J, File 203; I. du Pont to P. S. du Pont, June 8, 1934, IDP, Series J, File 292; *New York Times,* July 8, 1934, p. 21; Huthmacher, *Wagner,* pp. 167–68.

22. Shouse to Raskob, June 12, 1934, Raskob Papers, File 602; Fine, *Auto under the Blue Eagle,* p. 224; P. S. du Pont to FDR, June 26, 1934, I. du Pont to P. S. du Pont, June 26, 1934, Lammot du Pont to P. S. du Pont, June 27, 1934, PSDP, Series A, File 1173.

23. Crusaders to I. du Pont, June 15, 1934, IDP, Series J, File 292; I. du Pont to J. H. Rand, June 18, 1934, IDP, Series J, File 261; Raskob to Shouse, July 2, 1934, Shouse Papers; H. G. Haskell to Raskob, July 3, 1934, Raskob Papers, File 61; I. du Pont to P. S. du Pont, July 10, 1934, PSDP, Series A, File 771.

24. I. du Pont to P. S. du Pont, July 10, 1934, PSDP, Series A, File 771.

25. John W. Davis to Shouse, July 14, 1934, Shouse Papers; Milton W. Harrison to Raskob, July 16, 1934, Raskob Papers, File 61; S. W. Colgate to I. du Pont, July 23, 1934, IDP, Series J, File 292.

26. I. du Pont to Lammot du Pont, July 16, 1934, IDP, Series J, File 292.

27. Shouse to Raskob, July 20, 1934, Lammot du Pont to Raskob, July 27, 1934, IDP, Series J, File 292.

28. Donaldson Brown to Raskob, Shouse, Irénée, Lammot du Pont, Carpenter, Sloan, John Pratt, and John T. Smith, July 23, 1934, IDP, Series J, File 292. The accompanying DeBrul memo had been written on June 19, 1934, to Brown.

29. Sloan to Raskob, July 24, 1934, IDP, Series J, File 292; P. S. du Pont to Raskob, July 26, 1934, PSDP, Series A, File 771.

30. Raskob to P. S. du Pont, July 30, 1934, P. S. du Pont to Raskob, August 1, 1934, PSDP, Series A, File 771; Lammot du Pont to Raskob, July 27, 1934, IDP, Series J, File 292; Stayton to P. S. du Pont, July 30, 1934, P. S. du Pont to Stayton, August 3, 1934, PSDP, Series A, File 771. Stayton drafted at least seven solicitation letters to former AAPA directors, dated August 2, 7, 9, 13, 16, 21 and 24, 1934, IDP, Series J, File 292.

31. Brown to Raskob, August 3, 1934, IDP, Series J, File 292.

32. Crusaders, "Report of Conferences with Leaders of Industrial Groups Relative to Determining the Extent of Their Financial Participation," August 1, 1934, Raskob to Shouse, August 3, 1934, Raskob Papers, File 61.

33. Raskob to Davis, August 3, 1934, Church to Raskob, August 10, 1934, Raskob Papers, File 61.

34. P. S. du Pont to Stayton, August 3, 1934, PSDP, Series A, File 771.

35. Wolfskill, *Revolt of the Conservatives*, pp. 9–19; Shouse to Carter Glass, August 1, 1934, Glass to Shouse, August 1, 1934, Shouse Papers; Carpenter to P. S. du Pont, August 1, 1934, PSDP, Series A, File 765; P. S. du Pont to Lloyd K. Garrison, August 10, 1934, PSDP, Series A, File 1173.

36. Davis to Raskob, August 8, 1934, Brown to Raskob, August 16, 1934, Raskob Papers, File 61; Stayton, "Memorandum concerning the activities of the American Liberty League from its organization (August 1934) to June 1938" (henceforth cited as "Liberty League"), pp. 5–7, PSDP, Series A, File 771.

37. Fine, *Sit-Down*, pp. 33–34; Shouse, "Memorandum for the personal files of Jouett Shouse," August 16, 1934, Shouse Papers.

38. Shouse, "Memorandum," p. 4, Shouse Papers.

9. Launching the Liberty League

1. Shouse statement attached to letter from Benjamin Marsh to I. du Pont, August 23, 1934, IDP, Series J, File 292; Stayton, "Liberty League," p. 7, PSDP, Series A, File 771; Wolfskill, *Revolt of the Conservatives*, pp. 20–23.

2. Raskob to Byrd, August 21, 1934, Byrd to Raskob, August 24, 1934, Raskob Papers, File 602; I. du Pont to Raskob, August 17, 1934, I. du Pont to Walter J. Kohler, August 18, 1934, I. du Pont to Colgate, August 18, 1934, David Lawrence to I. du Pont, August 18, 1934, IDP, Series J, File 292; Wolfskill, *Revolt of the Conservatives*, p. 26.

3. P. S. du Pont to Russell E. Watson, August 24, 1934, P. S. du Pont to S. Clay Williams, August 24, 1934, P. S. du Pont to Donald Richberg, August 28, 1934, PSDP, Series A, File 1173.

4. Donald R. McCoy, *Coming of Age: The United States during the 1920's and 1930's* (Baltimore: Penguin Books, 1973), p. 225; La Follette Committee, *Hearings*, Exhibit No. 3799; "I. du Pont Political Contributions, January 1, 1919–September 11, 1934," IDP, Series J, File 203.

5. Wolfskill, *Revolt of the Conservatives,* p. 19; FDR to P. S. du Pont, August 18, 1934, PSDP, Series A, File 1173.
6. Wolfskill, *Revolt of the Conservatives,* pp. 34–35; Stayton, "Liberty League," p. 8, PSDP, Series A, File 771; Washington *Post,* August 24, 1934, p. 1.
7. Wolfskill, *Revolt of the Conservatives,* pp. 28–30, 33.
8. Ibid., pp. 31–33; *New York Times,* August 28, 1934, p. 15.
9. Wolfskill, *Revolt of the Conservatives,* pp. 33–34; Raoul Desvernine to Shouse, August 30, 1934, Shouse Papers; Stayton, "Liberty League," pp. 9–11; Church to P. S. du Pont, August 27, 1934, P. S. du Pont to Church, September 4, 1934, PSDP, Series A, File 771. A draft of Lawrence's column is included with Lawrence to Raskob, September 3, 1934, Raskob Papers, File 61.
10. P. S. du Pont to Shouse, August 24, 1934, PSDP, Series A, File 771.
11. I. du Pont to Harold Boericke, August 27, 1934, I. du Pont to Earl Reeves, September 1, 1934, IDP, Series, J, Files 292.
12. Shouse to Raskob, August 16, 1934, Farley to Shouse, August 28, 1934, Raskob to Farley, September 4, 1934, Shouse to Farley, October 2, 1934, Raskob to Farley, November 5, 1934, Raskob Papers, File 602.
13. Stayton, "Liberty League," p. 10, PSDP, Series A, File 771; Richard Whitney to Raskob, August 23, 1934, Raskob Papers, File 61; H. B. Rust to I. du Pont, September 25, 1934, IDP, Series J, File 292.
14. Sloan to Raskob, September 19, 1934, Walter Parker to Shouse, September 17, 1934, Desvernine to Raskob, September 13, October 11, 1934, Raskob Papers, File 61; I. du Pont to Shouse, August 30, 1934, G. d'Andelot Belin to I. du Pont, September 6, 1934, IDP, Series J, File 292; Desvernine to Shouse, September 29, 1934, Shouse Papers.
15. Shouse to Raskob, September 14, 1934, I. du Pont to Sloan, September 19, 1934, Sloan to Raskob, September 20, 1934, I. du Pont to Shouse, September 20, October 12, 1934, IDP, Series J, File 292.
16. Stayton to "25 of the Leading Citizens of the State," September 24, 1934, Stayton to I. du Pont, October 25, 1934, Alice Belin du Pont to Pauline Morton Sabin, September 27, 1934, IDP, Series A; P. S. du Pont to John Hemphill, September 27, 1934, P. S. du Pont remarks, September 17, 1934, P. S. du Pont to Gerard, September 18, 1934, PSDP, Series A, File 771.
17. Taylor and Sudnik, *Du Pont,* p. 147; Desvernine to Shouse, September 8, 1934, Shouse Papers. The best study of the Nye Committee investigations is John E. Wiltz, *In Search of Peace: The Senate Munitions Inquiry* (Baton Rouge: Louisiana State University Press, 1963).
18. *New York Times,* September 15, 1934, p. 1, September 16, 1934, p. 30; I. du Pont to Shouse, September 20, 1934, IDP, Series J, File 292.
19. I. du Pont to Shouse, September 27, 1934, Raskob to I. du Pont, September 28, 1934, IDP, Series J, File 292; "I. du Pont–Political Contributions," IDP, Series J, File 203; I. du Pont to New York State Economic Council, September 24, 1934, I. du Pont to Amos A. Fries, September 24, 1934, Earl Reeves to I. du Pont, September 17, October 6, 1934, IDP, Series J, File 292.
20. Wolfskill, *Revolt of the Conservatives,* pp. 57–58; I. du Pont speech, "Why America Needs the Liberty League," October 4, 1934, I. du Pont to Will Clayton, October 8, 1934, Desvernine to Raskob, September 27, 1934, IDP, Series J, File 292; Stayton to former AAPA executive committee members, October

11, 1934, PSDP, Series A, File 771; E. F. Hutton to Shouse, October 8, 1934, Shouse Papers.

21. Wolfskill, *Revolt of the Conservatives,* pp. 229–230.
22. Raskob to Shouse, October 18, 1934, Raskob Papers, File 61; Wolkskill, *Revolt of the Conservatives,* p. 230; I. du Pont to Voice of the Air, October 30, 1934, Howard Heinz to I. du Pont, October 31, 1934, IDP, Series J, File 292.
23. E. Willard Jensen to Raskob, October 2, 1934, Raskob to Lammot du Pont, October 18, 1934, Raskob Papers, File 61; Roper to Raskob, October 18, 1934, Business Advisory and Planning Council, "Confidential Bulletin" to Roper, November 7, 1934, Raskob to Morris Leeds, November 1, 1934, Raskob Papers, File 310; Raskob to Farley, November 25, 1934, Raskob Papers, File 602; P. S. du Pont to Brooks Darlington, October 17, 1934, Darlington to P. S. du Pont, October 21, 1934, PSDP, Series A, File 771; Hawley, *New Deal and the Problem of Monopoly,* p. 153.
24. I. du Pont to Daniel Willard, October 23, 1934, I. du Pont to Lammot du Pont, October 31, 1934, I. du Pont to Shouse, November 1, 1934, Shouse to I. du Pont, November 3, 1934, I. du Pont to F. H. Fechtig, November 6, 1934, Hiram Evans to I. du Pont, November 1, 1934, I. du Pont to Shouse, November 6, 1934, Stayton to Raskob, November 6, 1934, IDP, Series J, File 292.
25. *New York Times,* October 30, 1934; Bernstein, *A Caring Society,* p. 71. Irénée retained Shouse as his personal attorney in case of libel actions stemming from his activity in the League or the Nye hearings. I. du Pont to Shouse, November 7, 1934, IDP, Series J, File 292.
26. I. du Pont to Thomas J. Sullivan, November 6, 1934, I. du Pont to Frank Schoonover, November 7, 1934, IDP, Series J, File 292; Stayton, "Liberty League," p. 11, PSDP, Series A, File 771.
27. William A. Tissock to Shouse, November 5, 1934, I. du Pont to Lammot du Pont, November 7, 1934, IDP, Series J, File 292; Stayton to Shouse, November 9, 1934, Raskob Papers, File 61; I. du Pont to Stayton, November 8, 1934, IDP, Series J, File 292.
28. Stayton, "Liberty League," pp. 11–15, PSDP, Series A, File 771.
29. Shouse to Raskob, November 5, 1934, Shouse to I. du Pont, November 14, 1934, I. du Pont to William Randolph Hearst, November 20, 1934, IDP, Series J, File 292; Asa V. Call to Raskob, November 15, 1934, Raskob to Hearst, November 21, 1934, Raskob Papers, File 61.
30. *New York Times,* November 15, 1934; Will Rogers to E. F. Hutton, n.d., attached to letter from Hutton to I. du Pont, April 15, 1935, Shouse to I. du Pont, November 10, 1934, I. du Pont to Evans, November 20, 1934, IDP, Series J, File 292.
31. I. du Pont address, November 21, 1934, IDP, Series A; J. Ernest Smith to P. S. du Pont, November 14, 1934, Raskob to P. S. du Pont, November 22, 28, 1934, PSDP, Series A, File 765.
32. Colby, *Du Pont Dynasty,* pp. 368–369.
33. J. S. Cullinan to Stayton, November 13, 1934, PSDP, Series A, File 771. Among the various accounts of the "Legion Plot" are George Seldes, *One Thousand Americans* (New York: Boni and Gaer, 1947), pp. 209–210, 287–291; Jules Archer, *The Plot to Seize the White House* (New York: Hawthorn Books,

1973); and Colby, *Du Pont Dynasty*, pp. 324–330, all of which accept Butler's charges at face value, and Wolfskill, *Revolt of the Conservatives*, pp. 80–101, who is far more skeptical. This author weighs in with Wolfskill. The official record of the investigation is U.S. Congress, House, Special Committee on Un-American Activities, *Investiation of Nazi Propaganda Activities and Investigation of Certain Other Propaganda Activities: Hearings*, 73rd Cong., 2d sess. (1934), and *Final Report*, February 15, 1935.

34. Archer, *Plot to Seize the White House*, pp. 22–34, 152–163.

35. Wolfskill, *Revolt of the Conservatives*, pp. 86–94; Archer, *Plot to Seize the White House*, pp. 6–22, 140–152. Partial corroboration of the attempt to produce an American Legion endorsement of the gold standard in 1933 is in Val O'Ferrell to Louis M. Howe, December 11, 1933, FDR Papers as President, PPF File 6728.

36. Wolfskill, *Revolt of the Conservatives*, pp. 94–95.

37. Archer, *Plot to Seize the White House*, pp. 33–34, 164–168, 172–174.

38. Wolfskill, *Revolt of the Conservatives*, pp. 95–97; Archer, *Plot to Seize the White House*, pp. 169–191, 194; Samuel Dickstein to FDR, November 26, 1934, FDR to Dickstein, November 30, 1934, FDR Papers as President, PPF File 314.

39. The Liberty League shared the National Press Building as a headquarters with the extremist organization America First, Inc., a group headed by James True with the aim of giving "X-ray exposure" to the New Deal's "subversive activities"; Wolfskill and Hudson, *All But the People*, p. 94. According to Shouse's later claims to George Wolfskill, any blame for the "Legion plot," even in limited form, lay with the "loose cannon" MacGuire rather than with Murphy, who subsequently fired him. Shouse attributed the more grandiose of Butler's charges to his intense "dry" convictions earlier on prohibition, his hatred of the more "militaristic" American Legion, and his mental instability. Shouse to Wolfskill, June 6, 1961, Shouse Papers; Wolfskill, *Revolt of the Conservatives*, pp. 98–101; "American Liberty League Cash Statement," December 19, 1934, Robert E. Jackson to I. du Pont, November 22, 1934, IDP, Series J, File 292.

40. Karl T. Compton to Stayton, November 19, 1934, PSDP, Series A, File 771; Raskob to Shouse, November 23, 1934, Shouse to I. du Pont, November 24, 1934, "ALL Cash Statement," December 19, 1934, Hearst to I. du Pont, November 28, 1934, IDP, Series J, File 292.

41. H. C. Spratt to I. du Pont, November 28, 1934, I. du Pont to Shouse, December 1, 1934, I. du Pont to Spratt, December 1, 1934, IDP, Series J, File 292.

42. *New York Times*, December 9, 1934; Shouse to I. du Pont, November 24, 1934, IDP, Series J, File 292; Shouse to Mrs. James Ross Todd, November 24, 1934, PSDP, Series A, File 771.

43. Stayton, "Liberty League," p. 16, PSDP, Series A, File 771; P. S. du Pont, "Memorandum in Regard to Certain Labor Conditions," November 15, 1934, PSDP, Series A, File 765; P. S. du Pont to Cullinan, November 21, 1934, Cullinan to P. S. du Pont, November 26, 1934, Stayton to P. S. du Pont, November 27, 1934, Cullinan to P. S. du Pont, December 12, 1934, PSDP, Series A, File 771.

44. Desvernine to Shouse, September 21, 1934, Shouse Papers; Clayton to Shouse, December 4, 1934, IDP, Series J, File 292; Stayton to P. S. du Pont, November

23, 1934, P. S. du Pont to Stayton, November 26, 1934, P. S. du Pont to John E. Zimmerman, November 26, 1934, Zimmerman to P. S. du Pont, December 3, 1934, Stayton to P. S. du Pont, December 5, 1934, P. S. du Pont to Zimmerman, December 10, 1934, PSDP, Series A, File 771.

45. *New York Times,* December 6, 21, 1934; Colby, *Du Pont Dynasty,* pp. 344–345; *Bronx Home News,* December 17, 1934; I. du Pont to Shouse, December 15, 1934, IDP, Series J, File 292.

46. "Congress of American Industry and National Association of Manufacturers—Platform and Resolutions," December 5–6, 1934, Raskob Papers, File 462; *Time,* December 17, 1934, p. 59.

47. Stayton, "Liberty League," p. 17, PSDP, Series A, File 771; "Report to the Executive Committee of the American Liberty League," December 20, 1934, pp. 1–10, IDP, Series J, File 292.

48. "Report," December 20, 1934, pp. 11–27, IDP, Series J, File 292; Stayton, "Liberty League," pp. 17–18, PSDP, Series A, File 771.

49. Stayton, "Liberty League," Exhibit VIII, PSDP, Series A, File 771; Shouse to I. du Pont, December 21, 1934, I. du Pont to Shouse, December 24, 1934, I. du Pont to Evans, December 28, 1934, I. du Pont to ALL Executive Committe, December 31, 1934, IDP, Series J, File 292.

50. Hutton to Raskob, December 28, 1934, Raskob Papers, File 61; Raskob to Farley, January 2, 1935, Raskob Papers, File 602; Raskob to C. B. Ames, January 3, 1935, Raskob Papers, File 462; Raskob to H. P. Kendall, January 9, 1935, Raskob Papers, File 310; Raskob to P. S. du Pont, January 14, 1935, Raskob Papers, File 61.

10. Disintegration and Rebirth

1. Wolfskill, *Revolt of the Conservatives,* pp. 58–60; Washington *Daily News,* January 9, 1935. By January 1935, the executive committee included Al Smith, John W. Davis, James Wadsworth, Pauline Sabin, J. Howard Pew, H. B. Rust, Colby Chester, Mrs. Henry B. Joy, Joseph Proskauer, Colonel A. A. Sprague of Chicago, Mills Lane of Savannah, Mrs. James Ross Todd of Louisville, Frank C. Rand of the International Shoe Company, and Dr. Edwin N. Kemmerer.

2. J. Howard Pew to I. du Pont, January 4, 1934, IDP, Series J, File 292; Pew to Al Smith, January 4, 1935, Smith Papers; Davis to Shouse, January 3, 1935, Shouse Papers; Church to Rust, January 10, 1935, Raskob to Hutton, January 8, 1935 Raskob Papers, File 61; Stayton, "Liberty League," pp. 19–20, PSDP, Series A, File 771.

3. American Liberty League (henceforth ALL) Document 10, *The Budget Message,* January 10, 1935; Huthmacher, *Wagner,* pp. 182–184.

4. ALL Administrative Committee, "Minutes," January 11, 24, 1935, Joseph V. Baker to I. du Pont, January 25, 1935, IDP, Series J, File 292.

5. Stayton, "Liberty League," pp. 18, 21–24, PSDP, Series A, File 771; Baltimore *Sun,* January 16, 1935; ALL Doc. 10, *The Budget Message,* January 10, 1935; ALL Doc. 11, *The NRA,* January 1935.

6. The meeting minutes of the Relief Commission, Inc., of Wilmington (and its

public successor) are in PSDP, Series A, File 1164, under that title, up to and including the April 16, 1937, session.

7. Hutton to I. du Pont, January 26, 1935, IDP, Series J, File 292.
8. ALL Doc. 13, *Economic Security*, February 4, 1935; ALL Doc. 14, *Democracy or Bureaucracy*, February 4, 1935; ALL Doc. 17, *Inflation*, February 1935; Stayton, "Liberty League," pp. 23–26, PSDP, Series A, File 771.
9. Leff, *Limits of Symbolic Reform*, pp. 70–72; Raymond Pitcairn to P. S. du Pont, February 7, 1935, PSDP, Series A, File 771; Pitcairn to I. S. du Pont, February 7, 1935, IDP, Series J, File 292; P. S. du Pont to Pitcairn, February 11, 1935 PSDP, Series A, File 771; I. du Pont to Pitcairn, February 19, 1935, IDP, Series J, File 292.
10. Stayton, "Liberty League," Exhibit XXIX, Stayton to P. S. du Pont, January 16, 1935, P. S. du Pont to Shouse, February 7, 1935, PSDP, Series A, File 771; Stayton to I. du Pont, February 6, 1935, I. du Pont to Frank Kent, February 19, 1935, IDP, Series J, File 292.
11. Archer, *Plot to Seize the White House*, pp. 192–194, 209–211.
12. I. du Pont to Hutton, February 20, 1935, Hutton to I. du Pont, February 27, 1935, Frank Kent to I. du Pont, February 23, 1935, I. du Pont to Shouse, February 20, 1935, Shouse to I. du Pont, February 22, 1935, IDP, Series J, File 292.
13. Stayton, "Liberty League," pp. 26–27, Zimmerman to P. S. du Pont, February 7, 1935, P. S. du Pont to Zimmerman, February 11, 1935, PSDP, Series A, File 771; Shouse to I. du Pont, March 12, 1935, IDP, Series J, File 292; I. du Pont to Townsend, March 8, 1935, I. du Pont to Howard W. Smith, March 13, 1935, IDP, Series J, File 261.
14. Rust to I. du Pont, March 6, 1935, I. du Pont to ALL Executive Committee, February 19, 1935, I. du Pont to Shouse, March 8, 1935, Shouse to I. du Pont, March 9, 1935, Sewell Avery to I. du Pont, March 16, 1935, IDP, Series J, File 292; George May to Frank Kent, March 6, 1935, IDP, Series A.
15. Stayton to I. du Pont, March 18, 1935, I. du Pont note, March 19, 1935, I. du Pont to Shouse, March 26, 1935, I. du Pont to George Whitney, March 12, 1935, Stayton to I. du Pont, March 15, 1935, I. du Pont to Stayton, March 19, 1935, I. du Pont to Shouse, March 27, 1935, IDP, Series J, File 292.
16. I. du Pont to Earl Babst, March 25, 1935, I. du Pont to Zimmerman, March 30, 1935, IDP, Series J, File 292.
17. ALL Doc. 24, *Price Control*, March 28, 1935; Huthmacher, *Wagner*, pp. 190–191.
18. Huthmacher, *Wagner*, p. 191; P. S. du Pont to E. T. Stannard, April 10, 1935, P. S. du Pont to Jacob Billikopf, March 13, 1935, PSDP, Series A, File 1173; ALL Doc. 27, *The Labor Relations Bill*, April 15, 1935.
19. Neil Carouthers, "Government by Experiment," April 7, 1935, Ray Bert Westerfield, "How Inflation Affects the Average Family," April 18, 1935, Walter Spahr, "Political Banking," April 26, 1935, IDP, Series A; ALL Doc. 30, *The AAA Amendments*, April 18, 1935; Ernest T. Weir, "Present Relations of Business to Government," *Vital Speeches 1* (April 22, 1935), pp. 476–478.
20. Stayton to I. du Pont, April 13, 1935, IDP, Series J, File 292; P. S. du Pont to Raskob, April 15, 16, 1935, Stayton to P. S. du Pont, April 18, 19, 1935, PSDP, Series A, File 771.

21. Hutton to I. du Pont, April 24, 1935, IDP, Series J, File 292; Raskob to P. S. du Pont, confidential, April 30, 1935, PSDP, Series A, File 771; I. du Pont to Shouse, May 16, 1935, IDP, Series J, File 292.

22. Carpenter to I. du Pont, April 5, 1935, George Stuart Patterson to I. du Pont, April 25, 1935, IDP, Series J, File 292; Pitcairn to P. S. du Pont, May 7, 1935, PSDP, Series A, File 765.

23. Leuchtenburg, *FDR and the New Deal*, pp. 146–150; Wolfskill, *Revolt of the Conservatives*, p. 163.

24. Hawley, *New Deal and the Problem of Monopoly*, p. 154; ALL Doc. 32, *Bituminous Coal Bill*, April 29, 1935; Stayton to P. S. du Pont, April 26, 1935, PSDP, Series A, File 771.

25. Stayton to P. S. du Pont, April 26, 1935, PSDP, Series A, File 771.

26. Hal Roach to Grayson Murphy, May 21, 1935, Shouse to I. du Pont, April 22, 1935, Stayton to I. du Pont, April 25, 1935, I. du Pont to Shouse, April 29, 1935, I. du Pont to Stayton, May 3, 1935, Stayton to I. du Pont, May 25, 1935, IDP, Series J, File 292.

27. Ralph Shaw to Shouse, May 13, 1935, Wadsworth to I. du Pont, May 18, 1935, IDP, Series J, File 292.

28. P. S. du Pont to Amos Pinchot, May 14, 1935, PSDP, Series A, File 1173; I. du Pont to A. B. Echols, May 9, 1935, Shouse to I. du Pont, May 10, 1935, IDP, Series J, File 292.

29. Shouse to I. du Pont, May 17, 1935, I. du Pont to Shouse, May 21, 1935, IDP, Series J, File 292; G. W. Dyer, "Regimenting the Farmers," May 5, 1935, Raoul Desvernine, "Human Rights and the Constitution," May 16, 1935, IDP, Series A; ALL Doc. 34, *Extension of the NRA*, May 13, 1935; Huthmacher, *Wagner*, pp. 188–189; ALL Doc. 36, *The Farmers' Home Bill*, May 16, 1935; Shouse to I. du Pont, May 21, 1935, IDP, Series J, File 292; Shouse to P. S. du Pont, May 21, 1935, PSDP, Series A, File 771; P. S. du Pont to FDR, May 24, 1935, PSDP, Series A, File 765; FDR to P. S. du Pont, May 27, 1935, FDR Papers as President, PPF Box 348; ALL Doc. 37, *The TVA Amendments*, May 26, 1935.

30. La Follette Committee, *Hearings*, pt. 45, pp. 16791–16792, 16811; Huthmacher, *Wagner*, pp. 192–198; P. S. du Pont to Billikopf, May 13, 1935, PSDP, Series A, File 1173.

31. Bellush, *Failure of the NRA*, p. 173; Huthmacher, *Wagner*, p. 198; Bernstein, *A Caring Society*, p. 69; Stayton to I. du Pont, June 3, 1935, Thomas Bayard to I. du Pont, June 6, 1935, IDP, Series J, File 292; William E. Borah, "How to Meet the Issue," June 2, 1935, IDP, Series A.

32. Penciled notation on letter from Shouse to I. du Pont, June 4, 1935, ALL Executive Committee, "Minutes," June 11, 1935, IDP, Series J, File 292.

33. Among the prominent members of the Lawyers' Committee were John W. Davis, Joseph Proskauer, James Beck, former Massachusetts governor Joseph B. Ely, Frank J. Hogan of Washington, D.C., Forney Johnston of Alabama, Ralph Shaw, and even, ironically, former "dry" adversary George W. Wickersham. P. S. du Pont to I. du Pont *et al.*, June 12, 1935, Shouse to P. S. du Pont, June 17, 1935, Stayton, "Liberty League," p. 31, Stayton to P. S. du Pont, June 21, 1935, PSDP, Series A, File 771; Shouse, "To all members of the American Liberty League," June 27, 1935, Shouse Papers.

34. Shouse, "You Are the Government," June 13, 1935, Shouse Papers; Wolfskill and Hudson, *All But the People,* p. 146; Stayton to P. S. du Pont, May 27, 1935, P. S. du Pont to Stayton, June 3, 1935, Stayton to P. S. du Pont, June 21, 1935, PSDP, Series A, File 771; Shouse to I. du Pont, June 25, 1935, IDP, Series J, File 292; Raskob to Shouse, June 18, 1935, Stayton to Raskob, June 21, 1935, Raskob Papers, File 61.
35. Leff, *Limits of Symbolic Reform,* pp. 91, 109.
36. Ibid., pp. 93–94, 145; Shaw to Shouse, June 21, 1935, Shouse Papers; Wolfskill and Hudson, *All But the People,* pp. 69, 190–191.
37. Wolfskill, *Revolt of the Conservatives,* p. 62; A. Felix du Pont to Stayton, June 27, 1935, I. du Pont to Gifford, June 21, 1935, I. du Pont to Hutton, June 25, 1935, Sloan to I. du Pont, July 2, 1935, IDP, Series J, File 292.
38. Shouse to I. du Pont, June 26, 1935, I. du Pont to Desvernine, July 1, 1935, Desvernine to I. du Pont, July 3, 1935, IDP, Series J, File 292; ALL, "Resolution," July 2, 1935, PSDP, Series A, File 771; I. du Pont to Shouse, July 5, 1935, Shouse to I. du Pont, July 6, 1935, IDP, Series J, File 292; Huthmacher, *Wagner,* p. 198.
39. Sloan to P. S. du Pont, June 14, 1935, PSDP, Series A, File 771; Wolfskill, *Revolt of the Conservatives,* pp. 69–70; Stayton, "Liberty League," p. 32, PSDP, Series A, File 771.
40. Shouse to I. du Pont, June 18, 1935, I. du Pont to Fred A. Howland, July 17, 1935, Howland to I. du Pont, July 25, 1935, Grayson Murphy to Stayton, July 19, 1935, Rust to I. du Pont, July 26, 1935, IDP, Series J, File 292.
41. I. du Pont to Stayton, July 31, 1935, IDP, Series J, File 292; ALL Doc. 57, *Expanding Bureaucracy,* July 1935; ALL Doc. 60, *Lawmaking by Executive Order,* July 1935; ALL Doc. 63, *New Deal Laws in Federal Courts,* August 1935; Leff, *Limits of Symbolic Reform,* p. 158; Huthmacher, *Wagner,* pp. 199–201; Arthur M. Schlesinger, Jr., *The Age of Roosevelt: The Politics of Upheaval* (Boston: Houghton Mifflin, 1960), pp. 448–449.
42. Samuel I. Rosenman, comp., *The Public Papers and Addresses of Franklin D. Roosevelt* (New York: Random House, 1938–1950), vol. 4, pp. 297–298.

11. Mobilizing for Armageddon

1. Wolfskill and Hudson, *All But the People,* pp. 5–8.
2. For a detailed expression of the League's public ideology, the reader should consult the organization's leaflet, monthly bulletin, and, in particular, pamphlet series (indicated in this volume by the label "ALL Document"). Some 134 such pamphlets, including reprints of members' speeches and research studies, were published from the League's founding until September 1936. IDP, Series A.
3. Wolfskill and Hudson, *All But the People,* p. 121; Lopata, "John J. Raskob," p. 213.
4. P. S. du Pont to F. K. Reybold, August 29, 1935, PSDP, Series A, File 765; P. S. du Pont to Shouse, September 18, November 29, 1935, PSDP, Series A, File 771; P. S. du Pont to W. M. Newton, October 7, 1935, PSDP, Series A, File 1173; I. du Pont to Raskob, October 10, 1935, Raskob Papers, File 1624.
5. I. du Pont to Stayton, September 9, 1935, Shouse to P. S. du Pont, September

16, 1935, Charles A. Meade to I. du Pont, August 30, 1935, IDP, Series J, File 292; P. S. du Pont to Shouse, September 17, 1935, P. S. du Pont to Stayton, October 17, 1935, PSDP, Series A, File 771; P. S. du Pont to Joseph Foster, October 28, 1935, P. S. du Pont to Joseph McCoy, December 19, 1935, PSDP, Series A, File 765.

6. Wolfskill, *Revolt of the Conservatives,* pp. 66–67; Shouse, "Breathing Spells," September 16, 1935, IDP, Series A; Stayton, "Liberty League," p. 34, PSDP, Series A, File 771.

7. Stayton, "Liberty League," p. 35, PSDP, Series A, File 771; I. du Pont to Shouse, October 2, 1935, IDP, Series J, File 292; ALL Doc. 67, *Consumers and the AAA,* October 1935; ALL Doc. 68, *Straws Which Tell,* October 1935; ALL Doc. 71, *Budget Prospects,* October 1935; ALL Doc. 72, *Dangerous Experimentation,* October 1935; ALL Doc. 75, *Economic Planning—Mistaken But Not New,* November 1935; ALL Doc. 78, *Work Relief,* November 1935; ALL Doc. 80, *The AAA and Our Form of Government,* December 1935.

8. Brainbridge Colby to Al Smith, May 29, 1935, Smith Papers; P. S. du Pont to I. du Pont, June 28, 1935, PSDP, Series A, File 771; Howland to I. du Pont, July 25, 1935, IDP, Series J, File 292.

9. Keller, *In Defense of Yesterday,* pp. 267–269; Beck to Hearst, July 8, August 10, 1935, Hearst to Beck, August 18, 1935, Beck Papers; Wolfskill and Hudson, *All But the People,* p. 151; Rust to I. du Pont, July 26, 1935, IDP, Series J, File 292; P. S. du Pont to Joseph Baker, August 8, 1935, PSDP, Series A, File 765.

10. Wolfskill and Hudson, *All But the People,* p. 239; Carpenter to I. du Pont, August 16, 1935, I. du Pont to Stayton, August 20, 1935, Stayton to I. du Pont, August 23, 1935, IDP, Series J, File 292; Schlesinger, *Politics of Upheaval,* p. 518.

11. Wolfskill and Hudson, *All But the People,* p. 240. The best biography of Long is T. Harry Williams, *Huey Long* (New York: Alfred A. Knopf, 1969).

12. Wolfskill, *Revolt of the Conservatives,* pp. 240–241; John Henry Kirby to Lammot du Pont, August 17, 1935, I. du Pont to Stayton, September 16, 1935, Stayton to I. du Pont, September 25, 1935, IDP, Series J, File 292.

13. *New York Times,* August 15, 1935; Wolfskill, *Revolt of Conservatives,* pp. 71–73.

14. National Lawyer's Committee, "Report on the Constitutionality of the National Labor Relations Act," September 5, 1935, ALL press release, September 16, 1935, IDP, Series A; La Follette Committee, *Hearings,* pt. 45, pp. 16811–16812; Wolfskill, *Revolt of the Conservatives,* p. 72.

15. Bernstein, *Turbulent Years,* p. 646; La Follette Committee, *Hearings,* pt. 17, "Employer Associations and Citizens' Committees" Exhibit 3799.

16. Wolfskill, *Revolt of the Conservatives,* p. 73.

17. Ibid.; I. du Pont to Desvernine, October 2, 1935, Rust to Stayton, October 2, 1935, IDP, Series J, File 292.

18. Wolfskill, *Revolt of the Conservatives,* pp. 74–78; FDR to Farley, September 28, 1935, FDR Papers as President; Desvernine to I. du Pont, October 8, 1935, IDP, Series J, File 292.

19. Wolfskill, *Revolt of the Conservatives,* pp. 75–77.

20. George Creel, "Thunder on the Right," *Colliers,* November 2, 1935; Wolfskill and Hudson, *All But the People,* pp. 191, 309; Wolfskill, *Revolt of the Conservatives,*

p. 203. A sympathetic portrait of Landon is presented in Donald R. McCoy, *Landon of Kansas* (Lincoln: University of Nebraska Press, 1966).

21. Wolfskill, *Revolt of the Conservatives*, pp. 230–232, 234; Pitcairn to Raskob, November 18, 1935, Raskob Papers, File 1624.

22. Lammot du Pont to P. S. du Pont, November 14, 1935, PSDP, Series A, File 765.

23. Raskob speech to National Business Conference Committee, October 24, 1935, Raskob Papers, File 1624.

24. E. T. Weir to Raskob, September 13, 1935, Lammot du Pont to Raskob, November 8, 1935, Raskob Papers, File 1624; *New York Times*, November 26, 1935; Wolfskill and Hudson, *All But the People*, p. 156; Hawley, *New Deal and the Problem of Monopoly*, p. 162.

25. Taylor and Sudnik, *Du Pont*, p. 148; I. du Pont to A. L. Green, December 3, 1935, IDP, Series J, File 292.

26. Wolfskill, *Revolt of the Conservatives*, pp. 61–61, 65–66; Shouse to I. du Pont, November 26, 1935, Stayton to I. du Pont, December 19, 1935, ALL Administrative Committee, "Minutes," December 5, 1935, IDP, Series J, File 292.

27. "ALL executive contributions—1935," PSDP, Series A, File 771; Wolfskill, *Revolt of the Conservatives*, p. 63.

28. Stayton, "Liberty League," Exhibit VIII, PSDP, Series A, File 771; La Follette Committee, *Hearings*, pt. 17, Exhibit 3799; Seldes, *One Thousand Americans*, p. 205.

29. Wolfskill, *Revolt of the Conservatives*, pp. 118–119.

30. Wolfskill and Hudson, *All But the People*, p. 240.

31. ALL press release, December 26, 1935, Shouse Papers; Stayton, "Liberty League," pp. 36–37, PSDP, Series A, File 771.

32. Forney Johnston to Desvernine, December 28, 1935, Johnston to Shouse, December 30, 1935, Shouse Papers.

33. I. du Pont to Pew, December 24, 1935, IDP, Series J, File 292; P. S. du Pont to James P. Warburg, December 26, 1935, PSDP, Series A, File 765; P. S. du Pont to Henry P. Kendall, December 27, 1935, PSDP, Series A, File 1173; C. G. Williams to P. S. du Pont, December 23, 1935, P.S. du Pont to Williams, December 24, 1935, PSDP, Series A, File 765; P.S. du Pont to Shouse, December 31, 1935, PSDP, Series A, File 771.

34. P. S. du Pont to Lardner Howell, December 20, 1935, P. S. du Pont to Williams, December 24, 1935, PSDP, Series A, File 765.

12. Taking a Walk

1. Wolfskill and Hudson, *All But the People*, p. 240; Wolfskill, *Revolt of the Conservatives*, pp. 163, 166.

2. Wolfskill, *Revolt of the Conservatives*, pp. 143–144.

3. Washington *Post*, January 2, 1936; *New York Times*, January 2, 3, 1936.

4. Wolfskill and Hudson, *All But the People*, p. 241; *New York Times*, January 4, 1936.

5. Wolfskill, *Revolt of the Conservatives*, pp. 146–147; Shouse to Desvernine, De-

cember 27, 1935, Desvernine to Shouse, January 2, 1936, Shouse Papers; ALL Doc. 86, *The 1937 Budget,* January 1936.

6. Wolfskill and Hudson, *All But the People,* p. 242; Wolfskill, *Revolt of the Conservatives,* pp. 166–167; Stayton to P. S. du Pont, January 9, 1936, P. S. du Pont to Stayton, January 10, 1936, PSDP, Series A, File 771.

7. *New York Times,* January 7, 1936.

8. Wolfskill, *Revolt of the Conservatives,* pp. 147–148.

9. *New York Times,* January 12, 1936; Wolfskill, *Revolt of the Conservatives,* pp. 144–145; Lopata, "John J. Raskob," p. 249; Raskob to John G. Grimes, January 10, 1936, Raskob Papers, File 602; Baltimore *Sun,* January 17, 1936; New York *American,* January 12, 1936; New York *Herald-Tribune,* Februray 14, 1936. An Associated Press story of February 8 claimed that Raskob had been billed by the Treasury Department for over a million dollars in unreported income.

10. Wolfskill, *Revolt of the Conservatives,* pp. 167–168; ALL Doc. 91, *Professors and the New Deal,* January 20, 1936; P. S. du Pont to L. E. Staplin, January 16, 1936, P. S. du Pont to Atwood, January 27, 1936, PSDP, Series A, File 765; George H. May to I. du Pont, January 8, 1936, IDP, Series J, File 292. As late as 1938 for the President refreshed his memory on the du Pont–Raskob stock transactions, apparently for political ammunition if needed. See "Du Pont–Raskob transactions," February 11, 1938, FDR Papers as President.

11. *Congressional Record,* 74th Cong., 2d sess., January 23, 1936, pp. 925–930.

12. William H. Harbaugh, *Lawyer's Lawyer: The Life of John W. Davis* (New York: Oxford University Press, 1973), p. 353; ALL Doc. 93, *The Redistribution of Power,* January 24, 1936; Wolfskill, *Revolt of the Conservatives,* pp. 142–143, 150, 152; Stayton, "Liberty League," pp. 39–40, PSDP, Series A, File 771.

13. Wolfskill, *Revolt of the Conservatives,* pp. 115–116, 151; Frederick H. Harvey to Shouse, February 4, 1936, Shouse Papers; Stayton, "Liberty League," p. 40, PSDP, Series A, File 771.

14. Stayton, "Liberty League," pp. 40–41, PSDP, Series A, File 771; Wolfskill, *Revolt of the Conservatives,* pp. 151–152.

15. Wolfskill, *Revolt of the Conservatives,* pp. 152–157, 160–161; Stayton, "Liberty League," pp. 41A–B, PSDP, Series A, File 771.

16. Raskob to P. S. du Pont, January 9, 1936, Raskob to Shouse, January 10, 1936, Hooven Letters to Raskob, January 11, 1936, Sloan to Raskob, January 15, 1936, Raskob to GM and Du Pont stockholders, January 30, 1936, Shouse to Raskob, February 6, 14, March 7, 1936, Raskob Papers, File 61; New York *Herald-Tribune,* February 1, 1936; Wolfskill, *Revolt of the Conservatives,* pp. 62, 68; John A. Creps to P. S. du Pont, January 24, 1936, P. S. du Pont to Creps, January 30, 1936, PSDP, Series A, File 771; P. S. du Pont to Minute Men and Women of Today, January 21, February 1, 1936, PSDP, Series A, File 765.

17. New York *Post,* January 25, 1936; Wolfskill, *Revolt of the Conservatives,* pp. 225–226; I. du Pont to George S. Brown, February 7, 1936, IDP, Series J, File 292; Stayton, "Liberty League," p. 42, PSDP, Series A, File 771; McIntyre to Frank Walker, January 25, 1936, Walker to McIntyre, January 27, 1936, FDR Papers as President.

18. Wolfskill, *Revolt of the Conservatives,* pp. 157–160; Cordell Hull to FDR, January

27, 1936, FDR to George Foster Peabody, February 19, 1936, FDR Papers as President; Schlesinger, *Politics of Upheaval*, pp. 510–520.

19. Henry P. DuBois to Raskob, February 4, 1936, Beck to Raskob, February 4, 1936, Raskob Papers, File 61; *New York Times*, February 4, 1936.

20. Wolfskill and Hudson, *All But the People*, pp. 44, 91, 105, 166; Schlesinger, *Politics of Upheaval*, pp. 521–522; P. S. du Pont to Shouse, July 1, 1936, Shouse to P. S. du Pont, July 8, 1936, PSDP, Series A, File 771; Wolfskill, *Revolt of the Conservatives*, pp. 175–178, 242.

21. Wolfskill, *Revolt of the Conservatives*, pp. 178, 232–233.

22. George Creel to McIntyre, March 16, 1936, FDR Papers as President; P. S. du Pont to Shouse, January 24, 1936, P. S. du Pont to Stayton, January 30, 1936, PSDP, Series A, File 771.

23. P. S. du Pont to Erwin H. Schell, February 11, 1936, P. S. du Pont to W. M. Newton, February 17, 1936, PSDP, Series A, File 765; P. S. du Pont to Thomas A. Painter, February 13, 1936, PSDP, Series A, File 1173.

24. Pittsburgh *Press*, February 4, 1936; McIntyre to George M. Kimberly, February 10, 1936, FDR Papers as President.

25. Wolfskill, *Revolt of the Conservatives*, pp. 211–213.

26. Ibid., pp. 198–200; DuBois to Henry Fletcher, February 21, 1936, IDP, Series J, File 292.

27. Wolfskill, *Revolt of the Conservatives*, pp. 178–179; *U.S. News*, March 16, 1936; Shouse to Ernest N. May, February 24, 1936, Shouse Papers.

28. ALL Doc. 107, *The Story of an Honest Man*, March 1936; *Congressional Record*, 74th Cong., 2d sess. (March 10, 1936), p. 3494.

29. Stayton, "Liberty League," pp. 42–43, PSDP, Series A, File 771; Washington *Star*, March 22, 1936; Shouse, "The Right of Petition," March 6, 1936, IDP, Series A.

30. Wolfskill, *Revolt of the Conservatives*, pp. 228, 236–238; Stayton, "Liberty League," pp. 43–44, PSDP, Series A, File 771; Shouse, "The New Inquisition," March 27, 1936, IDP, Series A; New York *Daily News*, March 31, 1936.

31. Shouse to P. S. du Pont, March 23, 1936, P. S. du Pont to Shouse, March 31, 1936, PSDP, Series A, File 771; Evans to I. du Pont, March 31, 1936, I. du Pont to Evans, April 8, 1936, IDP, Series J, File 292.

32. Wolfskill, *Revolt of the Conservatives*, p. 68; I. du Pont to Hutton, April 10, 1936, Stayton to I. du Pont, April 13, 1936, I. du Pont to Stayton, April 14, 1936, I. du Pont to Desvernine, April 7, 1936, IDP, Series J, File 292.

33. P. S. du Pont to Charles S. Roberts, March 31, 1936, P. S. du Pont to Atwood, April 10, 1936, P. S. du Pont to V. C. Lathrop, March 23, 1936, PSDP, Series A, File 765.

34. Keller, *In Defense of Yesterday*, p. 271; Shouse, "Abuses of Power," April 8, 1936, IDP, Series A; Wolfskill, *Revolt of the Conservatives*, pp. 228–242; U.S. Congress, Senate, Committee to Investigate Lobbying Activities, *Investigation of Lobbying Activities: Hearings*, 74th Cong., 2d sess. (1936), pp. 1751–2075. (The panel is henceforth referred to as the Black Committee.).

35. Schlesinger, *Politics of Upheaval*, p. 523; Wolfskill, *Revolt of the Conservatives*, pp. 239–240; P. S. du Pont to Frank E. Cheadle, May 29, 1936, PSDP, Series A, File 765; Baltimore *Evening Sun*, April 10, 1936; New York *Herald-Tribune*, April

11, 1936; Washington *Star,* April 14, 15, 1936; Black Committee, *Hearings,* pp. 1835–1957.

36. Black Committee, *Hearings,* pp. 2047–2095; Harry H. Smith to P. S. du Pont, April 24, 1936, P. S. du Pont to Smith, May 6, 1936, Stayton to P. S. du Pont, May 12, 1936, PSDP, Series A, File 771; P. S. du Pont to Vance Muse, May 6, 1936, PSDP, Series A, File 765; Seldes, *One Thousand Americans,* pp. 205, 293–297; Colby, *Du Pont Dynasty,* pp. 356–357.

37. Wolfskill, *Revolt of the Conservatives,* p. 233; Walter Chrysler to Raskob, April 25, 1936, IDP, Series J, File 292.

38. Seldes, *One Thousand Americans,* p. 205; Wolfskill, *Revolt of the Conservatives,* pp. 242–245; Bernstein, *Turbulent Years,* pp. 646, 652; *New York Times,* April 15, 1936; Washington *Post,* April 15, 1936.

39. Wolfskill, *Revolt of the Conservatives,* p. 213; Robert L. Lund to Raskob, April 7, 1936, Raskob to Lund, April 9, 1936, Raskob Papers, File 1624; *New York Times,* April 24, 1936.

40. Sloan to Raskob, April 27, 1936, Raskob to P. S. du Pont, January 30, 1936, Raskob to Couzens, April 15, 24, 1936, Couzens to Raskob, February 6, April 16, 1936, Raskob to Robert W. Johnson, April 28, 1936, Raskob Papers, File 61.

41. St. Louis *Globe-Democrat,* January 5, 1936; B. A. Tompkins to Raskob, April 17, 1936, Raskob Papers, File 61; Wolfskill, *Revolt of the Conservatives,* pp. 179–180.

42. Wolfskill, *Revolt of the Conservatives,* p. 181.

43. "Twenty-eight Facts about the New Deal," May 5, 1936, IDP, Series A; ALL Doc. 125, *You Owe Thirty-One Billion Dollars,* May 19, 1936; P. S. du Pont to Stayton, June 1, 1936, PSDP, Series A, File 771; Bernstein, *A Caring Society,* pp. 128–129; Desvernine to I. du Pont, May 12, 1936, IDP, Series J, File 292.

44. Stayton to P. S. du Pont, April 6, 1936, PSDP, Series A, File 771; Henry A. Wallace to Dodd, Mead & Co., May 14, 1936, Desvernine to Wallace, May 19, 1936, Raskob Papers, File 61; *New York Times,* June 21, 1936; I. du Pont to Desvernine, June 24, 1936, IDP, Series J, File 292.

45. E. E. Lincoln to P. S. du Pont, confidential, May 11, 1936, PSDP, Series A, File 771; Shouse to I. du Pont, June 4, 1936, IDP, Series J, File 292.

46. P. S. du Pont to Kirby, May 15, 1936, P. S. du Pont to Painter, May 15, 1936, PSDP, Series A, File 765; Shouse to Don Baum, May 21, 1936, Shouse Papers.

47. Bernstein, *A Caring Society,* p. 130; New York *Evening Post,* June 1, 1936; *New York Times,* June 2, 1936; New York *Daily Worker,* June 1, 1936.

48. La Follette Committee, *Hearings,* pt. 45, pp. 16798–16799, 16810; Bernstein, *Turbulent Years,* p. 652.

49. Wolfskill, *Revolt of the Conservatives,* p. 206; Pew to Shouse, April 28, 1936, Shouse to P. S. du Pont, June 6, 1936, P. S. du Pont to Lammot du Pont, June 11, 1936, PSDP, Series A, File 771.

50. P. S. du Pont to Lammot du Pont, June 11, 1936, PSDP, Series A, File 771; P. S. du Pont to I. du Pont, June 11, 1936, IDP, Series J, File 292; I. du Pont to P. S. du Pont, June 10, 1936, Stayton to Pew, June 8, 1936, P. S. du Pont

to Stayton, June 12, 1936, PSDP, Series A, File 771; I. du Pont to Stayton, June 11, 1936, IDP, Series J, File 292.

51. *New York Times,* June 11, 1936; Wolfskill and Hudson, *All But the People,* pp. 246–248; Wolfskill, *Revolt of the Conservatives,* pp. 201–206.

52. Buck to Raskob, June 6, 20, 1936, Raskob to Buck, June 8, 1936, Raskob Papers, File 602; Cullinan to Shouse, June 15, 1936, P. S. du Pont to Cullinan, June 18, 1936, PSDP, Series A, File 765.

53. Huthmacher, *Wagner,* pp. 203–207, 215; Wolfskill and Hudson, *All But the People,* p. 243; Baltimore *Sun,* June 21, 1936.

54. Shouse, "The New Deal vs. Democracy," June 20, 1936, IDP, Series A; Wolfskill, *Revolt of the Conservatives,* pp. 182–183.

55. Wolfskill, *Revolt of the Conservatives,* pp. 183–186; Norman Hapgood to FDR, June 22, 1936, FDR to Hapgood, June 27, 1936, FDR Papers as President.

56. Wolfskill, *Revolt of the Conservatives,* pp. 187–188; Rosenman, *Public Papers of FDR,* vol. 4, pp. 283–285.

13. A Rout and a Valley Forge

1. Shouse to I. du Pont, June 26, 1936, IDP Series J, File 292; Shouse to Raskob, June 26, 1936, Raskob Papers, File 61; Wolfskill and Hudson, *All But the People,* pp. 243–245.

2. I. du Pont to Wadsworth, July 2, 1936, Wadsworth to I. du Pont, July 7, 1936, Howard Heinz to I. du Pont, July 14, 1936, Wadsworth to I. du Pont, July 23, 1936, IDP, Series J, File 292.

3. Pierre made contributions to the Bronx County Republican Committee, the Ohio Republican Central Committee, the New York County Republican Committee, the Queens County Republican Committee, the Maine State Republican Committee, the Delaware State Republican Committee, The New York State Republican Committee, the Illinois Republican Citizens Organization, the Kings County Republican Committee, the Republican Senatorial Campaign Committee, and the Republican National Committee. P. S. du Pont, "Political Contributions in 1936" (data accompanying letter to Senator Augustine Lonergan, Chairman of the Senate Committee to Investigate Campaign Expenditures), October 2, 1936, PSDP, Series A, File 765. Irénée's gifts were to the Philadelphia Republican City Committee, the Allegheny County Republican Committee, the Ohio Republican Party, the National Republican Club, the Kings County, Bronx County, and Queens County Republican chapters, the Pennsylvania State Republican Committee, the Townsend Senate reelection campaign in Delaware, the Illinois and Maine GOP organizations, and the National Republican Congressional Committee. I. du Pont, "Political Contributions in 1936" (similarly sent to Lonergan Committee), IDP, Series J, File 100; La Follette Committee, *Hearings,* pt. 45, p. 16873.

4. Wolfskill, *Revolt of the Conservatives,* pp. 193–194; Wolfskill and Hudson, *All But the People,* p. 251. An excellent biography of Smith is Glen Jeansonne, *Gerald L. K. Smith, Minister of Hate* (New Haven: Yale University Press, 1988).

5. Wolfskill, *Revolt of the Conservatives,* p. 195.

6. Ibid., pp. 196–198; Lammot du Pont to I. du Pont, undated note attached

to letter from I. du Pont to E. E. Lincoln, August 7, 1936, IDP, Series J, File 292.

7. I. du Pont to Lincoln, August 7, 1936, I. du Pont to Shouse, August 25, 1936, IDP, Series J, File 292; Shouse statement, July 17, 1936, Stayton, "Liberty League," p. 49, PSDP, Series A, File 771; Wolfskill, *Revolt of the Conservatives*, pp. 198, 214.

8. Wolfskill, *Revolt of the Conservatives*, pp. 195–196; Mrs. Mabel Jacques Eichel to Alfred M. Landon, July 2, 1936, Landon Papers; Shouse Statement, July 17, 1936, IDP, Series A; I. du Pont to G. D. Gurley, July 29, 1936, IDP, Series J, File 261.

9. P. S. du Pont to William C. Murphy, Jr., August 6, 1936, PSDP, Series A, File 771; Wolfskill and Hudson, *All But the People*, p. 249. As examples of the Breckinridge-Landon communication, see Breckinridge to Landon, August 10, 11, 14, 17, September 3, 1936, Landon Papers.

10. Breckinridge to Landon, August 10, 11, 14, 17, 1936, Landon Papers; Lincoln to P. S. du Pont, August 26, 1936, PSDP, Series A, File 765; I. du Pont to Stayton, August 24, 1936, Stayton to I. du Pont, September 4, 1936, IDP, Series J, File 292.

11. I. du Pont to Kirby, September 8, 1936, IDP, Series J, File 292; P. S. du Pont to Shouse, September 1, 1936, Shouse to P. S. du Pont, September 14, 1936, PSDP, Series A, File 771; Shouse to Demarest Lloyd, September 21, 1936, Shouse Papers; P. S. du Pont, "Political Contributions, 1936," PSDP, Series A, File 765; I. du Pont, "Political Contributions, 1936," IDP, Series J, File 100.

12. Wolfskill, *Revolt of the Conservatives*, p. 220; P. S. du Pont, "Political Contributions, 1936," PSDP, Series A, File 765; I. du Pont, "Political Contributions, 1936," IDP, Series J, File 100.

13. P. S. du Pont to Stayton, October 19, 1936, Grayson Murphy to P. S. du Pont, September 18, 1936, P. S. du Pont to Murphy, September 22, 1936, P. S. du Pont, "Time Notes and Demand Notes" (attached to letter from I. du Pont to Stayton, April 25, 1935), PSDP, Series A, File 771; I. du Pont to holders of unpaid notes, September 23, 1936, I. du Pont to Shouse, September 22, 1936, IDP, Series J, File 292; P. S. du Pont to Shouse, September 21, 1936, Charles J. Dawson to Shouse, September 28, 1936, PSDP, Series A, File 771; H. B. Earhart to Shouse, September 25, 1936, Shouse to Earhart, September 29, 1936, Shouse Papers; Raskob to Colby Chester, September 21, 1936, Raskob Papers, File 1620.

14. Stayton, "Liberty League," pp. 20, 50, PSDP, Series A, File 771; Shouse to T. B. McLeod, September 17, 1936, Shouse Papers; Wolfskill, *Revolt of the Conservatives*, pp. 114–115, 117; ALL Doc. 131, *A Reply to Secretary Wallace's Question—Whose Constitution? The Dominant Issue of the Campaign*, August 1936; ALL Doc. 134, *The Dual Form of Government and the New Deal*, September 1936.

15. I. du Pont to Shouse, September 26, 1936, IDP, Series J, File 292; Lewis H. Brown to Raskob, September 9, 1936, Lund to Raskob, September 22, 1936, Raskob to Carpenter, September 24, 1936, Raskob to Davis, October 1, 1936, A. Felix du Pont to Raskob, September 30, 1936, I. du Pont to Raskob, September 25, 1936, P. S. du Pont to Raskob, September 25, 1936, Raskob Papers, File 602.

16. Smith to FDR, September 24, 1936, Smith Papers; Raskob to Lawyers Trust Co., September 29, 1936, Raskob Papers, File 602; Lund to P. S. du Pont, October 21, 1936, PSDP, Series A, File 765; Davis to Raskob, October 31, 1936, Raskob to Carpenter, November 12, 1936, Raskob to I. du Pont, November 12, 1936, Raskob Papers, File 602; Henry Davis to I. du Pont, November 12, 1936, I. du Pont to Raskob, November 14, 1936, IDP, Series J, File 292.

17. P. S. du Pont to Lonergan, October 2, 1936, P. S. du Pont, "Memorandum" (*re* October 1936 contributions), October 22, 1936, PSDP, Series A, File 765; I. du Pont to Lonergan, October 2, 1936, I. du Pont, "Political contributions, 1936," IDP, Series J, File 100.

18. Shouse to Roy Roberts, October 14, 1936, Shouse Papers; I. du Pont to Shouse, October 15, 1936, IDP, Series J, File 292; Shouse to ALL Executive Committee and Advisory Council, October 29, 1936, PSDP, Series A, File 771.

19. Harold J. Gallagher to Shouse, October 23, 1936, Shouse Papers; Raskob to Publicity Associates, October 30, 1936, Raskob Papers, File 602; Harbaugh, *Lawyer's Lawyer*, p. 354.

20. Wolfskill, *Revolt of the Conservatives*, pp. 208–209.

21. Ibid., pp. 221–222; Wolfskill and Hudson, *All But the People*, p. 184.

22. Lincoln to I. du Pont, October 28, 1936, IDP, Series J, File 292; P. S. du Pont to Wade H. Cooper, October 29, 1936, PSDP, Series A, File 765; Hawley, *New Deal and the Problem of Monopoly*, p. 157.

23. "FDR Speech Schedule," Folder 179b, Smith Papers; Wolfskill, *Revolt of the Conservatives*, pp. 218–219.

24. Colby, *Du Pont Dynasty*, p. 351; *New York Times*, October 18, 1936; "Investigation of Campaign Expenditures," Folder 683, Smith Papers.

25. Rosenman (comp.), *Public Papers of FDR*, vol. 5, pp. 566–573.

26. Shouse to David H. Robertson, November 2, 1936, Shouse Papers; Wolfskill, *Revolt of the Conservatives*, p. 222.

27. Colby, *Du Pont Dynasty*, p. 355; Wolfskill, *Revolt of the Conservatives*, pp. 62–63, 207; Lopata, "John J. Raskob," p. 253, "Investigation of Campaign Expenditures," Smith Papers; Stayton, "Liberty League," Exhibit VIII, PSDP, Series A, File 771; La Follette Committee, *Hearings*, pt. 17, Exhibit 3799; Raskob to P. S. du Pont, I. du Pont, November 12, 1936, I. du Pont to Lammot du Pont, November 13, 1936, I. du Pont to Raskob, November 14, 1936, IDP, Series J, File 292.

28. Desvernine to I. du Pont, November 4, 1936, IDP, Series J, File 292; Shouse, "The Campaign of 1936," undated, Shouse Papers; Breckinridge to Landon, November 18, 1936 (Smith remarks attached), David A. Reed to Landon, November 6, 1936, Landon Papers; John Hamilton to Raskob, November 25, 1936, Raskob Papers, File 1946; P. S. du Pont to William Z. Ripley, November 4, December 1, 1936, PSDP, Series A, File 765.

29. Wolfskill, *Revolt of the Conservatives*, pp. 254–257; Colby, *Du Pont Dynasty*, p. 362; Hamilton Basso, "The Liberty League Writes," *New Republic*, July 22, 1936, p. 320.

30. Stayton, "Liberty League," p. 51 and Exhibit XXV, Grayson Murphy to P. S. du Pont, November 24, 30, December 2, 1936, Stayton to P. S. du Pont, December 22, 1936, P. S. du Pont to Stayton, December 23, 1936, PSDP,

Series A, File 771; I. du Pont to William du Pont, December 14, 1936, I. du Pont to Stayton, December 24, 1936, IDP, Series J, File 292; ALL Executive Committee, "Items for Consideration," December 30, 1936, PSDP, Series A, File 771.

31. Cullinan to Shouse, October 20, 1936, Breckinridge to Raskob, November 18, 1936, Raskob Papers, File 602; Breckinridge to Landon, November 18, 1936, Landon Papers; Wolfskill, *Revolt of the Conservatives,* p. 247; Robertson to Shouse, November 11, 1936, Shouse to Shaw, December 5, 1936, Shouse Papers.

32. I. du Pont to Herbert Hoover, December 12, 1936, IDP, Series J, File 261; P. S. du Pont to William J. Rau, December 28, 1936, PSDP, Series A, File 1173.

14. A Last Hurrah

1. Wolfskill, *Revolt of the Conservatives,* pp. 67, 247; Stayton to P. S. du Pont, January 4, 1937, Stayton, "Liberty League," pp. 20, 51–51A, Exhibit VIII, PSDP, Series A, File 771.

2. For a comprehensive look at the origins and development of the 1937 sit-down strike at General Motors, see Fine, *Sit Down.* On GM's attempts to forestall a strike, see Fine, pp. 23–51, and Bernstein, *Turbulent Years,* pp. 516–524.

3. Fine, *Sit Down,* pp. 21–22; Bernstein, *Turbulent Years,* pp. 510–515; La Follette Committee, *Hearings,* pt. 17, pp. 7387, 7503, 7510, 7515, 7518, Exhibit 3799, and pt. 45, pp. 16844–16850.

4. Bernstein, *Turbulent Years,* pp. 524–550; Fine, *Sit Down,* pp. 332–334.

5. Colby, *Du Pont Dynasty,* p. 366. For a history of the La Follette Committee, the reader should consult Jerold S. Auerbach, *Labor and Liberty: The La Follette Committee and the New Deal* (Indianapolis: Bobbs Merrill, 1966).

6. I. du Pont to Richard C. McMullen, March 24, 1937, IDP, Series J, File 261; R. C. Schroeder, *The "Du Ponts" or the "Roosevelts"?* (Washington, D.C.: National Publicity Bureau, 1937), pp. 3–8, 15.

7. Huthmacher, *Wagner,* p. 221; Wolfskill, *Revolt of the Conservatives,* p. 250; Wolfskill and Hudson, *All But the People,* p. 195; Shouse to Grayson Murphy, February 27, 1937, Shouse Papers.

8. Al Smith to Shouse, February 18, 1937, Shouse to Smith, February 23, 1937, Shouse Papers; Stayton, "Liberty League," p. 51A, PSDP, Series A, File 771.

9. Wolfskill, *Revolt of the Conservatives,* pp. 190, 252; I. du Pont to Townsend, March 25, 1937, Townsend to I. du Pont, March 27, 1937, IDP, Series J, File 261; Sterling Edmunds to Shouse, January 29, 1937, Wolfskill to Shouse, June 24, 1959, Shouse to Wolfskill, June 30, 1959, Shouse Papers; Stayton to P. S. du Pont, February 13, 1937, PSDP, Series A, File 771; Mrs. Louis A. Drexler to Ewing Laporte, February 5, 1937, Laporte to Drexler, February 6, 1937, IDP, Series A; Stayton to P. S. du Pont, March 13, 1941, PSDP, Series A, File 771.

10. Stayton, "Liberty League," pp. 51A–80, PSDP, Series A, File 771; Drexler to Delaware ALL members, February 16, 1937, IDP, Series A; Wolfskill, *Revolt of the Conservatives,* pp. 250–253.

11. Wolfskill and Hudson, *All But the People,* p. 168; P. S. du Pont to Kirby,

February 12, 1937, P. S. du Pont to Mrs. Ephraim B. Cockrell, February 18, 1937, P. S. du Pont to Frank Gannett, February 22, 1937, P. S. du Pont to Mrs. Catherine Curtis, March 4, 1937, P. S. du Pont to L. M. Bailey, March 9, 1937, P. S. du Pont to Townsend, March 26, 1937, PSDP, Series A, File 765.

12. Townsend to I. du Pont, March 29, 1937, Series J, File 261; Wolfskill and Hudson, *All But the People,* p. 264; Huthmacher, *Wagner,* p. 223; Bernstein, *A Caring Society,* p. 132.

13. Desvernine to Shouse, June 16, 1937, Shouse Papers; Colby, *Du Pont Dynasty,* pp. 369–370; Wolfskill and Hudson, *All But the People,* p. 264.

14. William O. Lucas to Raskob, April 7, 1937, Lammot du Pont to Raskob, June 12, 1937, Raskob Papers, File 1624; Leff, *Limits of Symbolic Reform,* p. 202; Huthmacher, *Wagner,* pp. 232–234; Bernstein, *A Caring Society,* pp. 135–136.

15. Wolfskill and Hudson, *All But the People,* pp. 255, 268; Huthmacher, *Wagner,* p. 203. An excellent study of the emergence of the conservative coalition in Congress is James T. Patterson, *Congressional Conservatism and the New Deal* (Lexington: University of Kentucky Press, 1967).

16. G. T. Barnhill to Edmunds, April 22, 1937, IDP, Series J, File 261; Shouse to Edmunds, June 14, 1937, Desvernine to Shouse, June 16, 1937, Shouse Papers; Landon to Ely, May 20, 1937, Landon Papers; Desvernine to Raskob, March 1, 1937, Edmunds to Raskob, March 27, April 8, 1937, Raskob to Edmunds, April 9, 1937, Raskob Papers, File 602.

17. I. du Pont to Townsend, May 14, 1937, I. du Pont to James H. Hughes, May 14, 1937, IDP, Series J, File 261; P. S. du Pont to Joseph L. Richards, June 4, 1937, F. C. Evans, "Personal, for Pierre, Lammot du Pont," June 11, 1937, PSDP, Series A, File 765; I. du Pont to Shouse, June 14, 1937, IDP, Series J, File 292.

18. Colby to William S. Gregg, June 11, 1937, Walter B. Ditmars to I. du Pont, June 22, 1937, I. du Pont to Desvernine, June 23, 1937, Desvernine to I. du Pont, June 24, 1937, I. du Pont to Donaldson Brown, June 25, 1937, I. du Pont to Stayton, July 7, 1937, I. du Pont to Stayton, August 21, 1937, IDP, Series J, File 292.

19. I. du Pont to Desvernine, June 23, 1937, I. du Pont to Shouse, June 8, 1937, Thomas L. Chadbourne to I. du Pont, May 27, 1937, IDP, Series J, File 292; Stayton to P. S. du Pont, May 12, 1937, PSDP, Series A, File 771; Knudsen to I. du Pont, September 28, 1937, Raskob Papers, File 61.

20. Wolfskill and Hudson, *All But the People,* p. 264; Al Smith to Shouse, October 2, 1937, Shouse Papers; Leff, *Limits of Symbolic Reform,* p. 204; Bernstein, *A Caring Society,* pp. 105–112; I. du Pont to Hamilton, August 27, 1937, IDP, Series J, File 261.

21. I. du Pont to Hughes, October 5, 1937, IDP, Series J, File 261; Huthmacher, *Wagner,* p. 237; Bernstein, *A Caring Society,* pp. 136–139.

22. Lincoln to P. S. du Pont, October 13, 1937, PSDP, Series A, File 1164; P. S. du Pont to Percy W. Phillips, November 24, 1937, Stayton to P. S. du Pont, December 2, 1937, J. A. Arnold to I. du Pont, December 13, 1937, PSDP, Series A, File 1125; P. S. du Pont to Republican National Committee, December 22, 1937, PSDP, Series A, File 765; Stayton to P. S. du Pont, December 27, 1937, PSDP, Series A, File 1125.

23. Colby, *Du Pont Dynasty*, pp. 371–375.
24. I. du Pont to Townsend, December 2, 1937, I. du Pont to Stayton, December 3, 23,1937, IDP, Series J, File 261; Raskob to Shouse, December 23, 1937, Shouse to Mrs. Newton D. Baker, December 28, 1937, Shouse to I. du Pont, December 28, 1937, Shouse Papers.
25. Wolfskill and Hudson, *All But the People*, p. 277; Colby, *Du Pont Dynasty*, pp. 374–376; P. S. du Pont to Townsend, January 18, 1938, PSDP, Series A, File 765; Lammot du Pont to Desvernine, February 2, 1938, Desvernine to Lammot du Pont, February 11, 1938, Desvernine to I. du Pont, February 11, 1938, IDP, Series J, File 261.
26. Bernstein, *A Caring Society*, p. 112; Huthmacher, *Wagner*, pp. 245–246; Shouse statement, April 11, 1938, Shouse Papers.
27. Wolfskill and Hudson, *All But the People*, p. 277; Huthmacher, *Wagner*, pp. 246–247; Eugene du Pont to FDR, June 20, 1938, FDR Papers as President; Colby, *Du Pont Dynasty*, pp. 376–377; *New York Times*, June 27, 1938.
28. Leff, *Limits of Symbolic Reform*, pp. 234–240; Huthmacher, *Wagner*, pp. 203, 248; Bernstein, *A Caring Society*, p. 142; I. du Pont to William F. Allen, May 23, 1938, IDP, Series J, File 261.
29. Stayton to P. S. du Pont, June 22, 23, July 5, 21, 1938, PSDP, Series A, File 771; P. S. du Pont to Hughes, June 9, 1938, PSDP, Series A, File 765; Bernstein, *Turbulent Years*, pp. 647–648.
30. Edmunds to Raskob, April 20, 1938, Raskob to Edmunds, April 26, May 1, 1938, Raskob Papers, File 602; I. du Pont to Shouse, May 9, 1938, IDP, Series J, File 292; Stayton, "Liberty League," p. 81, PSDP, Series A, File 771; P. S. du Pont to Lammot du Pont, August 2, 1938, PSDP, Series A, File 765; Shouse to I. du Pont, October 11, 1938, IDP, Series J, File 292; I. du Pont to George T. Weymouth, May 10, 1939, IDP, Series J, File 261.
31. P. S. du Pont to Stayton, March 10, 31, April 13, 25, May 10, 27, June 10, 29, July 12, 26, August 10, September 9, 26, October 10, 27, November 10, 28, December 14, 1938, Stayton to I. du Pont, June 9, 15, 24, July 11, 1938, Stayton, "Liberty League," Exhibit VIII, Stayton to P. S. du Pont, August 9, 1938, PSDP, Series A, File 771; Colby, *Du Pont Dynasty*, p. 375.
32. The history referred to is Stayton's "Liberty League," PSDP, Series A, File 771, frequently cited in this work. Shouse to I. du Pont, November 17, 1938, I. du Pont to Frank Phillips, January 5, 1939, IDP, Series J, File 292; Stayton to I. du Pont, December 7, 1938, Stayton to P. S. du Pont, October 26, November 12, December 9, 1938, PSDP, Series A, File 771.
33. Taylor and Sudnik, *Du Pont*, pp. 150–153; Colby, *Du Pont Dynasty*, pp. 375–376.
34. P. S. du Pont to Richard K. Mellon, January 20, July 6, 1939, P. S. du Pont to Sewell Avery, January 20, 1939, Stayton to P. S. du Pont, March 18, 1939, P. S. du Pont to Knudsen, March 24, 1939, Knudsen to P. S. du Pont, March 29, 1939, PSDP, Series A, File 771; Shouse to I. du Pont, March 6, 1939, IDP, Series J, File 292.
35. Shouse to I. du Pont, April 3, 1939, I. du Pont to Shouse, April 12, 1939, Lammot du Pont, Jr., to I. du Pont, May 24, 1939, IDP, Series J, File 292; Shouse to P. S. du Pont, January 23, 1939, PSDP, Series A, File 771; Muse

to P. S. du Pont, June 16, 1939, Stayton to P. S. du Pont, June 21, 1939, P. S. du Pont to Stayton, June 30, 1939, PSDP, Series A, File 1125; T. C. Geesey to P. S. du Pont, August 21, 1939, P. S. du Pont to Shouse, August 29, 1939, PSDP, Series A, File 771; P. S. du Pont to James E. Clark, April 4, 1939, Shouse to P. S. du Pont, December 128, 1939, PSDP, Series A, File 765.

36. Shouse to P. S. du Pont, June 19, 22, 1939, PSDP, Series A, File 771; P. S. du Pont to David Van Pelt, July 18, 1939, PSDP, Series A, File 765; Lopata, "John J. Raskob," p. 256; FDR to Al Smith, October 1, 1939, FDR Papers as President.

37. Stayton to P. S. du Pont, October 9, December 11, 13, 18, 22, 1939, PSDP, Series A, File 771.

38. Hawley, "A Partnership Formed, Dissolved, and in Renegotiation: Business and Government in the Franklin D. Roosevelt Era," in Joseph R. Frese, S. J. Judd, and Jacob Judd, eds., *Business and Government: Essays in Twentieth Century Cooperation and Confrontation* (Tarrytown, N.Y.: Sleepy Hollow Press, 1985), pp. 205–208; I. du Pont to Arthur H. James, June 4, 1940, IDP, Series J, File 261; Stayton to P. S. du Pont, January 25, 1940, PSDP, Series A, File 771; Pew to Shouse, May 23, 1940, Shouse Papers.

39. Landon to Shouse, January 8, 17, 1940, Shouse to Landon, January 12, 1940, Shouse to Al Smith, January 25, February 13, 1940, Shouse to Walter George, January 27, 1940, Shaw to Shouse, February 10, 1940, Shouse to Shaw, February 12, 1940, Shouse Papers; Hastings to I. du Pont, December 4, 1939, IDP, Series J, File 261; P. S. du Pont to Wadsworth, February 21, 1940, PSDP, Series A, File 765.

40. Shouse to Willkie, January 27, April 5, 20, 1940, Willkie to Shouse, April 5, 1940, Raskob to Lammot du Pont, April 16, 1940, Shouse Papers; Lammot du Pont to Sloan, April 8, 1940, Lammot du Pont to Donald Despain, April 9, 1940, Lammot du Pont to I. du Pont, April 10, 1940, IDP, Series J, File 261; Stayton to P. S. du Pont, April 10, 29, May 1, 1940, PSDP, Series A, File 771. The best biography of Willkie is Barnard Ellsworth, *Wendell Willkie, Fighter for Freedom* (Marquette: Northern Michigan University Press, 1966).

41. Shouse to Willkie, May 17, 1940, Shouse Papers; Henry Carter, Patterson to P. S. du Pont, June 18, 24, 1940, P. S. du Pont to Patterson, June 20, 1940, P. S. du Pont to Delaware Republican delegates, June 27, 1940, PSDP, Series A, File 765; Dutton, *Du Pont*, p. 364.

42. Shaw to Shouse, July 5, 1940, Shouse to Shaw, August 26, 1940, Shouse to Raskob, July 23, 1940, Al Smith to Reed, July 23, 1940, Shouse Papers; Reed to Smith, July 27, 1940, Smith Papers; Shouse to Willkie, July 15, 29, 1940, Shouse Papers.

43. Smith to Shouse, September 13, 1940, Shouse to Smith, September 16, October 24, 1940, Shouse Papers; I. du Pont to Hamilton, August 9, 1940, I. du Pont to Mercantile Press, Inc., September 30, 1940, IDP, Series J, File 261; Stayton to P. S., I. du Pont, September 20, 1940, PSDP, Series A, File 1125.

44. Stayton to P. S. du Pont, April 10, July 8, October 8, 1940, I. du Pont to Shouse, August 15, 1940, I. du Pont to Stayton, August 28, 1940, P. S. du Pont to Stayton, October 11, 1940, PSDP, Series A, File 771; I. du Pont, "Memorandum," September 5, 1940, IDP, Series J, File 261; Geesey to Stay-

ton, September 25, October 13, 28, November 20, 1940, Stayton to P. S. du Pont, December 3, 14, 1940, P. S. du Pont to Stayton, December 16, 27, 1940, PSDP, Series A, File 771.

45. I. du Pont to Delaware Republic campaign committee, Tennessee Republican campaign committee, October 7, 1940, I. du Pont to West Virginia Republican State Committee, October 31, 1940, Despain to I. du Pont, October 26, 1940, I. du Pont to Despain, October 31, 1940, IDP, Series J, File 261; P. S. du Pont to Harry L. Cannon, October 30, 1940, PSDP, Series A,, File 765; Colby, *Du Pont Dynasty*, p. 384; Seldes, *One Thousand Americans*, p. 182; Leuchtenburg, *FDR and the New Deal*, pp. 321–322.

46. Hutton to I. du Pont, November 12, 1940, I. du Pont to Hutton, November 6, 1940, IDP, Series J, File 261; Smith to Willkie, November 12, December 9, 1940, Smith Papers; Stayton to P. S. du Pont, December 3, 1940, and attached, "List of ALL Note-Holders," PSDP, Series A, File 771.

15. Old Soldiers

1. Taylor and Sudnik, *Du Pont*, pp. 155–159.
2. Raskob to FDR, January 30, 1942, Charles Michelson to Early, January 31, 1942, FDR to Raskob, February 19, March 3, 1942, FDR meetings with Al Smith, June 23, 1942, March 16, 1943, FDR Papers as President; Bernstein, *A Caring Society*, pp. 113–116; Hawley, "A Partnership Formed," pp. 209–212. In the late spring of 1941, the du Ponts through Stayton had lobbied the President to establish U.S. convoy escorts to Britain. Stayton to P. S. du Pont, May 19, 1941, PSDP, Series A, File 1125.
3. Stayton to P. S. du Pont, January 31, May 3, 1941, PSDP, Series A, File 1125; P. S. du Pont to Stayton, January 10, 29, February 11, 24, 1941, Geesey to Stayton, March 7, 24, April 19, 28, May 8, 1941, Stayton memorandum, May 29, 1941, Stayton to P. S. du Pont, May 3, 12, 19, 1941, PSDP, Series A, File 771.
4. P. S. du Pont to Stayton, September 15, October 3, 13, 1941, Stayton to P. S. du Pont, September 24, 1942, PSDP, Series A, File 771; Stayton to Raskob, "Memorandum *re* ALL," October 1, 1941, Raskob Papers, File 61; I. du Pont to Stayton, December 30, 1941, I. du Pont to P. S. du Pont, August 12, 1942, IDP, Series J, File 292; Stayton to P. S. du Pont, October 13, December 27, 1941, March 2, 1942, P. S. du Pont to Stayton, March 3, 1942, P. S. du Pont to I. du Pont, July 21, 1942, I. du Pont to Shouse, August 12, 25, 1942, Laporte, "Memorandum *re* ALL," September 21, 1942, PSDP, Series A, File 771.
5. I. du Pont to Shouse, August 12, 1942, P. S. du Pont to Davis, Smith, I. du Pont, Chester, August 19, 1942, Laporte, "Memorandum *re* ALL on Completion of Liquidation," November 25, 1942, PSDP, Series A, File 771; P. S. du Pont to Joseph R. Hamlen, August 13, 1942, Shouse to P. S. du Pont, August 18, October 15, 1942, Shouse Papers; I. du Pont to P. S. du Pont, August 12, 1942, IDP, Series J, File 292.
6. Taylor and Sudnik, *Du Pont*, p. 158.
7. P. S. du Pont to Walter H. Schoeller, March 5, 1942, Geesey to P. S. du Pont,

July 22, 1942, PSDP, Series A, File 771; Shouse to P. S. du Pont, October 21, 1942, P. S. du Pont to Shouse, October 26, 30, 1942, Shouse Papers.

8. Shouse to P. S. du Pont, November 4, 1942, Desvernine to Shouse, November 6, 1942, Shouse Papers; I. du Pont to Shouse, December 2, 1942, IDP, Series J, File 292; Shouse to P. S. du Pont, December 7, 1942, P. S. du Pont to Shouse, November 25, 1942, PSDP, Series A, File 765.

9. Taylor and Sudnik, *Du Pont,* pp. 158, 161–167.

10. P. S. du Pont to Matthew J. Kurtz, March 11, 1943, PSDP, Series A, File 765; Shouse memorandum, March 4, 1943, Shouse to Willkie, March 5, 22, 23, 29, April 5, 9, 12, 16, August 12, September 7, October 18, 25, November 2, 8, 1943, January 11, 14, 20, February 17, 1944, Willkie to Shouse, March 25, 1943, Roy Roberts to Shouse, April 6, 1943, Shouse to P. S. du Pont, March 4, 23, April 17, 1943, P. S. du Pont to Shouse, March 8, July 22, 1943, Shouse to I. du Pont, October 25, 29, 1943, I. du Pont to Shouse, October 27, 1943, Shouse Papers.

11. Colby, *Du Pont Dynasty,* p. 401; FDR to Smith, September 13, 1944, FDR Papers as President; I. du Pont to Shouse, August 4, 9, 1944, Shouse Papers; Chandler and Salsbury, *Pierre S. du Pont,* p. 588.

12. Seldes, *One Thousand Americans,* pp. 221–228; U.S. Congress, House, Select Committee on Lobbying Activities, *Hearings, Foundation for Economic Education, Lobbying, Direct and Indirect, July 13, 1950,* 81st Cong., 2d sess. (Washington, D.C.: Government Printing Office, 1950), pp. 8, 15 (panel subsequently referred to as Buchanan Committee); I. du Pont to Merwin K. Hart, June 30, 1943, Lammot du Pont to I. du Pont, March 29, 1944, I. du Pont to Hart, April 22, 1944, IDP, Series J, File 100.

13. I. du Pont to Hutton, November 12, 1945, IDP, Series J, File 261; I. du Pont to Hart, April 28, July 19, November 15, 1945, Hart to I. du Pont, May 9, 1946, Lammot du Pont to I. du Pont, May 23, 1946, I. du Pont to Hart, May 24, 1946, IDP, Series J, File 100.

14. I. du Pont to Gilbert H. Montague, September 20, 1946, IDP, Series J, File 261; P. S. du Pont to Weir, February 7, 1946, Weir to P. S. du Pont, March 6, 1946, PSDP, Series A, File 765; Colby, *Du Pont Dynasty,* pp. 401–402.

15. Colby, *Du Pont Dynasty,* p. 402; Davis to Shouse, November 7, 1946, Shouse Papers; Taylor and Sudnik, *Du Pont,* pp. 181–183.

16. I. du Pont to Hart, January 6, May 20, July 14, 1947, IDP, Series J, File 100.

17. I. du Pont to Foundation for Freedom, Inc., September 24, 1947, IDP, Series J, File 100; Buchanan Committee, *Report, Expenditures by Corporations to Influence Legislation,* 81st Cong., 2d sess. (Washington, D.C.: Government Printing Office, 1950), pp. 277, 293–296; Buchanan Committee, *Hearings,* pp. 8, 15, 88; P. S. du Pont to Lammot du Pont, September 12, 1947, PSDP, Series A, File 765.

18. Buchanan Committee, *Report,* pp. 277, 293–296, and *Hearings,* pp. 8, 15; Hart to Raskob, January 12, 1948, Raskob Papers, File 1035; I. du Pont to Hutton, April 26, 1948, IDP, Series J, File 261; I. du Pont to Hart, January 7, July 19, 1948, IDP, Series A, File 100.

19. P. S. du Pont to Pitcairn, March 8, 1948, PSDP, Series A, File 765; I. du Pont to Buck, July 22, 1948, IDP, Series J, File 261.

20. Taylor and Sudnik, *Du Pont,* pp. 158–159.

21. Ibid., pp.. 167, 183–184.
22. Raskob to P. S. du Pont, August 31, 1948, PSDP, Series A, File 765; Colby, *Du Pont Dynasty,* pp. 413–414.
23. Buchanan Committee, *Report,* pp. 89–90, 277, and *Hearings,* pp. 8, 15; I. du Pont to Hart, November 29, 1948, May 26, July 12, September 27, 1949, January 20, May 12, 1950, "I. du Pont—Payments to NEC," June 22, 1950, IDP, Series J, File 100.
24. Buchanan Committee, *Report,* pp. 277–296, and *Hearings,* p. 8, 15.
25. P. S. du Pont to Hutton, November 3, 1949, P. S. du Pont to George Wharton Pepper, November 28, 1949, Pepper to P. S. du Pont, November 30, 1949, PSDP, Series A, File 765.
26. P. S. du Pont to Charles H. McCarthy, April 24, 1950, PSDP, Series A, File 765; P. S. du Pont to Shouse, January 25, 1950, Shouse Papers.
27. I. du Pont to Hart, July 12, 1949, IDP, Series J, File 100; Colby, *Du Pont Dynasty,* p. 384. See also the Buchanan Committee's *Hearings* and *Report,* cited above.
28. Taylor and Sudnik, *Du Pont,* pp. 157–159; Edward A. Rumley to P. S. du Pont, January 23, 1950, June 1, 1952, PSDP, Series A, File 765.
29. Taylor and Sudnik, *Du Pont,* pp. 167–168; I. du Pont to NEC, July 5, 1950, IDP, Series J, File 100; P. S. du Pont to G. A. Vollmer, September 25, 1951, Rumely to P. S. du Pont, August 19, 1951, P. S. du Pont to Rumely, September 25, 1951, P. S. du Pont to J. A. Danielson, October 25, 1951, Pitcairn to P. S. du Pont, November 5, 1951, PSDP, Series A, File 765.
30. Rumely to I. du Pont, February 23, 1952, I. du Pont to Rumely, July 17, 1952, IDP, Series J, File 100; Sumner Gerard to P. S. du Pont, October 17, 1952, PSDP, Series A, File 765; Gerard newsletter, March 1953, IDP, Series J, File 100; Shouse to P. S. du Pont, July 25, 1952, Shouse Papers.
31. I. du Pont to Frank V. du Pont, April 24, 1952, IDP, Series J, File 261; P. S. du Pont to Weymouth, June 16, 1952, PSDP, Series A, File 765; Shouse to Arthur Eisenhower, July 25, 1952, Shouse Papers.
32. Gerard newsletter, March 1953, P. S. du Pont to I. du Pont, April 15, 1953, I. du Pont to Rumely, December 29, 1953, July 8, 1954, I. du Pont to Rumely, September 13, 16, 1954, IDP, Series J, File 100.
33. Colby, *Du Pont Dynasty,* p. 416–417; Taylor and Sudnik, *Du Pont,* p. 184.
34. Colby, *Du Pont Dynasty,* p. 417; I. du Pont to Rumely, October 6, 1954, IDP, Series J, File 100; Shouse to I. du Pont, October 10, 23, 1956, IDP, Series J, File 261; Taylor and Sudnik, *Du Pont,* pp. 184–185.
35. Taylor and Sudnik, *Du Pont,* p. 185; Colby, *Du Pont Dynasty,* pp. 422–425, 434.
36. Taylor and Sudnik, *Du Pont,* pp. 185–187.
37. Colby, *Du Pont Dynasty,* p. 434; Kyvig, *Repealing National Prohibition,* p. 244, n. 26.
38. Taylor and Sudnik, *Du Pont,* pp. 197–206; Chandler and Salsbury, *Pierre S. du Pont,* pp. 598–603.
39. For a sampling of current scholarship on the twentieth-century evolution of corporate "liberal" and "conservative" thought and action, see Ellis W. Hawley, "The Discovery and Study of a 'Corporate Liberalism,' " *Business History Review* 52 (1978), pp. 309–320; Kim McQuaid, "Corporate Liberalism

in the American Business Community, 1920–1940," *Business History Review* 52 (1978), pp. 342–368, and "The Frustration of Corporate Revival during the Early New Deal," *The Historian* 41 (August 1979), pp. 682–704; and Louis Galambos and Joseph Pratt, *The Rise of the Corporate Commonwealth: United States Business and Public Policy in the Twentieth Century* (New York: Basic Books, 1988).

Index